Developing Issues in the Legal Status of Women

Cases and Commentaries

Howard L. Feinstein

Pearson Custom Publishing

Printed in the United States of America

10 9 8 7 6 5 4 3 2 1

This manuscript was supplied camera-ready by the author(s).

Please visit our website at www.pearsoncustom.com

ISBN 0–536–60006–6

BA 990506

PEARSON CUSTOM PUBLISHING
160 Gould Street/Needham Heights, MA 02494
A Pearson Education Company

To my mother, the late Roslyn Feinstein,
my wife, Karen Feinstein,
and my daughter, Rachel Feinstein:

three generations, three pioneers
in their own times, on their own paths

And to my students in Legal Status of Women
at the University of Maryland, in the hope that
they have learned half as much from me as I from them

TABLE OF CONTENTS

PREFACE

In a harbinger of a separate movement to come, there had been muffled contention over the role of women in the march. Without noticeable dissent, the planning committee barred Coretta King and the other wives of the male leaders from marching with their husbands. Diverting them to a separate procession down Independence Avenue, the committee scheduled no female speakers during the entire three-hour program. Yet women provided much of the afternoon's historical resonance. In a "Tribute to Women," Randolph introduced for bows what amounted to a women's roll call of the movement: Rosa Parks, Daisy Bates, Diane Nash Bevel, Gloria Richardson of Cambridge, Maryland. Few in the audience recognized the shy widow of Herbert Lee, who had been slain two years earlier during SNCC's first registration drive in Mississippi, but those who did cheered her all the more. Randolph also presented Josephine Baker, the expatriate singer who had flown in from Paris for the march wearing her Free French uniform. He introduced Marian Anderson to sing "He's Got the Whole World in His Hands," and finally, when the long procession of speakers had reduced the sun-drenched crowd to restless fatigue, he brought out Mahalia Jackson. Her first notes were a cry from the deepest wellsprings of culture. The song was "I Been 'Buked and I Been Scorned," a spiritual born of the slave experience, but Jackson also managed to stir emotions irresistible to whites. People fumbled for handkerchiefs, and responsive cries chased the echoes of her *a cappella* voice through the cavernous outdoors.

- Taylor Branch, *Parting the Waters: America in the King Years 1954-63* (Simon & Schuster: 1988), pp. 880-81

ABOUT THE AUTHOR

Howard L. Feinstein, B.A., University of California (1968), J.D., George Washington University (1972), teaches Legal Status Of Women and Civil Rights And The Constitution in the Government and Politics Department at the University of Maryland, and a variety of courses in the Legal Assistant Program at George Washington University. He spent much of his career investigating, litigating, and prosecuting a wide range of federal civil rights violations for the Civil Rights Division of the U.S. Department of Justice, where he also drafted federal sex discrimination regulations. He is a performing and recording rhythm and blues and jazz musician in the Washington, D.C. area.

ACKNOWLEDGMENTS

Many thanks to the following people:

Ronda Harvey, my teaching assistant at the University of Maryland and future attorney, for persistent and imaginative research, and invaluable substantive and organizational suggestions;

Cindy Gaye and her colleagues at the University of Maryland's Women's Studies Department, for the use of their superb library;

John O'Brien at Pearson Custom Publishing and Marybeth Forys at Prentice Hall, for their unfailing encouragement and technical assistance;

and Jonathan Wilkenfeld, Chair of the Government and Politics Department at the University of Maryland, who knew not what demons he was unleashing when he suggested that I stop complaining about the need for a suitable undergraduate textbook and write one myself.

INTRODUCTION

Developing Issues in the Legal Status of Women: Cases and Commentaries is designed primarily to serve as a textbook -- suitable for academic areas such as political science, women's studies, history, and other contemporary fields of study -- and as an overview for the general reader. While it relies heavily on traditional legal materials, especially Supreme Court opinions and other federal and state cases, this edition does not contain the procedural material and extensive official citation typical of a law school text. Rather, it presents key legal documents, and political and social commentaries, to highlight the past, present, and future of the legal movement for gender equality. This work does not purport to be strictly neutral, although many of the commentaries, and several judicial opinions, are paired in "pro and con" format, to illustrate opposing arguments that one would likely confront, legally or rhetorically, in addressing a particular issue.

At the turn of the century, the "modern" movement for women's equality is approximately thirty years old. While there have been many victories, fundamental frustrations remain, and opponents of women's rights have access to increasingly sophisticated strategies. Like generals or foot soldiers in any battle, it eventually becomes vital to reassess priorities to be sure that it is not the "last war" that is being fought. This volume makes extensive use of recent statistical data, to help determine where progress has been made and where future resources might be allocated most effectively. Similarly, a large number of the commentaries and judicial opinions selected are highly contemporary.

This collection of cases and commentaries tracks the women's rights movement in the legal and political arenas, rather than through the lens of theory. By looking closely at how past strategies have fared, the movement may learn from past setbacks, and anticipate and overcome future resistance. As in the "traditional," or race-based civil rights movement, these battles take place in all three branches of government, and at the federal, state, and local levels. There are no special "women's rights" or "civil rights" courts or legislatures. An understanding of the formal and unwritten rules at all key junctures of government, from the Constitution of the United States to a rural county's policy for rape investigations, is essential for both the student and the advocate. Neither Ruth Bader Ginsburg nor Thurgood Marshall could have achieved their victories without this mastery. The foregoing does not contemplate "realistic" or "practical" limitations for any of the issues addressed in this book, but instead stresses the importance of governmental knowledge for tangible progress, from the preliminary to the revolutionary.

Finally, this book unabashedly favors the non-discrimination principle. While reasonable individuals can (and most definitely do) disagree concerning the social or philosophical primacy of "equality," "difference," or other strands of feminism, it is the focus on equality which, as in the "traditional" civil rights movement, can aspire to succeed legally. This approach can have unintended consequences, as in the case of the economic fall-out from much "no-fault" divorce legislation. However, it has enabled girls to attend Philadelphia's historically boys-only, academically superior competitive high school; enjoined Los Angeles County from giving a low priority to "911" calls involving domestic violence; and established the right of female college and secondary students to participate in athletics and other activities on an equal opportunity basis. Given the overwhelming judicial and political consensus against affording special privileges on the basis of group characteristics, the non-discrimination principle would appear, at least for the foreseeable future, to be the only avenue for legal and political gains.

On a wider plain, the movement for women's legal equality, given the unique numerical nature of its natural constituency, just might, as Betty Friedan suggests in this book's final piece, become a catalyst for an even loftier goal:

> "We need a new political movement in America that puts the lives and interests of people first. It can't be done by separate, single-issue movements now, and it has to be political, to protect and translate our new empowerment with a new vision of community, with new structures that open the doors again to real equality of opportunity for the diverse interests of all our children - - a new evolution of democracy as we approach the new millennium."

Howard L. Feinstein, 1999

CHAPTER I

Constitutional Development and Legal Framework

A. THE FEDERAL SYSTEM AND JUDICIAL REVIEW

The Constitution of the United States

We the people of the United States, in order to form a more perfect Union, establish Justice, insure domestic Tranquility, provide for the common defence, promote the general Welfare, and secure the Blessings of Liberty to ourselves and our Posterity, do ordain and establish this CONSTITUTION for the United States of America.

Article I

SECTION 1

All legislative Powers herein granted shall be vested in a Congress of the United States, which shall consist of a Senate and House of Representatives.

SECTION 2

The House of Representatives shall be composed of Members chosen every second Year by the People of the several States, and the Electors in each State shall have the Qualifications requisite for Electors of the most numerous Branch of the State Legislature.

No Person shall be a Representative who shall not have attained to the Age of twenty-five Years, and been seven Years a Citizen of the United States, and who shall not, when elected, be an Inhabitant of that State in which he shall be chosen.

[Representatives and direct Taxes shall be apportioned among the several States which may be included within this Union, according to their respective Numbers, which shall be determined by adding to the whole Number of Free Persons, including those bound to Service for a Term of Years, and excluding Indians not taxed, three fifths of all other persons.][1] The actual Enumeration shall be made within three Years after the first Meeting of the Congress of the United States, and within every subsequent Term of ten Years, in such Manner as they shall by Law direct. The Number of Representatives shall not exceed one for every thirty thousand, but each State shall have at least one Representative; and until such enumeration shall be made, the State of New Hampshire shall be entitled to chuse three, Massachusetts eight, Rhode Island and Providence Plantations one, Connecticut five, New York six, New Jersey four, Pennsylvania eight, Delaware one, Maryland six, Virginia ten, North Carolina five, South Carolina five, and Georgia three.

When vacancies happen in the Representation from any State, the Executive Authority thereof shall issue Writs of Election to fill such Vacancies.

The House of Representatives shall chuse their Speaker and other Officers; and shall have the sole Power of Impeachment.

SECTION 3

The Senate of the United States shall be composed of two Senators from each State, chosen by the Legislature thereof,[2] for six Years; and each Senator shall have one Vote.

Immediately after they shall be assembled in Consequence of the first Election, they shall be divided as equally as may be into three Classes. The Seats of the Senators of the first Class shall be vacated at the Expiration of the second Year, of the Second Class at the Expiration of the fourth Year, and of the third Class at the Expiration of the sixth Year, so that one-third may be chosen every second Year; and if Vacancies happen by Resignation, or otherwise, during the Recess of the Legislature of any State, the Executive therefore may make temporary Appointments until the next Meeting of

[1] This provision was modified by the Sixteenth Amendment. The three-fifths reference to slaves was rendered obsolete by the Thirteenth and Fourteenth Amendments.

[2] See the Seventeenth Amendment.

the Legislature, which shall then fill such Vacancies.

No Person shall be a Senator who shall not have attained to the Age of thirty Years, and been nine Years a Citizen of the United States, and who shall not, when elected, be an Inhabitant of that State in which he shall be chosen.

The Vice President of the United States shall be President of the Senate, but shall have no vote, unless they be equally divided.

The Senate shall chuse their other Officers, and also a President pro tempore, in the absence of the Vice President, or when he shall exercise the Office of President of the United States.

The Senate shall have the sole Power to try all Impeachments. When sitting for that Purpose, they shall be on Oath or Affirmation. When the President of the United States is tried, the Chief Justice shall preside; And no Person shall be convicted without the Concurrence of two thirds of the Members present.

Judgment in Cases of Impeachment shall not extend further than to removal from Office, and disqualification to hold and enjoy any Office of honor, Trust or Profit under the United States; but the Party convicted shall nevertheless be liable and subject to Indictment, Trial, Judgment, and Punishment, according to Law.

SECTION 4

The Times, Places and Manner of holding Elections for Senators and Representatives, shall be prescribed in each State by the Legislature thereof; but the Congress may at any time by Law make or alter such Regulations, except as to the Places of chusing Senators.

The Congress shall assemble at least once in every Year, and such Meeting shall be on the first Monday in December, unless they shall by Law appoint a different Day.[3]

SECTION 5

Each House shall be the Judge of the Elections, Returns and Qualifications of its own Members, and a Majority of each shall constitute a Quorum to do Business; but a smaller Number may adjourn from day to day, and may be authorized to compel the Attendance of absent Members, in such Manner, and under such Penalties, as each House may provide.

Each House may determine the Rules of its Proceedings, punish its Members for disorderly Behavior, and, with the Concurrence of two thirds, expel a Member.

Each House shall keep a Journal of its Proceedings and from time to time publish the same, excepting such Parts as may in their Judgment require Secrecy; and the Yeas and Nays of the Members of either House on any question shall, at the Desire of one fifth of those Present, be entered on the Journal.

Neither House, during the Session of Congress, shall without the Consent of the other, adjourn for more than three days, nor to any other Place than that in which the two Houses shall be sitting.

SECTION 6

The Senators and Representatives shall receive a Compensation for their Services, to be ascertained by Law, and paid out of the Treasury of the United States. They shall in all Cases, except Treason, Felony, and Breach of the peace, be privileged from Arrest during their Attendance at the Session of their respective Houses, and in going to and returning from the same; and for any Speech or Debate in either House, they shall not be questioned in any other Place.

No Senator or Representative shall, during the Time for which he was elected, be appointed to any civil Office under the Authority of the United States, which shall have been created, or the Emoluments whereof shall have been encreased during such time; and no Person holding any Office under the United States shall be a Member of either House during his continuance in Office.

SECTION 7

All Bills for raising Revenue shall originate in the House of Representatives; but the Senate may propose or concur with Amendments as on other Bills.

Every Bill which shall have passed the House of Representatives and the Senate, shall, before it become a Law, be presented to the President of the United States; if he approve he shall sign it, but if not he shall return it, with his Objections to that House in which it shall have originated, who shall enter the Objections at large on their Journal, and proceed to reconsider it. If after such Reconsideration two thirds of that House shall agree to pass the Bill it shall be sent, together with the Objections, to the other House, by which it shall likewise be reconsidered, and if approved by two thirds of that House, it shall become a Law. But in all such Cases the Votes of both Houses shall be determined by Yeas and Nays, and the Names of the Persons voting for and against the Bill shall be entered on the

[3] See the Twentieth Amendment.

Journal of each House respectively. If any Bill shall not be returned by the President within ten Days (Sundays excepted) after it shall have been presented to him, the Same shall be a Law, in like Manner as if he had signed it, unless the Congress by their Adjournment prevent its Return, in which Case it shall not be a Law.

Every Order, Resolution, or Vote to which the Concurrence of the Senate and House of Representatives may be necessary (except on a question of Adjournment) shall be presented to the President of the United States; and before the Same shall take Effect, shall be approved by him, or being disapproved by him, shall be repassed by two thirds of the Senate and House of Representatives, according to the Rules and Limitations prescribed in the Case of a Bill.

SECTION 8

The Congress shall have Power To lay and collect Taxes, Duties, Imposts and Excises, to pay the Debts and provide for the common Defence and general Welfare of the United States; but all Duties, Imposts and Excises shall be uniform throughout the United States;

To borrow money on the Credit of the United States;

To regulate Commerce with foreign Nations, and among the several States, and with the Indian Tribes;

To establish an uniform Rule of Naturalization, and uniform Laws on the subject of Bankruptcies throughout the United States;

To coin Money, regulate the Value thereof, and of foreign Coin, and fix the Standard of Weights and Measures;

To provide for the Punishment of counterfeiting the Securities and current Coin of the United States;

To Establish Post Offices and Post Roads;

To promote the Progress of Science and useful Arts, by securing for limited Times to Authors and Inventors the exclusive Right to their respective Writings and Discoveries;

To constitute Tribunals inferior to the supreme Court;

To define and punish Piracies and Felonies committed on the high Seas, and Offenses against the Law of Nations;

To declare War, grant Letters of Marque and Reprisal, and make Rules concerning Captures on Land and Water;

To raise and support Armies, but no Appropriation of Money to that Use shall be for a longer Term than two Years;

To provide and maintain a Navy;

To make Rules for the Government and Regulation of the land and naval Forces;

To provide for calling forth the Militia to execute the Laws of the Union, suppress Insurrections and repel Invasions;

To provide for organizing, arming, and disciplining the Militia, and for governing such Part of them as may be employed in the Service of the United States, reserving to the States respectively, the Appointment of the Officers, and the Authority of training the Militia according to the discipline prescribed by Congress;

To exercise exclusive Legislation in all Cases whatsoever, over such District (not exceeding ten Miles square) as may, by Cession of particular States, and the acceptance of Congress, become the Seat of the Government of the United States, and to exercise like Authority over all Places purchased by the Consent of the Legislature of the State in which the Same shall be, for the Erection of Forts, Magazines, Arsenals, dock-Yards, and other needful Buildings;—And

To make all Laws which shall be necessary and proper for carrying into Execution the foregoing Powers, and all other Powers vested by this Constitution in the Government of the United States, or in any Department or Officer thereof.

SECTION 9

The Migration or Importation of such Persons as any of the States now existing shall think proper to admit, shall not be prohibited by the Congress prior to the Year, one thousand eight hundred and eight, but a tax or duty may be imposed on such Importation, not exceeding ten dollars for each person.

The privilege of the Writ of Habeas Corpus shall not be suspended, unless when in Cases of Rebellion or Invasion the public Safety may require it.

No Bill of Attainder or ex post facto Law shall be passed.

No capitation, or other direct Tax shall be laid, unless in Proportion to the Census or Enumeration herein before directed to be taken.[4]

No Tax or Duty shall be laid on Articles exported from any State.

No Preference shall be given by any Regulation of Commerce or Revenue to the Ports of one State over those of another: nor shall Vessels bound to, or from one State, be obliged to enter, clear, or pay Duties in another.

[4] See the Sixteenth Amendment.

No Money shall be drawn from the Treasury, but in Consequence of Appropriations made by Law; and a regular Statement and Account of the Receipts and Expenditures of all public Money shall be published from time to time.

No Title of Nobility shall be granted by the United States:—And no Person holding any Office of Profit or Trust under them, shall, without the Consent of the Congress, accept of any present, Emolument, Office, or Title, of any kind whatever, from any King, Prince or foreign State.

SECTION 10

No State shall enter into any Treaty, Alliance, or Confederation; grant Letters of Marque and Reprisal; coin Money; emit Bills of Credit; make any Thing but gold and silver Coin a Tender in Payment of Debts; pass any Bill of Attainder, ex post facto Law, or Law impairing the Obligation of Contracts, or grant any Title of Nobility.

No State shall, without the Consent of the Congress, lay any Imposts or Duties on Imports or Exports, except what may be absolutely necessary for executing its inspection Laws: and the net Produce of all Duties and Imposts, laid by any State on Imports or Exports, shall be for the Use of the Treasury of the United States and all such Laws shall be subject to the Revision and Controul of the Congress.

No State shall, without the Consent of Congress, lay any duty of Tonnage, keep Troops, or Ships of War in time of Peace, enter into any Agreement or Compact with another State, or with a foreign Power, or engage in War, unless actually invaded, or in such imminent Danger as will not admit of delay.

Article II

SECTION 1

The executive Power shall be vested in a President of the United States of America. He shall hold his Office during the Term of four Years, and, together with the Vice-President, chosen for the same term, be elected, as follows.

Each State shall appoint, in such Manner as the Legislature thereof may direct, a number of Electors, equal to the whole number of Senators and Representatives to which the State may be entitled in the Congress; but no Senator or Representative, or Person holding an Office of Trust or Profit under the United States, shall be appointed an Elector.

The Electors shall meet in their respective States, and vote by Ballot for two persons, of whom one at least shall not be an Inhabitant of the same State with themselves. And they shall make a List of all the Persons voted for, and of the Number of Votes for each; which List they shall sign and certify, and transmit sealed to the Seat of the Government of the United States, directed to the President of the Senate. The President of the Senate shall, in the Presence of the Senate and House of Representatives, open all the Certificates, and the Votes shall then be counted. The Person having the greatest Number of Votes shall be the President, if such Number be a Majority of the whole Number of Electors appointed; and if there be more than one who have such Majority, and have an Equal Number of Votes, then the House of Representatives shall immediately chuse by Ballot one of them for President; and if no Person have a Majority, then from the five highest on the List the said House shall in like Manner chuse the President, but in chusing the President, the Votes shall be taken by States, the Representation from each State having one Vote; a quorum for this Purpose shall consist of a Member or Members from two-thirds of the States, and a Majority of all the States shall be necessary to a Choice. In every Case, after the Choice of the President, the Person having the greatest Number of Votes of the Electors shall be the Vice-President. But if there should remain two or more who have equal Votes, the Senate shall chuse from them by Ballot the Vice-President.[5]

The Congress may determine the Time of chusing the Electors, and the Day on which they shall give their Vote; which Day shall be the same throughout the United States.

No person except a natural born Citizen, or a Citizen of the United States, at the time of the Adoption of this Constitution, shall be eligible to the Office of President; neither shall any Person be eligible to that Office who shall not have attained to the Age of thirty-five Years, and been fourteen Years a Resident within the United States.

In Case of the Removal of the President from Office, or of his Death, Resignation, or Inability to discharge the Powers and Duties of the said Office, the same shall devolve on the Vice-President, and the Congress may by Law provide for the Case of Removal, Death, Resignation, or Inability, both of the President and Vice-President, declaring what Officer shall then act as President, and such Officer shall act accordingly, until the Disability be removed, or a President shall be elected.

The President shall, at stated Times, receive for

[5]This paragraph was superseded by the Twelfth Amendment.

his Services, a Compensation, which shall neither be encreased nor diminished during the Period for which he shall have been elected, and he shall not receive within that Period any other Emolument from the United States, or any of them.

Before he enters on the Execution of his Office, he shall take the following Oath or Affirmation: "I do solemnly swear (or affirm) that I will faithfully execute the Office of President of the United States, and will to the best of my Ability, preserve, protect and defend the Constitution of the United States."

SECTION 2

The President shall be Commander in Chief of the Army and Navy of the United States, and of the Militia of the several States, when called into the actual Service of the United States; he may require the Opinion in writing, of the principal Officer in each of the executive Departments, upon any subject relating to the Duties of their respective Offices, and he shall have Power to grant Reprieves and Pardons for Offenses against the United States, except in Cases of Impeachment.

He shall have Power, by and with the Advice and Consent of the Senate, to make Treaties, provided two-thirds of the Senators present concur; and he shall nominate, and by and with the Advice and Consent of the Senate, shall appoint Ambassadors, other public Ministers and Consuls, Judges of the supreme Court, and all other Officers of the United States, whose Appointments are not herein otherwise provided for, and which shall be established by Law: but the Congress may by Law vest the Appointment of such inferior Officers, as they think proper, in the President alone, in the Courts of Law, or in the Heads of Departments.

The President shall have Power to fill up all Vacancies that may happen during the Recess of the Senate, by granting Commissions which shall expire at the End of their next Session.

SECTION 3

He shall from time to time give to the Congress Information of the State of the Union, and recommend to their Consideration such Measures as he shall judge necessary and expedient: he may, on extraordinary Occasions, convene both Houses, or either of them, and in Cases of Disagreement between them, with Respect to the Time of Adjournment, he may adjourn them to such Time as he shall think proper; he shall receive Ambassadors and other public Ministers; he shall take Care that the Laws be faithfully executed, and shall Commission all the Officers of the United States.

SECTION 4

The President, Vice-President and all civil Officers of the United States, shall be removed from Office on Impeachment for, and Conviction of, Treason, Bribery, or other high Crimes and Misdemeanors.

Article III

SECTION 1

The judicial Power of the United States, shall be vested in one supreme Court, and in such inferior Courts as the Congress may from time to time ordain and establish. The Judges, both of the supreme and inferior Courts, shall hold their offices during good Behaviour, and shall, at stated Times, receive for their Services a Compensation, which shall not be diminished during their Continuance in Office.

SECTION 2

The judicial Power shall extend to all Cases, in Law and Equity, arising under this Constitution, the Laws of the United States and Treaties made, or which shall be made, under their Authority;—to all Cases affecting Ambassadors, other public Ministers and Consuls;—to all Cases of admiralty and maritime Jurisdiction;—to Controversies to which the United States shall be a Party;—to Controversies between two or more States;—between a State and Citizens of another State;[6]—Between Citizens of different States;—between Citizens of the same State claiming Lands under Grants of different States, and between a State, or the Citizens thereof, and foreign States, Citizens or Subjects.

In all Cases affecting Ambassadors, other public Ministers and Consuls, and those in which a State shall be a Party, the supreme Court shall have original Jurisdiction. In all the other Cases before mentioned, the supreme Court shall have appellate Jurisdiction, both as to Law and Fact, with such Exceptions, and under such Regulations as the Congress shall make.

The trial of all Crimes, except in Cases of Impeachment, shall be by Jury, and such Trial shall be held in the State where the said Crimes shall have been committed; but when not committed within any State, the Trial shall be at such Place or Places as the Congress may by Law have directed.

SECTION 3

Treason against the United States, shall consist only in levying War against them, or, in adhering to their

[6] See the Eleventh Amendment.

Enemies, giving them Aid and Comfort. No Person shall be convicted of Treason unless on the Testimony of two Witnesses to the same overt Act, or on Confession in open Court.

The Congress shall have Power to declare the Punishment of Treason, but no Attainder of Treason shall work Corruption of Blood, or Forfeiture except during the Life of the Person attainted.

Article IV

SECTION 1

Full Faith and Credit shall be given in each State to the public acts, Records, and judicial Proceedings of every other State. And the Congress may by general Laws prescribe the Manner in which such Acts, Records and Proceedings shall be proved, and the Effect thereof.

SECTION 2

The Citizens of each State shall be entitled to all Privileges and Immunities of Citizens in the several States.

A person charged in any State with Treason, Felony, or other Crime, who shall flee from Justice, and be found in another State, shall on demand of the executive Authority of the State from which he fled, be delivered up, to be removed to the State having Jurisdiction of the Crime.

No Person held to Service or Labour in one State, under the Laws thereof, escaping into another, shall, in Consequence of any Law or Regulation therein, be discharged from such Service or Labour, but shall be delivered up on Claim of the Party to whom such Service or Labour may be due.[7]

SECTION 3

New States may be admitted by the Congress into this Union; but no new States shall be formed or erected within the Jurisdiction of any other State; nor any State be formed by the Junction of two or more States, or parts of States, without the Consent of the Legislatures of the States concerned as well as of the Congress.

The Congress shall have Power to dispose of and make all needful Rules and Regulations respecting the Territory or other Property belonging to the United States; and nothing in this Constitution shall be so constructed as to Prejudice any Claims of the United States, or of any particular State.

[7] Obsolete. See the Thirteenth Amendment.

SECTION 4

The United States shall guarantee to every State in this Union a Republican Form of Government, and shall protect each of them against Invasion; and on Application of the Legislature, or of the Executive (when the Legislature cannot be convened) against domestic Violence.

Article V

The Congress, whenever two-thirds of both Houses shall deem it necessary, shall propose Amendments to this Constitution, or, on the Application of the Legislatures of two-thirds of the several States, shall call a Convention for proposing Amendments, which, in either Case, shall be valid to all Intents and Purposes, as part of this Constitution, when ratified by the Legislatures of three-fourths of the several States, or by Conventions in three-fourths thereof, as the one or the other Mode of Ratification may be proposed by the Congress; Provided that no Amendment which may be made prior to the Year One thousand eight hundred and eight shall in any Manner affect the first and fourth Clauses in the Ninth Section of the first Article; and that no State, without its Consent, shall be deprived of its equal Suffrage in the Senate.

Article VI

All Debts contracted and Engagements entered into, before the Adoption of this Constitution, shall be as valid against the United States under this Constitution, as under the Confederation.

This Constitution, and the Laws of the United States which shall be made in Pursuance thereof; and all Treaties made, or which shall be made, under the Authority of the United States, shall be the supreme Law of the Land; and the Judges in every State shall be bound thereby, any Thing in the Constitution or Laws of any State to the Contrary notwithstanding.

The Senators and Representatives before mentioned, and the Members of the several State Legislatures, and all executive and judicial Officers, both of the United States and of the several States, shall be bound by Oath or Affirmation, to support this Constitution; but no religious Test shall ever be required as a Qualification to any Office or public Trust under the United States.

Article VII

The Ratification of the Conventions of nine States shall be sufficient for the Establishment of this Constitution between the States so ratifying the Same.

AMENDMENTS[8]

Amendment I

Congress shall make no law respecting an establishment of religion, or prohibiting the free exercise thereof; or abridging the freedom of speech, or of the press; or the right of the people peaceably to assemble, and to petition the Government for a redress of grievances.

Amendment II

A well regulated Militia, being necessary to the security of a free State, the right of the people to keep and bear Arms, shall not be infringed.

Amendment III

No Soldier shall, in time of peace be quartered in any house, without the consent of the Owner, nor in time of war, but in a manner to be prescribed by law.

Amendment IV

The right of the people to be secure in their persons, houses, papers, and effects, against unreasonable searches and seizures, shall not be violated, and no Warrants shall issue, but upon probable cause, supported by Oath or affirmation, and particularly describing the place to be searched, and the persons or things to be seized.

Amendment V

No person shall be held to answer for a capital, or otherwise infamous crime, unless on a presentment or indictment of a Grand Jury, except in cases arising in the land or naval forces, or in the Militia, when in actual service in time of War or public danger; nor shall any person be subject for the same offense to be twice put in jeopardy of life or limb, nor shall be compelled in any criminal case to be a witness against himself, nor be deprived of life, liberty, or property, without due process of law; nor shall private property be taken for public use, without just compensation.

Amendment VI

In all criminal prosecutions, the accused shall enjoy the right to a speedy and public trial, by an impartial jury of the State and district wherein the crime shall have been committed, which district shall have been previously ascertained by law, and to be informed of the nature and cause of the accusation; to be confronted with the witnesses against him; to have compulsory process for obtaining witnesses in his favor, and to have the Assistance of Counsel for his defence.

Amendment VII

In suits at common law, where the value in controversy shall exceed twenty dollars, the right of trial by jury shall be preserved, and no fact tried by jury, shall be otherwise reexamined in any Court of the United States, than according to the rules of the common law.

Amendment VIII

Excessive bail shall not be required, nor excessive fines imposed, nor cruel and unusual punishments inflicted.

Amendment IX

The enumeration in the Constitution, of certain rights, shall not be construed to deny or disparage others retained by the people.

Amendment X

The powers not delegated to the United States by the Constitution, nor prohibited by it to the States, are reserved to the States respectively, or to the people.

Amendment XI (1798)

The Judicial power of the United States shall not be construed to extend to any suit in law or equity, commenced or prosecuted against one of the United States by Citizens of another State, or by Citizens or Subjects of any Foreign States.

[8] The first ten amendments were adopted in 1791 as the Bill of Rights.

Amendment XII (1804)

The Electors shall meet in their respective states and vote by ballot for President and Vice-President, one of whom, at least, shall not be an inhabitant of the same state with themselves; they shall name in their ballots the person voted for as President, and in distinct ballots the person voted for as Vice-President, and they shall make distinct lists of all persons voted for as president, and all persons voted for as Vice-President, and of the number of votes for each, which lists they shall sign and certify, and transmit sealed to the seat of the government of the United States, directed to the President of the Senate;—The President of the Senate shall, in the presence of the Senate and House of Representatives, open all the certificates and the votes shall then be counted;—The person having the greatest number of votes for President, shall be the President, if such number be a majority of the whole number of Electors appointed; and if no person have such majority, then from the persons having the highest numbers not exceeding three on the list of those voted for as President, the House of Representatives shall choose immediately, by ballot, the President. But in choosing the President, the votes shall be taken by states, the representation from each state having one vote; a quorum for this purpose shall consist of a member or members from two-thirds of the states, and a majority of all the states shall be necessary to a choice. And if the House of Representatives shall not choose a President whenever the right of choice shall devolve upon them, before the fourth day of March next following, then the Vice-President shall act as President, as in the case of the death or other constitutional disability of the President.—The person having the greatest number of votes as Vice-President, shall be the Vice-President, if such number be a majority of the whole number of Electors appointed, and if no person have a majority, then from the two highest numbers on the list, the Senate shall choose the Vice-President; a quorum for the purpose shall consist of two-thirds of the whole number of Senators, and a majority of the whole number shall be necessary to a choice. But no person constitutionally ineligible to the office of the President shall be eligible to that of Vice-President of the United States.

Amendment XIII (1865)

SECTION 1

Neither slavery nor involuntary servitude, except as a punishment for crime whereof the party shall have been duly convicted, shall exist within the United States, or any place subject to their jurisdiction.

SECTION 2

Congress shall have power to enforce this article by appropriate legislation.

Amendment XIV (1868)

SECTION 1

All persons born or naturalized in the United States and subject to the jurisdiction thereof, are citizens of the United States and of the State wherein they reside. No State shall make or enforce any law which shall abridge the privileges or immunities of citizens of the United States; nor shall any State deprive any person of life, liberty, or property, without due process of law; nor deny to any person within its jurisdiction the equal protection of the laws.

SECTION 2

Representatives shall be apportioned among the several States according to their respective numbers, counting the whole number of persons in each State, excluding Indians not taxed. But when the right to vote at any election for the choice of electors for President and Vice-President of the United States, Representatives in Congress, the Executive and Judicial Officers of a State, or the members of the Legislature thereof, is denied to any of the male inhabitants of such State, being twenty-one years of age, and citizens of the United States, or in any way abridged, except for participation in rebellion, or other crime, the basis of representation therein shall be reduced in the proportion which the number of such male citizens shall bear to the whole number of male citizens twenty-one years of age in such State.

SECTION 3

No person shall be a Senator or Representative in Congress, or elector of President and Vice-President, or hold any office, civil or military, under the United States, or under any State, who, having previously taken an oath, as a member of Congress, or as an officer of the United States, or as a member of any State legislature, or as an executive or judicial officer of any State, to support the Constitution of the United States, shall have engaged in insurrection or rebellion against the same, or given aid or comfort to the enemies thereof. But Congress may by a vote of two-thirds of each House, remove such disability.

SECTION 4

The validity of the public debt of the United States, authorized by law, including debts incurred for payment of pensions and bounties for services in suppressing insurrection or rebellion, shall not be questioned. But neither the United States nor any State shall assume or pay any debt or obligation incurred in aid of insurrection or rebellion against the United States, or any claim for the loss or emancipation of any slave; but all such debts, obligations, and claims shall be held illegal and void.

SECTION 5

The Congress shall have power to enforce, by appropriate legislation, the provisions of this article.

Amendment XV (1870)

SECTION 1

The right of citizens of the United States to vote shall not be denied or abridged by the United States or by any State on account of race, color, or previous condition of servitude.

SECTION 2

The Congress shall have the power to enforce this article by appropriate legislation.

Amendment XVI (1913)

The Congress shall have power to lay and collect taxes on incomes, from whatever source derived, without apportionment among the several States, and without regard to any census or enumeration.

Amendment XVII (1913)

The Senate of the United States shall be composed of two Senators from each State, elected by the people thereof, for six years, and each Senator shall have one vote. The electors in each State shall have the qualifications requisite for electors of the most numerous branch of the State legislatures.

When vacancies happen in the representation of any State in the Senate, the executive authority of such State shall issue writs of election to fill such vacancies: *Provided*, That the legislature of any State may empower the executive thereof to make temporary appointments until the people fill the vacancies by election as the legislature may direct.

This amendment shall not be so construed as to affect the election or term of any Senator chosen before it becomes valid as part of the Constitution.

Amendment XVIII (1919)[9]

SECTION 1

After one year from the ratification of this article the manufacture, sale, or transportation of intoxicating liquors within, the importation thereof into, or the exportation thereof from the United States and all territory subject to the jurisdiction thereof for beverage purposes is hereby prohibited.

SECTION 2

The Congress and the several States shall have concurrent power to enforce this article by appropriate legislation.

SECTION 3

This article shall be inoperative unless it shall have been ratified as an amendment to the Constitution by the legislatures of the several States, as provided in the Constitution, within seven years from the date of the submission hereof to the States by the Congress.

Amendment XIX (1920)

The right of citizens of the United States to vote shall not be denied or abridged by the United States or by any State on account of sex.

Congress shall have power to enforce this article by appropriate legislation.

Amendment XX (1933)

SECTION 1

The terms of the President and Vice-President shall end at noon on the 20th day of January, and the terms of Senators and Representatives at noon on the 3rd day of January, of the years in which such terms would have ended if this article had not been ratified; and the terms of their successors shall then begin.

SECTION 2

The Congress shall assemble at least once in every year, and such meeting shall begin at noon on the 3rd day of January, unless they shall by law appoint a different day.

SECTION 3

If, at the time fixed for the beginning of the term of the President, the President elect shall have

[9] Repealed by the Twenty-first Amendment.

died, the Vice-President elect shall become President. If a President shall not have been chosen before the time fixed for the beginning of his term, or if the President elect shall have failed to qualify, then the Vice-President elect shall act as President until a President shall have qualified; and the Congress may by law provide for the case wherein neither a President elect nor a Vice-President elect shall have qualified, declaring who shall then act as President, or the manner in which one who is to act shall be selected, and such person shall act accordingly until a President or Vice-President shall have qualified.

SECTION 4

The Congress may by law provide for the case of the death of any of the persons from whom the House of Representatives may choose a President whenever the right of choice shall have devolved upon them, and for the case of the death of any of the persons from whom the Senate may choose a Vice-President whenever the right of choice shall have devolved upon them.

SECTION 5

Sections 1 and 2 shall take effect on the 15th day of October following the ratification of this article.

SECTION 6

This article shall be inoperative unless it shall have been ratified as an amendment to the Constitution by the legislatures of three-fourths of the several States within seven years from the date of its submission.

Amendment XXI (1933)[10]

SECTION 1

The eighteenth article of amendment to the Constitution of the United States is hereby repealed.

SECTION 2

The transportation or importation into any State, Territory, or possession of the United States for delivery or use of intoxicating liquors, in violation of the laws thereof, is hereby prohibited.

SECTION 3

This article shall be inoperative unless it shall have been ratified as an amendment to the Constitution by conventions in the several States, as provided in the Constitution, within seven years from the date of the submission hereof to the states by the Congress.

[10] This is the only amendment to date to have been ratified not by state legislatures but by specially called conventions in the states.

Amendment XXII (1951)

SECTION 1

No person shall be elected to the office of the President more than twice, and no person who has held the office of President, or acted as President, for more than two years of a term to which some other person was elected President shall be elected to the office of President more than once. But this Article shall not apply to any person holding the office of President when this Article was proposed by the Congress, and shall not prevent any person who may be holding the office of President, or acting as President, during the term within which this Article becomes operative from holding the office of President, or acting as President during the remainder of such term.

SECTION 2

This article shall be inoperative unless it shall have been ratified as an amendment to the Constitution by the legislatures of three-fourths of the several States within seven years from the date of its submission to the States by the Congress.

Amendment XXIII (1961)

SECTION 1

The District constituting the seat of Government of the United States shall appoint in such manner as the Congress may direct:

A number of electors of President and Vice-President equal to the whole number of Senators and Representatives in Congress to which the District would be entitled if it were a State, but in no event more than the least populous State; they shall be in addition to those appointed by the States, but they shall be considered, for the purposes of the election of President and Vice-President, to be electors appointed by a state; and they shall meet in the District and perform such duties as provided by the twelfth article of amendment.

SECTION 2

The Congress shall have power to enforce this article by appropriate legislation.

Amendment XXIV (1964)

SECTION 1

The right of citizens of the United States to vote in any primary or other election for President or Vice-President, for electors for President or Vice-President, or for Senator or Representative in Congress, shall not be denied or abridged by the United States or any State by reason of failure to pay any poll tax or other tax.

SECTION 2

The Congress shall have power to enforce this article by appropriate legislation.

Amendment XXV (1967)

SECTION 1

In case of the removal of the President from office or his death or resignation, the Vice-President shall become President.

SECTION 2

Whenever there is a vacancy in the office of the Vice-President, the President shall nominate a Vice-President who shall take the office upon confirmation by a majority vote of both houses of Congress.

SECTION 3

Whenever the President transmits to the President pro tempore of the Senate and the Speaker of the House of Representatives his written declaration that he is unable to discharge the powers and duties of his office, and until he transmits to them a written declaration to the contrary, such powers and duties shall be discharged by the Vice-President as Acting President.

SECTION 4

Whenever the Vice-President and a majority of either the principal officers of the executive departments or of such other body as Congress may by law provide, transmit to the President pro tempore of the Senate and the Speaker of the House of Representatives their written declaration that the President is unable to discharge the powers and duties of his office, the Vice-President shall immediately assume the powers and duties of the office as Acting President.

Thereafter, when the President transmits to the President pro tempore of the Senate and the Speaker of the House of Representatives his written declaration that no inability exists, he shall resume the powers and duties of his office unless the Vice-President and a majority of either the principal officers of the executive department or of such other body as Congress may by law provide, transmit within four days to the President pro tempore of the Senate and the Speaker of the House of Representatives their written declaration that the President is unable to discharge the powers and duties of his office. Thereupon Congress shall decide the issue, assembling within 48 hours for that purpose if not in session. If the Congress, within 21 days after receipt of the latter written declaration, or, if Congress is not in session, within 21 days after Congress is required to assemble, determines by two-thirds vote of both houses that the President is unable to discharge the powers and duties of his office, the Vice-President shall continue to discharge the same as Acting President; otherwise, the President shall resume the powers and duties of his office.

Amendment XXVI (1971)

SECTION 1

The Right of Citizens of the United States, who are eighteen years of age or older, to vote shall not be denied or abridged by the United States or any State on account of age.

SECTION 2

The Congress shall have the power to enforce this article by appropriate legislation.

Amendment XXVII (1992)[11]

No law varying the compensation for the services of the Senators and Representatives shall take effect, until an election of Representatives shall have intervened.

[11] This is the so-called Lost Amendment, proposed in 1789 along with 11 others submitted to the states but, because of no limitation imposed on the time allowed for ratification, not adopted until more than two centuries later.

Note: Proposed Equal Rights Amendment adopted by Congress in 1972 but not ratified by the states: "Equality of rights under the law shall not be denied or abridged by the United States or by any state on account of sex."

AMERICAN JUDICIAL SYSTEM

U.S. SUPREME COURT

-Nine Justices, including Chief Justice
-Discretionary appellate jurisdiction
-Four votes required to hear a case

FEDERAL APPEALS COURTS

-12 Circuit Courts (Geographical)
plus special (subject matter) courts
-Appeal by right

STATE "HIGH" COURT

-Appeal by right if no intermediate appellate court
-Discretionary appeal from intermediate appellate court

STATE INTERMEDIATE APPELLATE COURT(S)

-Appeal by right

(if no intermediate appellate court)

FEDERAL DISTRICT COURTS

-94 District Courts
plus specialized (subject matter) courts
-Trial-level courts (jury, or judge only)

STATE TRIAL COURTS

-Judge or jury

*   *   *   *   *

FEDERAL ADMINISTRATIVE AGENCIES

-Specific subject-matter expertise
-Promulgate federal regulations
-Resolve certain disputes before federal agencies

STATE ADMINISTRATIVE AGENCIES

-Generally analogous to federal administrative agencies

FEDERAL GRAND JURIES

-Officially supervised by District Courts, but in control of federal prosecutor (U.S. Attorney)
-23 members; 12 votes to bring indictment

Federal judges (including Supreme Court Justices) are nominated by the President, subject to confirmation by majority vote of the U.S. Senate (after hearings before and vote of the Senate Judiciary Committee). Federal judges serve for life, subject to impeachment/trial by Congress.

The Supreme Court and Constitutional Interpretation

[Official Supreme Court Document]

"Equal Justice Under Law"-These words, written above the main entrance to the Supreme Court Building, express the ultimate responsibility of the Supreme Court of the United States. The Court is the highest tribunal in the nation for all cases and controversies arising under the Constitution or the laws of the United States. As the final arbiter of the law, the Court is charged with ensuring the American people the promise of equal justice under law, and thereby, also functions as guardian and interpreter of the Constitution.

The Supreme Court is "distinctly American in concept and function," as Chief Justice Charles Evans Hughes observed. Few other courts in the world have the same authority of constitutional interpretation and none have exercised it for as long or with as much influence. A century and a half ago, the French political observer Alexis de Tocqueville noted the unique position of the Supreme Court in the history of nations and of jurisprudence. "The representative system of government has been adopted in several states of Europe," he remarked, "but I am unaware that any nation of the globe has hitherto organized a judicial power in the same manner as the Americans . . . . A more imposing judicial power was never constituted by any people."

The unique position of the Supreme Court stems, in large part, from the deep commitment of the American people to the Rule of Law and to constitutional government. The United States has demonstrated an unprecedented determination to preserve and protect its written Constitution, thereby providing the American "experiment in democracy" with the oldest written constitution still in force.

The Constitution of the United States is a carefully balanced document. It is designed to provide for a national government sufficiently strong and flexible to meet the needs of the Republic, yet sufficiently limited and just to protect the guaranteed rights of citizens; it permits a balance between society's need for order and the individual's right to freedom. To assure these ends, the Framers of the Constitution created three independent and coequal branches of government. That this Constitution has provided continuous democratic government through the periodic stresses of more than two centuries illustrates the genius of the American system of government.

The complex role of the Supreme Court in this system derives from its authority to invalidate legislation or executive actions which, in the Court's considered judgment, conflict with the Constitution. This power of "judicial review" has given the Court a crucial responsibility in assuring individual rights, as well as in maintaining a "living Constitution" whose broad provisions are continually applied to complicated new situations.

While the function of Judicial Review is not explicitly provided in the Constitution, it had been anticipated before the adoption of that document. Prior to 1789, state courts had already overturned legislative acts which conflicted with state constitutions. Moreover, many of the Founding Fathers expected the Supreme Court to assume this role in regard to the Constitution; Alexander Hamilton and James Madison, for example, had underlined the importance of judicial review in the Federalist Papers, which urged adoption of the Constitution.

Hamilton had written that through the practice of judicial review the Court ensured that the will of the whole people, as expressed in their Constitution, would be supreme over the will of a legislature, whose statutes might express only the temporary will of part of the people. And Madison had written that constitutional interpretation must be left to the reasoned judgment of independent judges, rather than to the tumult and conflict of the political process. If every constitutional question were to be decided by public political bargaining, Madison argued, the Constitution would be reduced to a battleground of competing factions, political passion and partisan spirit.

Despite this background the Court's power of judicial review was not confirmed until 1803, when it was invoked by Chief Justice John Marshall in Marbury v. Madison. In this decision, the Chief Justice asserted that the Supreme Court's responsibility to overturn unconstitutional legislation was a necessary consequence of its sworn duty to uphold the Constitution. That oath could not be fulfilled any other way. "It is emphatically the province of the judicial department to say what the law is," he declared.

In retrospect, it is evident that constitutional interpretation and application were made necessary by the very nature of the Constitution. The Founding Fathers had wisely worded that document in rather general terms leaving it open to future elaboration to meet changing conditions. As Chief Justice Marshall noted in McCulloch v. Maryland, a constitution that attempted to detail every aspect of its own application "would partake of the prolixity of a legal code, and could scarcely be embraced by the human mind . . . . Its nature, therefore, requires that only its great outlines should be marked, its important objects designated and minor ingredients which compose those objects be deduced from the nature of the objects themselves."

The Constitution limits the Court to dealing with "Cases" and "Controversies." John Jay, the first Chief Justice, clarified this restraint early in the Court's history by declining to advise President George Washington on the constitutional implications of a proposed foreign policy decision. The Court does not give advisory opinions; rather, its function is limited only to deciding specific cases.

The Justices must exercise considerable discretion in deciding which cases to hear, since more than 6,500 civil and criminal cases are filed in the Supreme Court each year from the various state and federal courts. The Supreme Court also has "original jurisdiction" in a very small number of cases arising out of disputes between states or between a state and the federal government.

When the Supreme Court rules on a constitutional issue that judgment is virtually final; its decisions can be altered only by the rarely used procedure of constitutional amendment or by a new ruling of the Court. However, when the Court interprets a statute, new legislative action can be taken.

Chief Justice Marshall expressed the challenge which the Supreme Court faces in maintaining free government by noting: "We must never forget that it is a constitution we are expounding . . . intended to endure for ages to come, and consequently, to be adapted to the various crises of human affairs."

B. INTO THE FRAY: EARLY SUPREME COURT STEPS

It was not until the 1970's that the Supreme Court directly tackled challenges to sex discrimination under the Fourteenth Amendment's Equal Protection Clause. In the following four cases, the determining factor, in the majority's view, was whether the gender-specific statutory classification at issue was rationally related to a legitimate government objective. In two of the cases – *Reed v. Reed* and *Craig v. Boren,* the Court ruled that it did not, and these laws were held unconstitutional. However, in *Geduldig v. Aiello* and *Personnel Administrator of Massachusetts v. Feeney,* the Supreme Court refused to overturn state laws which impacted negatively on women.

In addition to the precariousness of this "rational relationship" test as a guarantor of equal rights for women, these early cases highlighted two other major aspects of gender-based constitutional jurisprudence:

- **Literality.** In *Reed*, the Idaho statute gave literal preference to males over females in the selection of estate administrators. In *Craig*, Oklahoma criminal law prohibited males under 21 and females under 18 from purchasing 3.2% beer. In both cases – in which there was no doubt that the gender-based disparate treatment was intentional, given the language of the statutes – the Court found Equal Protection violations by lopsided votes. By contrast, in *Geduldig*, the Court refused to invalidate California's exclusion of normal pregnancies from its employment disability insurance program, and in *Feeney*, the Massachusetts veterans' preference for state employment was upheld. The classifications in both cases impacted extremely disproportionately upon women, but the Court found non-gender-based reasons, rationally related to legitimate government objectives, for both: the financial soundness of the California disability scheme, and the compensation of veterans -- both male and female -- for service to their country. Although the Court gradually toughened the standard for gender-based classifications during the 1970's, it was apparent that a successful plaintiff was in a far better position if she could show **literal** discrimination.

Gender neutrality. Note that in *Craig*, the challenged 3.2% beer law operated to the detriment of males. Ruth Bader Ginsburg and other women's rights advocates successfully urged the Court to reject such disparate treatment, including those laws which purported to protect women or granted them "special privileges," based on stereotypes of traditional female roles. From early constitutional challenges to recent developments in the law of sexual harassment, the road to legal gender equality has often aided men as well as women.

REED v. REED, 404 U.S. 71 (1971)

Decided November 22, 1971

BURGER, C. J., delivered the opinion for a unanimous Court.

Richard Lynn Reed, a minor, died intestate in Ada County, Idaho, on March 29, 1967. His adoptive parents, who had separated sometime prior to his death, are the parties to this appeal. Approximately seven months after Richard's death, his mother, appellant Sally Reed, filed a petition in the Probate Court of Ada County, [404 U.S. 71, 72] seeking appointment as administratrix of her son's estate.1

Prior to the date set for a hearing on the mother's petition, appellee Cecil Reed, the father of the decedent, filed a competing petition seeking to have himself appointed administrator of the son's estate. The probate court held a joint hearing on the two petitions and thereafter ordered that letters of administration be issued to appellee Cecil Reed upon his taking the oath and filing the bond required by law. The court treated 15-312 and 15-314 of the Idaho Code as the controlling statutes and read those sections as compelling a preference for Cecil Reed because he was a male.

In issuing its order, the probate court implicitly recognized the equality of entitlement of the two applicants under 15-312 and noted that neither of the applicants was under any legal disability; the court ruled, however, that appellee, being a male, was to be preferred to the female appellant "by reason of Section 15-314 of the Idaho Code." In stating this conclusion, the probate judge gave no indication that he had attempted to determine the relative capabilities of the competing applicants to perform the functions incident to the administration of an estate. It seems clear the probate judge considered himself bound by statute to give preference to the male candidate over the female, each being otherwise "equally entitled."

Sally Reed thereupon appealed for review by this Court pursuant to 28 U.S.C. 1257 (2), and we noted probable jurisdiction. 401 U.S. 934. Having examined the record and considered the briefs and oral arguments of the parties, we have concluded that the arbitrary preference established in favor of males by 15-314 of the Idaho Code cannot stand in the face of the Fourteenth Amendment's command that no State deny the equal protection of the laws to any person within its jurisdiction. Section 15-314 is restricted in its operation to those situations where competing applications for letters of administration have been filed by both male and female members of the same entitlement class established by 15-312. In such situations, 15-314 provides that different treatment be accorded to the applicants on the basis of their sex; it thus establishes a classification subject to scrutiny under the Equal Protection Clause.

In applying that clause, this Court has consistently recognized that the Fourteenth Amendment does not deny to States the power to treat different classes of persons in different ways. Barbier v. Connolly, 113 U.S. 27 (1885); Lindsley v. Natural Carbonic Gas Co., 220 U.S. 61 (1911); Railway Express Agency v. New York, 336 U.S. 106 (1949); McDonald v. Board of Election Commissioners, 394 U.S. 802 (1969). The Equal Protection Clause of that amendment does, however, deny to States the power to legislate that different treatment be accorded to persons placed by a statute into [404 U.S. 71, 76] different classes on the basis of criteria wholly unrelated to the objective of that statute. A classification "must be reasonable, not arbitrary, and must rest upon some ground of difference having a fair and substantial relation to the object of the legislation, so that all persons similarly circumstanced shall be treated alike." Royster Guano Co. v. Virginia, 253 U.S. 412, 415 (1920). The question presented by this case, then, is whether a difference in the sex of competing applicants for letters of administration bears a rational relationship to a state objective that is sought to be advanced by the operation of 15-312 and 15-314.

In upholding the latter section, the Idaho Supreme Court concluded that its objective was to eliminate one area of controversy when two or more persons, equally entitled under 15-312, seek letters of administration and thereby present the probate court "with the issue of which one should be named." The court also concluded that where such persons are not of the same sex, the elimination of females from consideration "is neither an illogical nor arbitrary method devised by the legislature to resolve an issue that would otherwise require a hearing as to the relative merits . . . of the two or more petitioning relatives . . . ." 93 Idaho, at 514, 465 P.2d, at 638.

Clearly the objective of reducing the workload on probate courts by eliminating one class of contests is not without some legitimacy. The crucial question, however, is whether 15-314 advances that objective in a manner consistent with the command of the Equal Protection Clause. We hold that it does not. To give a mandatory preference to members of either sex over members of the other, merely to accomplish the elimination of hearings on the merits, is to make the very kind of arbitrary legislative choice forbidden by the Equal Protection Clause of the Fourteenth Amendment; and whatever may be [404 U.S. 71, 77] said as to the positive values of avoiding intrafamily controversy, the choice in this context may not lawfully be mandated solely on the basis of sex.

GEDULDIG v. AIELLO, 417 U.S. 484 (1974)

Decided June 17, 1974.

MR. JUSTICE STEWART delivered the opinion of the Court.

California's disability insurance system is funded entirely from contributions deducted from the wages of participating employees. Participation in the program is mandatory unless the employees are protected by a voluntary private plan approved by the State.2 Each employee is required to contribute one percent of his salary, up to an annual maximum of $85.3 These contributions are placed in the Unemployment Compensation Disability Fund, which is established and administered as a special trust fund within the state treasury.4 It is from this Disability Fund that benefits under the program are paid.

Appellant is the Director of the California Department of Human Resources Development.12 He is responsible for the administration of the State's disability insurance program. Appellees are four women who have paid sufficient amounts into the Disability Fund to be eligible for benefits under the program. Each of the appellees became pregnant and suffered employment disability as a result of her pregnancy. With respect to three of the appellees, Carolyn Aiello, Augustina Armendariz, and Elizabeth Johnson, the disabilities were attributable to abnormal complications encountered during their pregnancies.13 The fourth, Jacqueline Jaramillo, experienced a normal pregnancy, which was the sole cause of her disability.

At all times relevant to this case, 2626 of the Unemployment Insurance Code provided:

> "`Disability' or `disabled' includes both mental or physical illness and mental or physical injury. An individual shall be deemed disabled in any day in which, because of his physical or mental condition, he is unable to perform his regular or customary work. In no case shall the term `disability' or `disabled' include any injury or illness caused by or arising in connection with pregnancy up to the termination of such pregnancy and for a period of 28 days thereafter." (Emphasis added.) [417 U.S. 484, 490]

Appellant construed and applied the final sentence of this statute to preclude the payment of benefits for any disability resulting from pregnancy. As a result, the appellees were ruled ineligible for disability benefits by reason of this provision, and they sued to enjoin its enforcement. The District Court, finding "that the exclusion of pregnancy-related disabilities is not based upon a classification having a rational and substantial relationship to a legitimate state purpose," held that the exclusion was unconstitutional under the Equal Protection Clause. 359 F. Supp., at 801.

In ordering the State to pay benefits for disability accompanying normal pregnancy and delivery, the District Court acknowledged the State's contention "that coverage of these disabilities is so extraordinarily expensive that it would be impossible to maintain a program supported by employee contributions if these disabilities are included." 359 F. Supp., at 798. There is considerable disagreement between the parties with respect to how great the increased costs would actually be, but they [417 U.S. 484, 494] would clearly be substantial.18 For purposes of analysis the District Court accepted the State's estimate, which was in excess of $100 million annually, and stated: "[I]t is clear that including these disabilities would not destroy the program. The increased costs could be accommodated quite easily by making reasonable changes in the contribution rate, the maximum benefits allowable, and the other variables affecting the solvency of the program." Ibid.

Each of these "variables" - the benefit level deemed appropriate to compensate employee disability, the risks selected to be insured under the program, and the contribution rate chosen to maintain the solvency of the program and at the same time to permit low-income employees to participate with minimal personal sacrifice - represents a policy determination by the State. The essential issue in this case is whether the Equal Protection Clause requires such policies to be sacrificed or compromised in order to finance the payment of benefits to those whose disability is attributable to normal pregnancy and delivery.

We cannot agree that the exclusion of this disability from coverage amounts to invidious discrimination under the Equal Protection Clause. California does not discriminate with respect to the persons or groups which are eligible for disability insurance protection under the program. The classification challenged in this case relates to the asserted underinclusiveness of the set of risks that the State has selected to insure. Although California has created a program to insure most risks of employment [417 U.S. 484, 495] disability, it has not chosen to insure all such risks, and this decision is reflected in the level of annual contributions exacted from participating employees. This Court has held that, consistently with the Equal Protection Clause, a State "may take one step at a time, addressing itself to the phase of the problem which seems most acute to the legislative mind. . . . The legislature may select one phase of one field and apply a remedy there, neglecting the others. . . ." Williamson v. Lee Optical Co., 348 U.S. 483, 489 (1955); Jefferson v. Hackney, 406 U.S. 535 (1972). Particularly with respect to social welfare programs, so long as the line drawn by the State is rationally supportable, the courts will not interpose their judgment as to the appropriate stopping point. "[T]he Equal Protection Clause does not require that a State must choose between attacking every aspect of a problem or not attacking the problem at all." Dandridge v. Williams, 397 U.S. 471, 486-487 (1970).

These policies provide an objective and wholly non-invidious basis for the State's decision not to create a more comprehensive insurance program than it has. There is no evidence in the record that the selection of the risks insured by the program worked to discriminate against any definable group or class in terms of the aggregate risk protection derived by that group or class from the program.20 There is no risk from which men are protected [417 U.S. 484, 497] and women are not. Likewise, there is no risk from which women are protected and men are not.21

The appellee simply contends that, although she has received insurance protection equivalent to that provided all other participating employees, she has suffered discrimination because she encountered a risk that was outside the program's protection. For the reasons we have stated, we hold that this contention is not a valid one under the Equal Protection Clause of the Fourteenth Amendment.

CRAIG v. BOREN, 429 U.S. 190 (1976)

Decided December 20, 1976

MR. JUSTICE BRENNAN delivered the opinion of the Court.

The interaction of two sections of an Oklahoma statute, Okla. Stat., Tit. 37, 241 and 245 (1958 and Supp. 1976),1 [429 U.S. 190, 192] prohibits the sale of "nonintoxicating" 3.2% beer to males under the age of 21 and to females under the age of 18. The question to be decided is whether such a gender-based differential constitutes a denial to males 18-20 years of age of the equal protection of the laws in violation of the Fourteenth Amendment.

Analysis may appropriately begin with the reminder that Reed emphasized that statutory classifications that distinguish between males and females are "subject to scrutiny under the Equal Protection Clause." 404 U.S., at 75. To withstand constitutional challenge, previous cases establish that classifications by gender must serve important governmental objectives and must be substantially related to achievement of those objectives. Thus, in Reed, the objectives [429 U.S. 190, 198] of "reducing the workload on probate courts," id., at 76, and "avoiding intrafamily controversy," id., at 77, were deemed of insufficient importance to sustain use of an overt gender criterion in the appointment of administrators of intestate decedents' estates. Decisions following Reed similarly have rejected administrative ease and convenience as sufficiently important objectives to justify gender-based classifications. See, e. g., Stanley v. Illinois, 405 U.S. 645, 656 (1972); Frontiero v. Richardson, 411 U.S. 677, 690 (1973); cf. Schlesinger v. Ballard, 419 U.S. 498, 506-507 (1975). And only two Terms ago, Stanton v. Stanton, 421 U.S. 7 (1975), expressly stating that Reed v. Reed was "controlling," 421 U.S., at 13, held that Reed required invalidation of a Utah differential age-of-majority statute, notwithstanding the statute's coincidence with and furtherance of the State's purpose of fostering "old notions" of role typing and preparing boys for their expected performance in the economic and political worlds. 421 U.S., at 14-15.6

We accept for purposes of discussion the District Court's identification of the objective underlying 241 and 245 as the enhancement of traffic safety.7 Clearly, the protection [429 U.S. 190, 200] of public health and safety represents an important function of state and local governments. However, appellees' statistics in our view cannot support the conclusion that the gender-based distinction closely serves to achieve that objective and therefore the distinction cannot under Reed withstand equal protection challenge.

The appellees introduced a variety of statistical surveys. First, an analysis of arrest statistics for 1973 demonstrated that 18-20-year-old male arrests for "driving under the influence" and "drunkenness" substantially exceeded female arrests for that same age period.8 Similarly, youths aged 17-21 were found to be overrepresented among those killed [429 U.S. 190, 201] or injured in traffic accidents, with males again numerically exceeding females in this regard.9 Third, a random roadside survey in Oklahoma City revealed that young males were more inclined to drive and drink beer than were their female counterparts.10 Fourth, Federal Bureau of Investigation nationwide statistics exhibited a notable increase in arrests for "driving under the influence."11 Finally, statistical evidence gathered in other jurisdictions, particularly Minnesota and Michigan, was offered to corroborate Oklahoma's experience by indicating the pervasiveness of youthful participation in motor vehicle accidents following the imbibing of alcohol. Conceding that "the case is not free from doubt," 399 F. Supp., at 1314, the District Court nonetheless concluded that this statistical showing substantiated "a rational basis for the legislative judgment underlying the challenged classification." Id., at 1307.

Even were this statistical evidence accepted as accurate, it nevertheless offers only a weak answer to the equal protection question presented here. The most focused and relevant of the statistical surveys, arrests of 18-20-year-olds for alcohol-related driving offenses, exemplifies the ultimate unpersuasiveness of this evidentiary record. Viewed in terms of the correlation between sex and the actual activity that Oklahoma seeks to regulate - driving while under the influence of alcohol - the statistics broadly establish that .18% of females and 2% of males in that age group were arrested for that offense. While such a disparity is not trivial in a statistical sense, it hardly can form the basis for employment of a gender line as a classifying device. Certainly if maleness [429 U.S. 190, 202] is to serve as a proxy for drinking and driving, a correlation of 2% must be considered an unduly tenuous "fit."12 Indeed, prior cases have consistently rejected the use of sex as a decisionmaking factor even though the statutes in question certainly rested on far more predictive empirical relationships than this.13

Moreover, the statistics exhibit a variety of other shortcomings that seriously impugn their value to equal protection analysis. Setting aside the obvious methodological problems,14 the surveys do not adequately justify the salient [429 U.S. 190, 203] features of Oklahoma's gender-based traffic-safety law. None purports to measure the use and dangerousness of 3.2% beer as opposed to alcohol generally, a detail that is of particular importance since, in light of its low alcohol level, Oklahoma apparently considers the 3.2% beverage to be "nonintoxicating." Okla. Stat., Tit. 37, 163.1 (1958); see State ex rel. Springer v. Bliss, 199 Okla. 198, 185 P.2d 220 (1947). Moreover, many of the studies, while graphically documenting the unfortunate increase in driving while under the influence of alcohol, make no effort to relate their findings to age-sex differential as involved here.15 Indeed, the only survey that explicitly centered its attention upon young drivers and their use of beer - albeit apparently not of the diluted 3.2% variety - reached results that hardly can be viewed as impressive in justifying either a gender or age classification.16 [429 U.S. 190, 204]

There is no reason to belabor this line of analysis. It is unrealistic to expect either members of the judiciary or state officials to be well versed in the rigors of experimental or statistical technique. But this merely illustrates that proving broad sociological propositions by statistics is a dubious business, and one that inevitably is in tension with the normative philosophy that underlies the Equal Protection Clause.17 Suffice to say that the showing offered by the appellees does not satisfy us that sex represents a legitimate, accurate proxy for the regulation of drinking and driving. In fact, when it is further recognized that Oklahoma's statute prohibits only the selling of 3.2% beer to young males and not their drinking the beverage once acquired (even after purchase by their 18-20-year-old female companions), the relationship between gender and traffic safety becomes far too tenuous to satisfy Reed's requirement that the gender-based difference be substantially related to achievement of the statutory objective.

We hold, therefore, that under Reed, Oklahoma's 3.2% beer statute invidiously discriminates against males 18-20 years of age.

Both federal and state courts uniformly have declared the unconstitutionality of gender lines that restrain the activities of customers of state-regulated liquor establishments irrespective of the operation of the Twenty-first Amendment. See, e. g., White v. Fleming, 522 F.2d 730 (CA7 1975); Women's Liberation Union of R. I. v. Israel, 512 F.2d 106 (CA1 1975); Daugherty v. Daley, 370 F. Supp. 338 (ND Ill. 1974) (three-judge court); Seidenberg v. McSorleys' Old Ale House, Inc., 317 F. Supp. 593 (SDNY 1970); Commonwealth Alcoholic Beverage Control Bd. v. Burke, 481 S. W. 2d 52 (Ky. 1972); cf. Sail'er Inn, Inc. v. Kirby, 5 Cal. 3d 1, 485 P.2d 529 (1971); Paterson Tavern & G. O. A. v. Hawthorne, 57 N. J. 180, 270 A. 2d 628 (1970). Even when state officials have posited sociological or empirical justifications for these gender-based differentiations, the courts have struck down discriminations aimed at an entire class under the guise of alcohol regulation. In fact, social science studies that have uncovered quantifiable difference in drinking tendencies dividing along both racial and ethnic lines strongly suggest the need for application of the Equal Protection Clause in preventing discriminatory treatment that almost certainly would be perceived as invidious.22 In sum, the principles embodied in the Equal [429 U.S. 190, 209] Protection Clause are not to be rendered inapplicable by statistically measured but loose-fitting generalities concerning the drinking tendencies of aggregate groups. We thus hold that the operation of the Twenty-first Amendment does not alter the application of equal protection standards that otherwise govern this case. [429 U.S. 190, 210]

We conclude that the gender-based differential contained in Okla. Stat., Tit. 37, 245 (1976 Supp.) constitutes a denial of the equal protection of the laws to males aged 18-2023 and reverse the judgment of the District Court.24

PERSONNEL ADMINISTRATOR OF MASS. v. FEENEY, 442 U.S. 256 (1979)

Decided June 5, 1979.

MR. JUSTICE STEWART delivered the opinion of the Court.

This case presents a challenge to the constitutionality of the Massachusetts veterans' preference statute, Mass. Gen. Laws Ann., ch. 31, 23, on the ground that it discriminates against women in violation of the Equal Protection Clause of the Fourteenth Amendment. Under ch. 31, 23,1 all veterans who qualify for state civil service positions must be considered for appointment ahead of any qualifying nonveterans. The preference operates overwhelmingly to the advantage of males.

The veterans' hiring preference in Massachusetts, as in other jurisdictions, has traditionally been justified as a measure designed to reward veterans for the sacrifice of military service, to ease the transition from military to civilian life, to encourage patriotic service, and to attract loyal and well-disciplined people to civil service occupations.

The first Massachusetts veterans' preference statute defined the term "veterans" in gender-neutral language. See [442 U.S. 256, 268] 1896 Mass. Acts, ch. 517 1 ("a person" who served in the United States Army or Navy), and subsequent amendments have followed this pattern, see, e. g., 1919 Mass. Acts, ch. 150, 1 ("any person who has served . . ."); 1954 Mass Acts, ch. 627, 1 ("any person, male or female, including a nurse"). Women who have served in official United States military units during wartime, then, have always been entitled to the benefit of the preference. In addition, Massachusetts, through a 1943 amendment to the definition of "wartime service," extended the preference to women who served in unofficial auxiliary women's units. 1943 Mass. Acts, ch. 194.17

When the first general veterans' preference statute was adopted in 1896, there were no women veterans.18 The statute, however, covered only Civil War veterans. Most of them were beyond middle age, and relatively few were actively competing for public employment.19 Thus, the impact of [442 U.S. 256, 269] the preference upon the employment opportunities of non-veterans as a group and women in particular was slight.20

Notwithstanding the apparent attempts by Massachusetts to include as many military women as possible within the scope of the preference, the statute today benefits an overwhelmingly male class.

When this litigation was commenced, then, over 98% of the veterans in Massachusetts were male; only 1.8% were female. And over one-quarter of the Massachusetts population were veterans. During the decade between 1963 and 1973 when the appellee was actively participating in the State's merit selection system, 47,005 new permanent appointments were made in the classified official service. Forty-three percent of those hired were women, and 57% were men. Of the women appointed, 1.8% were veterans, while 54% of the men had veteran status. A large unspecified percentage of the female appointees were serving in lower paying positions for which males traditionally had not applied.22 [442 U.S. 256, 271] On each of 50 sample eligible lists that are part of the record in this case, one or more women who would have been certified as eligible for appointment on the basis of test results were displaced by veterans whose test scores were lower.

At the outset of this litigation appellants conceded that for "many of the permanent positions for which males and females have competed" the veterans' preference has "resulted in a substantially greater proportion of female eligibles than male eligibles" not being certified for consideration. The impact of the veterans' preference law upon the public employment opportunities of women has thus been severe. This impact lies at the heart of the appellee's federal constitutional claim.

Certain classifications, however, in themselves supply a reason to infer antipathy. Race is the paradigm. A racial classification, regardless of purported motivation, is presumptively invalid and can be upheld only upon an extraordinary justification. Brown v. Board of Education, 347 U.S. 483; McLaughlin v. Florida, 379 U.S. 184. This rule applies as well to a classification that is ostensibly neutral but is an obvious pretext for racial discrimination. Yick Wo v. Hopkins, 118 U.S. 356; Guinn v. United States, 238 U.S. 347; cf. Lane v. Wilson, 307 U.S. 268; Gomillion v. Lightfoot, 364 U.S. 339. But, as was made clear in Washington v. Davis, 426 U.S. 229, and Arlington Heights v. Metropolitan Housing Dev. Corp., 429 U.S. 252, even if a neutral law has a disproportionately adverse effect upon a racial minority, it is unconstitutional under the Equal Protection Clause only if that impact can be traced to a discriminatory purpose. [442 U.S. 256, 273]

Classifications based upon gender, not unlike those based upon race, have traditionally been the touchstone for pervasive and often subtle discrimination. Caban v. Mohammed, 441 U.S. 380, 398 (STEWART, J., dissenting). This Court's recent cases teach that such classifications must bear a close and substantial relationship to important governmental objectives, Craig v. Boren, 429 U.S. 190, 197, and are in many settings unconstitutional. Reed v. Reed, 404 U.S. 71;, Frontiero v. Richardson, 411 U.S. 677; Weinberger v. Wiesenfeld, 420 U.S. 636; Craig v. Boren, supra; Califano v. Goldfarb, 430 U.S. 199; Orr v. Orr, 440 U.S. 268; Caban v. Mohammed, supra. Although public employment is not a constitutional right, Massachusetts Bd. of Retirement v. Murgia, supra, and the States have wide discretion in framing employee qualifications, see, e. g., New York City Transit Authority v. Beazer, supra, these precedents dictate that any state law overtly or covertly designed to prefer males over females in public employment would require an exceedingly persuasive justification to withstand a constitutional challenge under the Equal Protection Clause of the Fourteenth Amendment.

The decision to grant a preference to veterans was of course "intentional." So, necessarily, did an adverse impact upon nonveterans follow from that decision. And it cannot seriously be argued that the Legislature of Massachusetts could have been unaware that most veterans are men. It would thus be disingenuous to say that the adverse consequences of this legislation for women were unintended, in the sense that they were not volitional or in the sense that they were not foreseeable. [442 U.S. 256, 279]

"Discriminatory purpose," however, implies more than intent as volition or intent as awareness of consequences. See United Jewish Organizations v. Carey, 430 U.S. 144, 179 (concurring opinion).24 It implies that the decisionmaker, in this case a state legislature, selected or reaffirmed a particular course of action at least in part "because of," not merely "in spite of," its adverse effects upon an identifiable group.25 Yet nothing in the record demonstrates that this preference for veterans was originally devised or subsequently re-enacted because it would accomplish the collateral goal of keeping women in a stereotypic and predefined place in the Massachusetts Civil Service.

To the contrary, the statutory history shows that the benefit of the preference was consistently offered to "any person" who was a veteran. That benefit has been extended to women under a very broad statutory definition of the term veteran.26 The preference formula itself, which is the focal [442 U.S. 256, 280] point of this challenge, was first adopted - so it appears from this record - out of a perceived need to help a small group of older Civil War veterans. It has since been reaffirmed and extended only to cover new veterans.27 When the totality of legislative actions establishing and extending the Massachusetts veterans' preference are considered, see Washington v. Davis, 426 U.S., at 242, the law remains what it purports to be: a preference for veterans of either sex over nonveterans of either sex, not for men over women.

The substantial edge granted to veterans by ch. 31, 23, may reflect unwise policy. The appellee, however, has simply failed to demonstrate that the law in any way reflects a purpose to discriminate on the basis of sex.

C. THE MARCH TO CONSTITUTIONAL EQUALITY

In another major case from the 1970's the Supreme Court came tantalizingly close to holding gender classifications to the same exacting standard as that for race. In invalidating different standards for spousal benefits for male and female military personnel in 1973 in *Frontiero v. Richardson*, four justices – one short of a majority of the Court – agreed that

> ...classifications based upon sex, like classifications based upon race, alienage, or national origin, are inherently suspect, and must therefore be subjected to strict judicial scrutiny. Applying the analysis mandated by that stricter standard of review, it is clear that the statutory scheme now before us is constitutionally invalid."
>
> *Frontiero*, 411 U.S. 677, 688.

While a majority of the Court has yet to take the formal step of equating gender discrimination with its racial counterpart, the standard continues to evolve, from the early "rational relationship" test, to an intermediate level of scrutiny, characterized initially as "substantial relationship" and eventually as "exceedingly persuasive justification."

The key cases establishing this burden of showing an exceedingly persuasive justification for gender-based classification were *Mississippi University for Women v. Hogan* in 1982, and the 1996 decision in *United States v. Virginia*. In *Hogan*, Justice O'Connor, having recently joined the Court as its first female member, struck down Mississippi's female-only admissions policy at its state nursing school. Once again, the Court focused on the *literal* classification based on gender, regardless of alleged motive. (Justice O'Connor also dismissed Mississippi's contention that supporting an all-female school for women was in essence a form of affirmative action for women rather than discrimination against men, noting that nursing was hardly on the list of professions historically closed to women). In the most sweeping sex discrimination case to date, Justice Ginsburg, the Court's second female Justice, held that Virginia Military Institute's historic male-only admissions policy could not survive the Equal Protection Clause. In her 1996 majority opinion, Justice Ginsburg noted the previous gender integration of the federal military academies, with no loss of educational or military quality.

It remains to be seen which, if any, gender-based governmental classifications might still be permissible in the wake of *United States v. Virginia*. One continuing exception to the general trend has been the area of military affairs; in its 1981 ruling in *Rostker v. Goldberg*, the court refused to invalidate the male-only draft, deferring to Congress and the President in matters of national defense.

FRONTIERO v. RICHARDSON, 411 U.S. 677 (1973)

Decided May 14, 1973

MR. JUSTICE BRENNAN announced the judgment of the Court and an opinion in which MR. JUSTICE DOUGLAS, MR. JUSTICE WHITE, and MR. JUSTICE MARSHALL join.

The question before us concerns the right of a female member of the uniformed services1 to claim her spouse as a "dependent" for the purposes of obtaining increased quarters allowances and medical and dental benefits under 37 U.S.C. 401, 403, and 10 U.S.C. 1072, 1076, on an equal footing with male members. Under these statutes, a serviceman may claim his wife as a "dependent" without regard to whether she is in fact dependent upon him for any part of her support. 37 U.S.C. 401 (1); 10 U.S.C. 1072 (2) (A). A servicewoman, on the other hand, may not claim her husband as a "dependent" under these programs unless he is in fact dependent upon her for over one-half of his support. [411 U.S. 677, 679] 37 U.S.C. 401; 10 U.S.C. 1072 (2) (C).2 Thus, the question for decision is whether this difference in treatment constitutes an unconstitutional discrimination against servicewomen in violation of the Due Process Clause of the Fifth Amendment. A three-judge District Court for the Middle District of Alabama, one judge dissenting, rejected this contention and sustained the constitutionality of the provisions of the statutes making this distinction. 341 F. Supp. 201 (1972). We noted probable jurisdiction. 409 U.S. 840 (1972). We reverse.

There can be no doubt that our Nation has had a long and unfortunate history of sex discrimination.13 Traditionally, such discrimination was rationalized by an attitude of "romantic paternalism" which, in practical effect, put women, not on a pedestal, but in a cage. Indeed, this paternalistic attitude became so firmly rooted in our national consciousness that, 100 years ago, a distinguished Member of this Court was able to proclaim:

> "Man is, or should be, woman's protector and defender. The natural and proper timidity and delicacy which belongs to the female sex evidently unfits it for many of the occupations of civil life. The constitution of the family organization, which is founded in the divine ordinance, as well as in the nature of things, indicates the domestic sphere as that which properly belongs to the domain and functions of womanhood. The harmony, not to say identity, of interests and views which belong, or should belong, to the family institution is repugnant to the idea of a woman adopting a distinct and [411 U.S. 677, 685] independent career from that of her husband. . . .
>
> ". . . The paramount destiny and mission of woman are to fulfil the noble and benign offices of wife and mother. This is the law of the Creator." Bradwell v. State, 16 Wall. 130, 141 (1873) (Bradley, J., concurring).

As a result of notions such as these, our statute books gradually became laden with gross, stereotyped distinctions between the sexes and, indeed, throughout much of the 19th century the position of women in our society was, in many respects, comparable to that of blacks under the pre-Civil War slave codes. Neither slaves nor women could hold office, serve on juries, or bring suit in their own names, and married women traditionally were denied the legal capacity to hold or convey property or to serve as legal guardians of their own children. See generally L. Kanowitz, Women and the Law: The Unfinished Revolution 5-6 (1969); G. Myrdal, An American Dilemma 1073 (20th anniversary ed. 1962). And although blacks were guaranteed the right to vote in 1870, women were denied even that right - which is itself "preservative of other basic civil and political rights"14 - until adoption of the Nineteenth Amendment half a century later.

It is true, of course, that the position of women in America has improved markedly in recent decades.15 [411 U.S. 677, 686] Nevertheless, it can hardly be doubted that, in part because of the high visibility of the sex characteristic,16 women still face pervasive, although at times more subtle, discrimination in our educational institutions, in the job market and, perhaps most conspicuously, in the political arena.17 See generally K. Amundsen, The Silenced Majority: Women and American Democracy (1971); The President's Task Force on Women's Rights and Responsibilities, A Matter of Simple Justice (1970).

Moreover, since sex, like race and national origin, is an immutable characteristic determined solely by the accident of birth, the imposition of special disabilities upon the members of a particular sex because of their sex would seem to violate "the basic concept of our system that legal burdens should bear some relationship to individual responsibility . . . ." Weber v. Aetna Casualty & Surety Co., 406 U.S. 164, 175 (1972). And what differentiates sex from such nonsuspect statuses as intelligence or physical disability, and aligns it with the recognized suspect criteria, is that the sex characteristic frequently bears no relation to ability to perform or contribute to society.18 As a result, statutory distinctions [411 U.S. 677, 687] between the sexes often have the effect of invidiously relegating the entire class of females to inferior legal status without regard to the actual capabilities of its individual members.

Here, however, there is substantial evidence that, if put to the test, many of the wives of male members would fail to qualify for benefits.23 And in light of the fact that the [411 U.S. 677, 690] dependency determination with respect to the husbands of female members is presently made solely on the basis of affidavits, rather than through the more costly hearing process,24 the Government's explanation of the statutory scheme is, to say the least, questionable.

In any case, our prior decisions make clear that, although efficacious administration of governmental programs is not without some importance, "the Constitution recognizes higher values than speed and efficiency." Stanley v. Illinois, 405 U.S. 645, 656 (1972). And when we enter the realm of "strict judicial scrutiny," there can be no doubt that "administrative convenience" is not a shibboleth, the mere recitation of which dictates constitutionality. See Shapiro v. Thompson, 394 U.S. 618 (1969); Carrington v. Rash, 380 U.S. 89 (1965). On the contrary, any statutory scheme which draws a sharp line between the sexes, solely for the purpose of achieving administrative convenience, necessarily commands "dissimilar treatment for men and women who are . . . similarly situated," and therefore involves the "very kind of arbitrary legislative choice forbidden by the [Constitution] . . . ." Reed v. Reed, 404 U.S., at 77, 76. We therefore conclude that, by according differential treatment to male and female members of the uniformed services for the sole purpose of achieving administrative [411 U.S. 677, 691] convenience, the challenged statutes violate the Due Process Clause of the Fifth Amendment insofar as they require a female member to prove the dependency of her husband.25

MISSISSIPPI UNIVERSITY FOR WOMEN v. HOGAN, 458 U.S. 718 (1982)

Decided July 1, 1982

JUSTICE O'CONNOR delivered the opinion of the Court.

Respondent, Joe Hogan, is a registered nurse but does not hold a baccalaureate degree in nursing. Since 1974, he has worked as a nursing supervisor in a medical center in Columbus, the city in which MUW is located. In 1979, Hogan applied for admission to the MUW School of Nursing's baccalaureate program.3 Although he was otherwise qualified, he [458 U.S. 718, 721] was denied admission to the School of Nursing solely because of his sex. School officials informed him that he could audit the courses in which he was interested, but could not enroll for credit. Tr. 26.4

We begin our analysis aided by several firmly established principles. Because the challenged policy expressly discriminates among applicants on the basis of gender, it is subject to scrutiny under the Equal Protection Clause of the Fourteenth Amendment. Reed v. Reed, 404 U.S. 71, 75 (1971). That this statutory policy discriminates against males rather than against females does not exempt it from scrutiny or reduce the standard of review.8 Caban v. Mohammed, [458 U.S. 718, 724] 441 U.S. 380, 394 (1979); Orr v. Orr, 440 U.S. 268, 279 (1979). Our decisions also establish that the party seeking to uphold a statute that classifies individuals on the basis of their gender must carry the burden of showing an "exceedingly persuasive justification" for the classification. Kirchberg v. Feenstra, 450 U.S. 455, 461 (1981); Personnel Administrator of Mass. v. Feeney, 442 U.S. 256, 273 (1979). The burden is met only by showing at least that the classification serves "important governmental objectives and that the discriminatory means employed" are "substantially related to the achievement of those objectives." Wengler v. Druggists Mutual Ins. Co., 446 U.S. 142, 150 (1980).9

Although the test for determining the validity of a gender-based classification is straightforward, it must be applied free [458 U.S. 718, 725] of fixed notions concerning the roles and abilities of males and females. Care must be taken in ascertaining whether the statutory objective itself reflects archaic and stereotypic notions. Thus, if the statutory objective is to exclude or "protect" members of one gender because they are presumed to suffer from an inherent handicap or to be innately inferior, the objective itself is illegitimate. See Frontiero v. Richardson, 411 U.S. 677, 684-685 (1973) (plurality opinion).

The State's primary justification for maintaining the single-sex admissions policy of MUW's School of Nursing is that it compensates for discrimination against women and, therefore, constitutes educational affirmative action. Brief for Petitioners 8.13 As applied to the School of Nursing, we find the State's argument unpersuasive. [458 U.S. 718, 728]

In limited circumstances, a gender-based classification favoring one sex can be justified if it intentionally and directly assists members of the sex that is disproportionately burdened. See Schlesinger v. Ballard, 419 U.S. 498 (1975). However, we consistently have emphasized that "the mere recitation of a benign, compensatory purpose is not an automatic shield which protects against any inquiry into the actual purposes underlying a statutory scheme." Weinberger v. Wiesenfeld, 420 U.S. 636, 648 (1975). The same searching analysis must be made, regardless of whether the State's objective is to eliminate family controversy, Reed v. Reed, 404 U.S. 71 (1971), to achieve administrative efficiency, Frontiero v. Richardson, 411 U.S. 677 (1973), or to balance the burdens borne by males and females.

Rather than compensate for discriminatory barriers faced by women, MUW's policy of excluding males from admission to the School of Nursing tends to perpetuate the stereotyped view of nursing as an exclusively woman's job.15 By assuring [458 U.S. 718, 730] that Mississippi allots more openings in its state-supported nursing schools to women than it does to men, MUW's admissions policy lends credibility to the old view that women, not men, should become nurses, and makes the assumption that nursing is a field for women a self-fulfilling prophecy. See Stanton v. Stanton, 421 U.S. 7 (1975). Thus, we conclude that, although the State recited a "benign, compensatory purpose," it failed to establish that the alleged objective is the actual purpose underlying the discriminatory classification.16

The policy is invalid also because it fails the second part of the equal protection test, for the State has made no showing that the gender-based classification is substantially and directly related to its proposed compensatory objective. To the contrary, MUW's policy of permitting men to attend classes as auditors fatally undermines its claim that women, at least those in the School of Nursing, are adversely affected by the presence of men. [458 U.S. 718, 731]

MUW permits men who audit to participate fully in classes. Additionally, both men and women take part in continuing education courses offered by the School of Nursing, in which regular nursing students also can enroll. Deposition of Dr. James Strobel 56-60 and Deposition of Dean Annette K. Barrar 24-26. The uncontroverted record reveals that admitting men to nursing classes does not affect teaching style, Deposition of Nancy L. Herban 4, that the presence of men in the classroom would not affect the performance of the female nursing students, Tr. 61 and Deposition of Dean Annette K. Barrar 7-8, and that men in coeducational nursing schools do not dominate the classroom. Deposition of Nancy Herban 6. In sum, the record in this case is flatly inconsistent with the claim that excluding men from the School of Nursing is necessary to reach any of MUW's educational goals.

Thus, considering both the asserted interest and the relationship between the interest and the methods used by the State, we conclude that the State has fallen far short of establishing the "exceedingly persuasive justification" needed to sustain the gender-based classification. Accordingly, we hold that MUW's policy of denying males the right to enroll for credit in its School of Nursing violates the Equal Protection Clause of the Fourteenth Amendment.17

UNITED STATES v. VIRGINIA

[June 26, 1996]

Justice Ginsburg delivered the opinion of the Court:

Founded in 1839, VMI is today the sole single sex school among Virginia's 15 public institutions of higher learning. VMI's distinctive mission is to produce "citizen soldiers," men prepared for leadership in civilian life and in military service. VMI pursues this mission through pervasive training of a kind not available anywhere else in Virginia. Assigning prime place to character development, VMI uses an "adversative method" modeled on English public schools and once characteristic of military instruction. VMI constantly endeavors to instill physical and mental

discipline in its cadets and impart to them a strong moral code. The school's graduates leave VMI with heightened comprehension of their capacity to deal with duress and stress, and a large sense of accomplishment for completing the hazardous course.

VMI has notably succeeded in its mission to produce leaders; among its alumni are military generals, Members of Congress, and business executives. The school's alumni overwhelmingly perceive that their VMI training helped them to realize their personal goals. VMI's endowment reflects the loyalty of its graduates; VMI has the largest per student endowment of all undergraduate institutions in the Nation.

Neither the goal of producing citizen soldiers nor VMI's implementing methodology is inherently unsuitable to women. And the school's impressive record in producing leaders has made admission desirable to some women. Nevertheless, Virginia has elected to preserve exclusively for men the advantages and opportunities a VMI education affords.

The heightened review standard our precedent establishes does not make sex a proscribed classification. Supposed "inherent differences" are no longer accepted as a ground for race or national origin classifications. See *Loving* v. *Virginia*, 388 U.S. 1 (1967). Physical differences between men and women, however, are enduring: "[T]he two sexes are not fungible; a community made up exclusively of one [sex] is different from a community composed of both." *Ballard* v. *United States*, 329 U.S. 187, 193 (1946).

"Inherent differences" between men and women, we have come to appreciate, remain cause for celebration, but not for denigration of the members of either sex or for artificial constraints on an individual's opportunity. Sex classifications may be used to compensate women "for particular economic disabilities [they have] suffered," *Califano* v. *Webster*, 430 U.S. 313, 320 (1977) *(per curiam)*, to "promot[e] equal employment opportunity," see *California Federal Sav. & Loan Assn.* v. *Guerra*, 479 U.S. 272, 289 (1987), to advance full development of the talent and capacities of our Nation's people. [n.7] But such classifications may not be used, as they once were, see *Goesaert*, 335 U. S., at 467, to create or perpetuate the legal, social, and economic inferiority of women.

Measuring the record in this case against the review standard just described, we conclude that Virginia has shown no "exceedingly persuasive justification" for excluding all women from the citizen soldier training afforded by VMI. We therefore affirm the Fourth Circuit's initial judgment, which held that Virginia had violated the Fourteenth Amendment's Equal Protection Clause. Because the remedy proffered by Virginia--the Mary Baldwin VWIL program--does not cure the constitutional violation, *i.e.*, it does not provide equal opportunity, we reverse the Fourth Circuit's final judgment in this case.

In sum, we find no persuasive evidence in this record that VMI's male only admission policy "is in furtherance of a state policy of 'diversity.' " See 976 F. 2d, at 899. No such policy, the Fourth Circuit observed, can be discerned from the movement of all other public colleges and universities in Virginia away from single sex education. See *ibid.* That court also questioned "how one institution with autonomy, but with no authority over any other state institution, can give effect to a state policy of diversity among institutions." *Ibid.* A purpose genuinely to advance an array of educational options, as the Court of Appeals recognized, is not served by VMI's historic and constant plan--a plan to "affor[d] a unique educational benefit only to males." *Ibid.* However "liberally" this plan serves the State's sons, it makes no provision whatever for her daughters. That is not *equal* protection.

Women's successful entry into the federal military academies, [n.13] and their participation in the Nation's military forces, [n.14] indicate that Virginia's fears for the future of VMI may not be solidly grounded. [n.15] The State's justification for excluding all women from "citizen soldier" training for which some are qualified, in any event, cannot rank as "exceedingly persuasive," as we have explained and applied that standard.

Virginia and VMI trained their argument on "means" rather than "end," and thus misperceived our precedent. Single sex education at VMI serves an "important governmental objective," they maintained, and exclusion of women is not only "substantially related," it is essential to that objective. By this notably circular argument, the "straightforward" test *Mississippi Univ. for Women* described, see 458 U. S., at 724-725, was bent and bowed.

The State's misunderstanding and, in turn, the District Court's, is apparent from VMI's mission: to produce "citizen soldiers," individuals

" `imbued with love of learning, confident in the functions and attitudes of leadership, possessing a high sense of public service, advocates of the American democracy and free enterprise system, and ready . . . to defend their country in time of national peril.' " 766 F. Supp., at 1425 (quoting Mission Study Committee of the VMI Board of Visitors, Report, May 16, 1986).

Surely that goal is great enough to accommodate women, who today count as citizens in our American democracy equal in stature to men. Just as surely, the State's great goal is not substantially advanced by women's categorical exclusion, in total disregard of their individual merit, from the State's premier "citizen soldier" corps. [n.16] Virginia, in sum, "has fallen far short of establishing the `exceedingly persuasive justification,' " *Mississippi Univ. for Women*, 458 U. S., at 731, that must be the solid base for any gender defined classification.

Virginia, in sum, while maintaining VMI for men only, has failed to provide any "comparable single gender women's institution." *Id.*, at 1241. Instead, the Commonwealth has created a VWIL program fairly appraised as a "pale shadow" of VMI in terms of the range of curricular choices and faculty stature, funding, prestige, alumni support and influence. See *id.*, at 1250 (Phillips, J., dissenting).

Virginia's VWIL solution is reminiscent of the remedy Texas proposed 50 years ago, in response to a state trial court's 1946 ruling that, given the equal protection guarantee, African Americans could not be denied a legal education at a state facility. See *Sweatt* v. *Painter*, 339 U.S. 629 (1950). Reluctant to admit African Americans to its flagship University of Texas Law School, the State set up a separate school for Herman Sweatt and other black law students. *Id.*, at 632. As originally opened, the new school had no independent faculty or library, and it lacked accreditation. *Id.*, at 633. Nevertheless, the state trial and appellate courts were satisfied that the new school offered Sweatt opportunities for the study of law "substantially equivalent to those offered by the State to white students at the University of Texas." *Id.*, at 632 (internal quotation marks omitted).

Before this Court considered the case, the new school had gained "a faculty of five full time professors; a student body of 23; a library of some 16,500 volumes serviced by a full time staff; a practice court and legal aid association; and one alumnus who ha[d] become a member of the Texas Bar." *Id.*, at 633. This Court contrasted resources at the new school with those at the school from which Sweatt had been excluded. The University of Texas Law School had a full time faculty of 16, a student body of 850, a library containing over 65,000 volumes, scholarship funds, a law review, and moot court facilities. *Id.*, at 632-633.

More important than the tangible features, the Court emphasized, are "those qualities which are incapable of objective measurement but which make for greatness" in a school, including "reputation of the faculty, experience of the administration, position and influence of the alumni, standing in the community, traditions and prestige." *Id.*, at 634. Facing the marked differences reported in the *Sweatt* opinion, the Court unanimously ruled that Texas had not shown "substantial equality in the [separate] educational opportunities" the State offered. *Id.*, at 633. Accordingly, the Court held, the Equal Protection Clause required Texas to admit African Americans to the University of Texas Law School. *Id.*, at 636. In line with *Sweatt*, we rule here that Virginia has not shown substantial equality in the separate educational opportunities the State supports at VWIL and VMI.

A generation ago, "the authorities controlling Virginia higher education," despite long established tradition, agreed "to innovate and favorably entertain[ed] the [then] relatively new idea that there must be no discrimination by sex in offering educational opportunity." *Kirstein*, 309 F. Supp., at 186. Commencing in 1970, Virginia opened to women "educational opportunities at the Charlottesville campus that [were] not afforded in other [State operated] institutions." *Id.*, at 187; see *supra*, at 20. A federal court approved the State's innovation, emphasizing that the University of Virginia "offer[ed] courses of instruction . . . not available elsewhere." 309 F. Supp., at 187. The court further noted: "[T]here exists at Charlottesville a `prestige' factor [not paralleled in] other Virginia educational institutions." *Ibid.*

VMI, too, offers an educational opportunity no other Virginia institution provides, and the school's "prestige"--associated with its success in developing "citizen soldiers"--is unequaled. Virginia has closed this facility to its daughters and, instead, has devised for them a "parallel program," with a faculty less impressively credentialed and less well paid, more limited course offerings, fewer opportunities for military training and for scientific specialization. Cf. *Sweatt*, 339 U. S., at 633. VMI, beyond question, "possesses to a far greater degree" than the VWIL program "those qualities which are incapable of objective measurement but which make for greatness in a . . . school," including "position and influence of the alumni, standing in the community, traditions and prestige." *Id.*, at 634. Women seeking and fit for a VMI quality education cannot be offered anything less, under the State's obligation to afford them genuinely equal protection.

VMI Freshmen Say Months of Terror Bonded Male and Female

LEXINGTON, Va., March 17—After seven months cloistered in barracks, the first women to attend the Virginia Military Institute broke their silence today and said the school's fabled Rat Line was intimidating and exhausting.

But it was equal-opportunity torment, they said—a relentless assault on their senses and muscles that was as blind to their gender as it was to their misery.

"I definitely think we have been treated the same way as the men as far as being yelled at and doing push-ups," said Alexis Abrams, 19, of Alexandria, one of 23 women who endured VMI's ritual of freshman abuse and harassment, which began in August and ended on Monday.

Several male freshmen agreed with that assessment. "From what I saw, the women did everything the men did," said Sean Collins, 18, of Gaithersburg.

VMI fought a losing battle against women's admission for six years through the courts, and some proponents of coeducation feared that school officials would make it especially difficult for this year's female cadets to succeed. That was not the case, the women said today.

Moreover, they said, the freshmen—known at VMI as rats—forged a strong bond with everyone in their class, regardless of their gender.

"You care for all your brother rats," said Angelia Pickett, 18, of Glasgow, Ky. "You make it through the day. And another day. And another day. And every day with your BRs, they become more important to you."

WASHINGTON POST - March 18, 1998

ROSTKER v. GOLDBERG, 453 U.S. 57 (1981)

Decided June 25, 1981

JUSTICE REHNQUIST delivered the opinion of the Court.

The question presented is whether the Military Selective Service Act, 50 U.S.C. App. 451 et seq. (1976 ed. and Supp. III), violates the Fifth Amendment to the United States Constitution in authorizing the President to require the registration of males and not females.

This case is quite different from several of the gender-based discrimination cases we have considered in that, despite appellees' assertions, Congress did not act "unthinkingly" or "reflexively and not for any considered reason." Brief for Appellees 35. The question of registering women for the draft not only received considerable national attention and was the subject of wide-ranging public debate, but also was extensively considered by Congress in hearings, floor debate, and in committee.

Congress determined that any future draft, which would be facilitated by the registration scheme, would be characterized by a need for combat troops. The Senate Report explained, in a specific finding later adopted by both Houses, that "[i]f mobilization were to be ordered in a wartime scenario, the primary manpower need would be for combat replacements.

Women as a group, however, unlike men as a group, are not eligible for combat. The restrictions on the participation of women in combat in the Navy and Air Force are statutory. Under 10 U.S.C. 6015 (1976 ed., Supp. III), "women may not be assigned to duty on vessels or in aircraft that are engaged in combat missions," and under 10 U.S.C. 8549 female members of the Air Force "may not be assigned to duty in aircraft engaged in combat missions." The Army and Marine Corps preclude the use of women in combat as a matter of established policy. See App. 86, 34, 58. Congress specifically recognized and endorsed the exclusion of women from [453 U.S. 57, 77] combat in exempting women from registration. In the words of the Senate Report:

Congress' decision to authorize the registration of only men, [453 U.S. 57, 79] therefore, does not violate the Due Process Clause. The exemption of women from registration is not only sufficiently but also closely related to Congress' purpose in authorizing registration. See Michael M., 450 U.S., at 472-473 (plurality opinion); Craig v. Boren, 429 U.S. 190 (1976); Reed v. Reed, 404 U.S. 71 (1971). The fact that Congress and the Executive have decided that women should not serve in combat fully justifies Congress in not authorizing their registration, since the purpose of registration is to develop a pool of potential combat troops. As was the case in Schlesinger v. Ballard, supra, "the gender classification is not individious, but rather realistically reflects the fact that the sexes are not similarly situated" in this case.

In light of the foregoing, we conclude that Congress acted well within its constitutional authority when it authorized the registration of men, and not women, under the Military Selective Service Act.

D. RECOMMENDED READING

M. Becker, C. Bowman, M. Torrey, *Feminist Jurisprudence* (West: 1994)

B.Babcock, A. Freedman, S. Ross, W. Williams, R. Copelon, D. Rhode, N. Taub, *Sex Discrimination and the Law* (Little, Brown: 1996)

CHAPTER II

Women in the Workplace

A. EMPLOYMENT DISCRIMINATION: PROGRESS AND CHALLENGES

In addition to the Constitution, the most important legal instrument in guaranteeing equal employment opportunity for women has been Title VII of the landmark Civil Rights Act of 1964. While the national focus was on race, Congress included gender in its prohibition of discriminatory employment practices:

> It shall be an unlawful employment practice for an employer to fail or refuse to hire or to discharge any individual, or otherwise to discriminate against any individual with respect to his compensation, terms, conditions, or privileges of employment, because of such individual's race, color, religion, **sex**, or national origin . . . or to limit, segregate, or classify his employees or applicants for employment in any way which would deprive or tend to deprive any individual of employment opportunities or otherwise adversely affect his status as an employee, because of such individual's race, color, religion, **sex**, or national origin.
>
> \- 42 U.S.C. 2000e *et seq.*

Enforcement of Title VII, through private law suits and in administrative and court proceedings through the regulatory avenue of the federal Equal Employment Opportunity Commission, has broken historical barriers to almost all occupations, but major challenges have remained. In a 1976 decision, *General Electric Co. v. Gilbert*, the Supreme Court, relying on its *Geduldig* ruling (see Ch. I), again refused to classify employment-related actions against women due to pregnancy as discriminatory. In reaction to these decisions, Congress passed the Pregnancy Discrimination Act of 1978, which amended Title VII to include discrimination on the basis of pregnancy. In 1987, in *California Federal S. & L. Ass'n v. Guerra,* the Supreme Court held that the pregnancy amendment to Title VII did not pre-empt states from going further than the federal government by affording additional protection to pregnant employees.

Despite these statutes and decisions, significant statistical disparities between men and women in the workplace have continued. Overall women's income relative to that of men has increased steadily since the modern movement began thirty years ago, but it had reached just 74.4% by the end of 1997. Progress in the percentage of female participation in various occupational fields has ranged from impressive (attorneys, journalists) to abysmal (airline pilots; most union construction work). Gender equality in many traditionally female fields (nurses, child-care workers) remains highly elusive.

The future path of the drive for gender-based equal employment opportunity is not clear. The Supreme Court was willing to invalidate traditional barriers to women in in the 1970's and 1980's -- in addition to the cases in Ch. I, *Johnson v. Transportation Agency* (1987) permitted an affirmative action plan for historically-underrepresented women in a county transportation agency, and *Dothard v. Rawlinson* (1977) rejected uniform height and weight requirements in a state corrections department, holding that they were not *bona fide occupational requirements* under Title VII. Given the Court's increasingly hostile stance on affirmative action and generally more conservative bent, future successes are uncertain. The effort to reform still-resistant occupations, and the general attack on the "glass ceiling", penetration of which is essential for increased earnings as well as power, will likely be a key 21st Century priority.

CALIFORNIA FEDERAL S. & L. ASSN. v. GUERRA, 479 U.S. 272 (1987)

Decided January 13, 1987

MARSHALL, J., announced the judgment of the Court

The question presented is whether Title VII of the Civil Rights Act of 1964, as amended by the Pregnancy Discrimination Act of 1978, pre-empts a state statute that requires [479 U.S. 272, 275] employers to provide leave and reinstatement to employees disabled by pregnancy.

California's Fair Employment and Housing Act (FEHA), Cal. Gov't Code Ann. 12900 et seq. (West 1980 and Supp. 1986), is a comprehensive statute that prohibits discrimination in employment and housing. In September 1978, California amended the FEHA to proscribe certain forms of employment discrimination on the basis of pregnancy. See Cal. Labor Code Ann. 1420.35, 1978 Cal. Stats., ch. 1321, 1, pp. 4320-4322 (West Supp. 1979), now codified at Cal. Gov't Code Ann. 12945(b)(2) (West 1980).1 Subdivision (b)(2) - the provision at issue here - is the only portion of the statute that applies to employers subject to Title VII. See [479 U.S. 272, 276] 12945(e).2 It requires these employers to provide female employees an unpaid pregnancy disability leave of up to four months. Respondent Fair Employment and Housing Commission, the state agency authorized to interpret the FEHA,3 has construed 12945(b)(2) to require California employers to reinstate an employee returning from such pregnancy leave to the job she previously held, unless it is no longer available due to business necessity. In the latter case, the employer must make a reasonable, good-faith effort to place the employee in a substantially similar job.4 The statute does not compel employers to provide paid leave to pregnant employees. Accordingly, the only benefit pregnant workers actually derive from 12945(b)(2) is a qualified right to reinstatement.

Title VII of the Civil Rights Act of 1964, 42 U.S.C. 2000e et seq., also prohibits various forms of employment [479 U.S. 272, 277] discrimination, including discrimination on the basis of sex. However, in General Electric Co. v. Gilbert, 429 U.S. 125 (1976), this Court ruled that discrimination on the basis of pregnancy was not sex discrimination under Title VII.5 In response to the Gilbert decision,

Congress passed the Pregnancy Discrimination Act of 1978 (PDA), 42 U.S.C. 2000e(k). The PDA specifies that sex discrimination includes discrimination on the basis of pregnancy.6 [479 U.S. 272, 278]

Petitioner California Federal Savings & Loan Association (Cal Fed) is a federally chartered savings and loan association based in Los Angeles; it is an employer covered by both Title VII and 12945(b)(2). Cal Fed has a facially neutral leave policy that permits employees who have completed three months of service to take unpaid leaves of absence for a variety of reasons, including disability and pregnancy. Although it is Cal Fed's policy to try to provide an employee taking unpaid leave with a similar position upon returning, Cal Fed expressly reserves the right to terminate an employee who has taken a leave of absence if a similar position is not available.

Lillian Garland was employed by Cal Fed as a receptionist for several years. In January 1982, she took a pregnancy disability leave. When she was able to return to work in April of that year, Garland notified Cal Fed, but was informed that her job had been filled and that there were no receptionist or similar positions available. Garland filed a complaint with respondent Department of Fair Employment and Housing, which issued an administrative accusation against Cal Fed on her behalf.7

Title VII, as amended by the PDA, and California's pregnancy disability leave statute share a common goal. The purpose of Title VII is "to achieve equality of employment opportunities and remove barriers that have operated in the past to favor an identifiable group of . . . employees over other employees." Griggs v. Duke Power Co., 401 U.S. 424, 429-430 (1971). See Hishon v. King & Spalding, 467 U.S. 69, 75, n. 7 (1984); Franks v. Bowman Transportation Co., 424 U.S. 747, 763 (1976); Alexander v. Gardner-Denver Co., 415 U.S. 36, 44 (1974); McDonnell Douglas Corp. v. Green, 411 U.S. 792, 800 (1973). Rather than limiting existing Title VII principles and objectives, the PDA extends [479 U.S. 272, 289] them to cover pregnancy.26 As Senator Williams, a sponsor of the Act, stated: "The entire thrust . . . behind this legislation is to guarantee women the basic right to participate fully and equally in the workforce, without denying them the fundamental right to full participation in family life." 123 Cong. Rec. 29658 (1977).

Section 12945(b)(2) also promotes equal employment opportunity. By requiring employers to reinstate women after a reasonable pregnancy disability leave, 12945(b)(2) ensures that they will not lose their jobs on account of pregnancy disability.27 California's approach is consistent with the dissenting opinion of JUSTICE BRENNAN in General Electric Co. v. Gilbert, which Congress adopted in enacting the PDA. Referring to Lau v. Nichols, 414 U.S. 563 (1974), a Title VI decision, JUSTICE BRENNAN stated:

> "[D]iscrimination is a social phenomenon encased in a social context and, therefore, unavoidably takes its meaning from the desired end products of the relevant legislative enactment, end products that may demand due consideration of the uniqueness of the `disadvantaged' individuals. A realistic understanding of conditions found in today's labor environment warrants taking pregnancy into account in fashioning disability policies." 429 U.S., at 159 (footnote omitted).

By "taking pregnancy into account," California's pregnancy disability-leave statute allows women, as well as men, to have families without losing their jobs. [479 U.S. 272, 290]
Thus, petitioners' facial challenge to 12945(b)(2) fails. The statute is not pre-empted by Title VII, as amended by the PDA, because it is not inconsistent with the purposes of the federal statute, nor does it require the doing of an act which is unlawful under Title VII.32

JOHNSON v. TRANSPORTATION AGENCY, 480 U.S. 616 (1987)

Decided March 25, 1987

JUSTICE BRENNAN delivered the opinion of the Court.

In December 1978, the Santa Clara County Transit District Board of Supervisors adopted an Affirmative Action Plan (Plan) for the County Transportation Agency. The Plan implemented a County Affirmative Action Plan, which had been adopted, declared the County, because "mere prohibition of discriminatory practices is not enough to remedy the effects of past practices and to permit attainment of an equitable representation of minorities, women and handicapped persons." App. 31.3 Relevant to this case, the Agency Plan provides that, in making promotions to positions within a traditionally segregated job classification in which women have [480 U.S. 616, 621] been significantly underrepresented, the Agency is authorized to consider as one factor the sex of a qualified applicant.

We next consider whether the Agency Plan unnecessarily trammeled the rights of male employees or created an absolute [480 U.S. 616, 638] bar to their advancement. In contrast to the plan in Weber, which provided that 50% of the positions in the craft training program were exclusively for blacks, and to the consent decree upheld last Term in Firefighters v. Cleveland, 478 U.S. 501 (1986), which required the promotion of specific numbers of minorities, the Plan sets aside no positions for women. The Plan expressly states that "[t]he `goals' established for each Division should not be construed as `quotas' that must be met." App. 64. Rather, the Plan merely authorizes that consideration be given to affirmative action concerns when evaluating qualified applicants. As the Agency Director testified, the sex of Joyce was but one of numerous factors he took into account in arriving at his decision. Tr. 68. The Plan thus resembles the "Harvard Plan" approvingly noted by JUSTICE POWELL in Regents of University of California v. Bakke, 438 U.S. 265, 316-319 (1978), which considers race along with other criteria in determining admission to the college. As JUSTICE POWELL observed: "In such an admissions program, race or ethnic background may be deemed a `plus' in a particular applicant's file, yet it does not insulate the individual from comparison with all other candidates for the available seats." Id., at 317. Similarly, the Agency Plan requires women to compete with all other qualified applicants. No persons are automatically excluded from consideration; all are able to have their qualifications weighed against those of other applicants.

In addition, petitioner had no absolute entitlement to the road dispatcher position. Seven of the applicants were classified as qualified and eligible, and the Agency Director was authorized to promote any of the seven. Thus, denial of the promotion unsettled no legitimate, firmly rooted expectation on the part of petitioner. Furthermore, while petitioner in this case was denied a promotion, he retained his employment with the Agency, at the same salary and with the same seniority, and remained eligible for other promotions.15 [480 U.S. 616, 639]

In evaluating the compliance of an affirmative action plan with Title VII's prohibition on discrimination, we must be mindful of "this Court's and Congress' consistent emphasis on `the value of voluntary efforts to further the objectives of the law.'" Wygant, 476 U.S., at 290 (O'CONNOR, J., concurring in part and concurring in judgment) (quoting Bakke, supra, at 364). The Agency in the case before us has undertaken such a voluntary effort, and has done so in full recognition of both the difficulties and the potential for intrusion on males and nonminorities. The Agency has identified a conspicuous imbalance in job categories traditionally segregated by race and sex. It has made clear from the outset, however, [480 U.S. 616, 641] that employment decisions may not be justified solely by reference to this imbalance, but must rest on a multitude of practical, realistic factors. It has therefore committed itself to annual adjustment of goals so as to provide a reasonable guide for actual hiring and promotion decisions. The Agency earmarks no positions for anyone; sex is but one of several factors that may be taken into account in evaluating qualified applicants for a position. 17 As both the Plan's language and its manner of operation attest, the Agency has no intention of establishing a work force whose permanent composition is dictated by rigid numerical standards.

We therefore hold that the Agency appropriately took into account as one factor the sex of Diane Joyce in determining [480 U.S. 616, 642] that she should be promoted to the road dispatcher position. The decision to do so was made pursuant to an affirmative action plan that represents a moderate, flexible, case-by-case approach to effecting a gradual improvement in the representation of minorities and women in the Agency's work force. Such a plan is fully consistent with Title VII, for it embodies the contribution that voluntary employer action can make in eliminating the vestiges of discrimination in the workplace.

DOTHARD v. RAWLINSON, 433 U.S. 321 (1977)

Decided June 27, 1977

MR. JUSTICE STEWART delivered the opinion of the Court.

At the time she applied for a position as correctional counselor trainee, Rawlinson was a 22-year-old college graduate whose major course of study had been correctional psychology. She was refused employment because she failed to meet the minimum 120-pound weight requirement established [433 U.S. 321, 324] by an Alabama statute. The statute also establishes a height minimum of 5 feet 2 inches.

Although women 14 years of age or older compose 52.75% of the Alabama population and 36.89% of its total labor force, they hold only 12.9% of its correctional counselor positions. In considering the effect of the minimum height and weight standards on this disparity in rate of hiring between the sexes, the District Court found that the 5'2"-requirement would operate to exclude 33.29% of the women in the United States between the ages of 18-79, while excluding only 1.28% of men between the same ages. The 120-pound weight restriction would exclude 22.29% of the women and 2.35% of the men in this age group. When the height and weight restrictions are combined, Alabama's statutory standards would exclude 41.13% of the female population [433 U.S. 321, 330] while excluding less than 1% of the male population. 12 Accordingly, the District Court found that Rawlinson had made out a prima facie case of unlawful sex discrimination.

The appellants argue that a showing of disproportionate impact on women based on generalized national statistics should not suffice to establish a prima facie case. They point in particular to Rawlinson's failure to adduce comparative statistics concerning actual applicants for correctional counselor positions in Alabama. There is no requirement, however, that a statistical showing of disproportionate impact must always be based on analysis of the characteristics of actual applicants. See Griggs v. Duke Power Co., supra, at 430. The application process itself might not adequately reflect the actual potential applicant pool, since otherwise qualified people might be discouraged from applying because of a self-recognized inability to meet the very standards challenged as being discriminatory. See Teamsters v. United States, 431 U.S. 324, 365-367. A potential applicant could easily determine her height and weight and conclude that to make an application would be futile. Moreover, reliance on general population demographic data was not misplaced where there was no reason to suppose that physical height and weight characteristics of Alabama men and women differ markedly from those of the national population. [433 U.S. 321, 331]

For these reasons, we cannot say that the District Court was wrong in holding that the statutory height and weight standards had a discriminatory impact on women applicants. The plaintiffs in a case such as this are not required to exhaust every possible source of evidence, if the evidence actually presented on its face conspicuously demonstrates a job requirement's grossly discriminatory impact. If the employer discerns fallacies or deficiencies in the data offered by the plaintiff, he is free to adduce countervailing evidence of his own. In this case no such effort was made.

> [*Note that while the Court invalidates the standard height and weight requires as lacking* bona fide occupational qualification *status, it does uphold the Alabama policy against permitting female prison guards to work in "direct contact" with male inmates, given the unusually volatile setting*]:

There was substantial testimony from experts on both sides of this litigation that the use of women as guards in "contact" positions under the existing conditions in Alabama maximum-security male penitentiaries would pose a substantial security problem, directly linked to the sex of the prison guard. On the basis of that evidence, we conclude that the District Court was in error in ruling that being male is not a bona fide occupational qualification for the job of [433 U.S. 321, 337] correctional counselor in a "contact" position in an Alabama male maximum-security penitentiary.

B. VITAL STATISTICS

Women's Earnings as a Percent of Men's, 1979–1997

Year	Hourly	Weekly	Annual	Year	Hourly	Weekly	Annual
1979	64.1%	62.5%	59.7%	1989	75.4%	70.1%	68.7%
1980	64.8	64.4	60.2	1990	77.9	71.9	71.6
1981	65.1	64.6	59.2	1991	78.6	74.2	69.9
1982	67.3	65.4	61.7	1992	80.3	75.8	70.8
1983	69.4	66.7	63.6	1993	80.4	77.1	71.5
1984	69.8	67.8	63.7	1994	80.6	76.4	72.0
1985	70.0	68.2	64.6	1995	80.8	75.5	71.4
1986	70.2	69.2	64.3	1996	81.2	75.0	73.8
1987	72.1	70.0	65.2	1997	80.8	74.4	—
1988	73.8	70.2	66.0				

Source: U.S. Women's Bureau.

Percent of Female Workers in Selected Occupations, 1975–96

Occupation	Women as percent of total employed 1975	1985	1996
Airline pilot	—	2.6%	1.4%
Auto mechanic	0.5%	0.6	1.2
Bartender	35.2	47.9	53.8
Bus driver	37.7	49.2	46.8
Cab driver, chauffeur	8.7	10.9	10.7
Carpenter	0.6	1.2	1.3
Child care worker	98.4	96.1	97.1
Computer programmer	25.6	34.3	30.8
Computer systems analyst	14.8	28.0	28.1
Data entry keyer	92.8	90.7	84.5
Data processing equipment repairer	1.8	10.4	18.3
Dentist	1.8	6.5	13.7
Dental assistant	100.0	99.0	79.8
Economist	13.1	34.5	54.4
Editor, reporter	44.6	51.7	55.7
Garage, gas station attendant	4.7	6.8	5.8
Lawyer, judge	7.1	18.2	29.0
Librarian	81.1	87.0	82.7
Mail carrier (Postal Service)	8.7	17.2	28.3
Office machine repairer	1.7	5.7	3.7
Physician	13.0	17.2	26.4
Registered nurse	97.0	95.1	93.3
Social worker	60.8	66.7	68.5
Teacher, college & university	31.1	35.2	43.5
Teacher, elementary school	85.4	84.0	83.3
Telephone installer, repairer	4.8	12.8	13.9
Telephone operator	93.3	88.8	90.5
Waiter/waitress	91.1	84.0	77.9
Welder	4.4	4.8	5.0

U.S. Census Bureau

Employment Status of the Population by Sex, 1960–1996 (numbers in thousands)

Year	Civilian non-institutional population[1]	Civilian labor force: Total	Percent of Population	Number employed	Employment/population ratio[2]	Percent unemployed
TOTAL						
1960	117,245	69,628	59.4%	65,778	56.1%	5.5%
1970	137,085	82,771	60.4	78,678	57.4	4.9
1980	167,745	106,940	63.8	99,303	59.2	7.1
1985	178,206	115,461	64.8	107,150	60.1	7.2
1990	188,049	124,787	66.4	117,914	62.7	5.5
1995[3]	198,584	132,304	66.6	124,900	62.9	5.6
1996[3]	200,591	133,934	66.8	126,708	63.2	5.4
MALE						
1960	55,662	46,388	83.3%	43,904	78.9%	5.4%
1970	64,304	51,228	79.7	48,990	76.2	4.4
1980	79,398	61,453	77.4	57,186	72.0	6.9
1985	84,469	64,411	76.3	59,891	70.9	7.0
1990	89,650	68,234	76.1	64,435	71.9	5.6
1995[3]	95,178	71,360	75.0	67,377	70.8	5.6
1996[3]	96,206	72,087	74.9	68,207	70.9	5.4
FEMALE						
1960	61,582	23,240	37.7%	21,874	35.5%	5.9%
1970	72,782	31,543	43.3	29,688	40.8	5.9
1980	88,348	45,487	51.5	42,117	47.7	7.4
1985	93,736	51,050	54.5	47,259	50.4	7.4
1990	98,399	56,554	57.5	53,479	54.3	5.4
1995[3]	103,406	60,944	58.9	57,523	55.6	5.6
1996[3]	104,385	61,857	59.3	58,501	56.0	5.4

Note: N.A.=Not Available. 1. Age 16 and over. 2. Civilians employed as a percent of the civilian noninstitutional population. 3. Data for 1995 and 1996 are not directly comparable with data for previous years because of a major redesign of the Current Population Survey

U.S. Census Bureau

Labor-force participation rates of married women, husband present, by presence and age of children, 1950–1996.

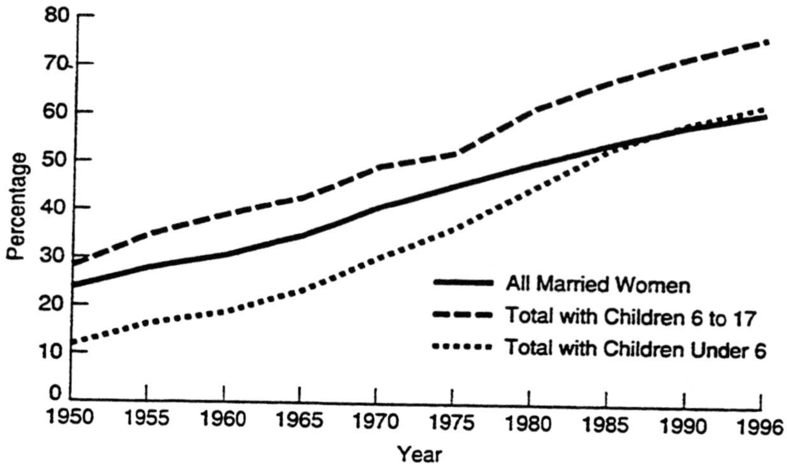

Source: U.S. Department of Labor, Bureau of Labor Statistics

Between 1951 and 1997, the proportion of wives who were in the labor force nearly tripled, from 23 percent to 62 percent.
The percentage of wage and salary recipients who were women increased from 32 percent in 1947 to 48 percent in 1997.

Since 1967, the proportion of full time, year-round workers who were women increased from 29 percent to 41 percent. Since 1960, the earnings of these women rose 54 percent to $24,973. The result is a female-to-male earnings ratio that is currently at an all-time high of 0.74.

In 1995, 55 percent of women aged 15 to 44 were in the labor force within a year of giving birth

About 4.5 million (43 percent) of America's 10.3 million preschool children received primary care from relatives other than their mothers in the fall of 1994. Fathers cared for 18 percent; grandparents, 16 percent; and other relatives such as siblings, aunts or uncles, 9 percent. In addition, some children (6 percent) received care from their mothers at their workplaces or while they were working in the home.

In contrast, 29 percent of preschoolers went to an organized facility such as a day care center (21 percent) or nursery school (8 percent).

Women-owned businesses hire proportionately more women. Thirty-five percent of women-owned employer firms reported 75 percent or more of their work force was female, compared to less than 24 percent of the nonminority male-owned firms.

U.S. Census Bureau

C. THE FAMILY AND MEDICAL LEAVE ACT

> My name is Liberia Johnson. In 1978, I was employed by a retail store in Charleston. South Carolina. . . . I became pregnant. . . . I tried to work because the income was so important to my family. My doctor told me that I was hypertensive and I had a thyroid problem. . . . If I did not stop working I would have a miscarriage. . . . The store manager . . . told me my job would be there after my baby was born. . . . I left at three months pregnant. I had a difficult pregnancy. I was in the hospital three times because I almost lost my baby. When I had my baby, I went and got my six weeks check up and the same day I went back to the store and asked for my job. . . . There was a new manager and he told me I don't have a job.[1]

On October 17, 1985, Ms. Johnson, married and the mother of five children, told her story to a joint oversight hearing on Disability and Parental Leave chaired by Congresswoman Patricia Schroeder (D-CO). Mary Rose Oakar (D-OH) and nine congressmen, six Democrats and three Republicans, attended part of the three-hour hearing that featured medical and academic experts, corporate and union representatives, and a local government official as well as another public witness, a single mother with an adopted daughter.

An oversight hearing is designed to attract attention from members of Congress, the press, and the public to an issue in hopes of gathering support for government action. Public witnesses like Liberia Johnson can play a brief, but significant, role. According to a veteran committee staff member, anecdotes are "the only thing that move people. A good public witness draws the rapt attention of the members."[2] They convince members of Congress in a very personal way that legislation is needed to remedy an injustice. The more heart-wrenching their stories, the better.

How did a black woman, who formerly worked a cash register and became a baker at a small hospital, get to tell her story to Congress? Public witnesses are usually located and coached by interest groups and subcommittee staff, but in this case the Congressional Caucus for Women's Issues (CCWI) was responsible along with the feminist National Women's Law Center (NWLC) and a subcommittee staff member. Several CCWI members, the CCWI staff, and a few interested attorneys led by the NWLC had been working on parental leave since early 1984. This issue illustrates the role of congresswomen and their caucus in developing and promoting a policy proposal to respond to the economic needs of women.

The House and Senate passed the FMLA in 1990 and again in 1992, but President Bush vetoed the bill both times and the Congress was unable to override either veto. Both chambers passed the bill again on February 4, 1993 and President Clinton signed it the next day, making it effective six months later

Provisions of the Family and Medical Leave Act (PL 103-3) Signed by President Clinton on February 5, 1993

1. Family leave—Employees may take up to 12 weeks of unpaid leave per year for the care of a newborn, newly adopted, or newly placed foster child, or for the care of a seriously ill child, parent, or spouse.
2. Medical leave—Employees may take up to 12 weeks of unpaid leave per year for their own serious medical condition. When medically necessary, employers must permit intermittent leave for treatment, but workers may be required to temporarily transfer to another equivalent position.
3. Exemption—Employers with fewer than 50 employees within 75 miles of a work site are exempt. Approximately 5 percent of all employers are covered and about 45 percent of all employees.
4. Coverage—Employees must have worked at least 12 months and at least 1,250 hours (an average of 25 hours per week) during the previous year to be eligible for leave. Highly paid workers (top 10 percent) in a firm may be denied reinstatement, if they received timely notice and the employer can demonstrate substantial and grievous economic injury would occur. Other eligible workers are entitled to the same or equivalent positions upon their return to work.

5. Conditions—Health insurance, if it is provided by the employer, must be continued on the same basis during the period of the leave. Employees are not entitled to more than 12 weeks leave in one year regardless of circumstances. Employees are required to give 30 days' notice when the need for leave is foreseeable. Employers may require that a health care provider certify the serious health condition of the employee or their family member in order to qualify for leave and reinstatement.
6. Paid leave—Workers may choose to substitute accrued paid vacation, personal or family leave for unpaid family leave mandated by the FMLA. Employers are not required to permit workers to take paid sick leave for the care of a new or ill family member. However, employers may require workers to substitute any paid leave they have accrued for all or part of their unpaid FMLA leave.
7. Enforcement—Administrative and civil procedures are available for enforcement under the supervision of the Wage and Hours Division of the Department of Labor. Violators are liable for lost wages, benefits and other compensation, or actual monetary losses sustained by the employee up to the equivalent of 12 weeks pay. If employers can demonstrate a good-faith effort to comply with the law, they will not be assessed an additional monetary penalty as punishment for the violation.
8. Federal employees—Federal government workers are also entitled to 12 weeks of family or medical leave after 12 months of employment. The Office of Personnel Management is responsible for enforcement.
9. Congressional employees—Employees of the House of Representatives and the Senate are eligible for 12 weeks of family or medical leave, the same as private employees. Previous employee rights bills have usually exempted congressional employees.

- From Joan Hulse Thompson, "The Family and Medical Leave Act: A Policy for Families," in Lois Duke Whitaker, *Women In Politics: Outsiders Or Insiders?*, Prentice Hall: 3rd ed. 1999

Make Time for Daddy

PARENTHOOD DID NOT COME EASILY TO KEVIN AND KIM Knussman. First there, was a painful year of fertility treatments. Then complications in Kim's pregnancy forced her doctors to induce labor prematurely, leaving her bedridden. Kevin, a trooper with the Maryland state police for 18 years, applied for extended leave to tend to his wife and infant, a request that fell under the federal Family and Medical Leave Act and a state law that provides paid leave for primary caregivers. He was allotted just 10 days, at the end of which his wife was still hemorrhaging and too weak to care for the baby. He asked for more time, but claims that the personnel manager responded, "Unless your wife is in a coma or dead, you can't be primary care provider."

When Kevin went back to work, he filed a complaint that he had been denied the leave solely because of his gender. Then he sought help from the American Civil Liberties Union, which sued the state on his behalf. Last week a jury sided with Kevin, awarding him $375,000 in the first-ever sex-discrimination case brought under the federal act. The state argued that Kevin did not alert the right people to his wife's condition and failed to prove that he was the primary care provider. "It was never a gender-based issue," says Maryland assistant attorney general Betty Stemley Sconion, who may appeal the verdict.

The long legal fight has turned Kevin into a poster dad for the Family and Medical Leave Act, now six years old. Though about 2 million people a year take parental leave under the act, only half a million of them are men. Kevin is working to even the scales. He has testified before a federal commission and even got a mention in Hillary Rodham Clinton's book *It Takes a Village*. But the biggest changes are back home. When he and his wife had their second child, in 1996, Kevin was granted a full 12 weeks of paid leave. "It's such a precious thing to hold that little life in your arms," he says. "And I lost that the first time." —*By Jodie Morse*

TIME, Feb. 15, 1999
vol. 153, no. 6

FAMILY LEAVE -- HOW THE U.S. MEASURES UP:

Number of fully-paid weeks of family leave in the following countries:
GROUP 1: India, Mexico, Pakistan; GROUP 2: Britain, Germany; GROUP 3: Austria, Costa Rica, Netherlands, Poland; GROUP 4: Chile, China, Denmark, Norway, South Korea, Venezuela; GROUP 5: Brazil, Bulgaria, Hungary; GROUP 6: Belarus, Ukraine; GROUP 7: Russia

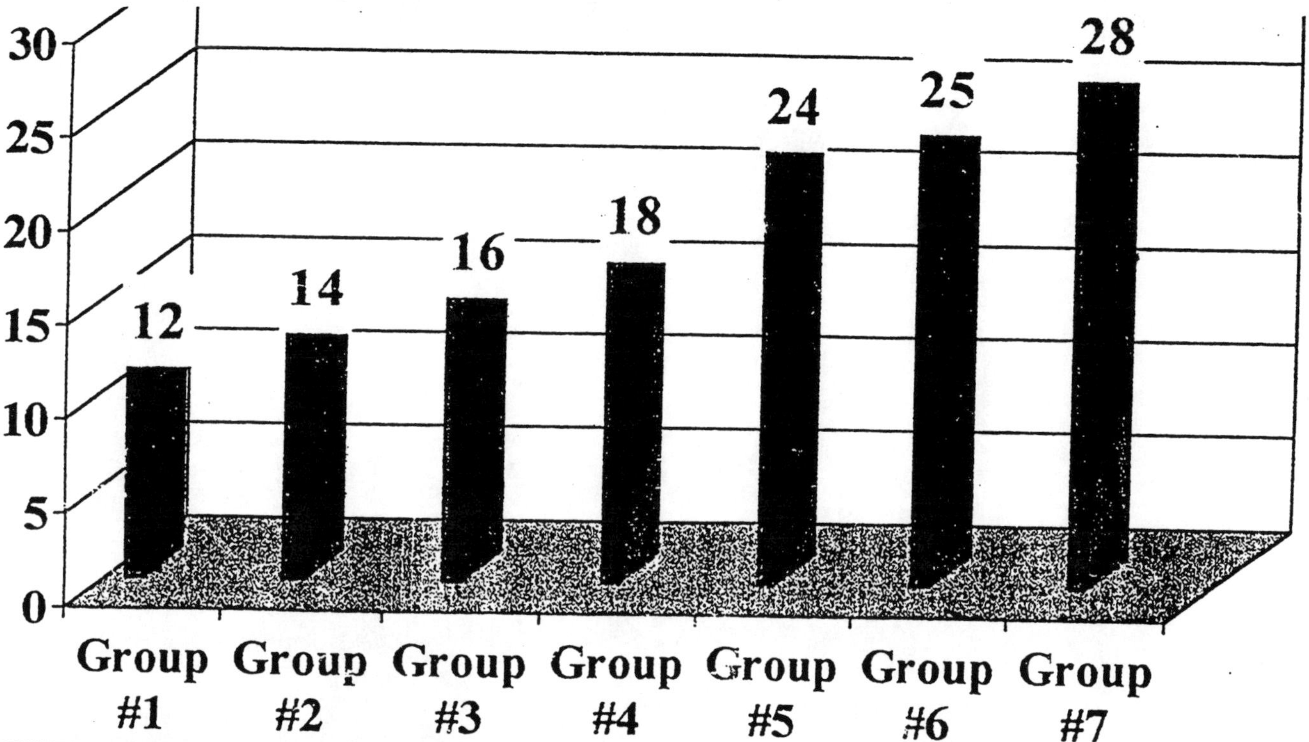

Other Selected Countries:

- 1997 United Nations Data

	Weeks Off	Percentage of Pay
Australia	52	none
Canada	15	55%
Italy	20	80
France	16	64
New Zealand	14	none
Japan	14	60
South Africa	12	45
Sweden	12	flat daily rate
United States	12	none

D. RECOMMENDED READING

R. Kelly, J. Bayes, eds., *Comparable Worth, Pay Equity, and Public Policy* (Greenwood Press: 1988)

S. Mezey, *In Pursuit of Equality: Women, Public Policy, and the Federal Courts* (St. Martin's Press: 1992)

L. Haas, *Equal Parenthood and Social Policy: A Study of Parental Leave in Sweden* (New York State University Press: 1992)

CHAPTER III

Equal Educational Opportunity

A. SINGLE-SEX SCHOOLS?

The constitutionality of single-sex education, even after Justice Ginsburg's opinion in *United States v. Virginia*, is still not completely settled. That opinion would appear to allow little room for gender-exclusive, publicly-funded schools, but it relied heavily on the substantially unequal female alternative to Virginia Military Institute proposed by the state. Some – but not all – courts have permitted male-only schools to exist when true equal educational opportunity is available to female students, but formulating a clear test is extremely difficult. In challenges to male-only public schools in Philadelphia and Detroit, two federal courts took very different approaches.

VORCHHEIMER v. SCHOOL DISTRICT OF PHILADELPHIA
532 F.2d 880 (3rd Cir. 1976)
aff'd by equally-divided S.Ct., 430 U.S. 703 (1977)

Do the Constitution and laws of the United States require that every public school, in every public school system in the Nation, be coeducational? Stated another way, do our Constitution and laws forbid the maintenance by a public school board, in a system otherwise coeducational, of a limited number of single-sex high schools in which enrollment is voluntary and the educational opportunities offered to girls and boys are essentially equal? This appeal presents those questions and, after careful consideration, we answer negatively. Accordingly, we vacate the district court's judgment which held that the school board policy was impermissible.[1]

Plaintiff is a teen-age girl who graduated with honors from a junior high school in Philadelphia. She then applied to Central High School, a public school in the city, but was refused admission because that institution is restricted to male students. After that setback, she filed this class action in the United States District Court seeking relief under 42 U.S.C. § 1983 from alleged unconstitutional discrimination. After a trial, the district court granted an injunction, ordering that she and other qualified female students be admitted to Central.

The Philadelphia School District offers four types of senior high schools: academic, comprehensive, technical and magnet. Although this suit is aimed at only an academic school, it is necessary to review the roles of other schools as well.

Comprehensive schools provide a wide range of courses, including those required for college admission, and offer advanced placement classes for students who are intellectually able to progress at a faster than average rate. The criterion for enrollment in the comprehensive schools is residency within a designated area. Although most of these schools are co-ed, two admit only males and one is restricted to female students. At the time the injunction was granted, plaintiff was enrolled at George Washington High School, a coeducational comprehensive school.

Academic high schools have high admission standards and offer only college preparatory courses. There are but two such schools in Philadelphia, and they accept students from the entire city rather than operating on a neighborhood basis. Central is restricted to males, and Girls High School, as the name implies, admits only females.

Central High School was founded in 1836 and has maintained a reputation for academic excellence. For some years before 1939, it was designated a comprehensive rather than an academic high school as it is presently. Its graduates both before and after 1939 have made notable contributions to the professions, business, government and academe.

Girls High has also achieved high academic standing. It was founded in 1848 and became an academic school in 1893. Its alumnae have compiled enviable records and have distinguished themselves in their chosen diverse fields. It now has a faculty of more than 100 and a student body of approximately 2,000, about the same as those of Central.

Enrollment at either school is voluntary and not by assignment. Only 7% of students in the city qualify under the stringent standards at these two schools, and it is conceded that plaintiff met the scholastic requirements of both. The Philadelphia school system does not have a co-ed academic school with similar scholastic requirements for admission.

The courses offered by the two schools are similar and of equal quality. The academic facilities are comparable, with the exception of those in the scientific field where Central's are superior. The district court concluded "that [generally] the education available to the female students at Girls is comparable to that available to the male students at Central." Moreover, "[g]raduates of both Central and Girls High, as well as the other senior high schools of Philadelphia," have been and are accepted by the most prestigious universities.

Equal educational opportunities should be available to both sexes in any intellectual field. However, the special emotional problems of the adolescent years are matters of human experience and have led some educational experts to opt for one-sex high schools. While this policy has limited acceptance on its merits, it does have its basis in a theory of equal benefit and not discriminatory denial.

The only occasion on which the Supreme Court ruled upon a gender classification in school admissions policy was in *Williams v. McNair,* 316 F.Supp. 134 (D.S.C.1970), *aff'd,* 401 U.S. 951, 91 S.Ct. 976, 28 L.Ed.2d 235 (1971), a case which was decided many years after *Sweatt, supra,* and *Brown, supra. Williams* was a summary affirmance of a three-judge district court, and we do not have the benefit of the Supreme Court's reasoning. Yet, the result does have precedential weight for us. *Hicks v. Miranda,* 422 U.S. 332, 95 S.Ct. 2281, 45 L.Ed.2d 223 (1975). The district court's opinion details a fact situation quite similar to that confronting us here, except that the plaintiffs were males who sought admission to a girls' state college. *Reed v. Reed, supra,* had not yet been decided and the district court therefore had no reason to discuss a substantial relationship test. Rather, it applied the traditional rational relationship guidelines. The court said:

> "While history and tradition alone may not support a discrimination, the Constitution does not require that a classification 'keep abreast of the latest' in educational opinion, especially when there remains a respectable opinion to the contrary; it only demands that the discrimination not be wholly wanting in reason." 316 F.Supp. at 137.

Believing the problem could not be considered in isolation, the court noted that the school involved was only one in an extensive state system which included several co-ed schools as well as an all male one.

We may not cavalierly disregard *Williams* although it predated *Reed* by a few months.[8] Indeed, the two cases are not inconsistent because the state schools' restrictive admissions policy applied to both sexes, a significant difference from the preferential statutory procedure in *Reed.* This distinction is enough to justify the use of the rational relationship test in *Williams* even though it is likely that the result would have been the same under the substantial relationship formula.

We do not accept *Williams* as being inapplicable merely because males were barred rather than females, as in the case *sub judice.* We are aware of the suggestion that disparity is likely to be favorably considered when it confers on the female some benefit tending to rectify the effects of past discrimination. For example, in *Kahn v. Shevin, supra,* a widow's tax exemption was permissible although no such benefit was provided for a widower. *See also* 1975 Duke L.J. 163, 179; Note, *The Supreme Court 1973 Term,* 88 Harv.L.Rev. 129 (1974). But we have no such exempting qualification here because there is no evidence of past deprivation of educational opportunities for women in the Philadelphia School District. Indeed, the factual findings establish that, for many years past and at the present, excellent educational facilities have been and are available to both sexes.[9]

Since there is no remedial measure at stake, we see no basis for differentiation between *Williams,* and the case at bar. Consequently, we differ with the district court's opinion that *Williams* has only a tenuous applicability here. In our view it is strong, if not controlling authority for denial of an injunction.

[6] The record does contain sufficient evidence to establish that a legitimate educational policy may be served by utilizing single-sex high schools. The primary aim of any school system must be to furnish an education of as high a quality as is feasible. Measures which would allow innovation in methods and techniques to achieve that goal have a high degree of relevance. Thus, given the objective of a quality education and a controverted, but respected theory that adolescents may study more effectively in single-sex schools, the policy of the school board here does bear a substantial relationship.

[7] We need not decide whether this case requires application of the rational or substantial relationship tests because, using either, the result is the same.[10] We conclude that the regulations establishing admission requirements to Central and Girls High School based on gender classification do not offend the Equal Protection Clause of the United States Constitution.

The gravamen of plaintiff's case is her desire to attend a specific school based on its particular appeal to her. She believes that the choice should not be denied her because of an educational policy with which she does not agree.

We are not unsympathetic with her desire to have an expanded freedom of choice, but its cost should not be overlooked. If she were to prevail, then all public single-sex schools would have to be abolished. The absence of these schools would stifle the ability of the local school board to continue with a respected educational methodology. It follows too that those students and parents who prefer an education in a public, single-sex school would be denied their freedom of choice. The existence of private schools is no more an answer to those people than it is to the plaintiff.

It is not for us to pass upon the wisdom of segregating boys and girls in high school.

GARRETT v. BOARD OF EDUCATION, DETROIT

U.S. District Court, 775 F.Supp. 1004 (E.D. Michigan 1991)

*** * * Plaintiffs are girls enrolled in Detroit public schools and their parents. Plaintiff Nancy Doe is a Detroit resident with daughters aged 11, 6, and 5, all of whom will attend Detroit public schools this fall.**

Three male academies ("Academies") are scheduled to open on August 26, 1991. The Academies offer special programs including a class entitled "Rites of Passage", an Afrocentric (Pluralistic) curriculum, futuristic lessons in preparation for 21st century careers,

an emphasis on male responsibility, mentors, Saturday classes, individualized counseling, extended classroom hours, and student uniforms

Plaintiffs contend that these special offerings (1) do not require a uniquely male atmosphere to succeed; and (2) address issues that face all children and adolescents, including females. Plaintiffs further charge that despite the stated goal of the Academies to address the high unemployment rates, school dropout levels and homicide among urban males, the Academies do not target "at-risk" males; rather, they serve a mix of boys from all achievement levels.

In Mississippi v. Hogan, the Supreme Court held that exclusion of an individual from a publicly-funded school because of his or her sex violates the Equal Protection Clause of the Fourteenth Amendment, unless the defendant can show the sex-based "classification serves 'important governmental objectives and that the discriminatory means employed'" are "substantially related to the achievement of those objectives."[4]

Plaintiffs maintain the Board cannot meet this standard because the Board's policy of excluding girls inappropriately relies on gender as a proxy for "at-risk" students.

The Board has proffered no evidence that the presence of girls in the classroom bears a substantial relationship to the difficulties facing urban males.

Accordingly, plaintiffs conclude that the male academies improperly use gender as a "proxy for other, more germane bases of classification," in this instance, for "at risk" students. Specifically, the gender specific data presented in defense of the Academies ignores the fact that all children in the Detroit public schools face significant obstacles to success. In fact, in its resolution establishing the Academies, the Board acknowledged an "equally urgent and unique crisis facing ... female students." Urban girls drop out of school, suffer loss of self esteem and become involved in criminal activity. Ignoring the plight of urban females institutionalizes inequality and perpetuates the myth that females are doing well in the current system. Accordingly, plaintiffs contend there is nc adequate justification for the Academies' exclusive focus on boys.

Plaintiffs also assert that the special curriculum proposed for the Academies suggests a false dichotomy between the roles and responsibilities of boys and girls. For example, the Rites of Passage curriculum teaches that "men need a vision and a plan for living," "men master their emotions," and "men acquire skills and knowledge to overcome life's obstacles." These issues confront all adolescents and are not rites peculiarly male. Therefore, they are insufficient to justify gender-based classification.

[T]he defendant here argues it has confirmed that the present delivery of education has resulted in substantially lower achievement levels for males than for females and that the Academies are the solution to this problem. The primary rationale for the Academies is simply that co-educational programs aimed at improving male performance have failed.

The Court is wary of accepting such a rationale.

Defendant argues that just because females also face academic performance problems does not weaken the importance of their objective in opening the male academies.

the objective of the male academies is important; but, the degree of importance does not eliminate the defendant's burden of showing that the second prong of the *Hogan* test is met.

Defendant argues in the alternative that the second prong, "substantially related" is satisfied for three reasons. First, the establishment of male academies is critical to expeditiously determine what curriculum and training programs will work to keep urban males out of the City's morgues and prisons. Second, the Board has already reviewed smaller scale experimental programs at two schools that specifically addressed the special needs of urban males and found them successful in improving the overall academic and behavioral aspects of the urban males' life style. Third, the Board knows that current co-ed programs do not work. Consequently, the Board finds that research supports the establishment of an experimental school with a specialized curriculum to address the special needs of urban males.

None of these findings meet the defendant's burden of showing how the exclusion of females from the Academies is necessary to combat unemployment, dropout and homicide rates among urban males.

Neither the Third Circuit Court of Appeal in *Vorchheimer,* nor the Federal District Court in *Garrett,* had the benefit of the Virginia Military Institute ruling. It is safe to say that today, a school system's *legal* burden in defending a gender-exclusive school would be extremely heavy. The *educational* and *social* aspects of the single-sex school controversy, however, are considerably more complex. Much of the statistical data (see Sec. B) demonstrates that female students have achieved parity in most indicators for secondary and college education, but recent studies, particularly "How Schools Shortchange Girls (1992) and "Gender Gaps: Where Schools Still Fail Our Children" (1998) by the American Association of University Women, argue that meaningful equal educational opportunity for women is not always a matter of numbers. Two views follow.

From Judy Mann, *The Difference* (Warner Books: 1994)

CHAPTER SIX

The Myth of Equal Education

Over the years I have written a number of columns about research that shows that boys and girls are treated differently in our classrooms. But what I did not realize until I started this book was the degree and extent to which this takes place, nor did I realize how clearly girls understand what is happening to them.

Some classroom sexism is subtle, but it is constant and pervasive. Some of it is so blatant, so ruthlessly destructive of our daughters' ambitions, that it ought to be indicted as malicious wounding. From the first years of elementary school through college and graduate schools, girls receive destructively different treatments in their classrooms. Girls know it, boys know it—and parents ought to know it as well. Our sons are at the center of the whole educational process, while our daughters are sitting on the sidelines—still waiting their turn, after all these years.

Among the pioneering researchers who have been sounding alarms about this have been David and Myra Sadker, both professors of education at American University in Washington, D.C. Myra is the author of *Sexism in Schools and Society*, a landmark work published in 1973. The Sadkers have been calling attention to sexism in the classroom for two decades now—long enough, one would think, for educators to have dispatched it once and for all. It's a good thing we haven't been holding our breath.

Blame for this continued crippling of girls in our schools must be shared by the Reagan administration. The great communicator's doorstep is by now littered with the detritus of many other scandals and failed policies. But while Reagan's followers were looting the savings and loan industry, his dreary ideologues were looting the futures of girls. They did it with a concerted, vicious, and unrelenting attack on a tiny federal program buried in the Department of Education.

The Women's Educational Equity Act (WEEA) program was the only federal program that promoted equal education for girls by raising gender issues among educators. It funded pilot programs to combat discrimination against girls and developed training manuals for parents, teachers, and school administrators. It was singled out as a hotbed of radical feminists by the Heritage Foundation and its henchmen in the seedier "new right" organizations that flourished around Reagan; WEEA was among the first targets of the Reagan administration's fierce backlash against the gains women made in the 1970s. Leslie Wolfe, a career civil servant who was WEEA's director, was backed by numerous liberal and moderate members of Congress in her courageous battle to preserve the program, but in the end WEEA's budget was gutted, its programs abolished, and Wolfe was forced to resign.

The result of the right wing's crude assault was that there was virtually no federal leadership for promoting educational equity. There would be no federal funds for retraining programs to redress unequal treatment in the classrooms. The subject simply fell off the radar screen. Even when President Bush misrepresented himself as the "education president," he never made the connection—at least not publicly—between the disparate classroom experience of boys and girls and how that ultimately wrecks girls' professional aspirations and capabilities.

The progress women had made in reforming the educational system was put into a state of suspended animation: People knew what had to be done to improve the classrooms for women, to give them adequate teacher attention and constructive feedback, but the will to do it, the leadership for reform, had vanished utterly.

Like so much sexism, classroom sexism is both insidious and ruinous. Even teachers who are committed to running honest classrooms are stunned when they see videotapes of the biased practices they are following. The Sadkers continue to be struck by how subtle these biases are, how unintentional they usually are, and how often the teachers themselves have no idea that they are responding differently to boys than they are to girls. "It goes undetected because we're living in a sea of bias," David Sadker once told me. They and other researchers investigating sexism in the classroom have found that males get more attention from teachers, they get more precise and challenging feedback, they get far more "air time" during classroom discussions, they interrupt more, they call out answers far more frequently than girls do, and girls are far more likely to be reprimanded for calling out answers than boys are. Boys are more likely to be praised for good work, and criticized and forced to produce better answers, and they are more likely to receive remedial help and be directed into special learning classes earlier than girls are.

The Sadkers were able to measure the disproportionate amount of attention that boys demand. In both elementary and secondary schools boys are eight times as likely as girls to call out and demand attention. Boys are called on from two to twelve times more often than girls in any class period, no matter the ratio of boys to girls or the sex of the instructor. The Sadkers concluded that boys are being trained to be assertive and girls to be passive.

Patterns of boys hogging classroom time, as well as equipment, are repeated throughout elementary school, high school, college, and graduate school. The same patterns have been found in the United States, Great Britain, and Australia.

The lesson is catastrophically clear: In classrooms, girls learn to be quiet.

To be passive.

To make do with less air time than boys get.

To get by with less feedback.

What they do not learn is how to accept criticism—since they don't get as much of it. From the lower grades on up, boys are more disruptive, and they get more attention from the teachers. In disciplining them, teachers give boys another learning experience that teaches them how to deal with criticism. Introducing an idea, taking ownership of it, and keeping it at the center of the class discussion is another experience that is largely denied to girls. Finally, girls do not get the experience of interrupting and taking over a conversation. Later, as adults, we see the results: One study found that 96 percent of the topics introduced by men were followed up in the course of conversation, while only 36 percent of topics introduced by women were developed further.[1] Men are much more frequently the ones to interrupt, and they interrupt women much more frequently than they interrupt other men. Men dominate professional meetings through interruption. Another way they gain verbal ascendancy is by answering questions not addressed to them—a way of seizing control of a meeting or conversation. Women, once interrupted, typically do not try to regain the floor.

TEACHERS' ATTENTION

The single most valuable resource in a classroom is the teacher's attention. If one group gets a disproportionately large share of that resource, it stands to reason that this group will have the most profitable educational experience. It came as no surprise to researchers that girls test as equal with or better than boys when they enter elementary school and yet fall behind at the end of high school. Such tests as the National Assessments of Educational Progress and the Scholastic Aptitude Tests uniformly document this retrogression. Small wonder. Given twelve years of such a thoroughly unequal educational experience—which gets progressively worse for girls as they leave elementary school and go through high school—it is remarkable that girls do as well as they do.

The Sadkers, Bernice Sandler, and other investigators have found that patterns established in elementary school and reinforced in high school persist in college. With one difference: They get worse. Since even fewer students actually participate in college classroom discussions, the cheating of women students becomes even more egregious. While a quarter of the children in elementary school classes did not interact with their teachers at all, the Sadkers found that this proportion doubled in college and university classes. Male students received significantly more attention. Another study found that college women speak two and a half times less often than their male classmates. In a review of the findings on women's experience in college that they did for the Association of American Colleges, Sandler and her colleague, Roberta Hall, found that professors are more likely to remember men's names, more likely to call on them in class and listen to their answers. Professors felt freer to interrupt women students and ask them less challenging questions.[2]

That is the bad news about what happens to girls who go to school full of hope and expectations about what they will learn, who they will meet, and what they can do—only to be diminished and sidelined in the classroom and, as we have seen, teased and harassed on the playground. The good news is that this can be fixed. Perhaps the most exciting aspect of the Sadkers' work is that by retraining teachers they have been able to promote equitable treatment of boys and girls in the classroom. By showing teachers videos of what they are doing wrong, the Sadkers alert them to the biases lurking in their classrooms. Having done that, they then teach them techniques for making sure that boys and girls participate equally. Simple techniques—such as "wait time," in which teachers wait a few seconds for both boys and girls to raise their hands, or alternating from boy to girl in selecting who will answer a question—promote greater participation of both groups. These routines help ensure that both boys and girls get access to the attention of teachers, and they create better teaching and learning environments overall. Boys who might have called out before learn to take turns. The Sadkers and other researchers are trying to get across one of the most fundamentally important lessons for parents, teachers, and children to learn: Equity in teaching promotes excellence.

THE FASTEST MOUTH GETS THE AIR TIME

Catherine G. Krupnick, director of the Harvard-Danforth Center Video Lab, led a research team that spent a year reviewing videotapes of twenty-four instructors at Harvard College. She observed a pattern that is familiar to all of us who have been in classrooms. A few people begin to dominate the classroom at the start of a class hour, asking questions, answering them, and becoming so engaged in running the discussion that the rest of the students drop out of the conversation. The pattern repeats itself day after day, and the less verbal students become more and more disconnected from the class. It is not the students who have the most thoughtful minds who run the class, but the ones with the fastest mouths.[3]

Krupnick concluded, as have others who have watched this pattern in classes, that instructors have to take a much firmer hand than they currently do in managing classrooms so that each student has an opportunity to talk. She suggests that teachers become close observers of their own classrooms—that they keep notes on who participates and how, have videos made, and ask colleagues to sit in and observe what goes on. Among steps teachers can take to encourage participation by everyone is to hold everyone responsible for each assignment, to call on all students—not just those who raise their hands—and to listen for interruptions and take pains to discourage them. United Nations Ambassador Madeleine Albright combated the interruption problem in her classes in the Georgetown School of Foreign Service with the opposite approach. She told me that she taught her women students to interrupt.

BOYS AGAINST GIRLS

Children segregate themselves by sex in school very early and they maintain an absolute minimum of cross-sex contact until they reach high school. Researchers who have studied this phenomenon believe that it has much deeper impact than commonly believed: The separation of the sexes contributes to stereotypes by reinforcing certain types of behavior in children and by labeling certain activities "masculine" or "feminine."

Researchers Marlaine E. Lockheed and Susan S. Klein believe that patterns of inequitable behavior we see in adult groups have their roots in elementary school. They reviewed eighteen studies of how students behaved in school situations, ranging from preschool through kindergarten and the eighth grade, and found a pervasive pattern of same-sex segregation in everything from selection of play partners and work partners, to seating patterns in cafeterias, to students' contacts with each other. Again the intensity of peer pressure showed up—and it showed up early. A study of preschoolers found that boys who had contacts with girls were criticized by other boys. They found that the children initiated the segregation and teachers rarely interfered. It was also evident that whatever contact boys and girls did have was characterized by a lack of cooperation and by male dominance.[4]

EYEWITNESS REPORTS

Do boys and girls understand what is going on in the classroom? Indeed they do.

The University of Michigan runs a summer science program for girls who are between the eighth and ninth grades. Carol Hollenshead, who runs the university's Center for the Education of Women, asked the girls to write brief comments describing their experiences in school. Many were acutely conscious of sexist teachers they had had in regular school. They were also keenly aware of whether their teachers had encouraged them, and were immensely appreciative. Some told of their own efforts to overcome sexism. These girls didn't pull any punches, and some of what they wrote about how teachers behave is downright shocking.

> "I have a science teacher who is all for Women in Science. He always supports whatever I do, and he even works for the Women in Science.
>
> "On the other hand, I have a U.S. History teacher who is sexist and advertises it."

> "This perverted teacher said to this girl, 'This class should be easy for you since you probably screwed every boy in this class.' He also wrote 'I love you' in my sister's notebook."

> "I had a science teacher once who would ignore you, not call on you, and generally pretend you were not there . . . especially if you were a girl. He would interrupt you in mid-sentence to try to prove you wrong with his own point even if you were right. I started a petition and got 100 signatures to the principal. He sure changed his train of thought about good teaching techniques."

> "I had a science teacher last year who very often would not call on me, even if I was the only person in the class with my hand up!"

> "In the sixth grade, I had a math teacher who refused to sign a recommendation for a pre-algebra course. He said, 'You, a girl in algebra. I don't think so.' I was persistent and prodded him and he eventually gave in."

Whether teachers call on boys eight times as often as they call on girls, whether they ask boys the tougher questions, whether they tolerate unruly behavior on the part of boys while squelching it mercilessly in girls—they are treating boys and girls unequally. Boys, who receive more and more teacher attention as they go through the educational system, retain their voice. Girls, who receive ever-diminishing amounts of attention from their teachers, lose theirs. Boys gain confidence in their ability to do math and science, while girls' confidence erodes. Boys see a dazzling array of occupations and possibilities spread out before them as they proceed from grade to grade. Girls find their options diminishing, their hopes dimming as they conclude there are certain things they simply can't do. They conclude that forays into the "masculine" fields of math and science aren't worth the social cost, the perceived loss of femininity that goes with being smart. Boys are being set up to be independent; girls are being set up to be dependent.

CHAPTER TEN

Reforming Schools for Girls

My day at Madeira provided eloquent arguments on behalf of single-sex girls' schools, but I was left with the question: How can Madeira's lessons be translated into public schools? How can public schools replicate the experience of academically strong girls' schools so that girls emerge feeling as confident, strong, and capable as boys do?

Well, for starters, public schools can make sure that assigned English readings offer women heroines and women authors, and that rite-of-passage stories so important to adolescents include girls as well as boys. Next, public schools should examine their science texts to make sure that girls are pictured doing experiments as often as boys are. Are their history books telling the history of men, wars, elections, and economic cycles, or are they depicting the history of an entire era, in which women played critical roles as pioneers, social reformers, inventors, and entrepreneurs? Young women need women of achievement as role models.

Public schools need to crunch their numbers and determine whether girls are doing as well in math and science courses as boys are. If they are not, public school administrators should consider segregated classes for both boys and girls. All of these fixes could be done quickly and cheaply—and almost certainly effectively.

Public schools can create a healthier atmosphere for girls by mandating teacher training about promoting equity in the classrooms. PTAs can pay for making videos of classrooms so teachers can see what they are doing. If the experience of educational researchers is any guide, even the most progressive teachers will be stunned at the gender bias they see in their own teaching. Are girls reinforced and supported in classes, or are they allowed to lapse into apathetic silence? Teachers can be taught to use simple techniques such as "wait time" and making boys and girls take turns to answer questions.

Public schools need to critique their own environment. What do girls and boys see when they enter the classroom? Pictures of women in outdated roles or pictures of women conducting a scientific experiment or directing a film or chairing a board meeting?

Public schools can incorporate the teaching techniques that top-flight girls' schools use, with heavy emphasis on collaboration, hands-on learning, and relevance, and cut down on the competitive style. "One of the things we do in math is to put four chairs together and the girls all correct their homework together," says Madeira's Betsy Griffith. She calls it "teaching on each other."

At the Emma Willard School, where Carol Gilligan has done her pioneering studies of how girls learn, one teacher changed the way she gave vocabulary tests—dividing the girls into groups to study vocabulary lists and to teach each other, and then giving them the test. Scores are averaged and the group score becomes the score of the individuals. Science teachers let students start working in pairs, and only when their confidence is strong do they move to individual work.

Paul Lamar, chair of the English division at the school, provides forums for students to state their points of view on controversial topics. Everyone is heard. Madeira provides forums for girls to talk about what is on their minds. Madeira has an issues book where students write down things that are bothering them and suggest solutions. Public schools can easily provide such avenues for making sure that girls' voices are heard.

Public schools need to pay more attention to the cultural and ethical atmosphere they are encouraging, or in some cases condoning. Girls' schools provide a model of respect and caring for other members of the school community that comes out of the emphasis that girls and women put on relationships. This, too, is something that public schools can work to foster in the classrooms and hallways. By emphasizing the validity of the female value system and its importance to the school community, public schools can offer a counterbalance to the machismo atmosphere that prevails—and too often creates a culture of violence—in public schools.

Public schools need to incorporate the findings of Gilligan and her associates in evaluating the school's atmosphere and how decisions are made on such matters as discipline. Is it very hierarchical, judgmental, and male? Or is discipline handled in a more open-ended manner, with an emphasis on justice? Is domination prized in classrooms, or is the mood one of tolerance and respect? This is probably the most important point of all, for it goes to the heart of the content of teaching, the style of teaching, and whose value systems are being perpetuated and honored.

Gilligan and her colleagues established in the Dodge Study, as their work at the Emma Willard School is known, that this sense of values, of what's important to girls, permeates every aspect of their learning experience. Their ethic of caring is the antithesis of the rigid male style that is obsessed with maintaining authority and discipline, no matter the cost to a child.

Lamar illustrated how this atmosphere of caring and mutual respect worked with the story of a girl who wrote a paper about a painful moment involving her brother. When she began to read it aloud, she broke down. Lydia, another student, went to her weeping classmate and asked if she could continue reading the paper aloud. It was, said Lamar, "one of the most human and authentic moments I've ever spent in a classroom."[1]

SINGLE SEX IN PUBLIC SCHOOLS

What cannot be translated to the public schools is the all-girls atmosphere and the benefits girls get when every decision is made with their welfare in mind. Perhaps the best way of providing that would be to offer single-sex environments within the framework of our public school system. It's an option worth considering, perhaps, but ironically the same law that has helped level the playing field in athletics for girls might be the biggest barrier to leveling the playing field in academics by providing girls with opportunities for separateness.

Title IX of the Education Amendments of 1972 bars discrimination on the basis of sex in any federally funded programs. The law rose out of the widely held perception that separate is not equal, a belief grounded in our sad history of racially segregated schools. In today's climate, separating students by gender in public schools runs counter to the powerful currents in social reform based on the idea that integration leads to equality and diversity leads to greater tolerance. Changing this deeply imbedded philosophy isn't going to be easy.

The courts have issued several ambiguous rulings in cases that have challenged the legality of running sex-segregated schools with public funds. Title IX does not directly forbid admission policies that segregate students by sex. It does not address admissions procedures at all. Title IX does forbid segregating by sex in programs that receive federal funds, once students are admitted to an institution. Thus, single-sex classrooms within a public elementary or secondary school are more clearly against the law than are separate admissions policies.

The Girls High School in Philadelphia survived a challenge to its sex segregation when the Third Circuit used a "separate but equal" analysis. The court found that Brown vs. Board of Education did not apply.

The court based its decision on findings that Central High (for boys) and Girls High were of equal quality and attendance was voluntary. It found that there was sufficient evidence to establish that legitimate educational goals could be served by single-sex schools in which young people could study better. Finally, the court did not find any evidence of anyone being harmed by the sex segregation, in contrast to the findings in Brown vs. Board of Education in which the court agreed that race segregation produced devastating psychological effects on black youngsters.[2]

The option of separating schools by race was foreclosed by the Brown vs. Board of Education decision, but the court has never spoken so forcefully on the matter of single-sex education, and there may be legal avenues that would allow communities to establish such schools. Certainly there is much evidence to support a claim that girls are not getting equal education in public schools. Are we to sacrifice the futures of girls to a legal standard designed to secure equal education for blacks—but which isn't doing it for girls? Does it not make more sense to revisit the issue and figure out how separate facilities or separate classes can be made to work so that both boys and girls get a top-flight education? What would be wrong with a magnet school for girls sharing a campus with a magnet school for boys, so that youngsters could take academic classes separately and perhaps share clubs and coed athletic teams—such as the swim team—and jointly sponsor school socials?

Another option could be to offer single-sex classes in math and science, and have the rest of the classes be mixed.

TESTING THE CLIMATE FOR GIRLS

Anne E. Bekebrede, headmistress of the MacDuffie School in Springfield, Massachusetts, has set forth ten criteria for picking out a school for girls. While her focus was private schools, her measurements can be generalized to all schools and can be helpful to parents who want to test how healthy the climate is at any schools, including colleges, their daughters are attending.[3] Distilled to their essence, here are her guidelines:

- Beware of schools where boys significantly outnumber girls. (This would be compounded if the school were a boarding school.)
- Parents should check on the ratio of females to males on the faculty. Women should be visible as department heads and administrators, bringing a feminine point of view to bear, and leading to greater equity in policies affecting boys and girls.
- What are the opportunities for girls to be student leaders?
- To what extent is the faculty engaged in ongoing discussions about the growing body of research on how schools shortchange girls—and, more important, what are they doing to repair their own environments?
- Is the faculty aware of the new research on how the intellectual and moral development of girls differs from that of boys? Are they assimilating this information into their teaching methods?
- Are girls' sports really getting their fair share of attention and resources? The message "comes through clearly about which group is important when the girls inherit the old gym and locker room and the boys get the new facilities," Bekebrede writes.
- Are there some facilities officially opened to all students that somehow become the special zones of males? Bekebrede notes that computer rooms can quickly become male preserves.

• Woodworking, shop, and mechanical drawing classes can enhance girls' comfort with science and disciplines that depend on spatial skills. Are girls encouraged to take these classes? Are girls taking the highest levels of math and science in proportions that reflect their presence in the student body?

• Does the school offer opportunities to boys and girls for service to others?

• Does the curriculum include one or more courses in women's studies? "Boys as much as girls should be encouraged to enroll in such classes," argues Bekebrede, "because equity in education ultimately depends on a widespread understanding of women in the past and where they are and should be in the world today."

A COMMITMENT TO EQUITY

Public schools and the communities they serve need to commit themselves to the proposition that all children deserve an equitable education and that sidelining girls into less demanding roles in school does them a lifelong disservice by tracking them into the low-paying end of the labor market.

Reform will not come about until teachers, administrators, and school boards, as well as parents and children, develop a much deeper and broader understanding about how schools continue to discriminate against girls. Teachers will have to become sophisticated enough about gender to spot discrimination in textbooks and then to lead classroom discussions about it. They will need to develop a teaching style that is a mixture of the individualistic and relational, drawing on the best of both styles, challenging both girls and boys to think, and enabling each to express their thoughts in a variety of ways. They will thus create a classroom atmosphere in which both boys and girls feel fully included.

Guidance counselors must be trained to encourage girls to pursue physics, chemistry, and the higher levels of math. They need to join forces with faculty members to make sure that career days feature women scientists and mathematicians, and that girls are encouraged to attend summer science programs and math enrichment programs that are offered at universities. Parents can support these efforts by lobbying to make sure that state universities offer these enrichment programs for girls. Many universities sponsor soccer and basketball camps during the summer. Surely math and science camps are just as worthwhile.

AGENTS OF CHANGE

Of course schools should not favor one gender over another. How dare they? Or, perhaps more to the point, why dare they? What earthly rationale can there be for favoring one style of learning over another? What equity, or practical good sense, is there in anointing one group of students as the norm and another group as "the other"?

Constipated careerist educators have no business prolonging "the longest war" by training boys to be sexually dominant and girls to be silent and submissive. If our free society is to fulfill its promise in an increasingly dangerous world, schools must be transformed into powerful agents of change, liberating both boys and girls from destructive hierarchical ways of learning and of devaluing other people. The connectedness girls cherish in human relations, the sense of caretaking that they bring to a classroom environment are prized in such superb schools as the Emma Willard School and the Madeira School. When a girl claims ownership of an idea she is asserting power and confidence in her intellect. When a girl goes to the aid of a troubled classmate, as Lydia did in Paul Lamar's class at the Emma Willard School, she showed what can and should be done to help a person who is in distress. Instead of averting her gaze, she looked anguish in the eye and moved to soothe it. When we create classrooms and schools in which the hand of learning bears this human touch, we bring about a society that values kindness. The best girls' schools produce high achievers because girls are constantly and consistently at the center of all the different considerations that go into running a school. Their needs are paramount; their values prevail.

In coeducational schools, however, the needs of boys are paramount and their values, their style of learning, and their noisy mode of communicating dominate. Academically demanding girls' schools can teach us a great deal about how to redress gender imbalance in public education, to find a new blend of styles that will benefit both boys and girls.

The goal of the best academic girls' schools is one all schools should strive for. That is to produce students—boys and girls—who emerge from the educational process as leaders and as smart, confident, and kind people who will go on to create a vastly improved society over what we have now.

And finally, isn't it time someone took a, yes, hard-headed look at that icon so cherished in male-dominated boardrooms, the bottom line? Can any society that dooms half of its pool of talent and energy to second-rate status hope to compete with truly progressive nations? Can a country whose public schools are obsessed with perpetuating unequal gender roles in classrooms truly survive and prosper in a new century so full of peril and promise?

Judith Kleinfeld, "Student Performance: Males versus Females" in The Public Interest, No. 134, Winter 1999

WOMEN'S advocacy groups have waged an intense media campaign to promote the idea that "schools shortchange girls." Their goal has been to convince the public that women are "victims" of an unfair educational system and that they deserve special treatment, extra funding, and heightened policy attention. Their sophisticated public-relations campaign has succeeded. The idea that girls are shortchanged by schools has become the common wisdom—what people take for granted, without a thought concerning whether or not it is true.

This idea that girls are not well served by our schools—that gender differences in performance result from institutional unfairness—received its greatest boost from a highly publicized report, *How Schools Shortchange Girls: A Study of Major Findings on Girls and Education*. Published in 1992 by the respected organization, the American Association of University Women (AAUW), along with a survey of self-esteem and aspirations among boys and girls, the AAUW report quickly became the basis for countless newspaper articles, magazine features, books, and university courses on gender and education. While a few voices challenged the report's findings—notably Christina Hoff Sommers, in *Who Stole Feminism?*—the mainstream media for the most part ignored dissenting views.

The AAUW report makes three principal claims: First, girls fall behind boys in science and mathematics; second, girls participate less than boys in class or, as it is said, are "silenced" in the classroom; and third, girls suffer a major decline in self-esteem at adolescence while adolescent boys gain in self-esteem. As the AAUW Executive Summary declares:

> The educational system is not meeting girls' needs. Girls and boys enter school roughly equal in measured ability. Twelve years later, girls have fallen behind their male classmates in key areas such as higher-level mathematics and measures of self-esteem.

And, in the 1998 study *Gender Gaps: Where Schools Still Fail Our Children*, the AAUW claimed that a gender gap was opening up in the field of computer science. "The failure to include girls in advanced-level computer science courses threatens to make women bystanders in the technological 21st century." Again, the accusation received great attention while dissenting opinions were ignored.

Certainly, the AAUW has done women and the nation a service in drawing attention to the gender gap in science and mathematics and in encouraging an array of policies and programs designed to boost female performance in these fields. But most of the other findings of the AAUW are either misleading or false, and even its findings on the math and science gap need to be put into perspective. Indeed, the fact is that policy makers should be as concerned about the educational progress of boys as girls. For it is boys, not girls, who lag behind in verbal skills, who are falling behind in college attendance, and who believe that schools are hostile to them. As the eminent researcher Jere Brophy reminds us, in a chapter written for the classic study *Gender Influences in Classroom Interaction*, neither boys nor girls have a lock on school success (or failure):

> Claims that one sex or the other is not being taught effectively in our schools have been frequent and often impassioned. From early in the century, criticism was usually focused on the treatment of boys, especially at the elementary level. Critics noted that boys received lower grades in all subjects and lower achievement test scores in reading and language arts. They insisted that these sex differences occurred because the schools were "too feminine" or the "overwhelmingly female" teachers were unable to meet boys' learning needs effectively.

Not so long ago, it was boys who were viewed as victims of the school system; today, it is the girls. The remedy proposed then was to encourage adult males to go into elementary school teaching; the remedy proposed today is a plethora of special policies and programs designed to help girls succeed. But the truth is, then as now, that males and females bring different developmental patterns, strengths, weaknesses, and interests to school, not that schools engage in institutional discrimination requiring national policy attention.

Who makes the grades?

If schools were shortchanging females, such gender discrimination should be easy to spot. Schools give clear and measurable rewards: grades, class rank, and academic honors and prizes. And these rewards are not inconsequential. They help determine who gains admission to selective colleges and graduate schools and who lands the best jobs. Which group—males or females—receives a disproportionate share of the school's institutional rewards? The answer is undisputed: females.

From grade school through graduate school, females receive higher grades, even in mathematics and the sciences. They also receive more academic honors in every field except science and mathematics. The female advantage in grades appears in virtually every study. In their essay, "Grades, Accomplishments and Correlates," which was published in *Gender and Fair Assessment*, Carol Dwyer and Linda Johnson put the matter clearly:

> Data from a wide variety of sources and educational settings show that females in all ethnic groups tend to earn higher grades in school than do males, across different ages and eras, and across different subject matter disciplines. Many researchers in past times and today consider this to be such an obvious fact that they treat

it as axiomatic.... Modern reviews of the subject are unanimous in their finding of higher grades for females.

In a nationally representative longitudinal study of the high-school class of 1992, discussed by Dwyer and Johnson, it was found that high-school girls outdistanced boys in making the honor roll, in getting elected to a class office, and in receiving writing awards and other academic honors. In the academic arena, boys outdistanced girls only in awards in science and mathematics competitions.

More recently, a 1998 report sponsored by the Horatio Alger Association came up with the same female grade advantage—this time a gap far larger than reported in earlier studies. In a survey of 1,195 randomly selected high-school students, one-third of the girls said that they had gotten "mostly A's on their last report card" compared to less than one-fifth of the boys. The students in the Horatio Alger study were divided into three groups: "Successful Students," who were doing well in school, "Strivers," who were working hard, and "Alienated Students," who were bitter and disillusioned. Of the successful students, two-thirds were girls; of the strivers, 55 percent were girls; of the alienated, 70 percent were boys.

Mathematics and science honors are the single area of male advantage, but females are catching up. Take performance on the Westinghouse Science Talent Search, a contest notable for producing winners who later receive the Nobel Prize. Westinghouse finalists used to be overwhelmingly male. From 1950 through 1959, for example, only 22 percent of the top 40 finalists were female. In the late 1990s, in contrast, close to 40 percent of the top 40 finalists were female; in 1997, the proportion of female finalists was 45 percent.

Testing males and females

Even though girls surpass boys in school grades, that does not necessarily mean they are learning more. Grades, after all, depend not only on how much students know but also on conformity to institutional demands, such as whether students follow the teacher's directions and turn in assignments on time. Scores on standardized tests provide a measure of school achievement less influenced by such subjective matters.

The research on gender differences in achievement test scores is complex and voluminous. But the Educational Testing Service recently consolidated numerous studies of nationally representative samples of twelfth graders on a variety of standardized tests, including the National Assessment of Educational Progress and the Preliminary Scholastic Aptitude Test. The final report, *Gender and Fair Assessment*, published by Lawrence Erlbaum in 1997, shows a clear pattern. Neither males nor females emerge as victors or victims; each group has its own distinctive strengths and weaknesses.

In a nutshell: On standardized achievement tests of basic school skills, females surpass males in writing ability and reading achievement while males surpass females in science and mathematics. Generally, these gender differences are small. The one exception is the significant female advantage in writing skills. *Indeed, the female advantage on standardized tests of reading and writing achievement substantially outstrips the male advantage on standardized tests of science and mathematics.*

As for the male advantage in mathematics and science, it is shrinking. The National Assessment of Educational Progress has measured the knowledge of 9-, 13-, and 17-year-olds in mathematics and science for over 20 years. In mathematics, the gender gap among 17-year-olds has declined significantly since the 1970s and no longer reaches statistical significance. In science, the gender gap has also declined.

Bell curves

In the general population then the mathematics and science gap is small. Another way of measuring gender inequality, however, is to see whether males or females dominate the top of each field. Are the conspicuous achievers, who for better or worse contribute most to our images of success, mostly male or female? Among students who take the Scholastic Assessment Test (SAT) and Advanced Placement (AP) Tests in mathematics and science, men do score substantially higher than women, especially in such areas as physics. Why?

The fundamental reason has less to do with bias than with a peculiarity of males as a group. On many human characteristics, not just math and physics, males display greater variability than females. This fact is well-known to researchers, and it goes a long way toward explaining what many in the public find disturbing, the greater number of males who end up at the top in most fields.

Bell-shaped curves with the identical averages can take different forms—high and peaked (low variability) or broad and spreading (high variability). The greater variability of males means that males more often appear in the far right-hand tail of the curve, among the top talent. This occurs even when male and female averages in the general population are the same. (Where males score higher on the average, as they do in science and mathematics, the male advantage in the far right-hand tail becomes even more extreme.) The practical result is that, in fields with small numbers of people, such as physics, few women will appear in the far right-hand tail, with the Albert Einsteins, Richard Feynmans, or Stephen Hawkings. This is unfortunate for women. But, as we shall see, this pattern has an unfortunate result for men as well. The greater variability of males means that more males also end up at the extreme left of the normal curve—the failures.

Do schools shortchange boys?

In virtually every category of educational, emotional, behavioral, and neurological impairment, males are overrepresented. Reviewing the literature on this phenomenon, Diane Halpern points out, in "Sex Differences in Intelligence," published in the *American Psychologist*, that "males are overrepresented at the low-ability end of many distributions, including the following examples: mental retardation (some types), majority of attention deficit disorders, delayed speech, dyslexia (even allowing for possible referral bias), stuttering, and learning disabilities, and emotional disturbances." Even the AAUW report acknowledges that "boys outnumber girls in special educational programs by startling percentages." According to the National Center for Education Statistics, more than double the number of males compared to females are enrolled in special-education programs.

The AAUW report predictably attributes such gender differences to school discrimination: Teachers are biased against badly behaved boys. The mislabeling of active boys may be part of the explanation. It may be true that too many boys are prescribed drugs like Ritalin to make them easier to control in class. But biology is also part of the explanation.

Gender differences appear long before children enter school and even before birth. As the physician Ruth Nass points out, in "Sex Differences in Learning Abilities and Disabilities," published in *Annals of Dyslexia*, obstetrical complications such as toxemia are more common with male fetuses (1.7:1) as is aburptio (2:1), spontaneous abortion (1.4:1), and birth trauma (1.8:1). Dyslexia, a reading and language disorder that has enormous impact on school success, and autism are both four times more common among males. Males are more apt to display virtually every neuro-developmental and psychiatric disorder of childhood.

The point is this: Just as the greater number of males at the top in science and mathematics does not necessarily mean that the schools are shortchanging girls, so too the greater number of males at the bottom in special-education classes does not necessarily mean that the schools are shortchanging boys. The fact is that males are more variable than females on many neurological dimensions.

While schools may not cause such gender differences, they may still have a significant role to play in ensuring that both sexes have the opportunity to develop a broad range of intellectual skills. Schools need to be attentive to the problems of males and females. Teachers should make sure that boys in the early grades, who may lag developmentally in reading skills, are not stigmatized as "slow learners" and assigned to classes where they receive lower-quality instruction. Teachers should also avoid labeling unruly boys as suffering from "attention deficit disorder" and prescribing drugs that depress their nervous systems and ability to learn. By the same token, girls should be encouraged to take mathematics and science courses and to participate in these classes more.

Mathematics and science education for girls has indeed improved. The National Science Foundation and other government agencies, private foundations, and universities have developed and funded an array of gender-equity programs designed to encourage young women in mathematics and the sciences. The Program for Women and Girls at the National Science Foundation alone has an annual budget of $9 million a year for such efforts. No comparable programs have targeted boys' academic deficiencies in, for example, reading and writing. And no program has been created to boost college attendance among males.

The policy that does the most to boost female achievement in math and science was, in fact, not designed specifically for girls. That policy is stricter requirements for high-school graduation. In the 1980s, high-school girls were far less likely than boys to take science and mathematics classes. According to the National Center for Educational Statistics, this particular gender gap has closed. Female high-school students now take as many mathematics and science classes as males do. The exception is physics: In 1994, 27 percent of males compared to 22 percent of females took a course in physics. But females surpassed males in taking courses in chemistry, algebra, geometry, precalculus, and biology. In trigonometry and calculus, the percentages of males and females are the same.

Increasing numbers of females are also enrolling in Advanced Placement (AP) courses in mathematics and science. We see again the familiar pattern of gender strengths and weaknesses. A greater proportion of the total number of students who take demanding AP examinations are female. More females take AP English and language tests while more males take AP mathematics and science tests. But since the proportion of females taking AP mathematics and science tests is increasing, we are also seeing an increase in the total number of talented, high-achieving women in mathematics and science.

Higher sex-ed

Ignored by the AAUW is another gender gap—a very serious one in college attendance and graduation. But this gender gap favors females. And the biggest losers are African-American males. In 1995, women were the majority of college students (55 percent), and women now earn the majority of both bachelor's and master's degrees. African-American college women (62 percent) vastly outnumber African-American college males. In some colleges, as the *Chronicle of Higher Education* has reported, the gender imbalance in favor of females has become such a serious problem that administrators have quietly developed affirmative-action programs for males, admitting them with lower grades and test scores.

Since the 1960s, women have made stunning progress in gaining professional and doctoral degrees too. In 1994, women attained over 40 percent of all professional degrees, up from almost none in 1961. Minority women made especially large gains, with African-American women receiving 57 percent of the professional degrees awarded to African Americans.

The professional field that most attracts women is law, an occupation that tends to reward strong verbal skills. In law, the gender gap is decreasing rapidly: In 1994, 43 percent of those receiving a law degree were female. In several professional fields, women now surpass men. More than 65 percent of degrees in veterinary medicine, for example, go to women. The number of MBAs awarded to women has increased more than a hundredfold. In 1965, women received only about 300 MBAs; 30 years later, women received almost 35,000 MBAs, almost 40 percent of the total awarded to American citizens. Similar progress has been made in doctoral degrees. Women in 1994 earned about 40 percent of all doctoral degrees. They received substantially more doctorates than men in such fields as health, psychology, English, and education.

Virtually unknown, given the continuing clamor over the gender gap in science and mathematics, is the great advance women have already made in these fields. In the biological and life sciences, women in 1994 received over 40 percent of the doctoral degrees. Even in mathematics and the physical sciences, women received over 20 percent of the doctorates, up from only 4 percent in 1961.

American women are actually making more progress in mathematics and the sciences than these historical analyses reveal. The reason is the increasing number of students from other countries, overwhelmingly male, who now receive doctorates from American universities. In 1994, more than one-third of all American doctorates and almost one-half of all mathematics and science doctorates went to students who were not American citizens. Among these foreign students, males outnumber females by more than three to one. By considering only the doctorates awarded to American citizens and resident aliens in recent years, we can see that the gender gap in doctoral degrees has almost closed. American women received 45 percent of all doctoral degrees in 1994. In the biological sciences, American women received 43 percent of the doctorates. Large gender gaps remain in mathematics, where American women received 24 percent of the doctorates, and in the physical sciences, where they received 22 percent of doctorates.

The federal government and private foundations have devoted considerable resources to closing the gender gap in mathematics and the physical sciences. What most people do not realize is just how few people this particular gender gap affects. In 1994, for example, only 450 American men received doctorates in mathematics compared to 146 American women. In the physical sciences, 2,335 American men received doctorates compared to 659 American women. The doctoral gender gap in mathematics and the physical sciences, in essence, affects the careers and prospects of fewer than 2,000 women each year. In a country of more than 265 million people, the math and science gender gap is far from a monumental social problem.

What most women want are professional degrees, not doctoral degrees in mathematics and the physical sciences. A 1996 study of college freshmen, done by the Higher Education Institute, shows that twice as many women (more than 20 percent) sought professional occupations compared to men (less than 10 percent). Almost the same proportion of men and women sought careers in the biological and natural sciences. A large gender gap did occur in engineering and the computer sciences, fast becoming the new frontier in gender-gap lobbying. But the significance of this new gap is hardly what the AAUW in its 1998 study *Gender Gaps* claims. That few women take advanced-level computer-science classes does not, as the report asserts, mean that women are not taking advantage of the new technologies in the work place. You don't need to take a computer-science course in order to work with computers any more than you need to be a car mechanic to drive a car. Besides, that more women prefer to be attorneys than cubicle-confined Dilberts hardly seems a social problem of great moment.

Silenced girls?

If girls make higher grades in school, get higher ranks in class, receive more academic honors, surpass boys on standardized tests in two subjects (reading and writing) and lag only a little behind in two other subjects (mathematics and science), enter and graduate from college in greater numbers than boys, attain more master's degrees, and are closing the gap in more advanced degrees, then what is the basis for the charge that schools shortchange girls? A fair judge might look at the evidence and call it a draw: Females do better in some academic areas and males do better in others.

Well, as it happens, the AAUW's charge that schools shortchange girls is based not on such objective and comprehensive measures of educational attainment but instead on soft criteria, like the supposed "silencing" of girls in the classroom. The AAUW report emphasizes dramatic, highly publicized findings by David and Myra Sadker who claim that "research spanning the past twenty years consistently reveals that males receive more teacher attention than do females." According to the AAUW report, the Sadkers "report that boys in one study of elementary and middle school students called out answers eight times more often than girls did." Even more inflammatory, the study supposedly found that when boys called out comments in class, the teacher usually listened; but when girls called out comments, the teacher socialized them into "good girl" behavior, making such comments as, "Please raise your hand if you want to speak."

The Sadkers' findings, if true, are indeed shocking, and the media have spread them with a vengeance. The problem is that the research on which these dramatic findings are based has strangely disappeared. When Christina Hoff Sommers pointed this out in *Who Stole Feminism?*, I was quite disturbed. Like many others, I had emphasized the Sadkers' work in my own university teaching. Is it possible for a study simply to disappear into thin air? Apparently it is: When I telephoned David Sadker to ask him for a copy of the research, he could not locate one.

Leaving aside the Sadkers' lost study, what other evidence do we have that teachers give more attention to boys or even that boys talk more in the classroom? This may seem like a straightforward question, but it actually contains a tangle of murky issues. First, the question carries a hidden assumption—that differences in teacher attention actually influence how much students learn. No study has shown that talking in class or getting attention from the teacher makes any difference in student achievement. Certainly, the objective criteria documenting the higher achievement of females—e.g., grades, test scores, college attendance—suggest otherwise.

Second, the meaning of "getting attention from the teacher" is unclear. Suppose, for example, that a teacher asks a fourth-grade boy a question in class. Is this a genuine academic question, which will help him learn the material? Or is the teacher's question actually a reprimand in disguise? The teacher may see that the boy is acting up and use the question to get him back on task.

Third, we do not have large, representative studies that objectively describe what goes on in different classrooms, different subject areas, and different locales. To get stable and reliable observational measures, a well-trained researcher must sit in the classroom for many hours and count who talks, who asks questions, and who answers questions. We have no such comprehensive studies. Most classroom-interaction studies, especially in recent years, have been conducted in classrooms where females are suspected to be, and may well be, at a disadvantage. These are high-school mathematics and science classrooms, subjects in which females do not do as well, and law-school classrooms, where aggressive classroom questioning, the "Socratic method," has been considered crucial to preparing students for combative legal discourse. The research on gender interaction in the classroom does not feature studies conducted in literature classes or in foreign language classes, areas of female strength. In these classrooms, girls may well participate more than boys.

What the research does show is that sex differences in classroom participation, as measured by observers, are small and inconsistent. Some studies show teachers favoring boys while others show teachers favoring girls. The classic study *Gender Influences in Classroom Interaction*, published in 1985, presents the results of the leading researchers who have examined patterns of classroom talk at a time when social expectations for girls were more stereotyped than they are today. In their "Overview," Janet Lindow, Cora Marrett, and Louise Cherry Wilkinson summarize the basic pattern. "Research conducted in elementary school classrooms shows rather consistently that teachers give more attention to boys than to girls although there is also research to the contrary. However, much of the contact with boys tends to be negative; it is managerial and disciplinary in nature." No consistent evidence was found that teachers give more *academic* attention to boys.

Observational studies of gender differences in classroom participation are difficult to conduct and interpret. But we have another valuable source of information on teacher favoritism—the perceptions of the students themselves. Research on student views of teacher bias—which the AAUW commissioned but did not release[1]—yields clear and consistent findings. In the views of elementary- and high-school students, teachers do show favoritism. But they are biased against boys.

Boys and girls reported receiving virtually identical amounts of attention—59 percent of girls and 57 percent of boys said that they "get called on often" in class. When asked specifically about teacher bias, boys and girls saw some bias, but the discrimination was directed against the boys: 59 percent of boys and 57 percent of girls said that teachers called more often on girls. When asked, "Who does the teacher pay more attention to?," 64 percent of boys and 57 percent of girls again said the preferred group was girls.

In short, the research on classroom interaction does not show any pattern of consistent teacher favoritism toward either boys or girls. Boys do get more attention in elementary schools, usually for disciplinary reasons. But we have no clear evidence that boys get more academic attention, and we have no clear evidence that talking in class boosts academic achieve-

---

[1] I discovered that gaining access to the data is difficult. While the AAUW's *How Schools Shortchange Girls* can be easily ordered for $16.95 by dialing an 800 number, obtaining the unpublished research on student views takes weeks of telephoning and a payment of $85.00. In *Who Stole Feminism?*, Christina Hoff Sommers reports a similar experience. Even more shocking is that she was asked to sign the following statement before she could get the report: "Please send a statement outlining how you plan to use the survey instrument and results, along with your payment for the full research report. If your review and analysis of the data results in a possible publication or presentation, that use of data must receive advance approval from AAUW."

ment. A few areas, such as participation in mathematics and science classrooms and law-school classrooms, may be exceptions. The field of classroom-participation research has become so politicized, however, that any data must be scrutinized with great care.

Self-esteem: girls versus boys

Another highly publicized AAUW message—that adolescent girls have lower self-esteem than boys—rests on equally shaky grounds. But the commercial success of psychologist Mary Pipher's pop-feminist book, *Reviving Ophelia: Saving the Selves of Adolescent Girls*, fueled parents' worries about the self-esteem of their daughters, reinforcing the AAUW's message. (That Pipher's conclusions were based on her clinical practice with disturbed girls went unnoticed.) Now so often aired, on "Oprah" and the "Today" show, and in *Time* and *Newsweek*, this message has become the received wisdom. Everyone now knows that girls have lower self-esteem than boys. Everyone now knows that girls suffer a severe drop in self-esteem at adolescence, that boys gain in self-assurance as they age while girls lose the vitality and sense of self they displayed in childhood. But is it true?

A careful review of the literature on gender, adolescence, and self-esteem reveals a picture far different from the message of the AAUW report. First, self-esteem itself turns out to be a muddled concept. No study shows that adolescent self-esteem depends on success in school; rather, it is rooted in friendships and physical appearance. Second, boys and girls (and young people from different ethnic groups) turn out to have quite different areas of proficiency in mind when they respond to vague questions such as, "I like most things about myself" (an item in the AAUW study of self-esteem). For example, Avril Thorne and Qhyrrae Michaelieu reported in *Child Development* that high and rising self-esteem among adolescent females was linked to memories about attempting to help female friends. High and rising self-esteem among adolescent males, in contrast, was linked to success in asserting themselves with male friends. Low and decreasing self-esteem among adolescent females was rooted in failing to win approval from friends while decreasing self-esteem among adolescent males was rooted in romantic failures. Other research shows the same. For most adolescents, school success is hardly paramount in their sense of self-worth.

On the vague and general questions that many surveys use to measure self-esteem, boys indeed are apt to score higher than girls. But the differences tend to be quite small and can be explained, in part, by the tendency of boys to choose the extreme response categories on multiple-choice questions. The Commonwealth Fund Survey of the Health of Adolescent Girls, released in 1997, and ballyhooed in the press as showing once again that adolescent girls lag behind adolescent boys in self-esteem, is a recent illustration.

What this survey actually shows is unreasonably high levels of self-confidence in both boys and girls, though boys are more apt to give extreme responses. But if the "strongly agree" and "somewhat agree" categories are added together, the much-lamented self-esteem gap disappears. As an example, on the question, "I feel that I have a number of good qualities," 70 percent of boys "strongly agree" and 67 percent of girls "strongly agree." If we add the category "somewhat agree," we find that exactly 87 percent of girls and 87 percent of boys believe that they "have a number of good qualities." This is the stuff of which the self-esteem gap is made!

In fact, problems with the concept of self-esteem have become so obvious that even feminist researchers have quietly retracted the original charge of a gender gap. This is evident in the much-publicized study, *The Girls' Report: What We Know and Need to Know About Growing Up Female.* The report was published in 1998 by the National Council for Research on Women, a coalition of 78 women's studies programs and women's research organizations, including the American Association of University Women Educational Foundation. *The Girls' Report* criticizes the very concept of self-esteem, though in prose so turgid that it is difficult to make out: "In popular discussion, as well as in much of the research literature, the complex and dynamic process of identity development is too often collapsed into an oversimplified concept of self-esteem, which is typically framed as an internal, psychological phenomenon or a static entity—someone has a lot or a little."

This pychobabble is obviously no more than a screen for the report's embarrassing failure to replicate earlier assertions of low self-confidence among teenage girls. The most careful research acknowledged in *The Girls' Report,* done by University of Denver psychologist Susan Harter, shows no gender differences in the self-esteem of adolescents. Harter examined "lack of voice" in approximately 900 boys and girls from grades 6 through 12. Contrary to the feminist argument that "voice" declines for females as they enter adolescence, Harter finds that "there is no evidence in our data for loss of voice among adolescent females as a group.... We have also found no evidence for *gender differences* favoring males." (emphasis in original)

Nor does Harter find that girls, any more than boys, are likely to suppress their opinions in school because they don't want to seem smart and aggressive. "Once again, we found no gender difference supporting the claims that this is merely a problem for girls," concludes Harter. "Anecdotal reports from within the high school suggest that certain boys are fearful of being considered 'nerds,' 'dorks,' or 'brains' if they are too smart, risking peer rejection." Some girls and some boys do lack self-confidence, Harter emphasizes, but this is an individual problem. "Reviving Ophelia is certainly a worthy goal," she tartly concludes, "however, Hamlet also displayed serious problems of indecision and lack of voice."

For many years, Metropolitan Life has supported studies of important issues facing the public schools. In 1997, their report focused on gender issues, based on a nationally representative sample of 1,306 students from grades 7 through 12 and 1,035 teachers in grades 6 through 12. The report concludes bluntly:

> •1) contrary to the commonly held view that boys are at an advantage over girls in school, girls appear to have an advantage over boys in terms of their future plans, teachers' expectations, everyday experiences at school and interactions in the classroom;
> •2) minority girls hold the most optimistic views of the future and are the group most likely to focus on educational goals;
>
> •3) minority boys are the most likely to feel discouraged about the future and the least interested in getting a good education; and
>
> •4) teachers nationwide view girls as higher achievers and more likely to succeed than boys.

The report received no attention from the media.

What's the harm?

But so what, a sensible person might say. What harm has been done by emphasizing—overemphasizing—the problems faced by females in education? After all, women have been at a historical disadvantage. Girls do lag behind in science and mathematics, at least at the top. All those federal programs for boosting female academic performance, such as summer programs that introduce minority girls to scientific fields, can't be a bad thing.

The harm is this: In their zeal to advance the interests of women and their own organizational interests, the AAUW and other feminist advocacy groups have distorted the achievements of women and the experience of girls and boys in schools. True, many of these groups are retracting some of their previous positions, acknowledging that the gap in adolescent self-esteem may not exist and that the math gap is, in fact, closing. But they are searching for new areas of female victimization, such as the low numbers of females in engineering and computer sciences. Meanwhile, resources and attention are drawn away from the group that the schools truly fail, African-American males. Unfortunately, the feminist agenda, because it is pushed so strongly and receives so much attention from media elites, distracts us from the real problem of low educational achievement among African-American males and boys more generally.

Recently, I was on a panel with several school counselors. The first question to the panel was the AAUW chestnut, "What can we do to help girls, who suffer such a loss of self-esteem at adolescence?" The first speaker, a school counselor, launched into a fiery description of the emotional problems of teenage girls. Adolescents she knew had changed from vital children who spoke their minds to bored and passive teenagers. This counselor was not aware that she was repeating chapter and verse from the AAUW report. These ideas were just in the air, promoted for years in teacher education workshops and university courses (such as the courses I myself taught).

I came next on the panel. Should I flat out contradict this counselor and tell the teachers in the audience that the research actually shows no differences in adolescent boys and girls in self-esteem, that this research has been politicized to serve a feminist agenda? As diplomatically as I could, I did so. The school counselor's reaction astonished me.

"I'm so glad you said that!" she proclaimed with fervent relief. "I know that boys have problems, too. But we just don't give the boys much attention." Other teachers chimed in. "Come to think of it, I have four suicidal adolescents in my classes this year, and all four are boys," one teacher said. "Get the word out," said the sole male teacher at the workshop. "We're too busy to read the professional literature. We didn't know this."

Teachers have limited attention, time, and energy. Schools are hectic, crowded worlds. Teachers are honing in on the problems of girls—and they are overlooking the problems of boys.

B. VITAL STATISTICS

College Enrollment by Selected Years

All	1986	1988	1990	1992	1994	1996
Total	10,985,600	12,086,800	13,818,600	14,278,800	14,261,800	14,367,500
Men	5,794,400	5,868,100	6,283,900	6,371,900	6,342,500	6,352,800
Women	5,191,200	6,218,700	7,534,700	7,906,900	7,919,200	8,014,700

Characteristics of Recipients of Doctorates, 1996

	All fields [1]	Arts and humanities [2]	Business and management	Education	Engineering	Life sciences	Physical sciences	Social sciences [3]	Professional fields [4]
Doctoral degrees conferred	42,415	5,116	1,276	6,772	6,305	8,255	6,675	6,814	1,163
Median age at conferral	33.8	35.2	36.4	44.3	31.7	32.5	31.1	33.7	39.6
Median number of years from bachelor's degree to doctorate	10.8	11.8	12.7	20.2	9.0	9.6	8.3	10.3	15.5
Median number of years registered as a graduate student	7.2	8.3	7.3	8.2	6.4	7.0	6.7	7.4	8.0
Proportion with bachelor's degree in same field as doctorate	54.8%	55.8%	35.1%	36.1%	80.2%	49.2%	65.6%	53.4%	30.3%
Sex									
Male	60.0%	50.3%	70.2%	38.3%	87.7%	56.5%	79.3%	48.4%	52.4%
Female	40.0	49.7	29.8	61.7	12.3	43.5	20.7	51.6	47.6

Highest Level of Educational Attainment of 1980 High-School Sophomores by 1992

	No high-school diploma	High-school diploma	Certificate	Associate degree	Bachelor's degree	Master's degree	Profes-sional degree	Doctoral degree
By sex								
Men	6.5%	53.5%	9.7%	6.7%	19.5%	2.6%	1.3%	0.2%
Women	5.0	49.5	12.4	9.1	20.5	2.8	0.5	0.1

Highest Level of Educational Attainment of 1989-90 Beginning Postsecondary Students by Spring 1994

	Enrolled in 1994, no degree	Not enrolled in 1994, no degree	Certificate	Associate degree	Bachelor's degree
By sex					
Men	15.6%	38.4%	11.3%	10.2%	24.5%
Women	11.2	35.4	14.4	12.1	26.9

COLLEGE STUDENTS: 1997

Enrollment:

At public 4-year institutions	5,806,036
At public 2-year institutions	5,314,463
At private 4-year institutions	2,998,157
At private 2-year institutions	248,864
Undergraduate	12,326,948
Graduate	1,742,260
Professional	298,312

Enrollment highlights:

Women	55.8%
Full-time	57.8%
Minority	26.2%
Foreign	3.2%

Above data from The Chronicle Of Higher Education, Vol. XLV, No. 1 - Aug. 28, 1998

The educational attainment levels in 1998 of women ages 25 to 29 exceeded those of men in the same age group. Ninety percent of young women had at least a high school diploma and 29 percent had a bachelor's degree or more. The respective percentages for young men were 87 percent and 26 percent.

Women constitute a rising share of people being awarded college and postgraduate degrees. In 1995, they represented 55 percent of people awarded bachelor's degrees, 55 percent of the masters', 39 percent of the doctorates, 39 percent of the M.D.'s and 43 percent of the law degrees. As recently as the early 1970s, the respective percentages were 43 percent, 40 percent, 14 percent, 8 percent and 5 percent.

- Back in 1971, very few of the bachelor's degrees awarded in business and management (9 percent) went to women. By 1995, the proportion had increased to 48 percent. Similarly impressive increases occurred over the period in engineering (from 1 percent to 16 percent) and biological and life sciences (from 29 percent to 52 percent).

—U.S. Census Bureau

C. COLLEGE FACULTY: A GLASS CEILING?

WASHINGTON – More women are becoming college professors but they get less pay and fewer promotions than male professors, a survey by a university faculty trade group finds.

In 1974-75, women made up 22.5 percent of all U.S. university faculty members. By 1997-98 the percentage had increased to 33.8.

But the study by the American Association of University Professors indicates that more than half the women are in lower positions such as lecturers and instructors, regardless of the type of institution.

In 1997-98, women represented 55.6 percent of lecturers, 58.6 percent of instructors and 46.8 percent of assistant professors – the profession's full-time entry level position.

But just 18.7 percent of full professors were women.

The data are based on an annual survey of about 2,500 public and private college administrators. The response rate is about 75 percent, researchers said.

Women also are more likely to work at community colleges, which generally pay less than four-year colleges and universities.

The report, released Tuesday by the group, was also published in the January-February 1999 issue of Academe, the group's journal.

Asociated Press, Feb. 2, 1999

Number of Full-Time Faculty Members by Sex, Rank

Rank	Total
Professor	
All	159,333
Men	130,940
Women	28,393
Associate professor	
All	125,082
Men	85,313
Women	39,769
Assistant professor	
All	129,682
Men	73,141
Women	56,541
Instructor	
All	66,708
Men	33,067
Women	33,641
Lecturer	
All	12,874
Men	5,889
Women	6,985
Other	
All	57,143
Men	31,800
Women	25,343
Total	
All	550,822
Men	360,150
Women	190,672

Chronicle Of Higher Education,
Vol. XLV, No. 1 - Aug. 28, 1998

While the student enrollment statistics demonstrate a promising trend for women, the status of faculty in higher education is not as sanguine. Composite female faculty percentages have achieved parity, but they continue to be clustered at lower academic ranks and pay scales. It remains to be seen whether the great disparities at the associate and full professor levels, as well as department chairs, will eventually recede as the pool of Ph.D.'s and assistant professors continues to grow. A landmark study of gender discrimination in the School of Science at Massachusetts Institute of Technology indicates that the passage of time alone will not be sufficient to grant female faculty meaningful equal opportunity (note the comparable gender disparities for other schools and offices at M.I.T.). M.I.T.'s recommended remedies for the discriminatory practices found by its Committee on Women Faculty in the School of Science would appear to comply with present Supreme Court affirmative action jurisprudence.

M.I.T. Numbers

Faculty By Gender and School

October 1998

	Architecture	Engineering	Management	Provost	Science	Humanities	VP Research	Athletics	Grand Total
Female	16	31	13	2	30	45		4	141
Male	53	296	74	13	230	100	6	10	782
	69	327	87	15	260	145	6	14	923

SUMMARY FROM THE FIRST REPORT OF THE COMMITTEE ON WOMEN FACULTY IN THE SCHOOL OF SCIENCE – 1996

The Committee reviewed the status and equitable treatment of women faculty in the School of Science and addressed the related question of why there are still so few women faculty. We used interviews with women faculty and Department Heads to obtain information about both tenured and untenured women faculty, and, in the case of tenured women faculty, we collected data pertaining to salary, amount of salary paid from grants, space, resources, teaching assignments, and outside professional activities for women vs men. We also obtained pipeline data on the number of men and women students, postdocs, and faculty in the School of Science at MIT to determine whether the number of women shows any signs of increasing.

The Committee learned that untenured women faculty feel that men and women faculty are treated equally in terms of resources, salary, and other material benefits. Most feel supported by their departments in their scientific endeavors, and feel included in departmental activities and in the types of intellectual networking needed to succeed in science. While the Committee did not collect equity data, nothing we learned contradicted the accuracy of this perception, and information obtained from interviews with department Heads supported it. While some junior women faculty experience what they suspect may be gender bias in their own treatment or in that of other women faculty, almost none believe that gender bias will impede their careers. Junior women faculty who have children believe, however, that the demands of family are a potential obstacle to success that may impact their careers differently from those of their male colleagues. The Committee believes that institutional changes could help to alleviate this inequality.

After tenure, many senior women faculty begin to feel marginalized, including those who felt well supported as junior faculty. They sense that they and their male colleagues may not be treated equally after all. Incidents in their own professional lives or differential treatment of their male and female colleagues may open their eyes to this reality. The Committee obtained strong evidence to support their perception, although considerable variation in departments was found. One department has no tenured women faculty, one had only one at the time of this analysis and she had not experienced difficulties, while a third department has several tenured women who feel involved and represented, although they have seen or experienced problems of marginalization and exclusion of women faculty from time to time in the past. Within three departments the Committee obtained evidence of subtle differences in the treatment of men and women faculty, evidence of exclusion, and, in some cases, evidence of apparent discrimination against women faculty. The Committee documented differences in salary in the recent past, in amount of 9-month salary paid from grants, in access to space, resources, and inclusion in positions of power and administrative responsibility within departments or within the broader MIT community. Differences resulted in women having less or in their being excluded from important professional opportunities. Interviews with women faculty revealed the tremendous toll that exclusion and marginalization take on their professional and personal lives. Problems appear to increase progressively as women approach the same age as their administrators. The Committee believes that problems flourish in departments where non-democratic practices, including administrative procedures whose basis is known only to a few, lead inevitably to cronyism and unequal access to the substantial resources of MIT.

The Committee learned that the percent of women faculty in the School of Science has not increased for at least a decade. As of 1994 there were 22 women faculty, 252 male faculty.

After the Committee submitted an Interim Report on its findings, the administration moved swiftly to improve the status and equitable treatment of senior women faculty and to increase the number of women faculty. These efforts have already significantly improved the professional lives and morale of many of the tenured women faculty. While considerable effort will be needed to sustain progress, success to date demonstrates that a collaboration between committed faculty and administrators can help to solve the long standing problem of integrating significant numbers of women into the faculty of MIT. Based on suggestions from the women faculty, the Committee prepared a set of recommendations to further improve the status and equitable treatment of women faculty.

RECOMMENDATIONS MADE TO THE MIT ADMINISTRATION IN THE FIRST REPORT OF THE COMMITTEE ON WOMEN FACULTY IN THE SCHOOL OF SCIENCE – 1996

To Improve the Status of, and Ensure Equity for, Senior Women Faculty

- Make the Committee on Women Faculty a standing committee. The Committee should:
  - Maintain and open channels of communication between Department Heads and women faculty
  - Collect equity data each year for inclusion in a written report, and disseminate a summary of the report to the MIT community
  - Raise community consciousness about the need for equity
- Seek out women for influential positions within Department and Institute administrations, including as Heads and as members and Chairs of key committees. Involve tenured women faculty in the selection of administrators, and consult with women faculty to ensure the continued commitment of administrators to women faculty issues.
- Review the compensation system, which has been shown to impact differentially on salaries of men and women faculty in recent years. In particular, review the reliance on outside offers. Review salary data and distribution of resources annually for gender equity.
- Replace administrators who knowingly practice or permit discriminatory practices against women faculty. Promptly end inequitable treatment of women faculty, and make appropriate corrections for inequities when they are discovered.
- Watch for, and intervene to prevent, the isolation and gradual marginalization of women faculty that frequently occurs, particularly after tenure.

To Improve the Professional Lives of Junior Women Faculty

- Take proactive steps, via department Heads and via the Committee on Women Faculty, to promote integration, and to prevent isolation of junior women faculty.
- Address the childbearing issue for junior women faculty:
  - Make the policy on maternity leave and tenure clock uniform throughout the Institute, and make the policies widely known so that they become routine
  - Take steps to change the presumption that women who have children cannot achieve equally with men or with women who do not have children

To Increase the Number of Women Faculty

- Advise Department Heads to place senior women faculty on appropriate search committees.
- When hiring faculty do not overlook women candidates from within MIT, particularly in the fields of Mathematics and Chemistry where the number of women candidates is small.
- Inform Department Heads each year that conscious effort is needed to identify and recruit outstanding junior and senior women faculty from outside MIT.
- Address the family-work conflict realistically and openly, relying on advice from appropriate women faculty, in order to make MIT more attractive to a larger pool of junior women faculty, and to encourage more women students and postdocs to continue in academic science.

From The Faculty Chair

Momentum of Report Needs to be Extended to Entire Institute

Lotte Bailyn

This report on the work of the Committees on Women Faculty in the School of Science and the response of the Dean to their findings, describes a model that can be used by the Institute as a whole to decrease the inequities that still exist, both in terms of numbers and in treatment. And though these data refer to women, the methods used and recommendations made can and should be adapted to faculty from underrepresented minorities.

The key conclusion that one gets from the report is that gender discrimination in the 1990s is subtle but pervasive, and stems largely from unconscious ways of thinking that have been socialized into all of us, men and women alike. This makes the situation better than in previous decades where blatant inequities and sexual assault and intimidation were endured but not spoken of. We can all be thankful for that. But the consequences of these more subtle forms of discrimination are equally real and equally demoralizing.

The women who worked on these issues over the past five years are all gifted scientists, themselves convinced that gender had nothing to do with their careers: if they succeeded it was on the basis of their competence, and recognition would certainly follow; if they didn't it was based on something they lacked and rewards weren't warranted. During their earlier years, this belief was continuously reinforced, but then something seemed to change. It was only when they came together, and with persistence and ingenuity, that they saw that as their careers advanced something else besides competence came into play, which for them meant an accumulation of slight disadvantages, with just the opposite for their male colleagues. Their ability to identify the inequities that resulted and the Dean's willingness to respond, have changed the environment for their work and enhanced their ability to contribute productively to the institution.

In order to keep the momentum of this effort, and to extend it to other parts of the Institute, we need to implement Institute-wide means of continuously tracking progress and to find ways to keep senior faculty women involved in the process. This is hard work. Our first instinct is to deny that a problem exists (if it existed, it would surely have been solved by now) or to blame it on the pipeline or the circumstances and choices of individual women. None of these, however, explains the inequities surfaced by the Committee. To ensure an equitable faculty environment, we need committees such as these (including also, as in the present case, male faculty with administrative experience) in all Schools of the Institute. Their task is not only to track and monitor, but also to keep underrepresented faculty closely tied to the administrators who make the Institute's critical decisions. As both President Vest and Dean Birgeneau emphasize in their comments, we have made progress, but there is still a long way to go.

A Study on the Status of Women Faculty in Science at MIT
From M.I.T. Faculty Newsletter, Vol. XI, No. 4 - March 1999

D. TITLE IX AND EQUAL ACCESS TO ATHLETICS

In 1972, Congress amended the 1964 Civil Rights Act to specifically prohibit sex discrimination in educational programs. This landmark legislation, generally referred to as "Title IX" [of the Education Amendments of 1972], has been enforced most significantly in the area of secondary and college-level athletics, where the disparities between male and female opportunities were massive when the legislation was passed:

> "No person in the United States shall, **on the basis of sex**, be excluded from participation in, be denied the benefits of, or be subjected to discrimination under any education program or activity receiving federal financial assistance."
>
> 20 U.S.C. 1621(a)

There have been a number of private Title IX lawsuits, although none have been decided by the Supreme Court; primary enforcement has been by the U.S. Department of Education's Office of Civil Rights, which promulgates regulations interpreting Title IX; investigates complaints; and issues reports on compliance by secondary schools and colleges. Office of Civil Rights regulations require that colleges afford women varsity athletic slots in substantially the same percentage as their numbers in the student body; that a school's percentage of female athletic scholarships be substantially identical to the female percentage of athletes; and that other program benefits -- including practice and dressing facilities, equipment and uniforms, travel and publicity opportunities – be substantially equivalent to those for men. Administrative enforcement of Title IX has toughened to the point that, in 1998, the Office of Civil Rights announced that "substantially" would be interpreted to mean a gender disparity of no greater than one per-cent.

Treatment of Women's Teams: How N.C.A.A. Divisions Compare

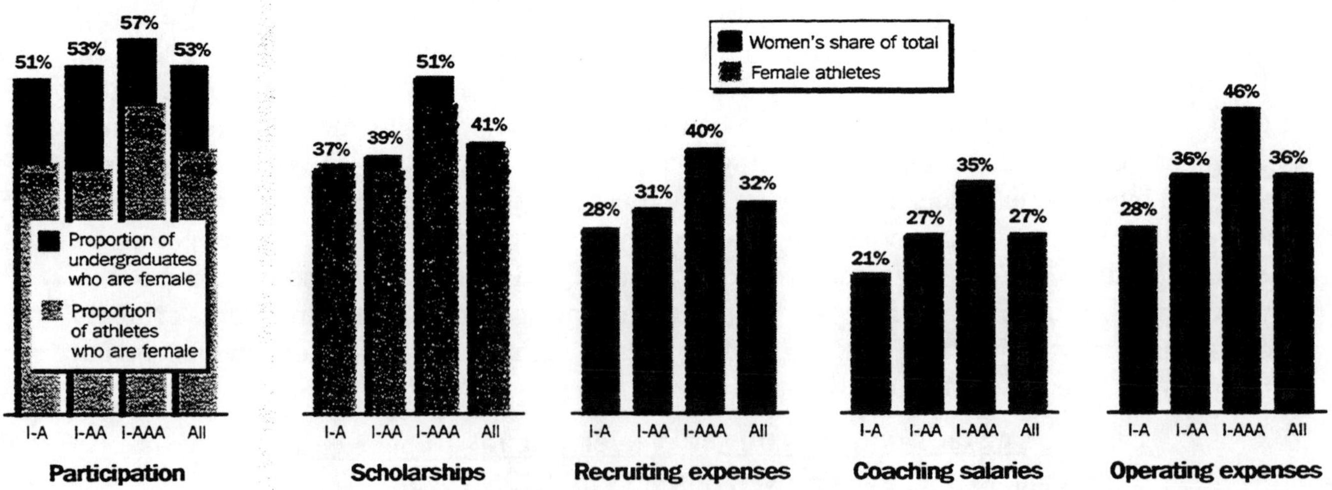

CHRONICLE OF HIGHER EDUCATION • MAY 21, 1999

During the 1996-1997 school year, 128,000 women took part in National Collegiate Athletic Association-sanctioned sports, comprising nearly 4 in 10 participants. The 7,684 female women's teams virtually equaled the number for male squads. - U.S. Census Bureau 1999

Janet Lee, "FAIR GAME - TITLE IX 25th ANNIVERSARY"

Women's Sports and Fitness, June 1997

Six years ago, freshmen Kate Lemos and Whitney Post joined Brown University's women's rowing team. At the time, it didn't bother them much that their locker room was the size of a closet or that they didn't have any shower facilities. They didn't really *expect* to have an entire floor to themselves as the men's team did. "It was never a sense of 'This is what we deserve,'" Lemos says. "It was more like, 'This is what we have.' Crew breeds you to tough anything out."

It wasn't until three years later, when Lemos and Post were co-captains of the team, that the facility was renovated and the women got their own locker room with showers and workout space. The university insists the action had nothing to do with the fact that it was embroiled in what has become the highest-profile Title IX lawsuit to date (brought by members of the women's gymnastics team). Post, now a member of the national lightweight rowing team, disagrees. "I'm sure it was a kick in the butt," she says.

Two years after the renovation, the women's rowing team won the national championships. It's a Cinderella story, but with a dark side. The Brown women's rowing team was acknowledged more than 20 years after the enactment of Title IX, the law that in 1971 mandated equal access to educational—and by association, athletic—programs for men and women in schools that receive federal funds.

June 23 is the 25th anniversary of Title IX. The date is an appropriate culmination of a yearlong period that opened with the Olympics and rolled on to see great advances for professional women athletes, particularly in team sports. But how far have women come overall in these 25 years? Athletes are still suing schools over inequities not unlike those the Brown rowers experienced, and defendants are still claiming that women don't deserve equal access because they're not as interested in sports as men are.

First Blush of Success

"It's a half-full, half-empty story," says Donna Lopiano, Ph.D., executive director of the Women's Sports Foundation. "The downside is it's taken 25 years, and the treatment of athletes is still uneven. The good news is that we've reached a critical mass of the first generation of mothers and fathers who grew up thinking it was fine for their daughters to play sports."

The U.S. women's Olympic soccer, basketball and softball teams, as well as standout performances by numerous other women athletes, are proof of this new generation. The athletes' success stories have propelled them from Atlanta to television commercials and print ads brimming with attitude. These athletes are lending their names to athletic shoes and clothing, and most notably, they're joining pro leagues that have emerged to take advantage of the sudden popularity of women's sports.

"It has taken 25 years to make a champion athlete," Lopiano says. "Twenty-five years of access to coaching, competition, scholarships and weight rooms. You're seeing the first blush of what happens when you give women the chance to play."

And it's not only professional women who are fanning the fervor. Although more quietly and with less publicity, the grooming grounds for these star athletes—our colleges and universities—are bolstering their women's sports programs with renewed zeal.

Out of fear or a sense of duty—or probably some of each—many schools are serving up women's sports with platters of scholarships and increased funding. The result is often packed sports arenas and, in some cases, women's teams like the Golden or "Lady" Buffs basketball team at the University of Colorado, that are more competitive—and more popular—than the men's teams. "Universities are realizing that that's what they have to do," says Christine Grant, Ph.D., women's athletic director at the University of Iowa. Grant has spent much of the past quarter century making sure Title IX succeeds. She's an expert on the law and has created a Web site (http://www.lib.uiowa.edu/proj/ge/) dedicated to the subject. "Universities are realizing that it will be less expensive and less damaging to their reputations to be in compliance [with the law]. They may be doing the right thing for the wrong reasons, but at this point, I don't care." In hot pursuit and with an eye toward protecting themselves from costly lawsuits in which precedent is against them, entire athletic conferences are devising action plans to get within spitting distance of full compliance in a few years. Some of those blueprints, enacted several years ago, are just now coming to fruition. The Big 10, for example, made a commitment in 1992 that its member schools would try to meet a 60–40 ratio of men's to women's participation by 1997. Five years later only four schools, Iowa, Michigan, Ohio State and Wisconsin, have complied. The law calls for participation ratios to approximate student enrollment ratios—close to 50–50 at most schools—but it's a start.

Some schools have come close to the goal. "We're in the third year of a five-year plan to achieve gender equity," says Bob Frederick, athletic director at the University of Kansas, a member of the Big 12 (formerly the Big 8). "In a number of respects, we've achieved that already." KU added women's soccer and rowing two years ago and plans to fully fund those sports at the end of three more years. At a school where the numbers of men and women students are roughly equal, 49 percent of women and 51 percent of men participate in nine men's sports and 11 women's sports. "I think there's been a tremendous amount of progress made," says Frederick. "In our situation, I've noticed a real change in attitude on the part of the fans and boosters. They realize this is the right thing to do."

The NCAA has made it its mission to ensure that members strive to meet the Title IX mandate. The organization published its second gender-equity study in April (results weren't yet available at press time), and Janet Justus, the NCAA's director of Education Outreach, predicted that participation numbers would be up. "The last time we did the study was in 1990–91. It was the first wake-up call in several years that there was still disparate treatment of men and women in athletics," she says. The NCAA has worked aggressively to reduce the disparities by educating its membership about the law. In addition to forming a gender-equity task force, they regularly offer gender-equity seminars and other educational programs.

In a surprise twist, the Clinton administration stepped in to pave the way for Title IX compliance. The Equity in Athletics Disclosure Act, passed October 1, 1996, makes it easier to find out how well each school is distributing its resources. The act requires coed colleges and universities that receive federal funds to make available to the public information about their sports programs. Schools must disclose statistics about male and female participation, athletic department budgets, scholarship programs, recruiting expenditures by gender and coach salaries. "Some institutions will be shamed into improving their compliance" is Grant's take on the new legislation.

Even before the equity act, things were looking up. The number of women's athletic teams per school is at an all-time high, according to the study "Women in Intercollegiate Sport," which looked at the 19-year period from 1977 to 1996.

The average number of teams per school (divisions I through III) has risen from 5.61 to 7.5. Since 1971, the number of women who participate in collegiate varsity sports has increased by nearly 250 percent, to more than 110,000. (It more than doubled by 1977, only two years after Title IX had been in effect.) And whereas one in 27 girls used to play sports in high school, now it's one in three.

It's not only the participation numbers that are up. In 1972, only $100,000 in college scholarship money was available to women nationwide, says Benita Fitzgerald Mosley, president of the Women's Sports Foundation and director of the ARCO Olympic Training Center in San Diego. That number had risen to $180 million in 1996. Men's programs, which have roughly 78,000 more participants than the women's, award twice that amount.

Sports and Courts

A growing body of legislation consistently supporting the principles of Title IX and the Supreme Court's 1992 ruling that plaintiffs could collect monetary damages in cases of intentional discrimination haven't kept lawsuits out of the courts. The Brown case could be appealed all the way to the Supreme Court, even though the plaintiffs have won all appeals to date. Attorney Deborah Brake, senior counsel at the National Women's Law Center in Washington, D.C., doubts that the high court will hear the case. "We should keep winning," she says. "The law is very strong in the courts." In fact, plaintiffs have not lost any cases to date.

That success rate is bittersweet; after all, a court of law is not the court an athlete wants to be making her play on. A quarter of a century after Title IX, perhaps the main reason only a handful of schools are in compliance is money. "I think the biggest stumbling block is that some schools are using the financial aspect of it as an excuse not to move more quickly," says Frederick. "Everybody—almost everybody—knows it's the right thing to do."

Lopiano agrees. "The existing competitive system in the schools favors football, basketball and one or two other men's sports," Lopiano says. 'It's like pulling teeth to get them to share [funds]." She blames the leaders of the universities, not just the athletic directors, for this reluctance. "The athletic departments won't [cut high-profile sports' budgets]; they won't put themselves in jeopardy like that."

Athletic directors, on the other hand, claim that cutting those budgets is akin to biting the hand that feeds all programs: Cut the marquee sports' budgets, and you cut revenue for all sports. "When you consider the income from the men's basketball tournament, from our football television contract and the bowl games, there's just a tremendous amount of revenue generated," Frederick counters. "We try to find alternate sources without cutting any sports."

And they have. For example, when the Big 8 expanded to become the Big 12, television revenues poured into members' coffers, money that spilled over into smaller athletic programs at each university. To fill in the gaps, the athletic departments aligned chancellors and athletic boards behind their efforts and ventured off campus to hit up corporate donors and sponsors.

High Hurdles

Without teeth to back it up, legal action can prove largely ineffective. And indeed, enforcement of Title IX has been lacking, critics say. Ensuring compliance with the act falls largely on the Office of Civil Rights (OCR). The Women's Sports Foundation recently released a study of the compliance reviews conducted by the OCR and found the office's performance to be less than acceptable. "The OCR is doing a horrible job," Lopiano says. "It has the ability to notify a school that it is out of compliance, yet they've not found one school out of compliance with Title IX."

But perhaps one of the biggest threats to the law, and one of the main reasons it leaves a nasty taste in the mouths of so many administrators and athletes, is the affirmative action stigma. The perceived similarity to quota rulings means that many assume it to be detrimental to nonrevenue men's sports. Lopiano has made the Women's Sports Foundation's stance on the issue clear, and many schools have followed suit. "We have always said that it is inappropriate for the Title IX solution to bring the level of men's sports down to the women's level," she says.

"There's been a backlash against a lot of the gains we've won," Brake says. "We're seeing the have-nots versus the have-nots. Instead of blaming football and basketball, which continue to hog resources, other men's sports like gymnastics and wrestling are blaming women." When lawyers start tossing out terms like quota and affirmative action, administrators start backpedaling, program plans sputter to a crawl and athletes—male and female—start questioning the fairness of legislating equity. Because of this, Brake thinks, many opponents are hoping that the Brown case will roll back Title IX or at least reveal a much-sought-after loophole. So far neither has happened.

In the end, the primary problem—one that dooms so much well-meaning legislation—is a lack of communication and broad-based commitment. "The biggest threat to Title IX is the unwillingness to sit down and resolve the many problems we have: financial, gender equity and the potential loss of men's minor sports," Grant says. "It will take a national will to do this."

The Future's So Bright

To some administrators, complying with Title IX is a daunting task that requires keeping track of every athlete, changing long-held prejudices and prying dollars out of already tight fists. Others, like Frederick, Grant and Justus, have seen the tide slowly changing and the momentum rising with it. Their jobs will get easier as America grows more used to seeing women as athletes, whether on their local high school field or on national television.

"I think the future is bright," Justus says. "I think the law will be a nontopic in 15 to 20 years." Angie Halbleib, a senior at KU who plays on the women's basketball team, agrees. "I think women's sports will be improving so much we won't have to say we *need* this money."

So there it stands. There will still be lawsuits, certainly, for years to come. There will still be people who think women aren't interested in athletics and don't deserve as many chances to participate in them. But there will also be the girls who idolize Sheryl Swoopes and Mia Hamm, who earn scholarships to play their favorite sports, who wear new uniforms and practice in state-of-the-art facilities. And perhaps ultimately there will be girls who won't need to think about their right to play. They'll just be out there playing.

Then, Title IX will be just another law that's served its purpose, a law that ultimately renders equity a moot point and is, in the end, forgotten.

E. RECOMMENDED READING

American Association Of University Women, *Gender Gaps: Where Schools Still Shortchange Our Children* (A.A.U.W.: 1972)

S. Klein, ed., *Handbook for Achieving Sex Equity Through Education* (Johns Hopkins University Press: 1985)

S. Gabriel, I. Smithson, eds., *Gender in the Classroom: Power and Pedagogy* (University of Illinois Press: 1990)

M. Chamberlain, ed., *Women in Academe: Progress and Prospects* (Russell Sage Foundation: 1991)

CHAPTER IV
Sexual Harassment

A. SOURCES AND EARLY DEVELOPMENT

The legal sources and theories at the heart of the modern struggle for gender equality are generally grounded in the American Constitution (e.g., the Fourteenth Amendment); common law tradition (marriage and family property laws); or broad-based anti-discrimination statutes (the 1964 Civil Rights Act). The concept of sexual harassment, however, is a singular product of the women's rights movement. Despite the passage and initial enforcement of the civil rights legislation of the 1960's and 1970's, many women continued to endure discrimination in the form of unwelcome sexual conduct and a hostile working environment. In its more personal form, this meant submitting to sexual advances or forfeiting one's job or job status. On a general level, women had to endure an often crudely sexualized workplace. Early lawsuits to combat this conduct met with little success.

In the 1970's, scholars such as Catherine MacKinnon and Lin Farley documented this pattern and called for an appropriate legal remedy. In 1980, pursuant to its administrative authority to enforce Title VII of the 1964 Civil Rights Act, the U.S. Equal Employment Opportunity Commission issued its ground-breaking sexual harassment regulations:

> (a) Harassment on the basis of sex is a violation of Sec. 703 of Title VII. Unwelcome sexual advances, requests for sexual favors, and other verbal or physical conduct of a sexual nature constitute sexual harassment when (1) submission to such conduct is made either explicitly or implicitly a term or condition of an individual's employment, (2) submission to or rejection of such conduct by an individual is used as the basis for employment decisions affecting such individual, or (3) such conduct has the purpose or effect of unreasonably interfering with an individual's work performance or creating an intimidating, hostile, or offensive working environment.
>
> (b) In determining whether alleged conduct constitutes sexual harassment, the Commission will look at the record as a whole and at the totality of the circumstances, such as the nature of the sexual advances and the context in which the alleged incidents occurred. The determination of the legality of a particular action will be made from the facts, on a case by case basis.

(d) With respect to conduct between fellow employees, an employer is responsible for acts of sexual harassment in the workplace where the employer (or its agents or supervisory employees) knows or should have known of the conduct unless it can show that it took immediate and appropriate corrective action.

(g) Other related practices: Where employment opportunities or benefits are granted because of an individual's submission to the employer's sexual advances or requests for sexual favors, the employer may be held liable for unlawful sex discrimination against other persons who were qualified for but denied that employment opportunity or benefit.

29 Code of Federal Regulations 1604.11

In two unanimous decisions, *Meritor Savings Bank v. Vinson* (1986) and *Harris v. Forklift Systems, Inc.* (1993), the Supreme Court interpreted the E.E.O.C. guidelines to permit causes of action based upon either *quid pro quo* (employment status dependent upon sexual favors) or hostile environment, when employer action was unwelcome, substantial, and continued after a victim's complaint. Pursuing individual and group remedies in federal court, however, continued to be a grueling struggle, illustrated by the story of pioneering workers at an iron ore mine in northern Minnesota.

MERITOR SAVINGS BANK v. VINSON, 477 U.S. 57 (1986)

Decided June 19, 1986

JUSTICE REHNQUIST delivered the opinion of the COURT:

In 1974, respondent Mechelle Vinson met Sidney Taylor, a vice president of what is now petitioner Meritor Savings Bank (bank) and manager of one of its branch offices. When respondent asked whether she might obtain employment at the bank, Taylor gave her an application, which she completed and returned the next day; later that same day Taylor called her to say that she had been hired. With Taylor as her supervisor, respondent started as a teller-trainee, and thereafter was promoted to teller, head teller, and assistant [477 U.S. 57, 60] branch manager. She worked at the same branch for four years, and it is undisputed that her advancement there was based on merit alone. In September 1978, respondent notified Taylor that she was taking sick leave for an indefinite period. On November 1, 1978, the bank discharged her for excessive use of that leave.

Respondent brought this action against Taylor and the bank, claiming that during her four years at the bank she had "constantly been subjected to sexual harassment" by Taylor in violation of Title VII. She sought injunctive relief, compensatory and punitive damages against Taylor and the bank, and attorney's fees.

At the 11-day bench trial, the parties presented conflicting testimony about Taylor's behavior during respondent's employment.Fn Respondent testified that during her probationary period as a teller-trainee, Taylor treated her in a fatherly way and made no sexual advances. Shortly thereafter, however, he invited her out to dinner and, during the course of the meal, suggested that they go to a motel to have sexual relations. At first she refused, but out of what she described as fear of losing her job she eventually agreed. According to respondent, Taylor thereafter made repeated demands upon her for sexual favors, usually at the branch, both during and after business hours; she estimated that over the next several years she had intercourse with him some 40 or 50 times. In addition, respondent testified that Taylor fondled her in front of other employees, followed her into the women's restroom when she went there alone, exposed himself to her, and even forcibly raped her on several occasions. These activities ceased after 1977, respondent stated, when she started going with a steady boyfriend.

[the] court stated that a violation of Title VII may be predicated on either of two types of sexual harassment: harassment that involves the conditioning of concrete employment benefits on sexual favors, and harassment that, while not affecting economic benefits, creates a hostile or offensive working environment. The court drew additional support for this position from the Equal Employment Opportunity Commission's Guidelines on Discrimination Because of Sex, 29 CFR 1604.11(a)
harassment claims.

Respondent argues, and the Court of Appeals held, that unwelcome sexual advances that create an offensive or hostile working environment violate Title VII. Without question, when a supervisor sexually harasses a subordinate because of the subordinate's sex, that supervisor "discriminate[s]" on the basis of sex

Since the Guidelines were issued, courts have uniformly held, and we agree, that a plaintiff may establish a violation of Title VII by proving that discrimination based on sex has created a hostile or abusive work environment. As the Court of Appeals for the Eleventh Circuit wrote in Henson v. Dundee, 682 F.2d 897, 902 (1982): [477 U.S. 57, 67]

> "Sexual harassment which creates a hostile or offensive environment for members of one sex is every bit the arbitrary barrier to sexual equality at the workplace that racial harassment is to racial equality. Surely, a requirement that a man or woman run a gauntlet of sexual abuse in return for the privilege of being allowed to work and make a living can be as demeaning and disconcerting as the harshest of racial epithets."

HARRIS v. FORKLIFT SYSTEMS, INC., 510 U.S. 17 (1993)

Decided November 9, 1993

JUSTICE O'CONNOR delivered the opinion of the Court.
Teresa Harris worked as a manager at Forklift Systems, Inc., an equipment rental company, from April, 1985, until October, 1987. Charles Hardy was Forklift's president.

The Magistrate found that, throughout Harris' time at Forklift, Hardy often insulted her because of her gender and often made her the target of unwanted sexual innuendos. Hardy told Harris on several occasions, in the presence of other employees, "You're a woman, what do you know" and "We need a man as the rental manager"; at least once, he told her she was "a dumb ass woman." App. to Pet. for Cert. A-13. Again in front of others, he suggested that the two of them "go to the Holiday Inn to negotiate [Harris'] raise." Id., at A-14. Hardy occasionally asked Harris and other female employees to get coins from his front pants pocket. [HARRIS v. FORKLIFT SYSTEMS, INC., ___ U.S. ___ (1993) , 2]

Ibid. He threw objects on the ground in front of Harris and other women, and asked them to pick the objects up. Id., at A-14 to A-15. He made sexual innuendos about Harris' and other women's clothing. Id., at A-15.

In mid-August, 1987, Harris complained to Hardy about his conduct. Hardy said he was surprised that Harris was offended, claimed he was only joking, and apologized. Id., at A-16. He also promised he would stop, and, based on this assurance Harris stayed on the job. Ibid. But in early September, Hardy began anew: While Harris was arranging a deal with one of Forklift's customers, he asked her, again in front of other employees, "What did you do, promise the guy . . . some [sex] Saturday night?" Id., at A-17. On October 1, Harris collected her paycheck and quit.

Harris then sued Forklift, claiming that Hardy's conduct had created an abusive work environment for her because of her gender.

Title VII of the Civil Rights Act of 1964 makes it "an unlawful employment practice for an employer . . . to discriminate against any individual with respect to his compensation, terms, conditions, or privileges of employment, because of such individual's race, color, religion, sex, or national origin." 42 U.S.C. 2000e-2(a)(1). As we made clear in Meritor Savings Bank v. Vinson, 477 U.S. 57 (1986), this language "is not limited to "economic" or "tangible" discrimination. The phrase "terms, conditions, or privileges of employment" evinces a congressional intent "to strike at the entire spectrum of disparate treatment of men and women" in employment," which includes requiring people to work in a discriminatorily hostile or abusive environment. Id., at 64, quoting Los Angeles Dept. of Water and Power v. Manhart, [HARRIS v. FORKLIFT SYSTEMS, INC., ___ U.S. ___ (1993) , 4] 435 U.S. 702, 707, n. 13 (1978) (some internal quotation marks omitted). When the workplace is permeated with "discriminatory intimidation, ridicule, and insult," 477 U.S., at 65, that is "sufficiently severe or pervasive to alter the conditions of the victim's employment and create an abusive working environment," id., at 67 (internal brackets and quotation marks omitted), Title VII is violated.

This standard, which we reaffirm today, takes a middle path between making actionable any conduct that is merely offensive and requiring the conduct to cause a tangible psychological injury. As we pointed out in Meritor, "mere utterance of an . . . epithet which engenders offensive feelings in a employee," ibid. (internal quotation marks omitted) does not sufficiently affect the conditions of employment to implicate Title VII. Conduct that is not severe or pervasive enough to create an objectively hostile or abusive work environment - an environment that a reasonable person would find hostile or abusive - is beyond Title VII's purview. Likewise, if the victim does not subjectively perceive the environment to be abusive, the conduct has not actually altered the conditions of the victim's employment, and there is no Title VII violation.

But Title VII comes into play before the harassing conduct leads to a nervous breakdown. A discriminatorily abusive work environment, even one that does not seriously affect employees' psychological wellbeing, can and often will detract from employees' job performance, discourage employees from remaining on the job, or keep them from advancing in their careers. Moreover, even without regard to these tangible effects, the very fact that the discriminatory conduct was so severe or pervasive that it created a work environment abusive to employees because of their race, gender, religion, or national origin offends Title VII's broad rule of workplace equality. The appalling conduct alleged in Meritor, [HARRIS v. FORKLIFT SYSTEMS, INC., ___ U.S. ___ (1993) , 5] and the reference in that case to environments "'so heavily polluted with discrimination as to destroy completely the emotional and psychological stability of minority group workers,'" supra, at 66, quoting Rogers v. EEOC, 454 F.2d 234, 238 (CA5 1971), cert. denied, 406 U.S. 957 (1972), merely present some especially egregious examples of harassment. They do not mark the boundary of what is actionable.

We therefore believe the District Court erred in relying on whether the conduct "seriously affect[ed] plaintiff's psychological wellbeing" or led her to "suffe[r] injury." Such an inquiry may needlessly focus the factfinder's attention on concrete psychological harm, an element Title VII does not require. Certainly Title VII bars conduct that would seriously affect a reasonable person's psychological wellbeing, but the statute is not limited to such conduct. So long as the environment would reasonably be perceived, and is perceived, as hostile or abusive, Meritor, supra, at 67, there is no need for it also to be psychologically injurious.

Into an Abyss of Sex Harassment At Eveleth Mine

By Kirstin Downey Grimsley
Washington Post Staff Writer

EVELETH, Minn.

In 1991, miner Patricia Kosmach won a legal victory that was hailed as marking a new era for women in the workplace. But three years later, when she died at 57 from Lou Gehrig's disease, the iron-willed redhead made a bitter last request.

From an airplane flying above the fierce terrain of Minnesota's Mesabi Iron Range, two friends emptied a box that contained Kosmach's ashes. Her remains drifted down over the Eveleth Taconite Mine and came to rest on the floor of the open-pit excavation where she had worked for 13 years, mixing indistinguishably with the iron ore dust.

"It was her way of saying, 'This is what you did to me,' " said Lois Jenson, Kosmach's longtime friend and co-worker.

Kosmach and Jenson had joined 19 other women in bringing a precedent-setting case, which legally established that the atmosphere of sexual harassment inside a company can be so pervasive and hostile that employees, as a class, can sue for relief. The class-action decision set a legal framework for others, including the current federal suit involving hundreds of women auto workers at Mitsubishi Motor Manufacturing of America Inc. in Normal, Ill.

The Eveleth case, only now winding down after

more than 12 years in Minnesota state and federal courts, documents violent and vulgar sexual harassment in a traditionally male workplace—and the failure of management and the union to stop such conduct. The women miners testified they were groped, grabbed, pressured for sex, threatened with rape, beaten, stalked and subjected to coarse sexual language and graffiti. One young boy, now in his early twenties, testified to watching his mother, Shirley Burton, pack her lunch box for work each day: knife, Mace, rope to tie shut the door to her work area, and food.

The case also documents how the legal system can create a second ordeal for women by allowing the most intimate details of their personal lives to be used in court to help discredit their allegations of harassment on the job. One plaintiff, in answering lawyers' questions, had to recount the horror of being molested by her grandfather at age 13. Another plaintiff's son learned for the first time through a court document that he was the product of a rape.

The women miners' legal battles still aren't over. In March a federal magistrate judge finally awarded them damages, ranging from $2,500 to $25,000 each—a fraction of what some experts say is the average jury award of $250,000 in such cases. The women appealed and a federal judge agreed in July to review the awards. A ruling is expected within the next few months.

The women won their case, but as yet they celebrate no victory.

The World of the Mines

Minnesota's Iron Range, about two hours south of the Canadian border, is one of the nation's major suppliers of iron ore, particularly a low grade of ore called taconite that is used in making steel. Eveleth Taconite, one of seven mines in that region, was launched in 1965 by Ford Motor Co. and Cleveland-based Oglebay Norton Co. to provide the raw materials for making cars. Oglebay Norton still manages the mine and makes all administrative decisions. Ownership now is shared with three other companies, AK Steel Corp., Stelco Inc. of Canada and Rouge Steel Co., a former Ford subsidiary. Ford no longer owns any share in the mine.

The mine, which sprawls across more than 8,000 acres near the tiny town of Eveleth, looks like the setting for a science fiction movie about mining operations on an alien planet. It is bitterly cold in the winter, with recorded temperatures dropping to 60 below zero, but workers labor outside round the clock, digging and blasting huge iron ore-laden rocks from the ground and carting them off in massive trucks that carry up to 120 tons at a time. Then the rocks are pulverized, processed, baked into iron ore pellets in a 2,400-degree blast furnace and shipped to other manufacturing plants.

Until the mid-1970s it was a man's world. The mine was staffed by second- and third-generation European immigrants, many of Scandinavian or Slavic descent, with sons following their fathers into the work. Their wives and mothers stayed home or helped tend family farms.

The Minnesota mines, including Eveleth Taconite, first began hiring women miners in the mid-1970s, at a time when the federal government was pressing employers generally to provide equal job opportunities. The jobs—then paying about $25,000 a year for a laborer, and now about $45,000 a year, with full health benefits and pensions—were far more lucrative than other work available in rural, northern Minnesota.

At the peak of female employment at the mine in 1984, 29 women hourly workers were employed there. Today, there are nine women out of a total hourly work force of 550.

The mine's leadership and many male workers strongly resisted the change, court testimony makes clear. Personnel Director Robert Raich, for example. He was responsible for hiring and promoting workers, and several employees testified that he told co-workers repeatedly that "women don't belong in the mines," and that women should be "barefoot and pregnant."

Raich did hire a few dozen women, many of whom he had identified as "hardship cases," without a husband or a father's support. The women said that he told them they would be accepted more readily by their male colleagues than married women.

Kosmach was hired to work in the mine's laboratory in 1976, allowing her to quit the two jobs she had been working after her husband stopped supporting her and their five children, according to Kosmach's testimony and interviews with her friends and family. She and her children were living in a dank, unfinished basement in an uncompleted house in rural Eveleth.

With Kosmach's new job, she could afford to move her family into a trailer. "She was really happy," her daughter Brenda, now 35, recalled. "For the first time, she was making some money."

Kosmach also was grateful to the union, which she saw as responsible for making such well-paying jobs possible. She became an active volunteer in Local 6860 of the United Steel Workers of America, co-chairing first the human services committee, where she helped people who had drug or alcohol problems get counseling; later, she joined the civil rights committee.

The women miners came to know Kosmach as a person they could go to with their problems.

Barrage of Bad Behavior

And those problems started almost immediately.

Lois Jenson, now 48, recalled her first day at the mine in 1975, as one of the first four women hired. A blizzard had hit the March weekend before she was to start, and the three other women had not arrived by the time she got there. Jenson said she walked into the lunchroom dressed in blue coveralls, work boots, hard hat and safety glasses.

She was met with dead silence. Men swiveled to stare. "They acted like they had never seen a woman before," she said. "They acted like I was nude."

According to court testimony, many of the male miners repeatedly harangued, threatened and assaulted the new women miners in ways that made clear they never would be treated as co-workers in the mine. The 21 women plaintiffs alleged these incidents:

Three times, a male worker masturbated into Judy Jarvela's locker and ejaculated onto her clothing. Several men exposed themselves. Joan Hunholz testified that John Jagunich exposed himself, and Lois Jenson testified that the same man broke into her house in the middle of the night, entered her bedroom and attempted to embrace her, exiting when she turned on the lights and started to scream.

Audrey Daniel testified that Leon Erickson slashed a gash in her pant leg, drawing blood. Marilyn Greiner testified that Hank Brown pressed his body against her and then put his hands around her throat. Marcia Steele claimed that LeRoy Stish menaced her with a huge red dildo he called "Big Red."

Contacted this month, Jagunich declined to comment on the allegation. Brown said he had been told by the company "not to talk" about what happened at the mine and was not asked to testify. Stish denied he had brought a red dildo to work and then hung up the phone, saying he didn't want to talk anymore. None of these three men testified in the trials in response to the women's allegations.

Erickson testified in court that he had a photo of a nude woman on his desk and that he did not believe women belonged working in the mines. He declined to comment in an interview this month on the knife-slashing incident.

None of these men was fired, and none was charged with any crimes. Only Brown was disciplined, with a five-day suspension.

The women workers' testimony drew a picture of widespread verbal and physical harassment. They were at times addressed with foul slang for parts of the female anatomy instead of by their names; they were sometimes denied bathroom facilities. Several reported their crotches were grabbed in what the men called a "horse bite." They were stalked by co-workers at home and at work.

Two women who worked in the same area were commonly referred to, even by supervisors, as "the dogs," with the red-haired worker called the "Irish setter" and the brunette called the "black Lab." When a woman miner who was an aspiring poet had some of her poems published, the men with whom she worked wrote sexual graffiti about her in rhyme.

The men taped sexually oriented posters, hand-rendered drawings and photographs on the walls throughout the mine, including depictions of women with their legs spread and naked women in an advanced stage of pregnancy. More than 30 of these pictures became exhibits in the trials.

Inside a locked, glass-paneled bulletin board where work schedules were posted by managers, a poster carried the message: "Sexual harassment in this area will not be reported. However it will be graded."

'Barefoot and Pregnant'

What could have triggered such behavior? One male employee, a manager who has worked at the mine for three decades, said in an interview that some of his co-workers are "male chauvinists who got off on" harassing and intimidating women. "They're not couth," he said, asking that his name not be used because it could jeopardize his job. "These are redneck guys, and back then they were young, and young guys do these things."

This manager said he never had any women in his group, but the harassing behavior by men in other parts of the mine was condoned by their managers, including officials at Oglebay Norton in Cleveland. "These are headstrong management people who are not aware of what's happening in the 20th century," he said. "They think it is still the 19th century."

Eugene Borgida, a social psychology professor at the University of Minnesota who served as an expert witness on behalf of the women, said his review of the men's depositions led him to believe the male miners had developed a pattern of group thinking after regularly reading pornographic literature at work, and that the men came to view the women not as co-workers but as potential sexual partners.

Oglebay Norton officials in Cleveland deny there was a widespread pattern of abusive behavior. During the long legal battle, their attorneys disputed many of the specific allegations. Top officials of the company declined repeated requests to comment for this story, but the attorney retained by their insurance companies who are paying the legal bills, David Jendrzejek, spoke on their behalf.

"The company feels strongly, and always has, they did not discriminate against the plaintiffs, and they were not subjected to sexual harassment or a hostile environment," Jendrzejek said. "The company doesn't believe it did anything wrong."

Jendrzejek alleged that some of the women bringing the claims had a "history of mental illness." He contended: "There is reason to question the veracity of those particular claimants." The company's lawyers presented these arguments in detail in court, in their efforts to challenge the women's claims for damages.

Some individual company officials also denied that they allowed rampant sexual harassment at the mine. Raich, the personnel director, was asked on the courtroom stand whether he had told mine employees that women should be "barefoot and pregnant" and didn't belong in the mine. Raich testified that he was unable to "recollect" what he had said.

"His most-used comment was women should be barefoot and pregnant," said Raich's secretary, Kathleen Tessier, who testified on behalf of the plaintiffs. She added Raich stated it as a fact, not as a joke. "He used that comment a lot when it came time for layoffs."

Several women alleged that Raich was himself a sexual harasser. One woman testified that she danced with him at a club, but when she rejected his sexual advances on the dance floor, he told her he could jeopardize her job. Another woman described in court how he fondled her, and a third told the court that Raich told her women would be hired at the mine when they could learn to urinate like men. Raich testified he could not recall saying or doing those things.

Raich, contacted at Sun Lakes, Ariz., where he has retired, said he could not comment about the case because he does not recall any details and does not remember testifying in court about the case. "When you retire you kind of go blank," Raich said.

Union officials testified that, when presented with the complaints, they didn't take action because they thought it was important to protect the men's jobs. Stanley Daniels, the union president, said in court testimony that he thought the women's complaints were a "bunch of BS."

"It's my job to represent the employees and the members of my union out there," Daniels testified. "And it's not my job to give discipline. It's my job to protect them from discipline."

Another of the mine's attorneys, Mary Stumo, said in an interview the presence of the union complicated the case because it made it harder to fire people.

But Milton Sundeen, president and grievance chairman at a nearby branch of the same union, Local 1938 of the United Steel Workers of America, which represents miners at the U.S. Steel facility, said in an interview that other mines in the region, including his, strongly disciplined or fired male workers who harassed female workers. He said the behavior he had heard about at Eveleth was not accepted elsewhere in the industry.

"If it were my mother or my sister, I wouldn't want to expose them to the level of embarrassment those ladies were put through," Sundeen said.

Defensive Tactics

The women miners at Eveleth testified they tried to handle the situation on their own. Some said they tried to laugh off or ignore rough antics. Others worked in pairs for mutual defense. Some said they gained weight on purpose to make themselves less attractive. Diane Hodge walked stiffly, like she was marching, she testified, so that nothing would wiggle.

Kosmach testified that she quickly learned not to smile. "When I went to work there I was fairly happy-go-lucky," she said in court. "I loved to smile. And shortly after working there I learned not to smile excessively . . . because someone was always misinterpreting you as to your smiling or who you were smiling at."

Others testified they began to believe their lives were in danger. Three of the women brought knives to work. Some began to keep loaded guns easily at reach in their homes or cars. Some quit, and ended up on welfare or financially dependent on relatives.

Dozens of women at the mine began to experience symptoms of severe stress, including some with conditions similar to those noted in combat veterans, according to their court testimony and that of medical experts called by their lawyers. The women described panic attacks, sleeplessness, exaggerated startle reflexes and a sense of vulnerability that made them afraid to venture outside. They became fearful of men. Some said they became perpetually enraged while others became depressed. Five ended up on Social Security disability.

The women initially took their concerns to Patricia Kosmach, who had become a volunteer union official. Kosmach testified she tried to get the union's leaders and mine managers to take action on numerous occasions, but they failed to do so. When top union officials were presented with the complaints, they generally would try to blame the women for behaving inappropriately or refuse to do anything at all, she testified.

Kosmach testified that she started to believe the harassment was becoming a life-and-death issue. After she heard that co-worker Don Cummings had angrily thrown work gloves at Michelle Mesich's crotch and told her she was lucky they were not his hands, Kosmach told him that his behavior was unacceptable. She testified that he responded by saying he would throw the "little bitch" into the concentrator bins, huge receptacles for mixing iron ore powder, which likely would cause a victim to suffocate or be crushed under the weight of the taconite.

"I was frightened for her," Kosmach testified, adding that she sought out a foreman to intervene. But, she said on the stand, Mesich was required to continue working with Cummings, who continued to harass her by writing explicit sexual graffiti about her on the walls of their work area.

Cummings, who no longer works at the mine and who did not testify in the trials, declined to comment when contacted earlier this month.

That incident was a turning point for Kosmach. She stopped believing that the union, the national leadership of which had been offering information and training on sexual harassment, would ever come to the defense of the women workers.

Judge Put Small Price On Pain

Damage Award Paled By Litigation Norms

EVELETH, Minn.

Judge Patrick McNulty's job in the precedent-setting sexual harassment case was to set a dollar value on the emotional, financial and physical damages 16 women suffered during more than a decade of sexual harassment.

McNulty, 74, a part-time federal magistrate judge in Duluth, Minn., decided their suffering wasn't worth much, by the standards of modern litigation. He awarded 16 women a combined $182,500. That's an average of about $11,400 each, at a time some experts say jury verdicts to individual plaintiffs in sexual harassment cases are averaging $250,000 each.

"That's what I felt they had proven in damages," McNulty said in a recent interview.

McNulty's ruling is being appealed by the women's attorneys.

In the Eveleth mine case, transcripts of McNulty's intermittent six-month trial and his detailed, 416-page report on the damages suggest that the semi-retired judge was skeptical of the women's stories.

McNulty wrote, for example, that he was puzzled about why Joan Hunholz was fearful when a man who she said had exposed himself to her several years earlier began driving his truck in circles, over and over, around her work area.

"This Court has difficulty understanding why the appearance of a suspected flasher outside the building in which she was working ... would cause great fear—of something—in a reasonable woman," McNulty wrote.

McNulty called it a "gigantic leap" for Judy Jarvela to view it as attempted rape when a man who had repeatedly and crudely propositioned her suddenly lunged at her one night at work with his arms spread, only stopping when she began screaming. "Equally as valid is a conclusion that he merely intended to say, 'boo,' " McNulty wrote.

According to the transcripts, McNulty allowed the mine's attorneys to probe intimate details of the women's lives. This is permitted by law, subject to a judge's discretion, when emotional damages are claimed by the plaintiffs. The mine got the women's complete medical records and obtained depositions from former husbands and former boyfriends, some of whom testified at trial on behalf of the mine.

This aggressive legal strategy is becoming increasingly common in sexual harassment cases. It's sometimes described jokingly as the "nuts or sluts" defense, in which women who have brought charges are portrayed as mentally ill or as instigators of the harassment, lawyers said.

"It's like the story of rape victims," said Mary Anne Sedey, president of the National Employment Lawyers Association, which represents employees. "When you report it, it becomes such a horrible experience that no woman wants to do it. That's what defense [lawyers] are trying to do in the sexual harassment arena."

McNulty concluded that the women were, variously, "histrionic," "paranoid," "had a tendency to exaggerate," "over-reactive," "emotionally dysfunctional" or "puritanical" for responding as negatively as they did to what they were experiencing at the mine. For example, McNulty wrote, when Jarvela three times found the clean clothes in her locker spotted with semen deposited by a male co-worker, it "colored her perception and mindset" and caused her to confuse "suspicions . . . with reality."

When Lois Jenson was assigned to cleaning duties because, she said she was told, women are better at cleaning, McNulty called her angry response an "overreaction to an imaginary slight."

McNulty placed into the report numerous intimate details of the women's physical and gynecological records. He also included a discussion of the birth of one plaintiff's child, which she had said was the result of a rape. McNulty instead decided, based on a notation in a 28-year-old hospital report and his own speculation, that the birth was most likely caused by consensual sex. McNulty cited the birth issue as an example of the woman's "propensity or inclination to favorably reconstruct events, by hindsight, to bend them to her advantage."

The woman who said she was raped asked not to be identified.

In the interview earlier this month, McNulty said he included the circumstances surrounding the child's birth on purpose. "I felt it had to be on the record," he said. "It became of extreme importance."

A Hostile Workplace

Second of two articles

EVELETH, Minn.

It was Lois Jenson, an electrician's helper, who finally brought a legal challenge to what she claimed was pervasive sexual harassment in the taconite mine here. She and 20 other women miners filed a class-action lawsuit in 1988 in federal district court in Minneapolis, naming as defendants the operators of the mine and Local 6860 of the United Steel Workers union.

Jenson quickly learned what her male co-workers thought of that pioneering lawsuit: When she returned to work at the mine, she found anti-female sexual epithets scrawled in chalk all over the machinery around her work area.

Then she saw, hanging directly over her work area, a hangman's noose made of thick rope, she testified. At first she tried to ignore it, she later recalled in an interview, and went on about her duties. But when she returned to the area again, she saw the noose had been moved to an even more visible position.

"I had a sick feeling," said Jenson, now 48. "My heart kind of jumped."

For Jenson and Patricia Kosmach, who joined in launching the first-of-its-kind case establishing that workers could challenge sexual harassment in the workplace through class-action lawsuits, the noose was only one of many signs of what was to come. For the next eight years, as the women plaintiffs traveled back and forth to Minneapolis 250 miles away to testify in depositions and at trial, they encountered a backlash of anger, retaliation and sabotage from their co-workers. In the small towns where they lived, the women became pariahs.

In court, the women testified to what they had endured in their work lives: being groped, grabbed, pressured for sex, threatened with rape, and subjected to coarse sexual language and graffiti. Some testified they had even been stalked at home and had begun carrying weapons to defend themselves against physical attacks. They testified that their appeals to the union and management to stop the harassment were mostly ignored, and that none of the men was fired for what he had done.

Their courtroom experience felt like a second wave of harassment, according to the women's friends and family. Probing lawyers were able to force open up their entire lives to public scrutiny. The federal rape shield law prevents such intimate details about sexual assault victims from being revealed in court, but it does not protect victims of sexual harassment if they are making damage claims.

The mine owners, using what has become a common legal strategy nationwide, sought to prove that the individual women were not entitled to financial damages because other events in their lives caused more psychological harm than what they experienced at work.

So it came out that one woman plaintiff's son was the product of a rape 28 years ago, which he had not known until federal magistrate Patrick McNulty made the information public knowledge by including it in his final court report. The mine's attorneys questioned another woman at length in open court about her husband's low sperm count, and whether she had turned to artificial insemination to become pregnant.

The women also found themselves criticized by many of their neighbors in Eveleth and surrounding towns. As layoffs hit the mine, many residents blamed the women miners for taking away men's jobs.

University of Minnesota social psychologist Eugene Borgida, who was an expert witness on behalf of the women and read many of their depositions, said in a recent interview the case left him troubled.

"I came away very sad," he said. "These women were victimized while they were working, victimized by the legal system and victimized in the community where they are living."

Filing for a Precedent

Jenson and Kosmach were among the first women hired at the Eveleth mine in the mid-1970s, and they testified later that the sexual harassment began almost immediately. At first they didn't have any way to explain what was happening to them. Then Jenson saw an article about sexual harassment in a women's magazine and went to the library to learn more about her legal rights.

The women took their complaints to the union and to the company, and in 1984, to the Minnesota Department of Human Rights. They wanted the mine to establish a training program and policy prohibiting such behavior. But four years later, they still hadn't obtained the relief they wanted. Many were continuing to work at the mine, but they found the conditions there deplorable.

Finally, in 1988, the women decided to file a class-action suit in federal court. Several lawyers turned them down, citing the potential expense of the case. They eventually found an advocate in Paul Sprenger, an attorney with offices in Minneapolis and Washington, who had heard about the case from the Minnesota attorney general's office. Sprenger said in an interview that he took the case because the facts seemed so extreme—yet provable—that the suit could establish a "hostile-work" environment as a precedent for class-action cases.

Sprenger filed a federal lawsuit on the women's behalf in August 1988, suing Cleveland-based Oglebay Norton Co. and the other companies that, at various times, owned shares in the mine. They also sued Local 6860 of the United Steel Workers of America, which they alleged had protected the jobs of male sexual harassers despite women's complaints. No money damages were sought from the union.

About two-thirds of the non-salaried women employed at the mine in 1988, ultimately 21 women in all, ended up joining the federal lawsuit.

Oglebay Norton denied the women's claims. "The company feels strongly, and always has, they did not discriminate against the plaintiffs, and they were not subjected to sexual harassment or a hostile environment," said David Jendrzejek, the attorney hired by the insurance companies to represent the mine. "The company doesn't believe it did anything wrong."

In court the mine's attorneys denied that there had been a pervasive environment of harassment. They argued that management had responded quickly and appropriately "in the few instances where incidents of harassing conduct were reported to management." They also contended that some of the women used coarse language themselves and that the sexually explicit pictures and graffiti were not as pervasive as the court exhibits indicated because the mine was spread over a large geographic area.

The four current owners of the mine—Oglebay Norton, Rouge Steel Co., Stelco Inc. of Canada and AK Steel Corp.—all declined to comment on the details of the litigation. A spokesman for Ford Motor Co., which formerly owned a share in the mine, said Ford's role had been in a "non-operating" capacity.

The Trials

The first phase of the case, in May 1991, sought to determine whether the alleged harassment had affected so many women at the mine that it could be pursued as a class-action case. Kosmach's testimony was key because, as a former union official, she had been privy to discussions between management and the union over sexually harassing behavior, and was able to corroborate some of the other women's accounts.

Late that year, in a precedent-setting opinion, U.S. District Court Judge James M. Rosenbaum, a Republican appointee named to the court in 1985, certified that the women could sue as a class. He concluded that, based on a standard of what a "reasonable woman" would find offensive, conditions at the mine constituted a hostile work environment for women.

In the next phase the women's lawyers sought to establish the mine's liability. U.S. District Court Judge Richard Kyle found a "sexualized and anti-female atmosphere" at the mine, as evidenced by numerous incidents of sexual harassment and widespread sexual graffiti.

"The court finds that the effect, and possibly the intent, of the sexualized environment that existed at Eveleth Mines was to inform women that they were perceived primarily as sexual objects and inferior to men, rather than as co-workers, and that these perceptions were an integral part of working at Eveleth Mines," Kyle ruled in May 1993.

Kyle said the mine had responded inadequately to the problem and he ordered it to establish a sexual harassment prevention program and procedures for reporting sexual harassment. He ordered that the women be awarded damages and that Oglebay Norton should pay their legal fees. In 1994 the mine established a sexual harassment training program.

In 1995 the case moved into its third phase, in which the court tried to determine the extent of the damages to the women—financial, physical and emotional. Kyle passed this phase of the case back to the federal court in Duluth.

McNulty's decision on damages, completed in last March, came in a 416-page report. That document revealed details he had gleaned about the women's lives.

He recommended the women be paid amounts ranging from $2,500 to $25,000 each. That was far below other sexual harassment awards, which have been averaging nationwide about $250,000, according to records compiled by the U.S. Equal Employment Opportunity Commission.

Mary Anne Sedey, president of the National Employment Lawyers Association, called the low damage awards in the mine case "appalling."

The women objected to McNulty's recommendations and asked Kyle to review it. He agreed to their request in July, and lawyers said this review could take several more months.

Resented and Ostracized

At the same time the lawsuit was proceeding slowly through the courts, the close-knit Eveleth area community turned against the women. The mine was the major local employer and jobs were being cut because of corporate reorganization, mechanization and competition from lower-cost Brazilian ore. The women said they became scapegoats. "We were called the mining whores," Mavie Maki, now 73, recalled in a recent interview. She had been in her sixties when she worked at the mine.

Everywhere they went, the women said, they were ostracized. Jenson moved from her apartment complex, she said, because the mother of one of the accused male harassers denounced Jenson to her elderly neighbors during senior citizen ceramic classes. The son of another accused harasser kicked Jenson's teenage son in the leg where he was wearing a cast for a compound fracture he had suffered, Jenson said.

Siblings turned against each other and parents against adult children. The company had a tradition of hiring family members, so many of the women claimants had relatives—brothers, fathers-in-law, even husbands—working at the mine. Judy Jarvela's brother still works there. Kathy Anderson's sister is married to Stan Daniels, the president of the union, which was a co-defendant with the company.

"It makes gatherings very sparse," said Anderson's brother, Milo Strom.

It was during this time that a poster first appeared inside a locked, glass-paneled bulletin board where work schedules were posted by mine managers. It read: "Sexual harassment in this area will not be reported. However it will be graded."

The mine's attorneys did not dispute that the poster had appeared there, but they said the glass had a fragile lock that could have been jimmied open, with the poster placed there by an unauthorized person.

Amid the hostility, Kosmach's health deteriorated rapidly. In October 1988, soon after the lawsuit was filed, she left work on disability. Three months later she was told she had Lou Gehrig's disease.

She testified in the first phase of the case and attended the second in 1993 in her wheelchair. She was not well enough to speak, though she had wanted to testify. Kosmach died in 1994 after a long hospitalization, still following the case closely but becoming increasingly bitter about how she had been treated by the mine's management and her male co-workers.

"She was consumed by it, totally consumed by it," said her friend and co-worker Michele Mesich, also a plaintiff. "It took a toll on her."

McNulty dismissed Kosmach's claim in the case, ruling that it could not survive her death and dismissing her daughter Susan Bonach's request to stand in behalf of her mother.

"It seems so unfair," another daughter, Brenda Kosmach, said. "Not just the money part of it. How they believed in it so much—and they got nowhere. Nowhere. Even when they win."

Sixteen women remain in the case, now awaiting the final word on the appeal of their damage amounts. Of the 21 original plaintiffs, only about one-third still work at the mine.

Four women dropped out of the lawsuit in the past two years. In 1994 Janice Wollin, whose testimony about her sexual harassment had been corroborated by co-workers, dropped out one morning as she went to face the mine's attorneys who were preparing to ask her personal questions about her family.

"I filed my initial claim in good faith, but I do not want to continue because of the stress of the proceeding," Wollin wrote in a letter to the court.

The next year, three more women left the case by settling with the mine. Connie Saari, a 17-year miner who had joined in the suit, said the final straw came during the depositions for the damages phase of the trial.

She was asked questions that were, as she put it, "totally stupid, like 'Is your son a homosexual?' 'Does anybody have AIDS?' I thought it was so wrong I got out of it. . . . I couldn't take it anymore."

Saari, who lost her job at the mine and now earns $5.50 an hour assembling air purifiers, dropped her part in the lawsuit in exchange for a settlement offer of $2,000. She accepted, but two years later, she said she has not received the money. Nor has she heard from the mine or the lawyers who negotiated the settlement with her. The two other women who settled also have not been paid.

Jendrzejek, the lawyer for the mine's insurance companies, said he had "no personal knowledge of any settlements." Attorney Goldstein blamed the failure to pay the settlement money on attorney Sprenger, who he said had not submitted his legal bills to the judge to free the claims of the three women. Sprenger, who still hasn't been compensated for what is now eight years of legal work, said the mine could pay the women if it chose.

Saari said she had become convinced that even if the women won, they would lose because the company had the ability to fight them in court for so many years.

"You could be dead by the time it's over," Saari said. "Pat Kosmach didn't make it."

Minn. Mining Firm Settles Lawsuit

After more than a decade of costly and acrimonious litigation, 15 female miners settled their precedent-setting class action sexual harassment lawsuit late last week against an iron ore mining company in Eveleth, Minn., that hired dozens of women in the 1970s.

Under the terms of the agreement, negotiated by lawyers on behalf of the plaintiffs and Fireman's Fund Insurance Co., which represented the company's former owners, both parties are barred from discussing the amount of the settlement. But sources said the amount exceeded $1 million, with at least four of the plaintiffs receiving more than $300,000 each, while others received less. Attorneys' fees still have to be set.

That would make the settlement one of the largest on record per person, because federal law caps sexual harassment awards at $300,000 per plaintiff, regardless of the amount awarded by the jury. The Eveleth suit was also tried under Minnesota law, which has no such limitations.

Lois Jenson, the lead plaintiff in the case, now 50, who was the second woman ever to be employed at the mine when she went to work there in 1975 and who first took the women's complaints to state human relations officials in 1984, said the plaintiffs were mostly "pleased and relieved," and said they had settled because it was "time."

"We reached a point where we'd proved everything we needed to prove," Jenson said.

Rochelle Walk, corporate secretary and director of corporate affairs at Oglebay Norton Co., the Cleveland-based shipping and mining firm that was controlling partner of the Eveleth Mines during the time the sexual harassment occurred, said executives there were "thrilled" it was over.

"I certainly hope the plaintiffs will be able to move forward with their lives and do what they want to do," Walk said. "It became a stumbling block for them to move forward in their lives. I hope that's no longer the case."

Walk said it's "a shame it took this long," adding that the company had wanted the case to settle earlier. "On the advice of counsel, the insurance company made their decisions," she said, adding that "it is conceivable the attorneys will end up being paid more than the plaintiffs."

She said few at Oglebay Norton now know first-hand about the case, as the company has completely changed its management team in the past two years. "The essence of Oglebay Norton is a very different place," she said. "There's nobody here now who was there at the time that took place."

Steve Buck, spokesman for Fireman's Fund Insurance, based in Novato, Calif., limited his comments to a short prepared statement. "The case has been settled to the satisfaction of all parties," he said.

The Eveleth mines case created the legal precedent for a class action sexual harassment case—where the environment is so hostile that it affects all women employees. It paved the way for the sexual harassment case against Mitsubishi Motor Manufacturing of America Inc., which settled in June for a record $34 million.

In three trials to determine liability and damages in the Eveleth case, three separate federal judges ruled that there was a pervasive pattern of sexual harassment at the mine.

About two dozen women, some of them former welfare recipients in their first good-paying jobs when hired at the mine, testified about being beaten, threatened with rape, terrorized with death threats, referred to as dogs, denied bathroom facilities, and having their crotches and breasts grabbed by male co-workers and supervisors.

They testified they armed themselves with knives and mace to go to work each morning. The company did not fire any of the men accused of the activities, and only disciplined one man with a five-day suspension.

Several of the women have since been diagnosed as suffering post traumatic stress syndrome, a mental ailment best known for afflicting combat veterans, and some have not worked for years.

The Eveleth case highlighted the use of the popular "nuts or sluts" defense strategy used by lawyers representing firms charged with tolerating sexual harassment, where they sought to aggressively investigate the women's personal, gynecological and medical histories to determine whether the women were emotionally damaged before they began work at the mine. The defense team obtained the women's medical records from birth and asked a barrage of intensely personal questions in open court.

The 8th U.S. Circuit Court of Appeals, reviewing the case, said the women had suffered additional damage during their long trials. "If our goal is to persuade the American people to utilize our courts as little as possible, we have furthered that objective in this case," wrote U.S. Circuit Court Judge Donald Lay in December 1997, ordering yet a new trial to determine what he called "adequate" damages to be awarded to the women.

On the eve of that fourth trial, scheduled to start tomorrow, the two sides abruptly achieved consensus after girding for battle yet again.

"The real clincher was, the judge ordered the vice president of the insurance company to show up [for mediation], and it was a woman, who had a fresh take on the situation and was able to alter their position," said lawyer Jean Boler, who represented the female miners.

B. SEXUAL HARASSMENT ON THE NATIONAL STAGE

The 1990's brought a national focus on the issue of sexual harassment at the highest levels of the federal government. In the 1991 Senate Judiciary Committee confirmation hearings on the nomination of Clarence Thomas, former Chair of the Equal Employment Opportunity Commission, to the Supreme Court, the key opposition witness was law professor Anita Hill, who testified that Thomas had engaged in a pattern of sexual harassment against her while she worked for him at E.E.O.C. Hill's testimony, and her aggressive questioning by members of the Committee, dominated the news nationwide, and sparked a significant increase in sexual harassment lawsuits and administrative complaints. Thomas survived a bitter confirmation battle on a tie vote in the Judiciary Committee, and by a 52-48 margin on the floor of the Senate. While no harassment claim was filed against Justice Thomas, the controversy surrounding Hill's testimony was galvanizing for the movement for women's rights.

In *Jones v. Clinton*, former Arkansas state employee Paula Jones sued President and former Arkansas Governor Clinton for sexual harassment stemming from an alleged 1991 incident in a Little Rock hotel room. Federal District Judge Susan Webber Wright ruled in the President's favor in 1998, but later found the President to be in civil contempt for testifying falsely in a pre-trial deposition, in which he denied having a sexual relationship with a White House intern. This denial, and the President's subsequent testimony before a Federal Grand Jury, led directly to his impeachment by the House, preceding Senate acquittal.

In a series of five sexual harassment decisions in 1998 and 1999, the Supreme Court gave additional guidance with regard to what constituted a legally sufficient claim of sexual harassment. In the two leading decisions, *Oncale v. Sundowner Offshore Services* (1998) and *Davis v. Monroe County Board of Education* (1999), the Court made clear that sexual harassment:

> does not reach genuine but innocuous differences in the ways men and women routinely interact with members of the same sex and with the opposite sex. The prohibition of harassment on the basis of sex requires neither asexuality nor androgyny in the workplace; it forbids only behavior so objectively offensive as to alter the "conditions" of the victim's employment. [*Oncale*]

In practical terms, however, far from narrowing the circumstances for colorable sexual harassment allegations, the Court expanded them. In *Oncale*, the Court found sexual harassment to be actionable when the victim and perpetrator were of the same sex, and in *Davis*, school district officials were held liable when they ignored evidence of student-on-student harassment.

JONES v. CLINTON

U.S. District Court, Eastern District of Arkansas

April 1, 1998

SUSAN WEBBER WRIGHT, U.S. DISTRICT JUDGE:

The plaintiff in this lawsuit, Paula Corbin Jones, seeks civil damages from William Jefferson Clinton, President of the United States, and Danny Ferguson, a former Arkansas State Police Officer, for alleged actions beginning with an incident in a hotel suite in Little Rock, Arkansas. This case was previously before the Supreme Court of the United States to resolve the issue of Presidential immunity but was remanded to this Court following the Supreme Court's determination that there is no constitutional impediment to allowing plaintiff's case to proceed while the President is in office.... Following remand, the President filed a motion for judgment on the pleadings and dismissal of the complaint pursuant to Rule 12(c) of the Federal Rules of Civil Procedure. Ferguson joined in the President's motion. By Memorandum opinion and Order dated August 22, 1997, this Court granted in part and denied in part the President's motion.... The Court dismissed plaintiff's defamation claim against the President, dismissed her due process claims for deprivation of a liberty interest based on false imprisonment and injury to reputation, but concluded that the remaining claims in plaintiff's complaint stated viable causes of action.... Plaintiff subsequently obtained new counsel and filed a motion for leave to file a first amended complaint, which the court granted, albeit with several qualifications.... The matter is now before the Court on motion of both the President and Ferguson for summary judgment pursuant to Rule 56 of the Federal Rules of Civil Procedure. Plaintiff has responded in opposition to these motions, and the President and Ferguson have each filed a reply to plaintiff's response to their motions. For the reasons that follow, the Court finds that the President's and Ferguson's motions for summary judgment should both be and hereby are granted.

I.

This lawsuit is based on an incident that is said to have taken place on the afternoon of May 8, 1991, in a suite at the Excelsior Hotel in Little Rock, Arkansas. President Clinton was Governor of the State of Arkansas at the time, and plaintiff was a State employee with the Arkansas Industrial Development Commission ("AIDC"), having begun her State employment on March 11, 1991. Ferguson was an Arkansas State Police officer assigned to the Governor's security detail.

According to the record, then-Governor Clinton was at the Excelsior Hotel on the day in question delivering a speech at an official conference being sponsored by the AIDC.... Plaintiff states that she and another AIDC employee, Pamela Blackard, were working at a registration desk for the AIDC when a man approached the desk and informed her and Blackard that he was Trooper Danny Ferguson, the Governor's bodyguard.... She states that Ferguson made small talk with her and Blackard and that they asked him if he had a gun as he was in street clothes and they "wanted to know." ... Ferguson acknowledged that he did and, after being asked to show the gun to them, left the registration desk to return to the Governor.... The conversation between plaintiff, Blackard, and Ferguson lasted approximately five minutes and consisted of light, friendly banter; there was nothing intimidating, threatening, or coercive about it....

Upon leaving the registration desk, Ferguson apparently had a conversation with the Governor about the possibility of meeting with plaintiff, during which Ferguson states the Governor remarked that plaintiff had "that come-hither look," i.e. "a sort of [sexually] suggestive appearance from the look or dress." ... He states that "some time later" the Governor asked him to "get him a room, that he was expecting a call from the White House and ... had several phone calls that he needed to make," and asked him to go to the car and get his briefcase containing the phone messages.... Ferguson states that upon obtaining the room, the Governor told him that if plaintiff wanted to meet him, she could "come up." ...

Plaintiff states that Ferguson later reappeared at the registration desk, delivered a piece of paper to her with a four-digit number written on it, and said that the Governor would like to meet with her in this suite number. ... She states that she, Blackard, and Ferguson talked about what the Governor could want and that Ferguson stated, among other things, "We do this all the time." ... Thinking that it was an honor to be asked to meet the Governor and that it might lead to an enhanced employment opportunity, plaintiff states that she agreed to the meeting and that Ferguson escorted her to the floor of the hotel upon which the Governor's suite was located....

Plaintiff states that upon arriving at the suite and announcing herself, the Governor shook her hand, invited her in, and closed the door. . . . She states that a few minutes of small talk ensued, which included the Governor asking her about her job and him mentioning that Dave Harrington, plaintiff's ultimate superior within the AIDC and a Clinton appointee, was his "good friend." . . . Plaintiff states that the Governor then "unexpectedly reached over to [her], took her hand, and pulled her toward him, so that their bodies were close to each other. . . . She states she removed her hand from his and retreated several feet, but that the Governor approached her again and, while saying, "I love the way your hair flows down your back" and "I love your curves," put his hand on her leg, started sliding it toward her pelvic area, and bent down to attempt to kiss her on the neck, all without her consent. . . . Plaintiff states that she exclaimed, "What are you doing?," told the Governor that she was "not that kind of girl," and "escaped" from the Governor's reach "by walking away from him." . . . She states she was extremely upset and confused and, not knowing what to do, attempted to distract the Governor by chatting about his wife. . . . Plaintiff states that she sat down at the end of the sofa nearest the door, but that the Governor approached the sofa where she had taken a seat and, as he sat down, "lowered his trousers and underwear, exposed his penis (which was erect) and told [her] to 'kiss it.' " . . . She states that she was "horrified" by this and that she "jumped up from the couch" and told the Governor that she had to go, saying something to the effect that she had to get back to the registration desk. . . . Plaintiff states that the Governor, "while fondling his penis," said, "Well, I don't want to make you do anything you don't want to do, and then pulled up his pants and said, "If you get in trouble for leaving work, have Dave call me immediately and I'll take care of it." . . . She states that as she left the room (the door of which was not locked), the Governor "detained" her momentarily, "looked sternly" at her, and said, "You are smart. Let's keep this between ourselves." . . .

Plaintiff states that the Governor's advances to her were unwelcome, that she never said or did anything to suggest to the Governor that she was willing to have sex with him, and that during the time they were together in the hotel suite, she resisted his advances although she was "stunned by them and intimidated by who he was." . . . She states that when the Governor referred to Dave Harrington, she "understood that he was telling her that he had control over Mr. Harrington and over her job, and that he was willing to use that power." . . . She states that from that point on, she was "very fearful" that her refusal to submit to the Governor's advances could damage her career and even jeopardize her employment. . . .

Plaintiff states that when she left the hotel suite, she was in shock and upset but tried to maintain her composure. . . . She states she saw Ferguson waiting outside the suite but that he did not escort her back to the registration desk and nothing was said between them. . . . Ferguson states that five or ten minutes after plaintiff exited the suite he joined the Governor for their return to the Governor's Mansion and that the Governor, who was working on some papers that he had spread out on the desk, said, "She came up here, and nothing happened." . . .

Plaintiff states she returned to the registration desk and told Blackard some of what had happened. . . . Blackard states that plaintiff was shaking and embarrassed. . . . Following the Conference, plaintiff states she went to the workplace of a friend, Debra Ballentine, and told her of the incident as well. . . . Ballentine states that plaintiff was upset and crying. . . . Later that same day, plaintiff states she told her sister, Charlotte Corbin Brown, what had happened and, within the next two days, also told her other sister, Lydia Corbin Cathey, of the incident. . . . Brown's observations of plaintiff's demeanor apparently are not included in the record. Cathey, however, states that plaintiff was "bawling" and "squalling," and that she appeared scared, embarrassed, and ashamed. . . .

Ballentine states that she encouraged plaintiff to report the incident to her boss or to the police, but that plaintiff declined, pointing out that her boss was friends with the Governor and that the police were the ones who took her to the hotel suite. . . . Ballentine further states that plaintiff stated she did not want her fiance to know of the incident and that she "just want[ed] this thing to go away." . . . Plaintiff states that what the Governor and Ferguson had said and done made her "afraid" to file charges. . . .

Plaintiff continued to work at AIDC following the alleged incident in the hotel suite. . . . One of her duties was to deliver documents to and from the Office of the Governor, as well as other offices around the Arkansas State Capitol. . . . She states that in June 1991, while performing these duties for the AIDC, she encountered Ferguson who told her that Mrs. Clinton was out of town often and that the Governor wanted her phone number and wanted to see her. . . . Plaintiff states she refused to provide her phone number to Ferguson. . . . She states that Ferguson also asked her how her fiance, Steve, was doing, even though she had never told Ferguson or the Governor his name, and that this "frightened" her. . . . Plaintiff states that she again encountered Ferguson following her return to work from maternity leave and that he said he had "told Bill how good looking you are since you've had the baby." . . . She also states that she was "accosted" by the Governor in the Rotunda of the Arkansas State Capitol when he "draped his arm over her, pulled her close to him and held her tightly to his body," and said to his bodyguard, "Don't we make a beautiful couple: Beauty and the Beast?" . . . Plaintiff additionally states that on an unspecified date, she was waiting in the Governor's outer office on a delivery run when the Governor entered the office, patted her on the shoulder, and in a "friendly fashion" said, "How are you doing, Paula?" . . .

Plaintiff states that she continued to work at AIDC "even though she was in constant fear that [the Governor] would retaliate against her because she had refused to have sex with him." . . . She states this fear prevented her from enjoying her job. . . . Plaintiff states that she was treated "very rudely" by certain superiors in AIDC, including her direct supervisor, Clydine Pennington, and that this "rude treatment" had not happened prior to her encounter with the Governor. . . . She states that after her maternity leave, she was transferred to a position which had much less responsibility and that much of the time she had nothing to do. . . . Plaintiff states that she was not learning anything, that her work could not be fairly evaluated, and that as a result, she could not be fairly considered for advancement and other opportunities. . . . She states that Pennington told her the reason for the transfer was that her prior position had been eliminated, but that she later learned this was untrue, as her former position was being occupied by another employee. . . . Plaintiff states that she repeatedly expressed to Pennington an interest in transferring to particular positions at a higher "grade" which involved more challenging duties, more potential for advancement, and more compensation, but that Pennington always discouraged her from doing so and told her she should not bother to apply for those positions. . . .

She goes on to state that her superiors exhibited hostility toward her by moving her work location, refusing to give her meaningful work, watching her constantly, and failing to give her flowers on Secretary's Day in 1992, even though all the other women in the office received flowers. . . .

Plaintiff voluntarily terminated her employment with AIDC on February 20, 1993, in order to move to California with her husband, who had been transferred. . . . She states that in January 1994, while visiting family and friends in Arkansas, she was informed of an article in *The American Spectator* magazine that she claims referred to her alleged encounter with the Governor at the Excelsior Hotel and incorrectly suggested that she had engaged in sexual relations with the Governor. . . . Plaintiff states that she also encountered Ferguson in a restaurant during this same time and that he indicated he was the source for the article and that he knew she had refused the Governor's alleged advances because, he said, "Clinton told me you wouldn't do anything anyway, Paula." . . .

On February 11, 1994, at an event attended by the media, plaintiff states that she publicly asked President Clinton to acknowledge the incident mentioned in the article in *The American Spectator*, to state that she had rejected his advances, and to apologize to her, but that the President responded to her request for an apology by having his press spokespersons deliver a statement on his behalf that the incident never happened and that he never met plaintiff. . . .

Thereafter, on May 6, 1994, plaintiff filed this lawsuit.

Plaintiff's amended complaint contains several claims, three of which remain at issue. . . . The first is a claim under 42 U.S. [Code] . . . in which plaintiff alleges that Governor Clinton, acting under color of state law, deprived her of her constitutional right to equal protection of the laws under the Fourteenth Amendment to the United States Constitution by sexually harassing her. The second is a claim under 42 U.S. [Code] . . . in which plaintiff alleges that Governor Clinton and Ferguson conspired to deprive her of her rights to equal protection of the laws and of equal privileges and immunities under the laws. The third is a state law claim in which plaintiff asserts a claim of intentional infliction of emotional distress or outrage against Governor Clinton, based primarily on the alleged incident at the hotel but also encompassing subsequent alleged acts.

II.

The President moves for summary judgment on the following grounds: (1) plaintiff cannot show either *quid pro quo* or hostile work environment sexual harassment under . . . because (a) the record plainly demonstrates that plaintiff did not suffer any tangible job detriment for purposes of establishing a *quid pro quo* claim, let alone one caused by her purported rejection of Mr. Clinton's alleged sexual advances, and (b) the alleged actions as described by plaintiff, even resolving all inferences and factual disputes in her favor, do not constitute severe or pervasive abusive conduct for purposes of establishing a hostile work environment claim; (2) if plaintiff's . . . claim fails, so too does her . . . conspiracy claim because (a) plaintiff has failed to show that any such conspiracy actually resulted in a deprivation of her constitutional rights, and (b) the undisputed facts do not show any agreement between Governor Clinton and Trooper Ferguson to deprive plaintiff of her constitutional rights; and (3) plaintiff's claim of intentional infliction of emotional distress or outrage fails because (a) by plaintiff's own testimony, the conduct at issue does not constitute intentional infliction of emotional distress or outrage under Arkansas law, and (b) plaintiff did not as a result of the alleged conduct suffer emotional distress so severe that no reasonable person could endure it. Ferguson, in turn, moves for summary judgment on grounds that (1) even if everything plaintiff has alleged were true, she does not have evidence to show either *quid pro quo* or hostile work environment sexual harassment, and (2) there was no conspiracy between the President and Ferguson to violate plaintiff's constitutional rights by sexually harassing her. The President and Ferguson both argue that there are no genuine issues of material fact with respect to any of these issues and that they are entitled to summary judgment as a matter of law.

To make a prima facie case of *quid pro quo* sexual harassment, this plaintiff must show, among other things, that her refusal to submit to unwelcome sexual advances or requests for sexual favors resulted in a tangible job detriment. . . . [Cites cases in which] (. . . to withstand summary judgment on *quid pro quo* claims, plaintiffs were required to produce evidence showing that the harassment complained of affected tangible aspects of their compensation, terms, conditions, or privileges of employment.) "[A] supervisor's mere threat or promise of job-related harm or benefits in exchange for sexual favors does not constitute *quid pro quo* harassment. . . ."

i.

Apparently recognizing the infirm ground upon which her assertion of tangible job detriments rest . . . plaintiff *first* argues that a showing of a tangible job detriment is not an essential element of an action for *quid pro quo* sexual harassment under Title VII. The Court rejects this argument as it conflicts with the Eighth Circuit's requirement that a refusal to submit to unwelcome sexual advances or requests for sexual favors resulted in a tangible job detriment . . . and conflicts with the majority of the other circuits on this point as well, including the recent decisions . . . (concluding that it is the essence of *quid pro quo* harassment when an employee is subjected to unwelcome sexual advances by a supervisor and her reaction to these advances affects tangible aspects of her compensation, terms, conditions, or privileges of employment); . . . (*quid pro quo* claim requires that the employee's reaction to the harassment affected tangible aspects of the employee's compensation, terms, conditions, or privileges of employment); . . . (noting that the gravamen of a *quid pro quo* claim is that a tangible job benefit or privilege is conditioned on an employee's submission to sexual blackmail and that adverse consequences follow from the employee's refusal); . . . (*quid pro quo* sexual harassment exists when adverse job consequences result from employee's refusal to submit to sexual advances); . . . (*quid pro quo* claim requires that the employee's reaction to the harassment affected tangible aspects of the employee's compensation, terms, conditions, or privileges of employment); . . . (no cause of action for *quid pro quo* sexual harassment where "the record [is] totally devoid of any evidence tending to demonstrate that plaintiff was denied a job benefit or suffered a job detriment as a result of her failure to engage in the activity suggested by [defendant]"). . . .

While it is true that the Seventh Circuit in *Jansen* concluded that a "clear and unambiguous" *quid pro quo* threat that "clearly conditions concrete job benefits or detriments on compliance with sexual demands" can constitute an actionable claim "even if the threat remains unfulfilled," . . . plaintiff acknowledges that no one, including Governor Clinton, ever told her that if she refused to submit to his alleged advances in order to receive job benefits, or that the Governor would use his relationship with AIDC Director Dave Harrington to penalize her in her job. . . . She merely states that "read[ing] between the lines," she "knew what [the Governor] meant" when he allegedly indicated in the hotel suite that Harrington was his good friend. . . . Be that as it may, the Governor's alleged statements do not in any way constitute a clear threat that clearly conditions concrete job benefits or detriments on compliance with sexual demands. Plaintiff's claim therefore would not survive a *Jansen* analysis, her "read[ing] between the lines" notwithstanding. . . .

Based on the foregoing, the Court finds that a showing of a tangible job detriment is an essential element of plaintiff's *quid pro quo* sexual harassment claim. It is that issue to which the Court now turns.

ii.

As evidence of tangible job detriments (or adverse employment action), plaintiff claims the following occurred after she resisted Governor Clinton's alleged advances on May 8, 1991: (1) she was discouraged from applying for more attractive jobs and seeking reclassification at a higher pay grade within the AIDC; (2) her job was changed to one with fewer responsibilities, less attractive duties and less potential for advancement—and the reason given for the change proved to be untrue; (3) she was effectively denied access to grievance procedures that would otherwise have been available to victims of sexual harassment; and (4) she was mistreated in ways having tangible manifestations, such as isolating her physically, making her sit in a location from which she was constantly watched, making her sit at her workstation with no work to do, and singling her out as the only female employee not to be given flowers on Secretary's Day. The Court has carefully reviewed the record in this case and finds nothing in plaintiff's employment records, her own testimony, or the testimony of her supervisors showing that plaintiff's reaction to Governor Clinton's alleged advances affected tangible aspects of her compensation, terms, conditions, or privileges of employment.

1.

Plaintiff's claim that she was discouraged from applying for more attractive jobs and seeking reclassification at a higher pay grade within the AIDC does not demonstrate any "tangible" job detriment as she has not identified a single specific job which she desired or applied for at AIDC but which she had been discouraged from seeking. . . . When asked for such specific information, plaintiff merely testified that the unidentified jobs she sought were "a grade higher" but that her supervisor "would always discourage me and make me believe that I could grow within the administrative services, which in fact I didn't. I got degrade—downgraded." . . . She further states that those "few" times that she would talk to her supervisor and receive discouragement, she "would go ahead and fill out an application maybe or something." . . . There is no record of plaintiff ever applying for another job within AIDC, however, and the record shows that not only was plaintiff never downgraded, her position was reclassified *upward* from a Grade 9 classification to a Grade 11 classification, thereby increasing her annual salary. . . . Indeed, it is undisputed that plaintiff received every merit increase and cost-of-living allowance for which she was eligible during her nearly two-year tenure with the AIDC and consistently received satisfactory job evaluations. . . . Specifically, on July 1, 1991, less than two months after the alleged incident that is the subject of this lawsuit, plaintiff received a cost-of-living increase and her position was reclassified from Grade 9 to Grade 11; on August 28, 1991, plaintiff received a satisfactory job evaluation from her supervisor, Clydine Pennington; on March 11, 1992, the one-year anniversary of her hire date with AIDC, plaintiff received another satisfactory evaluation from Pennington and Cherry Duckett, Deputy Director of AIDC, which entitled her to a merit raise. . . . In addition, plaintiff was given a satisfactory job review in an evaluation covering the period of March 1992 until her voluntary departure from the AIDC in February 1993. . . . Plaintiff signed this review on February 16, 1993, . . . and would have received another merit increase one month later in accordance with this review had she elected to continue her employment at AIDC. . . .

Although it is not clear why plaintiff failed to receive flowers on Secretary's Day in 1992, such an omission does not give rise to a federal cause of action in the absence of evidence of some more tangible change in duties or working conditions that constitute a material employment disadvantage. . . .

iii.

In sum, the Court finds that a showing of a tangible job detriment or adverse employment action is an essential element of plaintiff's . . . *quid pro quo* sexual harassment claim and that plaintiff has not demonstrated any tangible job detriment or adverse employment action for her refusal to submit to the Governor's alleged advances. The President is therefore entitled to summary judgment on plaintiff's claim of *quid pro quo* sexual harassment.

b.

The Court now turns to plaintiff's hostile work environment claim. Unlike *quid pro quo* sexual harassment, hostile work environment harassment arises when "sexual conduct has the purpose or effect of unreasonable interfering with an individual's work performance or creating an intimidating, hostile, or offensive working environment." ... To prevail on a hostile work environment cause of action, a plaintiff must establish, among other things, that she was subjected to unwelcome sexual harassment based upon her sex that affected a term, condition, or privilege of employment. ... The behavior creating the hostile working environment need not be overtly sexual in nature, but it must be " 'unwelcome' in the sense that the employee did not solicit or invite it, and the employee regarded the conduct as undesirable or offensive." ... The harassment must also be sufficiently severe or pervasive "to alter the conditions of employment and create an abusive working environment." ...

The President essentially argues that aside from the alleged incident at the Excelsior Hotel, plaintiff alleges only two other contacts with him, alleges only a few additional contacts with Ferguson, and contains conclusory claims that plaintiff's supervisors were rude. He argues that taken individually or as a whole, these contacts do not in any way constitute the kind of pervasive, intimidating, abusive conduct that courts require to establish a hostile work environment claim. The Court agrees.

In assessing the hostility of an environment, a court must look to the totality of the circumstances. ... Circumstances to be considered include "the frequency of the discriminatory conduct; its severity; whether it is physically threatening or humiliating, or a mere offensive utterance; and whether it unreasonably interferes with an employee's work performance." ... No single factor is determinative ... and the court "should not carve the work environment into a series of discrete incidents and then measure the harm occurring in each episode." ...

First, the Court finds plaintiff's reliance on her assertions of tangible job detriment as establishing a hostile work environment ... to be misplaced. In its August 22 Memorandum Opinion and Order, the Court noted that although the President's argument for outright dismissal of plaintiff's hostile work environment claim had "some force," further development of the record was nevertheless necessary. ... The Court based this conclusion in large part on plaintiff's representations that her rejection of the President's alleged advances caused her to suffer adverse employment actions, including being transferred to a position that had no responsible duties for which she could be adequately evaluated to earn advancement and failing to receive raises and merit increases. ... In this regard, the Court determined that the "totality" of the allegations alleged in this case were such that they could be said to have altered the conditions of plaintiff's employment and created an abusive work environment. ... However, development of the record has now established that plaintiff's allegations of adverse employment actions are without merit ... with her claim of failing to receive cost of living increases apparently having even been abandoned. ... Plaintiff received every merit increase and cost-of-living allowance for which she was eligible during her nearly two-year tenure with the AIDC, her job was upgraded from Grade 9 to Grade 11 (thereby increasing her salary), she consistently received satisfactory job evaluations, and her job responsibilities upon her return from maternity leave were not significantly different from prior to her taking leave and did not cause her any materially significant disadvantage. These facts are clearly established by the record and dispel the notion that she was subjected to a hostile work environment.

Plaintiff certainly has not shown under the totality of the circumstances that the alleged incident in the hotel and her additional encounters with Ferguson and the Governor were so severe or pervasive that it created an abusive working environment. ... She admits that she never missed a day of work following the alleged incident in the hotel, she continued to work at AIDC another nineteen months (leaving only because of her husband's job transfer), she continued to go on a daily basis to the Governor's Office to deliver items and never asked to be relieved of that duty, she never filed a formal complaint or told her supervisors of the incident while at AIDC, and she never consulted a psychiatrist, psychologist, or incurred medical bills as a result of the alleged incident. ... In addition, plaintiff has not shown how Ferguson's alleged comments, whether considered alone or in conjunction with the other alleged conduct in the case, interfered with her work, and she acknowledges that the Governor's statement about him and her looking like "beauty and the beast" was made "in a light vein" and that his patting her on the shoulder and asking her how she was doing was done in a "friendly fashion." ...

While the alleged incident in the hotel, if true, was certainly boorish and offensive, the Court has already found that the Governor's alleged conduct does not constitute sexual assault. ... This is thus not one of those exceptional cases in which a single incident of sexual harassment, such as an assault, was deemed sufficient to state a claim of hostile work environment sexual harassment. ...

Considering the totality of the circumstances, it simply cannot be said that the conduct to which plaintiff was allegedly subjected was frequent, severe, or physically threatening, and the Court finds that defendants' actions as shown by the record do not constitute the kind of sustained and nontrivial conduct necessary for a claim of hostile work environment.

One final matter concerns alleged suppression of pattern and practice evidence. Whatever relevance such evidence may have to prove other elements of plaintiff's case, it does not have anything to do with the issues presented by the President's and Ferguson's motions for summary judgment, *i.e.*, whether plaintiff *herself* was the victim of alleged *quid pro quo* or hostile work environment sexual harassment, whether the President and Ferguson conspired to deprive *her* of her civil rights, or whether *she* suffered emotional distress so severe in nature that no reasonable person could be expected to endure it. Whether other women may have been subjected to workplace harassment, and whether such evidence has allegedly been suppressed, does not change the fact that plaintiff has failed to demonstrate that *she* has a case worthy of submitting to a jury. Reduced to its essence, the record taken as a whole could not lead a rational trier of fact to find for the non-moving party and the Court therefore finds that there are no genuine issues for trial in this case.

JOSEPH ONCALE, PETITIONER *v.* SUNDOWNER OFFSHORE SERVICES,

[March 4, 1998]

Justice Scalia delivered the opinion of the Court.

The District Court having granted summary judgment for respondent, we must assume the facts to be as alleged by petitioner Joseph Oncale. The precise details are irrelevant to the legal point we must decide, and in the interest of both brevity and dignity we shall describe them only generally. In late October 1991, Oncale was working for respondent Sundowner Offshore Services on a Chevron U.S. A., Inc., oil platform in the Gulf of Mexico. He was employed as a roustabout on an eight-man crew which included respondents John Lyons, Danny Pippen, and Brandon Johnson. Lyons, the crane operator, and Pippen, the driller, had supervisory authority, App. 41, 77, 43. On several occasions, Oncale was forcibly subjected to sex-related, humiliating actions against him by Lyons, Pippen and Johnson in the presence of the rest of the crew. Pippen and Lyons also physically assulted Oncale in a sexual manner, and Lyons threatened him with rape.

Oncale's complaints to supervisory personnel produced no remedial action; in fact, the company's Safety Compliance Clerk, Valent Hohen, told Oncale that Lyons and Pippen "picked [on] him all the time too," and called him a name suggesting homosexuality. *Id.*, at 77. Oncale eventually quit–asking that his pink slip reflect that he "voluntarily left due to sexual harassment and verbal abuse." *Id.*, at 79. When asked at his deposition why he left Sundowner, Oncale stated "I felt that if I didn't leave my job, that I would be raped or forced to have sex." *Id.*, at 71.

Title VII's prohibition of discrimination "because of . . . sex" protects men as well as women, *Newport News Shipbuilding & Dry Dock Co.* v. *EEOC*, 462 U.S. 669, 682 (1983), and in the related context of racial discrimination in the workplace we have rejected any conclusive presumption that an employer will not discriminate against members of his own race. "Because of the many facets of human motivation, it would be unwise to presume as a matter of law that human beings of one definable group will not discriminate against other members of that group." *Castaneda* v. *Partida*, 430 U.S. 482, 499 (1977). See also *id.*, at 515—516 n. 6 (Powell, J., joined by Burger, C. J., and Rehnquist, J., dissenting). In *Johnson* v. *Transportation Agency, Santa Clara Cty.*, 480 U.S. 616 (1987), a male employee claimed that his employer discriminated against him because of his sex when it preferred a female employee for promotion. Although we ultimately rejected the claim on other grounds, we did not consider it significant that the supervisor who made that decision was also a man. See *id.*, at 624—625. If our precedents leave any doubt on the question, we hold today that nothing in Title VII necessarily bars a claim of discrimination "because of . . . sex" merely because the plaintiff and the defendant (or the person charged with acting on behalf of the defendant) are of the same sex.

We see no justification in the statutory language or our precedents for a categorical rule excluding same-sex harassment claims from the coverage of Title VII. As some courts have observed, male-on-male sexual harassment in the workplace was assuredly not the principal evil Congress was concerned with when it enacted Title VII. But statutory prohibitions often go beyond the principal evil to cover reasonably comparable evils, and it is ultimately the provisions of our laws rather than the principal concerns of our legislators by which we are governed. Title VII prohibits "discriminat[ion] . . . because of . . . sex" in the "terms" or "conditions" of employment. Our holding that this includes sexual harassment must extend to sexual harassment of any kind that meets the statutory requirements.

Respondents and their *amici* contend that recognizing liability for same-sex harassment will transform Title VII into a general civility code for the American workplace. But that risk is no greater for same-sex than for opposite-sex harassment, and is adequately met by careful attention to the requirements of the statute. Title VII does not prohibit all verbal or physical harassment in the workplace; it is directed only at "*discriminat[ion]* . . . because of . . . sex." We have never held that workplace harassment, even harassment between men and women, is automatically discrimination because of sex merely because the words used have sexual content or connotations. "The critical issue, Title VII's text indicates, is whether members of one sex are exposed to disadvantageous terms or conditions of employment to which members of the other sex are not exposed." *Harris, supra*, at 25 (Ginsburg, J., concurring).

As we emphasized in *Meritor* and *Harris*, the statute does not reach genuine but innocuous differences in the ways men and women routinely interact with members of the same sex and of the opposite sex. The prohibition of harassment on the basis of sex requires neither asexuality nor androgyny in the workplace; it forbids only behavior so objectively offensive as to alter the "conditions" of the victim's employment. "Conduct that is not severe or pervasive enough to create an objectively hostile or abusive work environment–an environment that a reasonable person would find hostile or abusive–is beyond Title VII's purview." *Harris*, 510 U.S., at 21, citing *Meritor*, 477 U.S. at 67. We have always regarded that requirement as crucial, and as sufficient to ensure that courts and juries do not mistake ordinary socializing in the workplace–such as male-on-male horseplay or intersexual flirtation–for discriminatory "conditions of employment."

We have emphasized, moreover, that the objective severity of harassment should be judged from the perspective of a reasonable person in the plaintiff's position, considering "all the circumstances." *Harris, supra,* at 23. In same-sex (as in all) harassment cases, that inquiry requires careful consideration of the social context in which particular behavior occurs and is experienced by its target. A professional football player's working environment is not severely or pervasively abusive, for example, if the coach smacks him on the buttocks as he heads onto the field—even if the same behavior would reasonably be experienced as abusive by the coach's secretary (male or female) back at the office. The real social impact of workplace behavior often depends on a constellation of surrounding circumstances, expectations, and relationships which are not fully captured by a simple recitation of the words used or the physical acts performed. Common sense, and an appropriate sensitivity to social context, will enable courts and juries to distinguish between simple teasing or roughhousing among members of the same sex, and conduct which a reasonable person in the plaintiff's position would find severely hostile or abusive.

DAVIS v. MONROE COUNTY BOARD OF EDUCATION

Decided May 24, 1999

Justice O'Connor delivered the opinion of the Court.

Petitioner brought suit against the Monroe County Board of Education and other defendants, alleging that her fifth-grade daughter had been the victim of sexual harassment by another student in her class. Among petitioner's claims was a claim for monetary and injunctive relief under Title IX of the Education Amendments of 1972 (Title IX), 86 Stat. 373, as amended, 20 U. S. C. §1681 *et seq.* The District Court dismissed petitioner's Title IX claim on the ground that "student-on-student," or peer, harassment provides no ground for a private cause of action under the statute. The Court of Appeals for the Eleventh Circuit, sitting en banc, affirmed. We consider here whether a private damages action may lie against the school board in cases of student-on-student harassment. We conclude that it may, but only where the funding recipient acts with deliberate indifference to known acts of harassment in its programs or activities. Moreover, we conclude that such an action will lie only for harassment that is so severe, pervasive, and objectively offensive that it effectively bars the victim's access to an educational opportunity or benefit.

Petitioner's minor daughter, LaShonda, was allegedly the victim of a prolonged pattern of sexual harassment by one of her fifth-grade classmates at Hubbard Elementary School, a public school in Monroe County, Georgia. According to petitioner's complaint, the harassment began in December 1992, when the classmate, G. F., attempted to touch LaShonda's breasts and genital area and made vulgar statements such as " `I want to get in bed with you' " and " `I want to feel your boobs.' " Complaint ¶ ;7. Similar conduct allegedly occurred on or about January 4 and January 20, 1993. *Ibid.* LaShonda reported each of these incidents to her mother and to her classroom teacher, Diane Fort. *Ibid.* Petitioner, in turn, also contacted Fort, who allegedly assured petitioner that the school principal, Bill Querry, had been informed of the incidents. *Ibid.* Petitioner contends that, notwithstanding these reports, no disciplinary action was taken against G. F. *Id.*, ¶ ;16.

G. F.'s conduct allegedly continued for many months. In early February, G. F. purportedly placed a door stop in his pants and proceeded to act in a sexually suggestive manner toward LaShonda during physical education class. *Id.*, ¶ ;8. LaShonda reported G. F.'s behavior to her physical education teacher, Whit Maples. *Ibid.* Approximately one week later, G. F. again allegedly engaged in harassing behavior, this time while under the supervision of another classroom teacher, Joyce Pippin. *Id.*, ¶ ;9. Again, LaShonda allegedly reported the incident to the teacher, and again petitioner contacted the teacher to follow up. *Ibid.*

Petitioner alleges that G. F. once more directed sexually harassing conduct toward LaShonda in physical education class in early March, and that LaShonda reported the incident to both Maples and Pippen. *Id.*, ¶ ;10. In mid-April 1993, G. F. allegedly rubbed his body against LaShonda in the school hallway in what LaShonda considered a sexually suggestive manner, and LaShonda again reported the matter to Fort. *Id.*, ¶ ;11.

The string of incidents finally ended in mid-May, when G. F. was charged with, and pleaded guilty to, sexual battery for his misconduct. *Id.*, ¶ ;14. The complaint alleges that LaShonda had suffered during the months of harassment, however; specifically, her previously high grades allegedly dropped as she became unable to concentrate on her studies, *id.*, ¶ ;15, and, in April 1993, her father discovered that she had written a suicide note, *ibid.* The complaint further alleges that, at one point, LaShonda told petitioner that she " `didn't know how much longer she could keep [G. F.] off her.' " *Id.*, ¶ ;12.

Nor was LaShonda G. F.'s only victim; it is alleged that other girls in the class fell prey to G. F.'s conduct. *Id.*, ¶ ;16. At one point, in fact, a group composed of LaShonda and other female students tried to speak with Principal Querry about G. F.'s behavior. *Id.*, ¶ ;10. According to the complaint, however, a teacher denied the students' request with the statement, " `If [Querry] wants you, he'll call you.' " *Ibid.*

Petitioner alleges that no disciplinary action was taken in response to G. F.'s behavior toward LaShonda. *Id.*, ¶ ;16. In addition to her conversations with Fort and Pippen, petitioner alleges that she spoke with Principal Querry in mid-May 1993. When petitioner inquired as to what action the school intended to take against G. F., Querry simply stated, " `I guess I'll have to threaten him a little bit harder.' " *Id.*, ¶ ;12. Yet, petitioner alleges, at no point during the many months of his reported misconduct was G. F. disciplined for harassment. *Id.*, ¶ ;16. Indeed, Querry allegedly asked petitioner why LaShonda " `was the only one complaining.' " *Id.*, ¶ ;12.

Nor, according to the complaint, was any effort made to separate G. F. and LaShonda. *Id.*, ¶ ;16. On the contrary, notwithstanding LaShonda's frequent complaints, only after more than three months of reported harassment was she even permitted to change her classroom seat so that she was no longer seated next to G. F. *Id.*, ¶ ;13. Moreover, petitioner alleges that, at the time of the events in question, the Monroe County Board of Education (Board) had not instructed its personnel on how to respond to peer sexual harassment and had not established a policy on the issue. *Id.*, ¶ ;17.

Where, as here, the misconduct occurs during school hours and on school grounds--the bulk of G. F.'s misconduct, in fact, took place in the classroom--the misconduct is taking place "under" an "operation" of the funding recipient. See *Doe* v. *University of Illinois*, 138 F. 3d, at 661 (finding liability where school fails to respond properly to "student-on-student sexual harassment that takes place while the students are involved in school activities or otherwise under the supervision of school employees"). In these circumstances, the recipient retains substantial control over the context in which the harassment occurs. More importantly, however, in this setting the Board exercises significant control over the harasser. We have observed, for example, "that the nature of [the State's] power [over public schoolchildren] is custodial and tutelary, permitting a degree of supervision and control that could not be exercised over free adults." *Vernonia School Dist. 47J* v. *Acton*, 515 U. S. 646, 655 (1995). On more than one occasion, this Court has recognized the importance of school officials' "comprehensive authority . . . , consistent with fundamental constitutional safeguards, to prescribe and control conduct in the schools." *Tinker* v. *Des Moines Independent Community School Dist.*, 393 U. S. 503, 507 (1969); see also *New Jersey* v. *T. L. O.*, 469 U. S. 325, 342, n. 9 (1985) ("The maintenance of discipline in the schools requires not only that students be restrained from assaulting one another, abusing drugs and alcohol, and committing other crimes, but also that students conform themselves to the standards of conduct prescribed by school authorities"); 74 F. 3d, at 1193 ("The ability to control and influence behavior exists to an even greater extent in the classroom than in the workplace . . ."). The common law, too, recognizes the school's disciplinary authority. See Restatement (Second) of Torts §152 (1965). We thus conclude that recipients of federal funding may be liable for "subject[ing]" their students to discrimination where the recipient is deliberately indifferent to known acts of student-on-student sexual harassment and the harasser is under the school's disciplinary authority.

School administrators will continue to enjoy the flexibility they require so long as funding recipients are deemed "deliberately indifferent" to acts of student-on-student harassment only where the recipient's response to the harassment or lack thereof is clearly unreasonable in light of the known circumstances.

The most obvious example of student-on-student sexual harassment capable of triggering a damages claim would thus involve the overt, physical deprivation of access to school resources. Consider, for example, a case in which male students physically threaten their female peers every day, successfully preventing the female students from using a particular school resource--an athletic field or a computer lab, for instance. District administrators are well aware of the daily ritual, yet they deliberately ignore requests for aid from the female students wishing to use the resource. The district's knowing refusal to take any action in response to such behavior would fly in the face of Title IX's core principles, and such deliberate indifference may appropriately be subject to claims for monetary damages. It is not necessary, however, to show physical exclusion to demonstrate that students have been deprived by the actions of another student or students of an educational opportunity on the basis of sex. Rather, a plaintiff must establish sexual harassment of students that is so severe, pervasive, and objectively offensive, and that so undermines and detracts from the victims' educational experience, that the victim-students are effectively denied equal access to an institution's resources and opportunities. Cf. *Meritor Savings Bank, FSB* v. *Vinson,* 477 U. S., at 67.

Whether gender-oriented conduct rises to the level of actionable "harassment" thus "depends on a constellation of surrounding circumstances, expectations, and relationships," *Oncale* v. *Sundowner Offshore Services, Inc.*, 523 U. S. 75, 82 (1998), including, but not limited to, the ages of the harasser and the victim and the number of individuals involved, see OCR Title IX Guidelines 12041-12042. Courts, moreover, must bear in mind that schools are unlike the adult workplace and that children may regularly interact in a manner that would be unacceptable among adults. See, *e.g.*, Brief for National School Boards Association et al. as *Amici Curiae* 11 (describing "dizzying array of immature . . . behaviors by students"). Indeed, at least early on, students are still learning how to interact appropriately with their peers. It is thus understandable that, in the school setting, students often engage in insults, banter, teasing, shoving, pushing, and gender-specific conduct that is upsetting to the students subjected to it. Damages are not available for simple acts of teasing and name-calling among school children, however, even where these comments target differences in gender. Rather, in the context of student-on-student harassment, damages are available only where the behavior is so severe, pervasive, and objectively offensive that it denies its victims the equal access to education that Title IX is designed to protect.

C. RECOMMENDED READING

C. MacKinnon, *Sexual Harassment of Working Women* (Yale University Press: 1979)

L.Farley, *Sexual Shakedown: The Sexual Harassment of Women on the Job* (McGraw-Hill: 1978)

J. Mayer, *Strange Justice: The Selling of Clarence Thomas* (Houghton Mifflin: 1994)

D. Brock, *The Real Anita Hill: The Untold Story* (Free Press: 1993)

CHAPTER V
Violence Against Women

A. RAPE: WHOSE TRIAL IS THIS ANWAY?

Like all but a few criminal offenses, rape is prosecuted overwhelmingly as a state, rather than a federal, offense; accordingly, prosecutions take place in fifty (plus the District of Columbia and territories) different state court systems, under fifty different laws, passed by fifty different state legislatures. Rape and sexual assault defendants are presumed legally innocent until proven guilty beyond a reasonable doubt by a unanimous jury. As in criminal cases generally, persons charged with rape are entitled to the protections of the Fourth, Fifth, Sixth [notably the right to confront and cross-examine the victim], and Eighth Amendments, and all other constitutional rights. A violation of any of these is grounds for appellate reversal in the event of a conviction. If the defendant is acquitted at trial, the Fifth Amendment's Double Jeopardy Clause bars appeal or retrial. In addition to the double ordeal that a rape victim must endure – the trauma of both the rape itself and an ensuing public trial – the legal burden on the prosecution is substantially greater than that for a civil plaintiff in a discrimination action; the margin for error is exceedingly thin.

Much of the effort to reform rape laws has centered on an element of state rape statutes that is generally absent in criminal prosecutions: the requirement that the prosecution prove that the defendant acted without the victim's consent, and that force or threat of force was used. Two Maryland cases illustrate how appellate courts can give highly divergent interpretations to these requirements, even in cases involving the same statute. An innovative reform proposal, which attempts to balance a victim's right to sexual autonomy with a defendant's constitutional rights, follows.

State v. Rusk

424 A.2d 720 (Md. 1981)
Md. Court of Appeals

MURPHY, C.J.:

Edward Rusk was found guilty by a jury . . . of second degree rape in violation of Maryland Code Art. 27, §463(a)(1), which provides in pertinent part:

> A person is guilty of rape in the second degree if the person engages in vaginal intercourse with another person; . . .
>
> (1) By force or threat of force against the will and without the consent of the other person. . . .

On appeal, the Court of Special Appeals, sitting en banc, reversed the conviction; it concluded by an 8-5 majority that in view of the prevailing law as set forth in Hazel v. State, 157 A.2d 922 (Md. 1960), insufficient evidence of Rusk's guilt had been adduced at the trial to permit the case to go to the jury. We granted certiorari to consider whether the Court of Special Appeals properly applied the principles of *Hazel*. . . .

At the trial, the 21-year-old prosecuting witness, Pat, testified that on the evening of September 21, 1977, she attended a high school alumnae meeting where she met a girl friend, Terry. After the meeting, Terry and Pat agreed to drive in their respective cars to Fells Point to have a few drinks. . . .

. . . They went to a bar where . . . Rusk approached and said "hello" to Terry. Terry, who was then conversing with another individual, momentarily interrupted her conversation and said "Hi, Eddie." Rusk then began talking with Pat and during their conversation both of them acknowledged being separated from their respective spouses and having a child. Pat told Rusk that she had to go home . . . [and] Rusk requested a ride to his apartment. Although Pat did not know Rusk, she thought that Terry knew him. She thereafter agreed to give him a ride. Pat cautioned Rusk on the way to the car that "I'm just giving a ride home, you know, as a friend, not anything to be, you know, thought of other than a ride,". . .

. . . After a twenty-minute drive, they arrived at Rusk's apartment. . . . Pat testified that she was totally unfamiliar with the neighborhood. She parked the car at the curb . . . but left the engine running. Rusk asked Pat to come in, but she refused. . . . Pat said that Rusk was fully aware that she did not want to accompany him to his room. Notwithstanding her repeated refusals, Pat testified that Rusk reached over and turned off the ignition to her car and took her car keys. He got out of the car, walked over to her side, opened the door and said, "Now, will you come up?" Pat explained her subsequent actions:

> . . . At that point, because I was scared, because he had my car keys. I didn't know what to do. I was someplace I didn't even know where I was. It was in the city. I didn't know whether to run. I really didn't think at that point, what to do.
>
> Now, I know that I should have blown the horn. I should have run. There were a million things I could have done. I was scared, at that point, and I didn't do any of them.

Pat testified that at this moment she feared that Rusk would rape her. She said: "[I]t was the way he looked at me, and said 'Come on up, come on up'; and when he took the keys, I knew that was wrong."

It was then about 1 A.M. Pat accompanied Rusk across the street into a totally dark house. . . . Rusk unlocked the door to his one-room apartment, and turned on the light. According to Pat, he told her to sit down. She sat in a chair beside the bed. Rusk sat on the bed. After Rusk talked for a few minutes, he left the room for about one to five minutes. Pat remained seated in the chair. She made no noise and did not attempt to leave. She said that she did not notice a telephone in the room. When Rusk returned, he turned off the light and sat down on the bed. Pat asked if she could leave; she told him that she wanted to go home and "didn't want to come up." She said, "Now, (that) I came up, can I go?" Rusk, who was still in possession of her car keys, said he wanted her to stay.

Rusk then asked Pat to get on the bed with him. He pulled her by the arms to the bed and began to undress her. . . . Pat removed the rest of her clothing, and then removed Rusk's pants because "he asked me to do it." After they were both undressed Rusk started kissing Pat as she was lying on her back. Pat explained what happened next:

> I was still begging him to please let, you know, let me leave. I said, "you can get a lot of other girls down there, for what you want," and he just kept saying, "no"; and then I was really scared, because I can't describe, you know, what was said. It was more the look in his eyes; and I said, at that point I didn't know what to say; and I said, "If I do what you want, will you let me go without killing me?" Because I didn't know, at that point, what he was going to do; and I started to cry; and when I did, he put his hands on my throat, and started lightly to choke me; and I said, "If I do what you want, will you let me go?" And he said, yes, and at that time, I proceeded to do what he wanted me to.

Pat testified that Rusk made her perform oral sex and then vaginal intercourse.

Immediately after the intercourse, Pat asked if she could leave. She testified that Rusk said, "Yes," after which she got up and got dressed and Rusk returned her car keys. She said that Rusk then "walked me to my car, and asked if he could see me again; and I said, 'Yes'; and he asked me for my telephone number; and I said, 'No, I'll see you down Fells Point sometime,' just so I could leave." Pat testified that she "had no intention of meeting him again." She asked him for directions out of the neighborhood and left.

. . . As she sat in her car reflecting on the incident, Pat said she began to "wonder what would happen if I hadn't of done what he wanted me to do. So I thought the right thing to do was to go report it, and I went from there to Hillendale to find a police car." She reported the incident to the police at about 3:15 A.M. . . .

Rusk and two of his friends, Michael Trimp and David Carroll, testified on his behalf. According to Trimp, they went in Carroll's car to Buggs' bar to dance, drink and "tr(y) to pick up some ladies." Rusk stayed at the bar, while the others went to get something to eat.

Trimp and Carroll next saw Rusk walking down the street arm-in-arm with a lady whom Trimp was unable to identify. . . .

Carroll's testimony corroborated Trimp's. He saw Rusk walking down the street arm-in-arm with a woman. He said "(s)he was kind of like, you know, snuggling up to him like. . . . She was hanging all over him then." Carroll was fairly certain that Pat was the woman who was with Rusk. . . .

According to Rusk, when they arrived in front of his apartment Pat parked the car and turned the engine off. They sat for several minutes "petting each other."... Rusk testified that Pat came willingly to his room and that at no time did he make threatening facial expressions.... Rusk explained that after the intercourse, Pat "got uptight."

> Well, she started to cry. She said that she said, "You guys are all alike," she says, "just out for," you know, "one thing."... And she said, that she just wanted to leave; and I said, "Well, okay;" and she walked out to the car. I walked out to the car. She got in the car and left.

Rusk denied placing his hands on Pat's throat or attempting to strangle her. He also denied using force or threats of force to get Pat to have intercourse with him.

In reversing Rusk's second degree rape conviction, the Court of Special Appeals, quoting from *Hazel*, noted that:

> Force is an essential element of the crime [of rape] and to justify a conviction, the evidence must warrant a conclusion either that the victim resisted and her resistance was overcome by force or that she was prevented from resisting by threats to her safety.

Writing for the majority, Judge Thompson said:

> In all of the victim's testimony we have been unable to see any resistance on her part to the sex acts and certainly can we see no fear as would overcome her attempt to resist or escape as required by *Hazel*. Possession of the keys by the accused may have deterred her vehicular escape but hardly a departure seeking help in the rooming house or in the street. We must say that "the way he looked" fails utterly to support the fear required by *Hazel*.

... Of course, due process requirements mandate that a criminal conviction not be obtained if the evidence does not reasonably support a finding of guilt beyond a reasonable doubt. However, as the Supreme Court made clear in Jackson v. Virginia, 443 U.S. 307 (1979), the reviewing court does not ask itself whether *it* believes that the evidence established guilt beyond a reasonable doubt; rather, the applicable standard is "whether, after viewing the evidence in the light most favorable to the prosecution, *any* rational trier of fact could have found the essential elements of the crime beyond a reasonable doubt." (emphasis in original)....

The Court [in *Hazel*] noted that lack of consent is generally established through proof of resistance or by proof that the victim failed to resist because of fear. The degree of fear necessary to obviate the need to prove resistance, and thereby establish lack of consent, was defined in the following manner:

> The kind of fear which would render resistance by a woman unnecessary to support a conviction of rape includes, but is not necessarily limited to, a fear of death or serious bodily harm, or a fear so extreme as to preclude resistance, or a fear which would well nigh render her mind incapable of continuing to resist, or a fear that so overpowers her that she does not dare resist.

We think the reversal of Rusk's conviction by the Court of Special Appeals was in error for the fundamental reason so well expressed in the dissenting opinion by Judge Wilner when he observed that the majority had "trampled upon the first principle of appellate restraint . . . (because it had) substituted (its) own view of the evidence (and the inferences that may fairly be drawn from it) for that of the judge and jury . . . (and had thereby) improperly invaded the province allotted to those tribunals." In view of the evidence adduced at the trial, the reasonableness of Pat's apprehension of fear was plainly a question of fact for the jury to determine. . . . Quite obviously, the jury disbelieved Rusk and believed Pat's testimony. From her testimony, the jury could have reasonably concluded that the taking of her car keys was intended by Rusk to immobilize her alone, late at night, in a neighborhood with which she was not familiar; that after Pat had repeatedly refused to enter his apartment, Rusk commanded in firm tones that she do so; that Pat was badly frightened and feared that Rusk intended to rape her; . . . that Pat was afraid that Rusk would kill her unless she submitted; that she began to cry and Rusk then put his hands on her throat and began "lightly to choke" her; that Pat asked him if he would let her go without killing her if she complied with his demands; that Rusk gave an affirmative response, after which she finally submitted.

Just where persuasion ends and force begins in cases like the present is essentially a factual issue. . . . Considering all of the evidence in the case, with particular focus upon the actual force applied by Rusk to Pat's neck, we conclude that the jury could rationally find that the essential elements of second degree rape had been established and that Rusk was guilty of that offense beyond a reasonable doubt.[9] . . .

GOLDBERG v. MARYLAND

Court of Special Appeals of Maryland, 1979.
41 Md.App. 58, 395 A.2d 1213.

On October 18, 1977, Randy Jay Goldberg, the appellant, was found guilty by a jury in the Circuit Court for Baltimore County, of rape in the second degree. The appellant was sentenced to a five year term, of which the first two years were to be served in a work release program at the jail and the remaining three years on probation.

* * *

The eighteen year old prosecuting witness was a high school senior who worked part-time as a sales clerk in the Merry-Go-Round clothing store at Towson Plaza. Around 1:00 P.M., on August 10, 1977, she was at work when the appellant, aged twenty-five, entered the store. The prosecuting witness started out trying to sell the appellant clothing but ended up being sold a story by the appellant that he was a free-lance agent and thought she was an excellent prospect to become a successful model. They arranged to meet at 5 o'clock when she got off from work.

When the appellant returned for her at 5:00 P.M., she asked him for "any ID to show me if you are who you say you are". He showed her his driving license with his picture on it. This satisfied her: "Well, I figured that he wouldn't ... if he was planning to harm me in any way ... wouldn't give his name like that, and I figured that, you know, he was who he said he was. I believed him". Despite some cautioning from her employer she drove off with the appellant at 5:10 P.M. in a silver-grey Cadillac Eldorado. The appellant was actually a student at Catonsville Community College and the car belonged to his mother. Appellant told her he was taking her to "a temporary studio" in the Pikesville area. When the "studio" was found to be closed, they drove to a condominium building on Slade Avenue. Upon arrival there she stayed in the car while appellant went inside. Shortly, he returned to the car and told her he had contacted a friend who said they could use his house for his "studio". When they arrived at the friend's house, she helped appellant find a door that was open. The door led to the kitchen which she described as "very dirty" and she "didn't, you know, understand why we were coming here". From the kitchen they walked into the bedroom which by contrast she described as being "really made up really nice" with "a queen sized bed, real big bed, with a red velvet bedspread, and a big backboard on the back." She was "pretty impressed by the room".

Soon after they entered the bedroom, appellant "motioned" her to sit beside him on the bed. Instead, she sat on a chair at the foot of the bed. Appellant then said it was hot in the room and took his shirt off. When asked her reaction to appellant's removing his shirt she responded: "He told me he was hot, so I figured—so I figured he was hot". She then stood up and appellant "came over to me and he started unbuttoning my blouse. He said this is what I want you to do". She pulled her blouse together and said "no". Asked to describe what happened next she said:

> "He just kept on smooth-talking me and saying I won't hurt you. This is what I do to all the models that I interview. And he, you know, started motioning me to take my blouse off and everything, and then I went through the same thing with every piece of clothing. It was like, you know, kept on trying to tell me to take it off, and I didn't want to. And he kept on trying to convince me that—he was still trying to convince me that this was this modeling job, and I knew that it wasn't any more."

She said she removed her clothes because she "was really scared of him". "There was nothing I could do". When asked what caused her fright she said: "Because he was—he was so much bigger than I was, and, you know, I was in a room alone with him, and there was nothing, no buildings around us, or anything, and I mean wouldn't helped if I wouldn't—help me if I didn't. It was like being trapped or something". On cross-examination she said she was "afraid" she was "going to be killed".

After her clothes were removed, the appellant "pushed" her down on the bed and tried "to move [her legs] in different ways, and [she] kept pulling them together, and telling him that [she] didn't want to do it, and just wanted to go home". He kept telling her that he wouldn't hurt her "and just to relax". But she was "just really scared" and she was "shaking and my voice was really shaking" and she "kept on telling him [she] wanted to go home", and that "[she] didn't want to do this"; that she "didn't want to be a model, and [she] didn't want to do it any more. Just to let [her] alone". When asked, "And what was his reaction?", she testified as follows:

"A. He was just—he was just really cool about the whole thing, telling me not to worry, and he wouldn't hurt me, and to relax.

Q. All right. Now, after you were on the bed, and he was moving your legs around, what, if anything, occurred next?

A. Well, he kept on trying to make me get in different positions, and kept on telling me to look sexual or something like that. I don't know what the word was.

Q. All right. And what, if anything, occurred after he said that?

A. He laid me down and placed his hands on my vagina and told me he was doing that to make me relax. I told him that it didn't make me relax.

Q. All right. Then what happened after he placed his hands on your vagina?

A. He went into the other room, and I couldn't see him. He wasn't facing me, and had his back to me, and his hands down by his belt buckle. And I realized what he was doing, and I jumped up and grabbed my clothes and started putting them on. Then he came in and pulled them away from me and said no.

Q. What did he say?

A. He said don't worry. What are you doing that for? I am not going to hurt you, and he kept telling me just to relax, and not to be nervous. And he laid me down on the bed and tried to get me to do that stuff again, and I told him I didn't want to do that.

Q. What happened then?

A. And then he put his arms up on my stomach and his torso was in between my legs. He said just take your time; take a deep breath. And then he moved up on me and placed his penis in my vagina.

Q. What were you doing when this occurred?

A. I squeezed my legs together and got really tense, and I just started crying real hard. And I told him not to do that to me.

Q. And what was his response?

A. He didn't say anything. Just stayed there. And then I felt him move.

Q. How long was he on top of you?

A. Not very long.

Q. How long was he moving?

A. I guess for about two minutes, and then I felt him. Just for about two minutes.

Q. Did the Defendant ejaculate to your knowledge?

A. Yes, I think he did.

Q. Now, what, if anything, occurred after the Defendant ejaculated?

A. He got up and he said that if I can't enjoy it, then he can't enjoy it."

The appellant then asked her to go to dinner with him but she declined and he drove her to her home where she lived with her parents. On the way home, the appellant gave her his telephone number which she wrote down on a piece of paper. At his request she gave him her telephone number by writing it on a piece of paper with her lipstick. Although she told him she "would never see him again", she said she gave him her correct telephone number because she "didn't want to get him suspicious of me". They had a "general conversation about sex" in which he told her that "girls act like they don't want to, but they really do". She told him that he "had the wrong impression of [her]"; that she "didn't want him to do that". She further testified, somewhat inconsistently as follows:

> "I told him I didn't want that. I told him I didn't like him doing that to me, and didn't let him. I didn't make him think that I enjoyed all of it, and that I ever wanted to do it again, because I know I would never do it again. Never. I know I would never get near him again."

The appellant let her off at her home at 6:25 P.M., 1¼ hours after she left her place of employment with him at 5:10 P.M. Before the appellant drove off she told him to "drive home safely . . . I guess I was being more sarcastic than anything". She estimated that they had been at the house where the alleged rape took place for 30 minutes.

When she arrived inside her house she "walked straight past my parents" to her upstairs room. She said nothing to them because she was "just scared, nervous, just you know, I wanted to go upstairs and just clean myself up and just forget, you know, about it. Just think". After cleaning herself and using a contraceptive, she called her boyfriend on the telephone and talked to him for "about three minutes". She did not tell him "what happened" because she "didn't know how he would take it". She then called her girlfriend and told her that she "had a problem, and that I was raped today. . . ." She did not relate the details of the "rape". She told her girlfriend not to tell anybody and not to tell her girlfriend's boyfriend, "but she told him anyways". She contemplated calling the police but said she "didn't know who to call", so she called her girlfriend back and asked what she should do. Shortly thereafter the girlfriend and the girlfriend's boyfriend came to her house and after picking up her own boyfriend the four young people eventually went to the police station where the "rape" was reported at approximately 9:00 P.M. According to the girlfriend, the prosecuting witness did not want to report the matter but "[w]e convinced her into going to the police".

After reporting the incident the prosecuting witness was taken to the Greater Baltimore Medical Center for a physical examination. The examining physician's "Impression" was "Recent sexual intercourse", but he found "no evidence of recent trauma" to any part of her body, including the "perineal and genital" areas.

Testifying in his own behalf, the appellant admitted having sexual relations with the prosecuting witness at the time and place alleged, but maintained that it was mutually consensual and that the prosecuting witness did not appear to be frightened at any time.

Prior to 1976, the Maryland rape statute was primarily a sentencing law, fixing the penalties without actually defining the crime. The common law definition of rape that has been applied in Maryland is: "the act of a man having unlawful carnal knowledge of a female over the age of ten years by force without the consent and against the will of the victim".

By Chapter 573 of the Laws of 1976, effective July 1, 1976, the Legislature * * * [has provided that:]

> "A person is guilty of rape in the second degree if the person engages in vaginal intercourse with another person: (1) By force or threat of force against the will and without the consent of the other person . . . ."

* * *

The terms "force," "threat of force," "against the will" and "without the consent" are not defined by the 1976 Act. We therefore look to the "judicially determined meaning" of these elements of the common law crime of rape. In doing so, we conclude that the evidence was legally insufficient to sustain the conviction and the judgment will be reversed. We reach this conclusion because on the record before us, viewing the evidence in the light most favorable to the State, we find legally insufficient evidence of the requisite element of "force or threat of force".

There was certainly no "threat of force". On the contrary, the prosecuting witness on numerous occasions in her testimony negated that element. As to actual force, the only arguable evidence is the prosecuting witness' testimony that after she herself had removed all her clothes, the appellant put his hands on her shoulders and "pushed" her down on the bed. This is negated, however, by her further testimony on cross-examination that "he didn't push but guided [her] on the bed". She admitted that she was not "injured or anything" by the encounter. This, of course, is consistent with the findings of the physician who subsequently examined her. Those findings so far as they relate to the use of any actual force were completely negative. But *actual physical* force is not an indispensable element of the crime of rape.

As said by the Court of Appeals:

> "Force is an essential element of the crime and to justify a conviction, the evidence must warrant a conclusion either that the victim resisted and her resistance was overcome by force *or that she was prevented from resisting by threats to her safety.* But no particular amount of force, either actual or constructive, is required to constitute rape. Necessarily that fact must depend upon the prevailing circumstances.... [F]orce may exist without violence. If the acts and threats of the defendant were reasonably calculated to create in the mind of the victim—having regard to the circumstances in which she was placed—a real apprehension, due to fear, of imminent bodily harm, serious enough to impair or overcome her will to resist, then such acts and threats are the equivalent of force." * * *

Since resistance is necessarily relative, the presence or absence of it must depend on the facts and circumstances in each case. But the real test, which must be recognized in all cases, is whether the assault was committed without the consent and against the will of the prosecuting witness.

we hold that the evidence is legally insufficient to warrant a finding by the jury that the prosecutrix exerted the necessary degree of resistance that was overcome by force or that she was prevented from resisting by fear based upon reasonable apprehension of bodily harm.

The State argues that the "totality of [the] circumstances" caused the prosecutrix's fear of being killed and that the fear was a reasonable fear, thus rendering more resistance than that exerted by her unnecessary. First of all, we find nothing in the record evidencing any real resistance by the prosecutrix to anything the appellant said or did. It is true that she *told* the appellant she "didn't want to do that [stuff]". But the resistance that must be shown involves not merely verbal but *physical* resistance "to the extent of her ability at the time". The State points to her testimony that when penetration occurred she "squeezed [her] legs together and got really tense". Assuming that this was evidence of her reluctance, even unwillingness, to engage in vaginal intercourse, it was not evidence that she resisted "to the extent of her ability" *before* the intercourse occurred.

We are left therefore with the question of whether the prosecutrix's lack of resistance was caused by fear based upon reasonable apprehension of physical harm. We find no legally sufficient evidence warranting an affirmative answer to that question. As we said [in an earlier case]: ". . . [W]here the victim's story could not be corroborated by wounds, bruises or disordered clothing, the lack of consent could be shown by fear based upon reasonable apprehension." * * *

On the record before us, we find the evidence legally insufficient to warrant a conclusion that the appellant's words or actions "were reasonably calculated to create in the mind of the victim" a reasonable fear that if she had resisted he would have harmed her, or that, faced with such resistance, he would have used force to overcome it. The prosecutrix swore that the reasons for her fear of being killed if she did not accede to appellant's advances were two-fold: 1) she was alone with the appellant in a house with no buildings close by and no one to help her if she resisted, and 2) the appellant was much larger than she was. In the complete absence of any threatening words or actions by the appellant, these two factors, as a matter of law, are simply not enough to have created a reasonable fear of harm so as to preclude resistance and be "the equivalent of force". Without proof of force, actual or constructive, evidenced by words or conduct of the defendant or those acting in consort with him, sexual intercourse is not rape. This is so even though the intercourse may have occurred without the actual consent and against the actual will of the alleged victim.

UNWANTED SEX

by

STEPHEN SCHULHOFER
Stephen Schulhofer ("Unwanted Sex") is the Julius Kreeger Professor of Law and Criminology at the University of Chicago.

THE ATLANTIC MONTHLY · OCTOBER 1998

The law protects our property, labor, privacy, and other fundamental interests, but sexual autonomy—the right to choose whether and when to be sexually intimate with another person—is too often ignored

A YOUNG Illinois woman stopped to rest while biking along an isolated reservoir near the town of Carbondale. A stranger approached and struck up a conversation. After chatting with him for a few minutes, she got on her bicycle and started to leave. At that point the man, Joel Warren, put his hand on her shoulder. When she said, "No, I have to go now," he replied, "This will only take a minute. My girlfriend doesn't meet my needs." He added, "I don't want to hurt you."

Perhaps Warren only meant "We'll both enjoy this." But to the woman his comment sounded ominous, a hint of what he might do if she resisted him. In any event she had little time to consider nuances. Warren quickly lifted her up and carried her into the woods. He was six feet three inches tall and weighed 185 pounds. With no one else in sight, the young woman, who was only five feet two and weighed 100 pounds, did not attempt to scream or fight back, actions that she feared might prompt him to start choking or beating her. Once Warren had her hidden from view, he pulled off her pants, pushed up her shirt to expose her breasts, and subjected her to several acts of oral sex.

The police eventually identified Warren, prosecutors charged him with sexual assault, and a jury found him guilty. Yet an Illinois court set aside the conviction, saying that "the record is devoid of any attendant circumstances which suggest that complainant was compelled to submit." The year was 1983, but the court's approach remains very much with us.

Despite decades of public discussion and numerous statutory reforms before and since decisions like this one, the problem of defining and protecting our sexual boundaries has not been solved. The reasons are many. Sometimes statutes are highly protective but ineffectively enforced. Whatever the law may say, jurors often assume that it is neither abnormal nor harmful for a man to make aggressive physical advances to a silent, passive, or openly reluctant woman—literally to sweep her off her feet, pull off her clothes, and penetrate her, all without any explicit indication of her consent. Some jurors assume that women who submit to these advances really want the sexual contact, that they could easily resist if they didn't, or that it would be unfair to punish a man who, after all, was only doing what (so they may think) nature intended.

But attitudes like these are no longer universal. Our sexual culture has changed. Prosecutors sometimes file charges and juries sometimes convict in cases that would have been laughed out of court twenty or thirty years ago. Yet the law itself continues to pose obstacles, blocking enforcement and denying remedies even when juries are prepared to condemn defendants' conduct as outrageous. With its many gaps and limits, the law even tends to validate and reinforce the strands within our culture that persist in seeing aggressive male sexuality as a biological given that poses no problems. Outmoded standards are especially evident in criminal law, but other remedies have many of the same failings.

Criminal law's most obvious weak spot is its continuing vagueness—a surprise after all the effort devoted to reform.

Rape law's most obvious weak spot is its continuing vagueness — a surprise after all the effort devoted to reform. This vagueness deters prosecutors from pursuing charges. And where criminal law is murky, the benefit of doubt usually goes to the defendant.

Standards remain extraordinarily murky, especially for determining when a man's behavior amounts to prohibited force or when a woman's conduct signals her consent. And where criminal law is murky, the benefit of the doubt usually goes to the defendant, in theory and often in practice. Acquittal rates are not noticeably lower for rape than they are for other serious felonies, but vague standards take their toll in other ways—deterring prosecutors from pursuing charges and deterring victims from filing complaints.

The number of cases affected is difficult to estimate, but a 1992 survey by researchers at the University of Chicago provides a chilling perspective on the problem. The survey found that 22 percent of American women felt they had been forced to have sex, yet only three percent of American men said they had ever forced a woman to have sex. After discounting the possibility that the men or the women had lied, or that a few men were responsible for forcing many different women, the researchers concluded that most of the men simply did not realize that their sexual partners were unwilling. The researchers wrote, "There seems to be not just a gender gap but a gender chasm in perceptions of when sex was forced."

But criminal-law rules are sometimes quite clear—especially when they *exclude* certain kinds of abuse. In the fall of 1988 a young Montana woman wrote an alarming letter to her school board. She claimed that two years earlier, during her senior year in high school, the school's principal had forced her to submit to intercourse by threatening to block her graduation. After an investigation by the county prosecutor, the principal was charged with two acts of "sexual intercourse without consent," a felony under Montana law.

Like many other cases of rape, indecent assault, or sexual harassment, the Montana case bristled with credibility questions. But the Montana Supreme Court decided that the victim's story, even if true, could not support criminal charges. In Montana, as in most states, a sexual-assault charge normally requires proof that the abuser used physical force or threatened the victim with physical injury. Submission to avoid other kinds of harm is not enough to meet the statutory requirement of intercourse "without consent." The court itself was appalled by the narrow scope of the statute. The judges dismissed the case "with a good deal of reluctance," noting their "strong condemnation of the alleged acts," and adding, "If we could rewrite the statutes to [punish] the alleged acts . . . we would willingly do so."

In a situation like the one in Montana, the victim has a hard choice to make. An exceptionally self-possessed young woman might just tell her principal to get lost. But if she submits to the man's sexual demands, then as far as criminal law is concerned, she has consented.

Rape laws have moved far since the days when women were required to resist "to the utmost." Today "reasonable" resistance is supposed to be sufficient. In the more progressive states no resistance is required at all. But in nearly all states intimidation short of physical threats is still treated as if it were mere "persuasion." When it succeeds, courts will usually say that the victim "consented."

We have all heard of cases in which the police, judge, or jury refused to believe that a woman's "no" really meant no. But the problems run deeper: even when jurors are convinced that a woman was unwilling, unwillingness is not enough. In the face of clearly expressed objections, intercourse is still not considered rape or any other form of felonious assault unless the assailant used physical force or threatened bodily injury. And the law's definition of physical force remains extremely strict. The physical acts of lifting a woman up or pushing her onto a bed and accomplishing sexual penetration usually aren't enough. The "force" must be something beyond the acts involved in intercourse—something that physically "compels" the woman to submit.

Because nearly all states require proof of physical force in prosecutions for rape or sexual assault, many serious abuses are classified as "nonviolent" and penal sanctions are assumed to be inappropriate. The abuses are not really nonviolent, of course. It is more accurate to say that they don't involve what the law regards as the *required kind* of force. The force they do involve is seen as normal and therefore permissible.

When men use only the "right kind" of force, prosecutors seldom bother to file charges. But sometimes such cases are brought to court, often because of an aggravating element such as the youth of the victim. When prosecutors bring these cases, judges usually take the occasion to remind them that the force requirement will be strictly observed.

In a 1982 Mississippi case a fourteen-year-old girl I will call Sally was visiting her married sister, Elizabeth, who had recently separated from her husband, Dennis McQueen. One day Dennis stopped by Elizabeth's house and asked to take their two-year-old baby for a ride in his truck. Elizabeth did not want to leave Dennis alone with the baby, so she asked Sally to go along. When they returned, Sally was shaking and crying. She told her sister that Dennis had pulled off onto a deserted road and told her to get out of the truck. He told her to take off her clothes, lie down on the front seat, and put her legs up on his shoulders. Sally explained that she was scared of him because he had been drinking, and was afraid he was going to hurt her. She said she complied, crying throughout, as Dennis penetrated her and quickly had intercourse.

Because Mississippi then set the age of consent for intercourse at fourteen, Dennis McQueen was not charged with statutory rape. He was prosecuted for forcible rape, and the jury found him guilty. But the Mississippi Supreme Court set aside the conviction, because McQueen "did not threaten to injure [Sally], did not forcibly remove her from the truck, did not remove her clothes, and did not forcibly make her lie down in the truck." In 1992 an Ohio court reversed a similar conviction, invoking the same principle: no proof of physical force.

When the victim is only fourteen, most states would be able to charge a man like McQueen with statutory rape. Earlier this year Mississippi raised its age of consent—to sixteen. But when a young woman reaches the age of sixteen, or in some states eighteen, statutory-rape charges are no longer possible; the man is likely to escape any criminal sanction.

The narrow scope of contemporary criminal law becomes especially significant when a woman confronts sexual pressure from a man who holds professional power over her. Women face recurrent sexual demands from teachers, job supervisors, psychotherapists, doctors, and lawyers who misuse their authority to compel sexual submission. The best available estimates suggest that each year roughly a million working women are pressured to have sex with their job supervisors, and thousands (probably hundreds of thousands) of college women face unwanted sexual demands from their professors. Thousands more women submit each year to unwanted sex with their psychotherapists and physicians. Yet rape law offers no help in these situations, because the tactics the men use, though sometimes flagrantly coercive, are not physically violent. And civil suits, along with administrative penalties, often prove ineffective as well. Men who abuse their status or professional authority to coerce sexual compliance often face no significant sanctions.

Karen (not her real name), the mother of three children, sought legal help to escape a troubled marriage. She hired a lawyer and paid him a $2,500 retainer. Later, distraught and insecure, she went to see him to discuss her case. He locked his office door, unzipped his pants, and asked her for oral sex. Convinced that he would drop her case and abandon her if she refused, Karen complied, and on two later occasions she submitted to his demands for intercourse. After several months she could no longer cope with the lawyer's sexual demands. She fired him and sued for malpractice. But in a 1990 decision an Illinois court said that she had no case, even if the lawyer had exploited her vulnerability and used his professional position to coerce her consent. The court ruled that lawyers can be held accountable for malpractice only when their misconduct has an adverse effect on their clients' *legal* problems. Emotional harm from coerced submission to repugnant sexual demands was, the court said, "insufficient"; the woman had no case because she "did not claim that her legal position in the divorce proceedings was harmed."

Alcohol can add another dimension to the problem. A widely reported 1996 trial involved a woman in upstate New York who had been drinking heavily on a date and passed out in a restaurant bathroom. Her date, waiting for her outside, fell asleep in his pickup truck. Meanwhile, five men carried the woman from the bathroom to a booth, where they undressed her. All five then allegedly raped her, left her in the booth, and returned to their beer and sandwiches.

The five men admitted the acts of intercourse, pleaded guilty to minor misdemeanor charges, and were fined $840 each. But after a political uproar over the leniency of the sentences, a special prosecutor managed to get the guilty pleas set aside and brought the first of the defendants to trial on felony rape charges. At the trial, *The New York Times* reported, the man's lawyer argued that "if the woman had consumed enough alcohol to be helpless, as she testified, then she could not be sure that she had not consented to sex." He didn't say, of course, that the men should be sure that she *had* consented. Genuine willingness on the part of the woman simply isn't required. The jury acquitted the man.

Criminal-law reforms often leave a false impression. For example, resistance requirements have supposedly been restricted or abolished. But when a woman says no, clearly and insistently, a man can still roll on top of her, remove her clothes, and penetrate her, all without committing rape. The obstacle in such a case is not conflicting versions of the truth or questions of credibility. The man can admit to the facts, more or less with impunity. His conduct remains perfectly legal, because he has not used what the law calls force—that is, physical power *in addition to* the force that may be intrinsic to intercourse.

The upshot is that resistance requirements remain in effect even where the law says they have been abolished. A woman's right to bodily integrity and sexual autonomy—her right to sexual choice—simply does not exist until she begins to scream or fight back physically.

Sexual-harassment suits provide an alternative for women who are coerced by tactics that stop short of physical force. It would be natural to assume that sexual-harassment laws fill the gap left by criminal law's strict force requirement, because these laws are so often portrayed as exceedingly restrictive. Vocal critics of these laws imply that they impose draconian sanctions on any man who dares to use off-color language or express the slightest hint of sexual interest in the presence of an exceptionally sensitive woman. In fact sexual-harassment laws do nothing of the kind. On the contrary, they remain limited in their coverage and effectiveness.

With few exceptions, sexual-harassment laws, state and federal, extend protection only to employees and students. They are no help at all when a patient is pressured for sex by her doctor or when a client in a divorce proceeding is coerced by a lawyer who threatens to stop working on her case if she won't meet his sexual demands.

Even in the workplace, sexual-harassment laws are at best only partly effective. The laws apply if a supervisor or a professor is stupid enough to tell a woman that he will hurt her career unless she submits to him. But sexual-harassment laws often ignore the pressure that lurks beneath the surface of sexual demands from a professor or a job supervisor. And even when an explicit threat can be proved, remedies are limited. The law permits civil damage suits against universities and companies, and such suits are often well publicized. What is less well known is that even when clear abuses are committed, the offender isn't personally liable for damages; sexual-harassment penalties apply only against the university or the business as an entity.

A series of Supreme Court decisions last spring made clear that women subjected to sexual harassment can sue even when they have not been fired or denied a promotion. But at the same time the Court created new defenses that will permit many corporations and school districts to escape responsibility for harassment by their employees, and it left in place the rule that the employees themselves are not personally liable. President Bill Clinton's position in the Paula Jones suit is an exception, because a public official can be sued personally, under a separate set of federal laws, if he or she uses governmental power to violate a citizen's civil rights. However, the ordinary supervisor or teacher who uses his position to gain sexual favors usually incurs no civil or criminal liability, even for acts blatantly interfering with the sexual autonomy of a subordinate.

THIS gap in the law is puzzling, but not simple to fill. It is a daunting task to define, clearly and specifically, what an appropriate system for protection of sexual autonomy should look like. It is not easy to set the boundaries for permissible conduct when positions of authority, threats, promises, alcohol, and abuses of trust have some effect on sexual interaction.

A prison guard's power clearly prevents an inmate from choosing freely whether to accept or refuse a sexual proposal, but do we say the same about a college professor and a nineteen-year-old student taking his course? Do we say the same about a corporate vice-president and a junior executive working in another division? There are problems in such relationships, to be sure. But if sexual interaction is ruled legally out of bounds every time one of the parties has any possible source of power over the other, our opportunities to find companionship and sexual intimacy will shrink drastically. To create a legal barrier to every relationship not formed on the purely neutral ground of the singles bar or the church social would be pathetic and absurd.

A woman too drunk to stand up should not be expected to resist physically or to protest explicitly—even if she downed all the drinks of her own accord and knew exactly what was in them. But do we say the same about a woman who has had just two or three drinks? Should we conclude that a woman's consent is invalid if she said "yes" because she was feeling relaxed and uninhibited after drinking a glass of wine? The law's willingness to find consent in cases of severe alcohol impairment should be considered intolerable, but a standard suggesting that rape occurred whenever alcohol played a part in sexual consent would be intolerable as well.

Respect for sexual autonomy requires safeguards against abuse and exploitation. But—equally important—it requires that the law protect our freedom to seek emotional intimacy and sexual fulfillment with willing partners. Despite decades of discussion and years of ambitious feminist reforms, adequate protection of sexuality remains elusive, in part because freedom from unwanted sex and the freedom to seek mutually desired sex sometimes seem to be in tension. A workable notion of sexual autonomy appears to require compromises and balancing—the kind of chore that lawyers and academics often regard as a technical problem of "line-drawing." But the problem is neither simple nor unimportant. What is at stake is nothing less than women's bodily security and every person's right to control the boundaries of his or her own sexual experience.

KNOWING CONSENT WHEN WE SEE IT

INTERCOURSE often "happens" after voluntary hugging, kissing, and sexual touching, without coercive threats but also without either of the parties ever saying "Yes, let's agree to have sex now." In one of the most frequent scenarios the woman remains silent and relatively passive; she may even push the man's hands away several times or say "No, don't." Traditional rape laws permit a defense of "consent," but they don't say what consent is.

For many, the often-heard feminist view—that "no" means no—now seems obvious and uninteresting. In fact it is neither. By repeating the mantra "'no' means no," anti-rape activists have sensitized many men and made some progress in changing assumptions about how women express interest in sex. But beneath the surface, in the messy, emotionally ambiguous real world of dating, petting, and sexual exploration, "no" doesn't always mean no.

A 1988 survey of undergraduates at Texas A & M University presents a detailed look at this problem. More than 600 women were asked whether they had ever engaged in acts of token resistance when they really wanted to have sex. Thirty-nine percent of the women reported that they sometimes said no even though they "had every intention to and were willing to engage in sexual intercourse." Of the sexually experienced women, 61 percent said that they had done so. Though these women were willing to engage in intercourse eventually, they didn't necessarily want the men to disregard their "no" and force them to submit right away; many wanted their dates to wait or "talk me into it." But when a woman's "no" is equivocal, it means that her date, if he reads her intention correctly, should continue to press her for sex, perhaps in a physically assertive way. In fact, some of the women said that they told a date no because they "want[ed] him to be more physically aggressive."

An obvious concern regarding this study is that the Texas A & M students may not be typical. The authors cautioned that the men tend to endorse gender roles that were prevalent in the 1950s. But subsequent studies elsewhere have reported strikingly similar findings, with no regional differences. A 1994 study of students at universities in Hawaii, Texas, and the Midwest found that 38 percent of the women sometimes said no when they meant yes. In a 1995 study at Penn State 37 percent of women reported having said no when they meant yes. For most women, most of the time, "no" does mean no. But sometimes it means "maybe" or "try harder." Sometimes, for some women, it means "get physical."

Some supporters of rape-law reform prefer to set aside these empirical findings. They probably fear that evidence of this sort will only reinforce society's willingness to tolerate male behavior that poses enormous risks for women. But sexual ambivalence and miscommunication, though they undoubtedly exist, do not automatically justify permissive legal standards. They need not dictate impunity for men who ignore women's verbal protests. Indeed, it is precisely because of these inconvenient realities that legal requirements such as "consent" and "reasonableness" solve so few of the difficulties.

THE SEARCH FOR SOLUTIONS

DESPITE their many disputes over theory and tactics, critics of existing rape law largely agree in tracing its inadequacies to its overly narrow conception of force. Protection of autonomy—a woman's right to make her own sexual choices—is not ignored; it remains the ultimate goal and a frequent rhetorical theme. Yet few reformers attempt to make autonomy or consent a formal legal requirement.

One reason is practical. Many anti-rape activists worry that evidence about the victim's personal life might become relevant and that extensive cross-examination of the victim might have to be permitted if legal proof focuses on her state of mind rather than on the defendant's behavior. There is a more basic point as well: a concern that autonomy simply has no meaning independent of some notion of coercion. Through all the reform struggles of the past, reformers and their critics alike shared the assumption that autonomy means—and can only mean—freedom from force or duress.

As a result, most contemporary reformers stress autonomy only in their rhetoric; they avoid making autonomous choice a formal requirement. Instead the leading proposals for change urge two distinct but complementary reforms. The first is to insist that "no" means no. The second aims to bridge the gaps in existing legal protection by expanding traditional notions of force, coercion, or duress. Both approaches have led the reform effort to unexpected dead ends.

The argument that a woman's "no" should always establish her unwillingness remains intensely controversial. But even if that argument is accepted, as it should be, it solves few of the problems. For example, a "no"-means-no rule doesn't clarify the standards of behavior that should apply *after* the woman says no. Is her "no" always final, or can a man ask again? Can he try to change her mind—and if so, how? Those problems return us to the elusive question of what should count as legally sufficient force. Winning legal recognition for the principle that "no" means no will not solve this puzzle.

Rape-law reformers have an answer. They hope to overcome the remaining problems by extending the definition of "force" from physical violence to other kinds of coercion. One obstacle here is the common practice of limiting rape prosecutions to cases involving an explicit threat to use force. But shifting the legal analysis to focus on implicit threats doesn't solve the problems; it only restates them. Courts still must identify some conduct that amounts to an unstated threat. If the implicit-threat standard requires evidence tied to the defendant's behavior at the time of the incident, verbal and physical details (flexing of the biceps, actual choking) will remain crucially important.

The problem is that even when implicit threats can count as force, the standard remains artificial because it focuses narrowly, in snapshot fashion, on specific comments and gestures made at the time of a rape incident. To escape that narrow focus, courts could consider the entire context, including the setting of the incident, the possibilities for running away or calling for help, the prior relationship between the parties, their relative size and strength, and so on.

This broader approach has clear advantages, but it poses a large problem. By shifting the force requirement from a man's threatening actions to his *capacity* to inflict harm, it makes the line between voluntary encounters and coercive sex hard to locate. If disparity in size, strength, and fighting ability is sufficient to establish force, then rape is implicit in most heterosexual relationships.

No court will permit a standard like this to extend to the limits of its logic, of course. The more serious concern is that a principle of this sort will seldom be used in practice. As long as the contextual approach fails to separate, in a roughly predictable way, what is legitimate from what is abusive, courts will bend over backward to ensure that men are not convicted of a serious offense unless they had fair warning that their conduct was criminal. Prosecutors, juries, and appellate courts will have no clear guidance and, much worse, no strong imperative to act. Underenforcement will be the all-too-foreseeable result.

Courts that accept the implicit-threat and inherent-capacity-to-harm standards keep those approaches within bounds by invoking a "reasonableness" limitation. An implicit threat or an intimidating capacity to inflict harm counts as force, and the woman does not have to resist physically—but her fears of injury must be considered "reasonable."

The reasonable-fear requirement seems a plausible limitation. Courts understandably consider it unfair to convict a man of rape when a woman who has cooperated in a sexual act has done so because of an unreasonable fear. Yet a reasonableness standard destroys most of the gains that the implicit-threat standard was supposed to achieve.

Reasonableness standards are common in law, and often work tolerably well, especially in highway driving and other areas of behavior in which norms of conduct are widely shared and moderately well understood. When norms are more controversial and stakes are high, as in the use of deadly force in self-defense, a general standard of reasonableness is seldom sufficient; the law uses elaborate rules to specify the kinds of threats that are serious enough to justify a lethal response, the circumstances that require the threatened person to shoot in defense rather than retreat, and so on.

In the case of sexual encounters, perceptions of danger can differ widely, and appropriate norms of behavior are intensely disputed. Our culture is at best ambivalent about whether a bit of physical aggression is attractive or unacceptable in male sexual initiatives. In these conditions a reasonableness standard doesn't just keep the implicit-threat approach within commonsense bounds. Instead it undercuts the effort to make traditional requirements of explicit force more realistic. A reasonableness standard does little to challenge our culture's willingness to condone men's physically assertive sexual advances. And a reasonableness standard makes it all the more difficult to see why that culture—and the behavior it encourages—poses dangers for women.

As a result, the reasonableness standard leaves legal requirements almost as narrow or unpredictable as they were before. Without some limitation, courts feel, reforms that extend force requirements from explicit to implicit threats and from actual conduct to inherent capabilities would have intolerable scope: they would render virtually all heterosexual sex coercive and therefore criminal. But with a limitation to "reasonable" fears, the move to include implicit threats and inherent capacities as forms of force ultimately achieves very little. The effort to stretch legal concepts of force cannot achieve what is needed—the recognition that sexual autonomy should be protected directly.

THE MISSING ENTITLEMENT— SEXUAL AUTONOMY

SEXUAL autonomy, like other rights, has two facets. The first is active—the right to decide on the kind of life one wishes to live and the kinds of activities one wishes to pursue, including sexual interaction with others who are willing. The second is the reverse—the right to safeguard and exclude, the freedom to refuse to have sex with any person at any time, for any reason or for no reason at all.

Protection from coercion and the protection of autonomy are closely related and thus sometimes hard to tell apart. Existing rape laws and all the leading reform efforts add to this confusion by treating the two concerns as if they were two sides of the same coin. But the differences between them are crucial. Physical coercion interferes with autonomy, but many interferences with autonomy involve no coercion, physical or otherwise.

These distinctions are familiar when interests other than sexuality are at stake. A person may take $100 from me by physical force, or he may take it by coercive but nonphysical threats—for example, if he threatens to spread false rumors that will ruin my business. A person may also get control over my property illegally without coercing me at all. He may take my $100 by stealth, or he may persuade me to give it to him by falsely promising something in return. In these cases his actions are illegal but not coercive. If our law of theft punished only coercive takings, we might try to say that takings by stealth or deception were in effect coercive—but we would know that the language was strained. The law of theft requires no such verbal contortions. It simply punishes takings by force (robbery), by coercive threats (extortion), by stealth (larceny), by breach of trust (embezzlement), and by deception (fraud and false pretenses). All these methods violate my rights because they impair—without adequate justification—my control over my property.

Much the same can be said for nearly all our most fundamental interests. The law protects our control over our labor and our votes, our right to receive honest services from professionals, and our privacy, including confidential information about ourselves. Contexts are important, and the details of legal rights vary, but the general point holds: the law protects our autonomy in regard to these interests—our freedom to retain them or dispose of them however we may choose. It prohibits interference with meaningful choice by force, by stealth, and, usually, by breach of trust or deception. The law does not strain to say that all these interferences are coercive; it simply treats them as impermissible infringements on the liberty and self-determination to which every person is entitled.

Sexual autonomy is treated differently. Few of our other personal rights and liberties—perhaps only our right to life itself—are as important as our right to decide whether and when we will become sexually intimate with another person. The emotional vulnerability and potential physical danger attached to sexual interaction make effective legal safeguards at least as important for sex as they are for the sale of land or the purchase of a used car. Strangely, in the list of fundamental entitlements that the law grants us as free and independent beings, sexual autonomy is somehow left out.

There is nothing intrinsic to sexuality that requires this constricted pattern of protection. Violent threats are just one possible source of a defect in consent, and the law already recognizes a few others in the context of sexual relations. The best-known example is immaturity: the law has long prohibited consensual intercourse with a girl who is below the legally prescribed age of consent. The law likewise punishes acts of intercourse with a woman who is sleeping, unconscious, mentally incompetent, or unaware that a sexual act is being performed.

Traditionally, the law draws no formal distinction between cases of physical violence and exceptional cases like the ones just mentioned; all are classified as rape. Yet our terminology keeps force in the forefront. In ordinary language "rape" *means* the imposition of intercourse by force. The terminology influences assumptions about the proper scope of rape or assault, for judges, legislators, ordinary citizens, and committed anti-rape activists alike. Rather than asking whether certain sexual advances unjustifiably impair freedom of choice, we have asked only whether the conduct is so bad that it is equivalent to violent compulsion—whether it is tantamount to rape.

Sexual autonomy should not exist so precariously. Attention should no longer focus exclusively on whether a man's behavior is aberrant, egregious, or potentially lethal. Instead the proper questions for debate are whether each participant in a sexual encounter had a meaningful opportunity to choose, and whether a meaningful choice was in fact made before sexual penetration occurred. In connection with criminal sanctions the law must also consider whether the defendant can fairly be considered culpable. But culpability cannot be confined to cases of aberrant physical violence; there is ample reason to find criminal responsibility when, for example, a man commits an act of sexual penetration ***knowing*** that he doesn't have the woman's consent.

Posing the issues in these terms will not by itself resolve them. Meaningful choice and the limits of permissible interference with autonomy must be determined by paying close attention to contexts. We have to consider the dynamics of sexual interaction in different settings and the possible impairment of decision-making capabilities under different circumstances. We have to consider as well the possibility of significant differences between the scope of protection appropriate for sexuality and the scope of protection appropriate for other interests protected by current laws. But the issue must be framed in terms of sexual autonomy itself, not in terms of a futile search for something we can squeeze under the rubric of "force."

Once the focus of legal concern shifts from force to sexual autonomy, a much broader range of individual misconduct is called into question. When one person interferes with another person's ability to choose freely in a sexual encounter, legal intervention is appropriate even in the absence of force—just as it is when one person impairs another person's autonomy in relation to property rights, privacy, or other entitlements recognized by law.

The starting point for any consideration of autonomy is the question of whether a person's consent is coerced. A focus on sexual autonomy enables us to distinguish legitimate inducements from threats or other sorts of pressure (sometimes in the form of offers) that should be criminally punishable.

Without explicit threats or other improper inducements, freedom of choice can still be affected by the distribution of power in particular settings. For sexual relationships between men or women and their teachers, job supervisors, psychotherapists, doctors, dentists, and lawyers, legal restrictions are needed even in the absence of explicit threats.

The capacity for meaningful choice can also be impaired by deception. Yet currently the law places no restrictions whatsoever on the use of fraudulent tactics to obtain consent to sex. Proposals for insisting on the same level of honesty in sexual exchange that we require as a matter of course in property transactions are usually dismissed as impractical or wildly out of touch with reality. At least in the case of egregiously deceptive inducements, the absence of legal sanctions is hard to justify.

Even if a relationship is completely free of threats, deception, disparities of power, or breaches of trust, sexual contact obviously violates autonomy when one of the parties does not consent. But the question of what counts as an expression of consent is intensely contested: Does "no" always mean no? Is physical resistance necessary to make clear the absence of consent? And can we infer willingness from silence or ambivalence—from *not* saying no?

COURTS that find consent despite a verbal protest will inevitably find consent if the woman didn't protest or physically resist. But even courts and juries that treat a verbal no as sufficient to signal unwillingness are likely to consider a woman's silence equivalent to consent. Only a handful of states have taken the next step and insisted that consent to sex requires "affirmative and freely given permission." To most courts, a refusal to infer consent when a woman lies still and utters no protest is overly fastidious and wildly unrealistic.

If a woman is unconscious or asleep, of course, her silence can't be equated with sexual willingness; a man who penetrates her will be guilty of rape. But when the woman is *able* to say no, the usual assumption is that if she remains silent, she must be willing; otherwise she would object. Or if she isn't really willing, it is considered fair to treat her as if she were. Consent may be actual, or it may be a justified fiction. The episode on the Illinois bike path is just one of countless illustrations of this point of view. The court that reversed the man's sexual-assault conviction said that the woman's "failure to resist when it was within her power to do so conveys the impression of consent."

The soundness of requiring some protest is usually accepted without question. Yet it is by no means clear that women in such situations do have a fair chance to protest. The Illinois woman, for example, was a foot shorter and weighed eighty-five pounds less than her attacker, and was startled by a stranger in an isolated setting, with no one else in sight. Her silence might mean enthusiastic willingness, but it is *at least* equally likely that she was terrified and paralyzed by fear.

The silence-means-consent assumption draws support even from some rape-law reformers. They worry that treating passivity or ambivalence as nonconsent will patronize women, who should be assumed to be capable of asserting their own wishes. But we seldom think it patronizing to insist on permission, not just silence, when the interests affected are ones that men can easily recognize. When a doctor asks if a patient wants a probe inserted into his rectum to check for tumors, the patient's silence is not assumed to indicate consent. The patient's willingness must be made explicit. Yet rape law doesn't require us to obtain actual permission for intercourse; it prohibits penetration only when there is clear evidence of *non*consent.

An insistence on proof of unwillingness has a certain logic within the framework of existing law. It serves not only to ensure that potential lawbreakers have fair warning but also to keep the criminal prohibition focused on conduct involving force. A requirement of actual permission, however, would not shift the burden of proof to the defendant or require doubts to be resolved against him. A defendant could be convicted only if he knew he did not have the woman's affirmative permission or if he was criminally negligent in thinking that he did. But silence, ambiguous behavior, and the absence of a clearly expressed preference would be evidence that affirmative consent was absent; they would no longer suggest, as they do under present law, that a defendant did nothing wrong in forging ahead to intercourse.

The significance of equivocal behavior should in effect be reversed. Equivocal behavior should reinforce prosecutors' claims that consent was absent, rather than serving (as under current law) to buttress defense claims that the woman never signaled her unwillingness. No standard can eliminate all factual uncertainty or swearing contests between witnesses. And some defendants would continue to avoid liability simply by telling elaborate lies. But facts that will often be quite clear—verbal protests, ambivalence, passivity, or silence—would by themselves be sufficient to establish an unambiguous offense against personal autonomy and an unambiguous basis for punishment. The important point is to shift the emphasis of the consent inquiry away from concern over whether the woman explicitly communicated her opposition. Sexual intimacy involves a profound intrusion on the physical and emotional integrity of the individual. Nothing less than positive willingness, clearly communicated, should ever count as consent.

In the few states—New Jersey, Wisconsin, Washington—where consent now means actual permission, not just the absence of protests, consent need not be in writing, of course. Permission can be communicated, these states' laws provide, by "actual words or conduct indicating freely given agreement to have sexual intercourse." Because body language can still count as an expression of consent, this approach (for better or worse) doesn't eliminate all the uncertainties of sexual communication. A world without ambiguity in erotic interaction might be a very dull place, after all. But ambiguity is also dangerous, especially for women who justifiably want the freedom to explore intimacy and sexual contact without losing their right to stop matters short of intercourse.

To minimize the risks, many reformers propose that nothing less than verbal permission—an explicit yes—should ever count as consent to intercourse. The drawbacks of such a rule are evident. If body language cannot be a legally effective way to express consent, many common modes of indicating a desire for intercourse will have to change radically, or—more likely—the verbal-permission requirement will simply be ignored by spouses, lovers, dating partners, and perhaps courts and juries as well.

To signal affirmative consent, body language must be unambiguous. Sexual petting does not in itself imply permission for intercourse, any more than does inviting a man in for coffee or permitting him to pay for dinner. A woman who engages in intense sexual foreplay should always retain the right to say no. If she doesn't say no, and if her silence is combined with passionate kissing, hugging, and sexual touching, it is usually sensible to infer actual willingness. A verbal-permission rule would reduce the risks of a possible misunderstanding in this situation, but at the cost of imposing a degree of formality and artificiality on human interactions in which spontaneity is especially important.

The verbal-yes rule thus seems many steps beyond the level of regulation that contemporary courts are likely to entertain. And a verbal-yes rule is not mandated by a commitment to respect sexual autonomy. The central point is that sexual intimacy must be chosen freely. The first priorities are to stop insisting on proof of the woman's opposition, and to stop requiring her to take actions clear enough to overcome the law's presumption that she is always interested in sex—at any time, in any place, with any person. The legal standard must move away from the demand for unambiguous evidence of her protests and insist instead that the man have affirmative indications that she chose to participate. So long as her choice is clearly expressed, by words or conduct, her right to control her sexuality is respected.

These important steps are not sufficient by themselves, however. In states that now require affirmative, "freely given" consent, the law still makes no effort to define which kinds of pressure prevent consent from being given "freely." Experience under New Jersey's relatively progressive rule has demonstrated that when the concepts of force and coercion are left undefined, prosecutors continue to insist on evidence of physical intimidation. The law must stop equating force with physical violence.

Without this change of focus, clear-cut abuses will continue to slip through the gaps in existing law. Men today are free, as in the Illinois case, to take advantage of strangers they accost in isolated settings. Lawyers in most states can exact sexual cooperation from clients who depend on them for essential help in divorce, child-custody, and criminal cases. A man in a bar or a fraternity house can get a woman drunk, undress her, and penetrate her before she can resist. In cases like these men continue to escape conviction by claiming that they never threatened physical violence and that the woman failed to make her unwillingness clear. Only when our laws and culture acknowledge the importance of affirmative, uncoerced permission will we afford women and men the right to control the boundaries of their own sexual lives. Until then sexual autonomy will remain the missing, unprotected entitlement.

Many rape law reform proponents believe that revising criminal laws along the lines suggested by Schulhofer and others might not only make convictions less difficult, but could help more victims come forward with rape complaints to the police. In their current form, all but a few state statutes effectively place the burden on the victim to prove lack of consent, a task particularly difficult when there is a pre-existing or "dating" relationship between victim and defendant. Allegations by some commentators that many claims of "date rape" are exaggerated have drawn sharp responses.

DATE RAPE'S OTHER VICTIM

By Katie Roiphe

New York Times Magazine, June 13, 1993

ONE IN FOUR COLLEGE WOMEN HAS BEEN THE victim of rape or attempted rape. One in four. I remember standing outside the dining hall in college, looking at a purple poster with this statistic written in bold letters. It didn't seem right. If sexual assault was really so pervasive, it seemed strange that the intricate gossip networks hadn't picked up more than one or two shadowy instances of rape. If I was really standing in the middle of an "epidemic," a "crisis" — if 25 percent of my women friends were really being raped — wouldn't I know it?

These posters were not presenting facts. They were advertising a mood. Preoccupied with issues like date rape and sexual harassment, campus feminists produce endless images of women as victims — women offended by a professor's dirty joke, women pressured into sex by peers, women trying to say no but not managing to get it across.

This portrait of the delicate female bears a striking resemblance to that 50's ideal my mother and other women of her generation fought so hard to leave behind. They didn't like her passivity, her wide-eyed innocence. They didn't like the fact that she was perpetually offended by sexual innuendo. They didn't like her excessive need for protection. She represented personal, social and intellectual possibilities collapsed, and they worked and marched, shouted and wrote to make her irrelevant for their daughters. But here she is again, with her pure intentions and her wide eyes. Only this time it is the feminists themselves who are breathing new life into her.

IS THERE A RAPE CRISIS ON CAMPUS? MEASURING rape is not as straightforward as it might seem. Neil Gilbert, a professor of social welfare at the University of California at Berkeley, questions the validity of the one-in-four statistic. Gilbert points out that in a 1985 survey undertaken by Ms. magazine and financed by the National Institute of Mental Health, 73 percent of the women categorized as rape victims did not initially define their experience as rape; it was Mary Koss, the psychologist conducting the study, who did.

One of the questions used to define rape was: "Have you had sexual intercourse when you didn't want to because a man gave you alcohol or drugs." The phrasing raises the issue of agency. Why aren't college women responsible for their own intake of alcohol or drugs? A man may give her drugs, but she herself decides to take them. If we assume that women are not all helpless and naive, then they should be held responsible for their choice to drink or take drugs. If a woman's "judgment is impaired" and she has sex, it isn't necessarily always the man's fault; it isn't necessarily always rape.

As Gilbert delves further into the numbers, he does not necessarily disprove the one-in-four statistic, but he does clarify what it means — the so-called rape epidemic on campuses is more a way of interpreting, a way of seeing, than a physical phenomenon. It is more about a change in sexual politics than a change in sexual behavior. Whether or not one in four college women has been raped, then, is a matter of opinion, not a matter of mathematical fact.

That rape is a fact in some women's lives is not in question. It's hard to watch the solemn faces of young Bosnian girls, their words haltingly translated, as they tell of brutal rapes; or to read accounts of a suburban teen-ager raped and beaten while walking home from a shopping mall. We all agree that rape is a terrible thing, but we no longer agree on what rape is. Today's definition has stretched beyond bruises and knives, threats of death or violence to include emotional pressure and the influence of alcohol. The lines between rape and sex begin to blur. The one-in-four statistic on those purple posters is measuring something elusive. It is measuring her word against his in a realm where words barely exist. There is a gray area in which one person's rape may be another's bad night. Definitions become entangled in passionate ideological battles. There hasn't been a remarkable change in the number of women being raped; just a change in how receptive the political climate is to those numbers.

The next question, then, is who is identifying this epidemic and why. Somebody is "finding" this rape crisis; and finding it for a reason. Asserting the prevalence of rape lends urgency, authority to a broader critique of culture.

In a dramatic description of the rape crisis, Naomi Wolf writes in "The Beauty Myth" that "Cultural representation of glamorized degradation has created a situation among the young in which boys rape and girls get raped *as a normal course of events.*"

The italics are hers. Whether or not Wolf really believes rape is part of the "normal course of events" these days, she is making a larger point. Wolf's rhetorical excess serves her larger polemic about sexual politics. Her dramatic prose is a call to arms. She is trying to rally the feminist troops. Wolf uses rape as a red flag, an undeniable sign that things are falling apart.

From Susan Brownmiller — who brought the politics of rape into the mainstream with her 1975 best seller, "Against Our Will: Men, Women and Rape" — to Naomi Wolf, feminist prophets of the rape crisis are talking about something more than forced penetration. They are talking about what they define as a "rape culture." Rape is a natural trump card for feminism. Arguments about rape can be used to sequester feminism in the teary province of trauma and crisis. By blocking analysis with its claims to unique pandemic suffering, the rape crisis becomes a powerful source of authority.

Dead serious, eyes wide with concern, a college senior tells me that she believes one in four is too conservative an estimate. This is not the first time I've heard this. She tells me the right statistic is closer to one in two. That means one in two women are raped. It's amazing, she says, amazing that so many of us are sexually assaulted every day.

What is amazing is that this student actually believes that 50 percent of women are raped. This is the true crisis. Some substantial number of young women are walking around with this alarming belief: a hyperbole containing within it a state of perpetual fear.

"Acquaintance Rape: Is Dating Dangerous?" is a pamphlet commonly found at counseling centers. The cover title rises from the shards of a shattered photograph of a boy and girl dancing. Inside, the pamphlet offers a sample date-rape scenario. She thinks:

"He was really good looking and he had a great smile. . . . We talked and found we had a lot in common. I really liked him. When he asked me over to his place for a drink I thought it would be O.K. He was such a good listener and I wanted him to ask me out again."

She's just looking for a sensitive boy, a good listener with a nice smile, but unfortunately his intentions are not as pure as hers. Beneath that nice smile, he thinks:

"She looked really hot, wearing a sexy dress that showed off her great body. We started talking right away. I knew that she liked me by the way she kept smiling and touching my arm while she was speaking. She seemed pretty relaxed so I asked her back to my place for a drink. . . . When she said 'Yes' I knew that I was going to be lucky!"

These cardboard stereotypes don't just educate freshmen about rape. They also educate them about "dates" and about sexual desire. With titles like "Friends Raping Friends: Could It Happen to You?" date-rape pamphlets call into question all relationships between men and women. Beyond warning students about rape, the rape-crisis movement produces its own images of sexual behavior, in which men exert pressure and women resist. By defining the dangerous date in these terms — with this type of male and this type of female, and their different expectations — these pamphlets promote their own perspective on how men and women feel about sex: men are lascivious, women are innocent.

The sleek images of pressure and resistance projected in rape-education movies, videotapes, pamphlets and speeches create a model of acceptable sexual behavior. The don'ts imply their own set of do's. The movement against rape, then, not only dictates the way sex *shouldn't* be but also the way it *should* be. Sex should be gentle, it should not be aggressive; it should be absolutely equal, it should not involve domination and submission; it should be tender, not ambivalent; it should communicate respect, it shouldn't communicate consuming desire.

In "Real Rape," Susan Estrich, a professor of law at the University of Southern California Law Center, slips her ideas about the nature of sexual encounters into her legal analysis of the problem of rape. She writes: "Many feminists would argue that so long as women are powerless relative to men, viewing a 'yes' as a sign of true consent is misguided. . . . Many women who say yes to men they know, whether on dates or on the job, would say no if they could. . . . Women's silence sometimes is the product not of passion and desire but of pressure and fear."

Like Estrich, most rape-crisis feminists claim they are not talking about sex; they're talking about violence. But, like Estrich, they are also talking about sex. With their advice, their scenarios, their sample aggressive male, the message projects a clear comment on the nature of sexuality: women are often unwilling participants. They say yes because they feel they have to, because they are intimidated by male power.

The idea of "consent" has been redefined beyond the simple assertion that "no means no." Politically correct sex involves a yes, and a specific yes at that. According to the premise of "active consent," we can no longer afford ambiguity. We can no longer afford the dangers of unspoken consent. A former director of Columbia's date-rape education program told New York magazine, "Stone silence throughout an entire physical encounter with someone is not explicit consent."

This apparently practical, apparently clinical proscription cloaks retrograde assumptions about the way men and women experience sex. The idea that only an explicit yes means yes proposes that, like children, women have trouble communicating what they want. Beyond its dubious premise about the limits of female communication, the idea of active consent bolsters stereotypes of men just out to "get some" and women who don't really want any.

Rape-crisis feminists express nostalgia for the days of greater social control, when the university acted in loco parentis and women were protected from the insatiable force of male desire. The rhetoric of feminists and conservatives blurs and overlaps in this desire to keep our youth safe and pure.

By viewing rape as encompassing more than the use or threat of physical violence to coerce someone into sex, rape-crisis feminists reinforce traditional views about the fragility of the female body and will. According to common definitions of date rape, even "verbal coercion" or "manipulation" constitute rape. Verbal coercion is defined as "a woman's consenting to unwanted sexual activity because of a man's verbal arguments not including verbal threats of force." The belief that "verbal coercion" is rape pervades workshops, counseling sessions and student opinion pieces. The suggestion lurking beneath this definition of rape is that men are not just physically but also intellectually and emotionally more powerful than women.

Imagine men sitting around in a circle talking about how she called him impotent and how she manipulated him into sex, how violated and dirty he felt afterward, how coercive she was, how she got him drunk first, how he hated his body and he couldn't eat for three weeks afterward. Imagine him calling this rape. Everyone feels the weight of emotional pressure at one time or another. The question is not whether people pressure each other but how our minds and our culture transform that pressure into full-blown assault. There would never be a rule or a law or even a pamphlet or peer counseling group for men who claimed to have been emotionally raped or verbally pressured into sex. And for the same reasons — assumption of basic competence, free will and strength of character — there should be no such rules or groups or pamphlets about women.

In discussing rape, campus feminists often slip into an outdated sexist vocabulary. But we have to be careful about using rape as metaphor. The sheer physical fact of rape has always been loaded with cultural meaning. Throughout history, women's bodies have been seen as property, as chaste objects, as virtuous vessels to be "dishonored," "ruined," "defiled." Their purity or lack of purity has been a measure of value for the men to whom they belonged.

"Politically, I call it rape whenever a woman has sex and feels violated," writes Catharine MacKinnon, a law professor and feminist legal scholar best known for her crusade against pornography. The language of virtue and violation reinforces retrograde stereotypes. It backs women into old corners. Younger feminists share MacKinnon's vocabulary and the accompanying assumptions about women's bodies. In one student's account of date rape in the Rag, a feminist magazine at Harvard, she talks about the anguish of being "defiled." Another writes, "I long to be innocent again." With such anachronistic constructions of the female body, with all their assumptions about female purity, these young women frame their experience of rape in archaic, sexist terms. Of course, sophisticated modern-day feminists don't use words like honor or virtue anymore. They know better than to say date-rape victims have been "defiled." Instead, they call it "post-traumatic stress syndrome." They tell the victim she should not feel "shame," she should feel "traumatized." Within their overtly political psychology, forced penetration takes on a level of metaphysical significance: date rape resonates through a woman's entire life.

Combating myths about rape is one of the central missions of the rape-crisis movement. They spend money and energy trying to break down myths like "She asked for it." But with all their noise about rape myths, rape-crisis feminists are generating their own. The plays, the poems, the pamphlets, the Take Back the Night speakouts, are propelled by the myth of innocence lost.

All the talk about empowering the voiceless dissolves into the image of the naive girl child who trusts the rakish man. This plot reaches back centuries. It propels Samuel Richardson's 18th-century epistolary novel, "Clarissa": after hundreds of pages chronicling the minute details of her plight, her seduction and resistance, her break from her family, Clarissa is raped by the duplicitous Robert Lovelace. Afterward, she refuses to eat and fades toward a very virtuous, very religious death. Over a thousand pages are devoted to the story of her fall from innocence, a weighty event by 18th-century standards. But did these 20th-century girls, raised on Madonna videos and the 6 o'clock news, really trust that people were good until they themselves were raped? Maybe. Were these girls, raised on horror movies and glossy Hollywood sex scenes, really as innocent as all that? Maybe. But maybe the myth of lost innocence is a trope — convenient, appealing, politically effective.

As long as we're taking back the night, we might as well take back our own purity. Sure, we were all kind of innocent, playing in the sandbox with bright red shovels — boys, too. We can all look back through the tumultuous tunnel of adolescence on a honey-glazed childhood, with simple rules and early bedtimes. We don't have to look at parents fighting, at sibling struggles, at casting out one best friend for another in the Darwinian playground. This is not the innocence lost; this is the innocence we never had.

The idea of a fall from childhood grace, pinned on one particular moment, a moment over which we had no control, much lamented, gives our lives a compelling narrative structure. It's easy to see why the 17-year-old likes it; it's easy to see why the rape-crisis feminist likes it. It's a natural human impulse put to political purpose. But in generating and perpetuating such myths, we should keep in mind that myths about innocence have been used to keep women inside and behind veils. They have been used to keep them out of work and in labor.

It's not hard to imagine Clarissa, in jeans and a sweatshirt, transported into the 20th century, at a Take Back the Night march. She would speak for a long time about her deception and rape, about verbal coercion and anorexia, about her ensuing post-traumatic stress syndrome. Latter-day Clarissas may worry more about their "self esteem" than their virtue, but they are still attaching the same quasi-religious value to the physical act.

"CALLING IT RAPE," a play by Sonya Rasminsky, a recent Harvard graduate, is based on interviews with date-rape victims. The play, which has been performed at Harvard and may be taken into Boston-area high schools, begins with "To His Coy Mistress," by the 17th-century poet Andrew Marvell. Although generations of high-school and college students have read this as a romantic poem, a poem about desire and the struggle against mortality, Rasminsky has reinterpreted it as a poem about rape. "Had we but world enough, and time, this coyness, lady, were no crime." But what Andrew Marvell didn't know then, and we know now, is that the real crime is not her coyness but his verbal coercion.

Farther along, the actors recount a rape that hinges on misunderstanding. A boy and girl are watching videos and he starts to come on to her. She does not want to have sex. As the situation progresses, she says, in an oblique effort to communicate her lack of enthusiasm, "If you're going to [expletive] me, use a condom." He interprets that as a yes, but it's really a no. And, according to this play, what happens next, condom or no condom, is rape.

This is a central idea of the rape-crisis movement: that sex has become our tower of Babel. He doesn't know what she wants (not to have sex) and she doesn't know what he wants (to have sex) — until it's too late. He speaks boyspeak and she speaks girlspeak and what comes out of all this verbal chaos is a lot of rapes. The theory of mixed signals and crossed stars has to do with more than gender politics. It comes in part, from the much-discussed diversity that has so radically shifted the social composition of the college class since the 50's.

Take my own Harvard dorm: the Adams House dining hall is large, with high ceilings and dark paneling. It hasn't changed much for generations. As soon as the students start milling around gathering salads, ice cream and coffee onto green trays, there are signs of change. There are students in jeans, flannel shirts, short skirts, girls in jackets, boys in bracelets, two pierced noses and lots of secondhand clothes.

Not so many years ago, this room was filled with boys in jackets and ties. Most of them were white, Christian and what we now call privileged. Students came from the same social milieu with the same social rules and it was assumed that everyone knew more or less how they were expected to behave with everyone else. Diversity and multiculturalism were unheard of, and if they had been, they would have been dirty words. With the shift in college environments, with the introduction of black kids, Asian kids, Jewish kids, kids from the wrong side of the tracks of nearly every railroad in the country, there was an accompanying anxiety about how people behave. When ivory tower meets melting pot, it causes tension, some confusion, some need for readjustment. In explaining the need for intensive "orientation" programs, including workshops on date rape, Columbia's assistant dean for freshmen stated in an interview in The New York Times: "You can't bring all these people together and say, 'Now be one big happy community,' without some sort of training. You can't just throw together somebody from a small town in Texas and someone from New York City and someone from a conservative fundamentalist home in the Midwest and say, 'Now without any sort of conversation, be best friends and get along and respect one another.' "

Catharine Stimpson, a University Professor at Rutgers and longtime advocate of women's studies programs, once pointed out that it's sometimes easier for people to talk about gender than to talk about class. "Miscommunication" is in some sense a word for the friction between the way we were and the way we are. Just as the idea that we speak different languages is connected to gender — the arrival of women in classrooms, in dorms and in offices — it is also connected to class.

When the Southern heiress goes out with the plumber's son from the Bronx, when the kid from rural Arkansas goes out with a boy from Exeter, the anxiety is that they have different expectations. The dangerous "miscommunication" that recurs through the literature on date rape is a code word for difference in background. The rhetoric surrounding date rape and sexual harassment is in part a response to cultural mixing. The idea that men don't know what women mean when women say no stems from something deeper and more complicated than feminist concerns with rape.

PEOPLE HAVE ASKED ME if I have ever been date-raped. And thinking back on complicated nights, on too many glasses of wine, on strange and familiar beds, I would have to say yes. With such a sweeping definition of rape, I wonder how many people there are, male or female, who haven't been date-raped at one point or another. People pressure and manipulate and cajole each other into all sorts of things all of the time. As Susan Sontag wrote, "Since Christianity upped the ante and concentrated on sexual behavior as the root of virtue, everything pertaining to sex has been a 'special case' in our culture, evoking peculiarly inconsistent attitudes." No human interactions are free from pressure, and the idea that sex is, or can be, makes it what Sontag calls a "special case," vulnerable to the inconsistent expectations of double standard.

With their expansive version of rape, rape-crisis feminists are inventing a kinder, gentler sexuality. Beneath the broad definition of rape, these feminists are endorsing their own utopian vision of sexual relations: sex without struggle, sex without power, sex without persuasion, sex without pursuit. If verbal coercion constitutes rape, then the word rape itself expands to include any kind of sex a woman experiences as negative.

When Martin Amis spoke at Princeton, he included a controversial joke: "As far as I'm concerned, you can change your mind before, even during, but just not after sex." The reason this joke is funny, and the reason it's also too serious to be funny, is that in the current atmosphere you *can* change your mind afterward. Regret can signify rape. A night that was a blur, a night you wish hadn't happened, can be rape. Since "verbal coercion" and "manipulation" are ambiguous, it's easy to decide afterwards that he manipulated you. You can realize it weeks or even years later. This is a movement that deals in retrospective trauma.

Rape has become a catch-all expression, a word used to define everything that is unpleasant and disturbing about relations between the sexes. Students say things like "I realize that sexual harassment is a kind of rape." If we refer to a whole range of behavior from emotional pressure to sexual harassment as "rape," then the idea itself gets diluted. It ceases to be powerful as either description or accusation.

Some feminists actually collapse the distinction between rape and sex. Catharine MacKinnon writes: "Compare victims' reports of rape with women's reports of sex. They look a lot alike. . . . In this light, the major distinction between intercourse (normal) and rape (abnormal) is that the normal happens so often that one cannot get anyone to see anything wrong with it."

There are a few feminists involved in rape education who object to the current expanding definitions of sexual assault. Gillian Greensite, founder of the rape prevention education program at the University of California at Santa Cruz, writes that the seriousness of the crime "is being undermined by the growing tendency of some feminists to label all heterosexual miscommunication and insensitivity as acquaintance rape." From within the rape-crisis movement, Greensite's dissent makes an important point. If we are going to maintain an *idea* of rape, then we need to reserve it for instances of physical violence, or the threat of physical violence.

But some people want the melodrama. They want the absolute value placed on experience by absolute words. Words like "rape" and "verbal coercion" channel the confusing flow of experience into something easy to understand. The idea of date rape comes at us fast and coherent. It comes at us when we've just left home and haven't yet figured out where to put our new futons or how to organize our new social lives. The rhetoric about date rape defines the terms, gives names to nameless confusions and sorts through mixed feelings with a sort of insistent consistency. In the first rush of sexual experience, the fear of date rape offers a tangible framework to locate fears that are essentially abstract.

When my 55-year-old mother was young, navigating her way through dates, there was a definite social compass. There were places not to let him put his hands. There were invisible lines. The pill wasn't available. Abortion wasn't legal. And sex was just wrong. Her mother gave her "mad money" to take out on dates in case her date got drunk and she needed to escape. She had to go far enough to hold his interest and not far enough to endanger her reputation.

Now the rape-crisis feminists are offering new rules. They are giving new political weight to the same old no. My mother's mother told her to drink sloe gin fizzes so she wouldn't drink too much and get too drunk and go too far. Now the date rape pamphlets tell us: "Avoid excessive use of alcohol and drugs. Alcohol and drugs interfere with clear thinking and effective communication." My mother's mother told her to stay away from empty rooms and dimly lighted streets. In "I Never Called It Rape," Robin Warshaw writes, "Especially with recent acquaintances, women should insist on going only to public places such as restaurants and movie theaters."

There is a danger in these new rules. We shouldn't need to be reminded that the rigidly conformist 50's were not the heyday of women's power. Barbara Ehrenreich writes of "re-making love," but there is a danger in re-making love in its old image. The terms may have changed, but attitudes about sex and women's bodies have not. Rape-crisis feminists threaten the progress that's been made. They are chasing the same stereotypes our mothers spent so much energy escaping.

One day I was looking through my mother's bookshelves and I found her old battered copy of Germaine Greer's feminist classic, "The Female Eunuch." The pages were dogeared and whole passages marked with penciled notes. It was 1971 when Germaine Greer fanned the fires with "The Female Eunuch" and it was 1971 when my mother read it, brand new, explosive, a tough and sexy terrorism for the early stirrings of the feminist movement.

Today's rape-crisis feminists threaten to create their own version of the desexualized woman Greer complained of 20 years ago. Her comments need to be recycled for present-day feminism. "It is often falsely assumed," Greer writes, "even by feminists, that sexuality is the enemy of the female who really wants to develop those aspects of her personality. . . . It was not the insistence upon her sex that weakened the American woman student's desire to make something of her education, but the insistence upon a passive sexual role [Greer's italics]. In fact, the chief instrument in the deflection and perversion of female energy is the denial of female sexuality for the substitution of femininity or sexlessness."

It is the passive sexual role that threatens us still, and it is the denial of female sexual agency that threatens to propel us backward. ■

Not Just Bad Sex

Katha Pollitt

"Stick to straight liquor," my father advised me when I left for college, in the fall of 1967. "That way, you'll always know how drunk you are." I thought he was telling me that real grown-ups didn't drink brandy Alexanders, but of course what he was talking about was sex. College boys could get totally plastered, and the worst that would happen to them would be hangovers and missed morning classes. But if I didn't carefully monitor my alcohol intake one of those boys might, as they used to say, take advantage of me. Or, as they say now, date-rape me.

Veiled parental warnings like the one my father gave me—don't go alone to a boy's room, always carry "mad money" on a date, just in case—have gone the way of single-sex dorms, parietal hours, female-only curfews, and the three-feet-on-the-floor rule, swept away like so much Victorian bric-a-brac by the sexual revolution, the student movement, and the women's movement. The kids won; the duennas and fussbudgets lost. Or did they? In *The Morning After: Sex, Fear, and Feminism on Campus,* Katie Roiphe, a twenty-five-year-old Harvard alumna and graduate student of English at Princeton, argues that women's sexual freedom is being curtailed by a new set of hand-wringing fuddy-duddies: feminists. Antirape activists, she contends, have manipulated statistics to frighten college women with a nonexistent "epidemic" of rape, date rape, and sexual harassment, and have encouraged them to view "everyday experience"—sexist jokes, professorial leers, men's straying hands and other body parts—as intolerable insults and assaults. "Stranger rape" (the intruder with a knife) is rare; true date rape (the frat boy with a fist) is even rarer. As Roiphe sees it, most students who say they have been date raped are reinterpreting in the cold gray light of dawn the "bad sex" they were too passive to refuse and too enamored of victimhood to acknowledge as their own responsibility. Camille Paglia, move over.

These explosive charges have already made Roiphe a celebrity. The *New York Times Magazine* ran an excerpt from her book as a cover story: "Rape Hype Betrays Feminism." Four women's glossies ran respectful prepublication interviews; in *Mirabella* she was giddily questioned by her own mother, the writer Anne Roiphe. Clearly, Katie Roiphe's message is one that many people want to hear: Sexual violence is anomalous, not endemic to American society, and appearances to the contrary can be explained away as a kind of mass hysteria, fomented by man-hating fanatics.

How well does Roiphe support her case? *The Morning After* offers itself as personal testimony, with Roiphe—to use her own analogy—as a spunky, commonsensical Alice at the mad women's-studies-and-deconstructionism tea party familiar from the pages of Paglia and Dinesh D'Souza. As such, it's hard to challenge. Maybe Roiphe's classmates really are as she portrays them—waiflike anorexics, male-feminist wimps, the kind of leftist groupthinkers who ostracize anyone who says Alice Walker is a bad writer. Maybe Roiphe was, as she claims, "date raped" many times and none the worse for it. The general tone of her observations is unpleasantly smug, but in her depiction of a tiny subculture on a few Ivy League campuses, she may well be onto something. The trouble is that *The Morning After*, although Roiphe denies this, goes beyond her own privileged experience to make general claims about rape and feminism on American campuses, and it is also, although she denies this, too, a "political polemic." In both respects, it is a careless and irresponsible performance, poorly argued and full of misrepresentations, slapdash research, and gossip. She may be, as she implies, the rare grad student who has actually read *Clarissa*, but when it comes to rape and harassment, she has not done her homework.

Have radical feminists inundated the nation's campuses with absurd and unfounded charges against men? Roiphe cites a few well-publicized incidents: At Princeton, for example, a student told a Take Back the Night rally that she had been date raped by a young man she eventually admitted she had never met. But Roiphe's claim that such dubious charges represent a new norm rests on hearsay and a few quotations from the wilder shores of feminist theory. "Recently," she writes, "at the University of Michigan, a female teaching assistant almost brought a male student up on charges of sexual harassment," because of some mildly sexist humor in a paper. When is "recently"? In what department of the vast University of Michigan did this incident occur? How does Roiphe know about it—

after all, it only "almost" happened—and know that she got it right? Roiphe ridicules classmates for crediting and magnifying every rumor of petty sexism, but she does the same: Hysterical accusations are always being made at "a prominent university." Don't they teach the students at Harvard and Princeton anything about research anymore?

Where I was able to follow up on Roiphe's sources, I found some fairly misleading use of data. Roiphe accuses the legal scholar Susan Estrich of slipping "her ideas about the nature of sexual encounters into her legal analysis" in *Real Rape,* her study of acquaintance rape and the law—one such idea being that women are so powerless that even *yes* does not necessarily constitute consent to sex. In fact in the cited passage Estrich explicitly lays that view aside to pursue her own subject, which is the legal system's victimization of women who say no. Nowhere does Roiphe acknowledge that—whatever may happen in the uncritical, emotional atmosphere of a Take Back the Night rally or a support-group meeting for rape survivors (a term she mocks)—in the real world women who have been raped face enormous obstacles in obtaining justice in the courts or sympathy from their friends and families. Nor does she seem to realize that it is the humiliation and stigmatization and disbelief reported by many rape victims, and documented in many studies, that have helped to produce the campus climate of fear and credulity she deplores. Indeed the only time Roiphe discusses an actual court case, it is to argue that the law veers too far to the victim's side:

> In 1992 New Jersey's Supreme Court upheld its far-reaching rape laws. Ruling against a teenager charged with raping his date, the court concluded that signs of force or the threat of force is [*sic*] not necessary to prove the crime of rape—no force, that is, beyond that required for the physical act of penetration. Both the plaintiff and the defendant admitted that they were sexually involved, but the two sides differed on whether what happened that night was rape. It's hard to define anything that happens in that strange, libidinous province of adolescence, but this court upheld the judgment that the girl was raped. If the defendant had been an adult, he could have gone to jail for up to ten years. Susan Herman, deputy public defender in the case, remarked, "You not only have to bring a condom on a date, you have to bring a consent form as well."

Roiphe should know better than to rely on a short item in the Trenton *Times* for an accurate account of a complicated court case, and she misrepresents even the sketchy information the article contains: The girl was not the boy's "date," and they did not both "admit" they were "sexually involved." The two indeed disagreed about the central facts of the case. The article does mention something Roiphe chose to omit: The girl was fifteen years old. The Supreme Court opinion further distinguishes this case from Roiphe's general portrait of date-rape cases: the hypersensitive female charging an innocently blundering male with a terrible crime for doing what came naturally and doing it without a peep from her. The offender, it turns out, was dating another girl living in the house where the rape took place, and not the victim, who, far from passively enduring his assault, did what Roiphe implies she did not: She slapped him, demanded that he withdraw, and, in the morning, told her mother, whereupon they went immediately to the police. It is absurd to use this fifteen-year-old victim—who had surely never heard of Catharine MacKinnon or Take Back the Night—as an example of campus feminism gone mad. And it is equally absurd to suggest that the highly regarded New Jersey Supreme Court, which consists of one woman and six middle-aged men, issued a unanimous decision in the victim's favor because it had been corrupted by radical feminism.

The court did affirm that "signs of force or the threat of force" —wounds, torn clothes, the presence of a weapon—were not necessary to prove rape. This affirmation accords with the real-life fact that the amount of force necessary to achieve penetration is not much. But it is not true that the court opened the door to rape convictions in the kinds of cases Roiphe takes for the date-rape norm: sex in which the woman says yes but means no, or says yes, means yes, but regrets it later. The court said that consent, which need not be verbal, must be obtained for intercourse. It's easy to parody this view, as the defense counsel did with her joke about a "consent form"—but all that it really means is that a man cannot penetrate a woman without some kind of go-ahead. Roiphe ridicules this notion as "politically correct" and objects to educational materials that remind men that "hearing a clear sober 'yes' to the question 'Do you want to make love?' is very different from thinking, 'Well, she didn't say no.' " But is that such terrible advice? Roiphe herself says she wants women to be more vocal about sex, yet here she is dismissive of the suggestion that men ought to listen to them.

Roiphe's attempt to debunk statistics on the frequency of rape is similarly ill informed. A substantial body of research, by no means all of it conducted by feminists, or even by women, supports the contention that there is a staggering amount of rape and attempted rape in the United States and that most incidents are not reported to the police—especially when, as is usually the case, victim and offender know each other. For example the National Women's Study, conducted by the Crime Victims Research and Treatment Center at the Medical University of South Carolina, working under a grant from the National Institute of Drug Abuse, which released its results last year, found that 13 percent of adult American women—one in eight—have been raped at least once, 75 percent by someone they knew. (The study used the conservative legal definition of rape which Roiphe favors: "an event that occurred without the woman's consent, involved the use of force or threat of force, and involved sexual penetration of the victim's vagina, mouth or rectum.") Other researchers come up with similar numbers or even higher ones, and are supported by studies querying men about their own behavior: in one such study, 15 percent of the college men interviewed said they had used force at least once to obtain intercourse.

Roiphe does not even acknowledge the existence of this sizable body of work—and it seems she hasn't spent much time studying the scholarly journals in which it appears. Instead she concentrates on a single 1985 article in *Ms.* magazine, which presented a preliminary journalistic account of an acquaintance-rape study conducted by Dr. Mary Koss, a clinical psychologist now at the University of Arizona. Relying on opinion pieces by Neil Gilbert, a professor of social welfare at Berkeley, Roiphe accuses Koss of inflating her findings—one in eight students raped, one in four the victims of rape or attempted rape—by including as victims women who did not describe their experience as rape, although it met a widely accepted legal definition. It is unclear what Roiphe's point is—that women don't mind being physically forced to have sex as long as no one tells them it's rape? Surely she would not argue that the victims of other injustices—fraud, malpractice, job discrimination—have suffered no wrong as long as they are unaware of the law. Roiphe also accuses Koss of upping her numbers by asking respondents if they had ever had sex when they didn't want to because a man gave them alcohol or drugs. "Why aren't college women responsible for their own intake of alcohol or drugs?" Roiphe asks, and it may be fair to say that the alcohol question in the study is ambiguously worded. But it's worth noting that the question doesn't come out of feminist fantasyland. It's keyed to a legal definition of rape that in many states includes sex obtained by intentional incapacitation of the victim with intoxicants—the scenario envisioned by my father. Be that as it may, what happens to Koss's figures if the alcohol question is dropped? The number of college women who have been victims of rape or attempted rape drops from one in four to one in five.

One in five, one in eight—what if it's "only" one in ten or twelve? Social science isn't physics. Exact numbers are important, and elusive, but surely what is significant here is that lots of different studies, with different agendas, sample populations, and methods, tend in the same direction. Rather than grapple with these inconvenient data, Roiphe retreats to her own impressions: "If I was really standing in the middle of an epidemic, a crisis, if 25 percent of my female friends were really being raped, wouldn't I know about it?" (Roiphe forgets that the one-in-four figure includes attempts, but let that pass.) As an experiment, I applied Roiphe's anecdotal method myself, and wrote down what I knew about my own circle of acquaintance: eight rapes by strangers (including one on a college campus); two sexual assaults (one Central Park, one Prospect Park); one abduction (woman walking down street forced into car full of men); one date rape involving a Mickey Finn, which resulted in pregnancy and abortion; and two stalkings (one ex-lover, one deranged fan); plus one brutal beating by a boyfriend, three incidents of childhood incest (none involving therapist-aided "recovered memories"), and one bizarre incident in which a friend went to a man's apartment after meeting him at a party and was forced by him to spend the night under the shower, naked, while he debated whether to kill her, rape her, or let her go. The most interesting thing about this tally, however, is that when I mentioned it to a friend, he was astonished—he himself knew of only one rape victim in his circle, he said—but he knows several of the women on my list.

It may be that Roiphe's friends have nothing to tell her. Or it may be that they have nothing to tell *her*. With her adolescent certainty that bad things don't happen, or that they happen only to weaklings, she is not likely to be on the receiving end of many painful, intimate confessions. The one time a fellow student tells her about being raped (at knifepoint, so it counts), Roiphe cringes like a high school vegetarian dissecting her first frog: "I was startled. . . . I felt terrible for her. I felt like there was nothing I could say." Confronted with someone whose testimony she can't dismiss or satirize, Roiphe goes blank.

Roiphe is right to point out that cultural attitudes toward rape, harassment, coercion, and consent are slowly shifting. It is certainly true that many women today, most of whom would not describe themselves as feminists, feel outraged by male behavior that previous generations—or even those women themselves not so long ago—quietly accepted as "everyday experience." Roiphe may even be right to argue that it muddies the waters when women colloquially speak of "rape" in referring to sex that is caddish or is obtained through verbal or emotional pressure or manipulation, or when they label as "harassment" the occasional leer or off-color comment. But if we lay these terms aside, we still have to account for the phenomenon they point to: that women in great numbers—by no means all on elite campuses, by no means all young—feel angry at and exploited by behavior that many men assume is within bounds and no big deal. Like many of those men, Roiphe would like to short-circuit this larger discussion, as if everything that doesn't meet the legal definition of crime were trivial, and any objection to it mere paranoia. For her, sex is basically a boys' game, with boys' rules, like football, and if a girl wants to make the team—whether by "embracing experience" in bed or by attending a formerly all-male college—she has to play along and risk taking some knocks. But why can't women change the game and add a few rules of their own? What's so "utopian" about expecting men to act as though there are two people in bed and two sexes in the classroom and in the workplace?

Roiphe gives no consistent answer to this question. Sometimes she dismisses the problems as inconsequential: Coerced intercourse is bad sex, widespread sexual violence a myth. Sometimes she suggests that the problem is real but is women's fault: They should be more feisty and vociferous, be more like her and her friends, one of whom she praises for dumping a glass of milk on a boy who grabbed her breast. (Here, in a typical muddle, Roiphe's endorsement of assertive behavior echoes the advice of the antirape educational materials she excoriates.) Sometimes she argues that the women's movement has been so successful in moving women into the professions that today's feminists are whining about nothing. And sometimes she argues that men, if seriously challenged to change their ways and habits, will respond with a backlash, keeping women students at arm's length out of a fear of lawsuits, retreating into anxious nerdhood, like her male-feminist classmates, or even, like the male protagonist of David Mamet's *Oleanna,* becoming violent: "Feminists, Mamet warns, will conjure up the sexist beast if they push far enough."

Coming from a self-proclaimed bad girl and sexual rebel, this last bit of counsel is particularly fainthearted: now who's warning women about the dangers of provoking the savage male? When Roiphe posits a split between her mother's generation of feminists—women eager to enter the world and seize sexual freedom—and those of today, who emphasize the difficulties of doing either, she has it wrong, and not just historically. (Sexual violence was a major theme of seventies feminism, in whose consciousness-raising sessions women first realized that rape was something many of them had in common.) The point she misses is that it was not the theories of academics or of would-be Victorian maidens masquerading as Madonna fans that made sexual violence and harassment an issue. It was the movement of women into male-dominated venues—universities, professions, blue-collar trades—in sufficiently great numbers to demand real accommodation from men both at work and in private life. If Roiphe's contention that focusing on "victimhood" reduces women to passivity were right, the experience of Anita Hill would have sent feminists off weeping, en masse, to a separatist commune. Instead it sparked a wave of activism that revitalized street-level feminism and swept unprecedented numbers of women into Congress.

Roiphe is so intent on demonizing the antirape movement that she misses an opportunity to address a real deficiency of much contemporary feminism. The problem isn't that acknowledging women's frequent victimization saps their get-up-and-go and allows them to be frail flowers; it's that the discourse about sexuality says so little about female pleasure. Unfortunately Roiphe, too, is silent on this subject. We hear a lot about heavy drinking, late nights, parties, waking up in strange beds, but we don't hear what made those experiences worth having, except as acts of rebellion. In a revealing anecdote, she cites with approval a friend who tells off obscene phone callers by informing them that she was her high school's "blow-job queen." Not to detract from that achievement, but one wonders at the unexamined equation of sexual service and sexual selfhood. Do campus bad girls still define their prowess by male orgasms rather than their own?

It's sad for Roiphe and her classmates that they are coming of age sexually at a time when sex seems more fraught with danger and anxiety than ever. Indeed AIDS is the uneasily acknowledged specter hovering over *The Morning After*—the condom, not the imaginary consent form, is what really put a damper on the campus sex scene. Certainly AIDS gives new urgency to the feminist campaign for female sexual self-determination and has probably done a lot, at both conscious and unconscious levels, to frame that quest in negative rather than positive terms. But that's just the way we live now—and not only on campus. Rape, coercion, harassment, the man who edits his sexual history and thinks safe sex kills passion, the obscene phone call that is no longer amusing because you're not in the dorm anymore but living by yourself in a not-so-safe neighborhood and it's three in the morning. It's not very hard to understand why women sometimes sound rather grim about relations between the sexes.

It would be wonderful to hear more from women who are nonetheless "embracing experience," retaining the vital spark of sexual adventure. Roiphe prefers to stick to the oldest put-down of all: Problems? What problems? It's all in your head.

B. VITAL STATISTICS

- In the United States, 1.3 women are raped every minute. That results in 78 rapes each hour, 1872 rapes each day, 56160 rapes each month and 683,280 rapes each year.
- The United States has the world's highest rape rate of the countries that publish such statistics---4 times higher than Germany, 13 times higher than England, and 20 times higher than Japan.
- 1 out of every 3 American women will be sexually assaulted in her lifetime.
- 1 in 7 women will be raped by her husband.
- 61% of all rape cases are victims less than 18 years old. 22% are between the ages of 18 and 24.
- 78% of rape victims know the attacker.
- In a survey of college women, 38% reported sexual victimizations which met the legal definition of a rape or attempted rape, yet only 1 out of every 25 reported their assault to the police.
- 1 in 4 college women have either been raped or suffered attempted rape.
- In a study of college students, 35% of men indicated some likelihood that they would commit a violent rape of a woman who had fended off an advance if they were assured of getting away with it.
- 1 in 12 male students surveyed had committed acts that met the legal definition of rape. Furthermore, 84% of the men who had committed such acts said what they had done was definitely not rape.
- 75% of male students and 55% of female students involved in acquaintance rape had been drinking or using drugs.

- Rape has a devastating impact on the mental health of victims. 31% of all victims develop Rape-Related Post Traumatic Stress Disorder (RR-PTSD) sometime in their lifetimes. Based on U.S. Census reports on the number of women in the United States, 1.3 million women currently have RR-PTSD, 3.8 million women have previously had RR-PTSD and roughly 211,000 women will develop RR-PTSD each year.
- When compared with nonvictims, rape victims have been found to be 8.7 times more likely to attempt suicide.
- Only 16% of rapes are ever reported to the police. In a survey of victims who did not report rape or attempted rape to the police, the following was found as to why no report was made: 43% thought nothing could be done, 27% felt it was a private matter, 12% were afraid of police response, and 12% felt it was not important enough.

From National Victim Center

Domestic violence is the leading cause of injury to women. 1 out of every 3 women will be victims of domestic violence in their lives. A woman is battered every 15 seconds in this country.

- **Women sustain an average of 2.5 million violent crimes each year. In 29% of all violence against women by a lone offender, the perpetrator was a husband, ex-husband, boyfriend or ex-boyfriend an intimate. Compared to men, women were about 6 times more likely to experience violence committed by an intimate.**
- **Women annually reported about 500,000 rapes and sexual assaults. This only accounts for about half of the rapes and sexual assaults that actually occur, since many women do not report sexual crimes. Friends or acquaintances of the victims committed over half of these rapes or sexual assaults. Strangers were responsible for about 1 in 5.**
- **Women were significantly more likely to be killed by an intimate. Nearly 30% of all female homicide victims were known to have been killed by their husbands, ex-husbands or boyfriends in 1992. In contrast, 3% of male homicide victims were known to have been killed by their wife, ex-wife or girlfriend.**
- **Violence against women perpetrated by intimates is consistent across racial and ethnic boundaries.**
- **Compared to other age groups, women ages 19 through 29 reported more incidents of violence by intimates.**
- **Women suffering violent victimizations were twice as likely to be injured if their attacker was an intimate.**
- **Among victims of violence committed by an intimate, the victimization rate of women separated from their husbands was about 3 times higher than that of divorced women and about 25 times higher than that of married women.**
- **25%-45% of battered women were battered while they were pregnant.**
- **32% of battered women are re-victimized within six months.**
- **Men who witnessed violence in their childhood homes are three times as likely to batter their wives and/or girlfriends. 75% of batterers witnessed violence in their childhood homes. 63% of males incarcerated between the ages of 12-20 were there for assaulting or killing their mother's abuser.**

– from the Bureau of Justice Statistics Nation Crime Victimization Survey, August 1995, and the Maryland Network Against Domestic Violence Recruit Curriculum, 1997.)

COMPARISON OF FBI HATE CRIME STATISTICS 1991- 1996

	1991	1992	1993	1994	1995	1996
Participating Agencies	***2,771***	***6,181***	***6,551***	***7,356***	***9,584***	***11,355***
Total Hate Crime Incidents Reported	4,558	6,623	7,587	5,932	7,947	8,734
Number of States, including D.C.	***32***	***42***	***47***	***44***	***46***	***50***
Percentage of U.S. Population Agencies Represent	N/A	51	58	58	75	84

OFFENDERS' REPORTED MOTIVATION

(In Percentages of Offenses)

	1991	1992	1993	1994	1995	1996
Racial Bias	***62.3***	***60.7***	***62.4***	***59.8***	***60.7***	***61.6***
Anti-Black	35.5	34.7	37.1	36.6	37.6	41.9
Anti-White	18.7	20.3	19.4	17	15.4	12.6
Religious Bias	***19.3***	***17.5***	***17.1***	***17.9***	***16.1***	***15.9***
Anti-Semitic	16.7	15.4	15.1	15.1	13.3	12.7
Anti-Semitic as Percentage of Religious Bias	***86.4***	***87.5***	***88.1***	***86.2***	***82.9***	***79.2***
Ethnicity	9.5	10.1	9.2	10.8	10.2	10.7
Sexual Orientation	***8.9***	***11.6***	***11.3***	***11.5***	***12.8***	***11.6***

State Hate Crimes Statutory Provisions

Alabama - Idaho

	AL	AK	AZ	AR	CA	CO	CT	DC	DE	FL	GA	HI	ID
Bias-Motivated Violence and Intimidation	✓	✓	✓		✓	✓	✓	✓	✓	✓			✓
Civil Action				✓	✓	✓	✓	✓		✓			✓
Criminal Penalty	✓	✓	✓		✓	✓	✓	✓	✓	✓			✓
Race, Religion, Ethnicity [1]	✓	✓	✓		✓	✓	✓	✓	✓	✓			✓
• Sexual Orientation			✓		✓		✓	✓	✓	✓			
• Gender		✓	✓		✓			✓					
Other [2]	✓	✓	✓		✓			✓	✓				
Institutional Vandalism	✓		✓	✓	✓	✓	✓	✓	✓	✓	✓	✓	
Data Collection [3]			✓		✓		✓	✓		✓			✓
Training for Law Enforcement Personnel [4]			✓		✓								

Illinois - Missouri

	IL	IN	IA	KS	KY	LA	ME	MD	MA	MI	MN	MS	MO
Bias-Motivated Violence and Intimidation	✓		✓			✓	✓	✓	✓	✓	✓	✓	✓
Civil Action	✓		✓			✓			✓	✓	✓		✓
Criminal Penalty	✓		✓			✓	✓	✓	✓	✓	✓	✓	✓
Race, Religion, Ethnicity [1]	✓		✓			✓	✓	✓	✓	✓	✓	✓	✓
• Sexual Orientation	✓		✓			✓	✓		✓		✓		
• Gender	✓		✓			✓	✓			✓	✓	✓	
Other [2]	✓		✓			✓	✓		✓		✓		
Institutional Vandalism	✓	✓		✓	✓	✓	✓	✓	✓	✓	✓	✓	✓
Data Collection [3]	✓		✓		✓	✓	✓	✓	✓	✓	✓		
Training for Law Enforcement Personnel [4]	✓		✓		✓	✓			✓		✓		

Montana - Pennsylvania

	MT	NE	NV	NH	NJ	NM	NY	NC	ND	OH	OK	OR	PA
Bias-Motivated Violence and Intimidation	✓	✓	✓	✓	✓		✓[5]	✓	✓	✓	✓	✓	✓
Civil Action		✓	✓		✓					✓	✓	✓	✓
Criminal Penalty	✓	✓	✓	✓	✓		✓	✓	✓	✓	✓	✓	✓
Race, Religion, Ethnicity [1]	✓	✓	✓	✓	✓		✓	✓	✓	✓	✓	✓	✓
• Sexual Orientation		✓	✓	✓	✓							✓	
• Gender		✓		✓	✓		✓		✓				
Other [2]		✓	✓	✓	✓		✓				✓		
Institutional Vandalism	✓		✓		✓	✓		✓		✓	✓	✓	✓
Data Collection [3]		✓	✓		✓						✓	✓	✓
Training for Law Enforcement Personnel [4]												✓	

Rhode Island - Wyoming

	RI	SC	SD	TN	TX	UT	VT	VA	WA	WV	WI	WY
Bias-Motivated Violence and Intimidation	✓		✓	✓	✓[6]	✓[7]	✓	✓	✓	✓	✓	
Civil Action	✓		✓	✓			✓	✓	✓		✓	
Criminal Penalty	✓		✓	✓	✓	✓	✓	✓	✓	✓	✓	
Race, Religion, Ethnicity [1]	✓		✓	✓			✓	✓	✓	✓	✓	
• Sexual Orientation	✓						✓		✓		✓	
• Gender	✓						✓		✓	✓		
Other [2]	✓						✓		✓	✓	✓	
Institutional Vandalism	✓	✓		✓	✓			✓	✓		✓	
Data Collection [3]	✓				✓			✓	✓			
Training for Law Enforcement Personnel [4]	✓								✓			

From Federal Bureau of Investigation;Anti-Defamation League, 1999

C. DOMESTIC VIOLENCE

Like "date rape," domestic violence is generally not prosecuted as a crime in itself, but rather under general assault, battery, and other state criminal statutes. In 1994, Congress passed the Violence Against Women Act (Public Law 103-322), which provides federal funds for investigation and prosecution of domestic violence; allows victims to bring federal lawsuits for damages and injunctive relief against perpetrators; and permits federal criminal prosecution of persons who cross state lines to commit acts of domestic violence. The latter provision has been held to be an unconstitutional infringement of the prerogative of the states by the Fourth U.S. Circuit Court of Appeals; even if this decision is ultimately reversed by the Supreme Court, the overwhelming majority of domestic violence prosecutions, like rape and sexual assault cases, will continue to be brought in state courts.

All states have domestic violence prevention networks or coalitions, which collect data and conduct public education, law enforcement training, and lobby state legislatures for more effective investigation, prosecution, and victim protection. It is at the local level, where police and prosecutors handle these cases, that innovative measures and prompt official response can be crucial. In the Washington, D.C. area, recent steps have included free distributions of cell-phones to victim for emergency contact in Arlington County, Virginia, and a special weekly domestic violence court docket in Montgomery County, Maryland [Washington Post, Feb. 16, 1998; April 1, 1999]. In a landmark June, 1999 ruling, the Ninth U.S. Circuit Court of Appeals, in *Navarro v. Block,* found that Los Angeles County's policy of assigning a low priority to domestic violence-relate "911" calls violated the Equal Protection Clause of the Fourteenth Amendment.

NAVARRO v. BLOCK

U.S. Court of Appeals, Ninth Circuit

Case No. 95-55699

Decided June 3, 1999

PREGERSON, Circuit Judge:

Denise Navarro and other relatives of decedent Maria Navarro ("the Navarros") appeal the district court's grant of judgment on the pleadings in favor of the defendants under Federal Rule of Civil Procedure 12(c). The Navarros sued Defendants under 42 U.S.C. S 1983 for allegedly giving lower priority to domestic-violence 9-1-1 calls than to non-domestic-violence 9-1-1 calls.

[1] It does not matter whether it is rational to distinguish between in-progress calls and not-in-progress calls because that was not the distinction that Defendants allegedly made. The Navarros allege that Defendants distinguished between domestic-violence 9-1-1 calls and non-domestic-violence 9-1-1 calls regardless of whether the violence was in progress.

[2] Moreover, whether domestic violence "rarely" results in death or severe injury does not, by itself, end the matter. The critical issue is whether domestic-violence crimes result in severe injury or death less frequently than non=domestic= violence crimes that are considered 9-1-1 emergencies. See Cleburne v. Cleburne Living Center, 473 U.S. 432, 439 (1985) (indicating that the Equal Protection Clause requires the same treatment of "similarly situated" persons).2 Nothing in the pleadings suggests that victims of domestic violence are less likely to suffer severe injury or death than are victims of other 9=1=1 emergency crimes.3

[3] Hence, the district court erred by equating domestic violence calls with not-in-progress calls and equating non-domestic violence calls with in-progress calls, and by assuming that domestic-violence crimes are less injurious than non-domestic-violence crimes. Because these assumptions formed the basis of the district court's conclusion, the district court also erred when it concluded, as a matter of law, that Defendants' domestic-violence/non-domestic-violence classification was rational and reasonable under equal-protection analysis.

2 Additionally, if the Navarros can prove at trial that Defendants dispatch peace officers to prevent crimes that pose less (or equal) risk of death or severe injury than that posed by domestic violence crimes, then the Navarros would establish that Defendants' asserted justification is a pretext. If Defendants' justification for discriminating against domestic-violence crimes is nothing more than pretextual, then Defendants' actions are arbitrary and violate the Equal Protection Clause.

MYTHS ABOUT DOMESTIC VIOLENCE

- Battering affects only a small percentage of the population.
- Battering is only a momentary loss of control.
- Battered women are masochistic; they like the violence.
- Battering does not produce serious injuries.
- Drinking causes people to batter.
- Therapy will stop the violence. ("If he/she gets into therapy, I will be safe at home.")
- Religious faith will prevent further battering
- It is easy for battered spouses to leave their abuser.
- Even if the spouse is violent, it is better for the children to have two parents.
- If you are battered by one spouse/loved one, you will be battered by the next.
- Victims of abuse are crazy.
- Middle and upper class victims do not get battered as frequently or as violently as poorer victims.
- Batterers are violent in all of their relationships.
- Batterers are unsuccessful and lack resources to cope with the world.
- Batterers are psychopathic personalities.
- The batterer is not a loving partner.
- Victims of domestic violence deserve to get beaten.
- Battering will stop "when we get married."
- Domestic violence is a private family matter. Officials are acting in the best interest of the family by not interfering.
- Domestic violence is usually precipitated by the victim's provoking statements or actions.

WHY DO ABUSED SPOUSES STAY IN A VIOLENT RELATIONSHIP?

Usually, there is not one reason for staying in a violent relationship, but several overlapping reasons. Reasons cited by abused spouses include:

1. Fear that leaving will precipitate even more violent incidents of abuse directed toward themselves or their children;

2. Emotional dependency on marital relationship, accompanied by feelings of low self-esteem and self-blame;

3. Lack of financial resources and employment income necessary to establish and maintain an independent household;

4. Concern about the effects of separation or divorce on the children (e.g., a "broken" home will jeopardize the children's future);

5. Concern about the loss of economic security and benefits, such as retirement income and health insurance;

6. Feelings of love toward the spouse, coupled with hopes that the relationship will improve and violence will cease;

7. Denial of the potential for severe abuse, rationalizations and excuses for the abuser's behavior, as well as the inability to assess accurately the risks of the situation;

8. Physical and/or social isolation from family, friends and community resources (isolation is an even greater problem for victims who live in rural areas and for foreign-born wives);

9. Concern about the negative implication of divorce on career;

10. Strong cultural and religious beliefs about the importance of maintaining a marriage, regardless of "marital" problems;

11. Feeling of shame about the occurrence of violence in the relationship, preventing requests for help;

12. Acceptance of violence as "normal" in families because of exposure to violent episodes as a child;

13. Lack of, or perceived lack of, police protection and other forms of intervention;

14. Lack of information regarding legal rights, legal options and resources available for victims, such as emergency shelters; and

15. Prior unsuccessful attempts to obtain help from extended family or from the law enforcement, legal and social service systems.

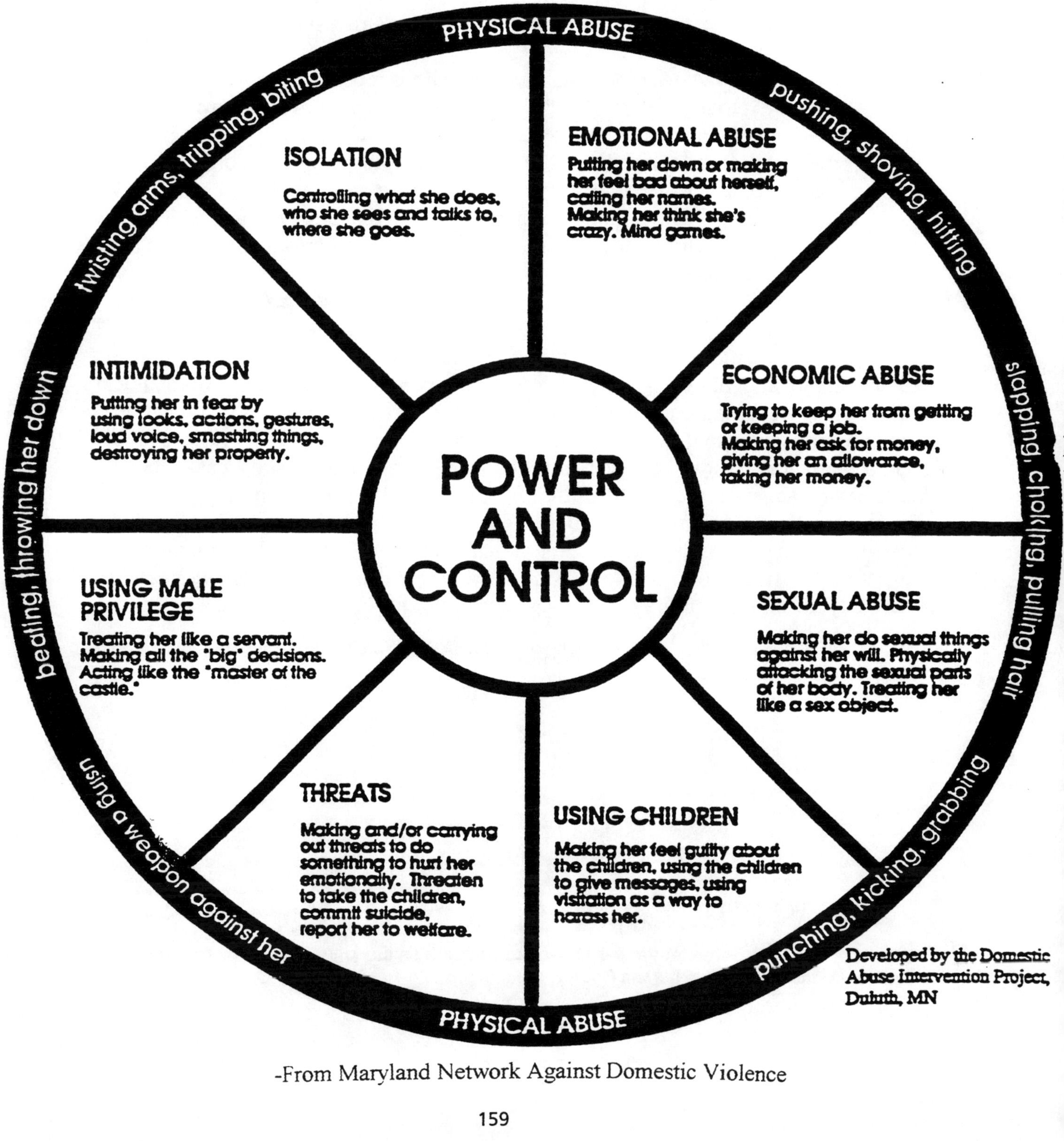

-From Maryland Network Against Domestic Violence

D. BATTERED WOMAN SYNDROME AND THE LAW

The preceding material from the Maryland Network Against Domestic Violence and other states emanates in great measure from studies pioneered by Lenore Walker. In works such as *The Battered Woman* (Harper & Row: 1979) and *Terrifying Love: Why Battered Women Kill and How Society Responds* (Harper & Row: 1989), Walker was instrumental in developing the medical, and ultimately legal concept of battered woman's syndrome, a form of post-traumatic stress syndrome:

> "A battered woman is a woman who is repeatedly subjected to any forceful physical or psychological behavior by a man in order to coerce her to do without any concern for her rights. Battered women include wives or women in any form of intimate relationships with men. Furthermore, in order to be classified as a battered woman, the couple must go through the battering cycle at least twice. Any woman may find herself in an abusive relationship with a man once. If it occurs a second time, and she remains in the situation, she is defined as a battered woman."
>
> Walker, *The Battered Woman* at p. xv

While the battered woman syndrome has not met with universal medical or political approval, it has been a critical defense weapon in prosecutions of women who kill their abusers, because it allows expert witnesses to explain to jurors why a battered woman would continue to stay in such a relationship. Unique among the various mental and physiological "syndrome" defenses – of which jurors are often skeptical -- the battered woman syndrome is perhaps the only one in which there is no truly innocent victim, because the "victim" of the homicide is the person who is responsible for the existence of the syndrome. Two decisions by the Supreme Court of Wyoming show how legislative recognition of the battered woman syndrome can present a jury with crucial, previously inadmissible testimony.

Edith **BUHRLE,** Appellant (Defendant below), v. **STATE** of Wyoming, Appellee (Plaintiff below)

No. 5425

Supreme Court of Wyoming

627 P.2d 1374; 1981 Wyo. LEXIS 338

May 13, 1981

OPINIONBY: BROWN

OPINION: [*1375] Defendant-appellant was convicted by a jury of murder in the second degree, in the Seventh Judicial District, in and for Natrona County, Wyoming.

We find that the trial judge did not commit reversible error and, therefore, we affirm.

Kenneth Buhrle, the victim, and appellant had been married eighteen years at the time of Mr. Buhrle's death. During this time appellant suffered numerous instances of physical and mental abuse. On September 24, 1979, Mr. Buhrle had his lawyer draw up papers to institute a divorce action, and he also executed an affidavit in order to obtain a restraining order against his wife. The next day Mr. Buhrle and appellant got into an argument and during the altercation appellant threatened her husband with a shovel. Mr. Buhrle responded by beating his wife about the head, neck and shoulders with a pair of work boots. The following day Mr. Buhrle moved out of the family home and into the Bel Air Motel.

[*1376] Appellant testified that her husband returned to the family home in the late afternoon of October 2, 1979, and requested that appellant drive out to the motel where he was staying so they could talk. When appellant [**3] arrived at the motel she had a hunting rifle and a pair of rubber gloves in her possession. Mr. Buhrle kept the night chain on the door of his motel room the entire time that the two talked. After standing outside her husband's motel room for an hour and forty-five minutes while they argued over money and the divorce, appellant shot her husband.

After appellant shot her husband she pushed open the motel room door and was kneeling over Mr. Buhrle when the people from the adjoining rooms arrived at the scene. Appellant then began shouting that someone had shot her husband. In addition, while appellant asserts that she made no effort to flee, she did attempt to conceal the pair of rubber gloves she was seen wearing shortly after the shooting and she hid the rifle underneath a nearby trailer-house. At the time that appellant was arrested she had her husband's wallet in her possession.

At trial appellant relied upon the theory of self-defense. Edith Buhrle took the stand and told of a history of violence on the part of the deceased towards her, her children and the household furnishings. She further testified that when she shot her husband she had thought that he was reaching for [**4] the gun that he customarily kept under his bed so that he could kill her. No gun, however, was found in Mr. Buhrle's motel room.

EXCLUSION OF THE TESTIMONY OF A DEFENSE PSYCHOLOGIST

The criteria to be used in determining the admissibility of an expert witness' testimony are set out in *Dyas v. United States,* 376 A.2d 827, 832 (D.C.C.A. 1977), cert. denied 434 U.S. 973, 98 S. Ct. 529, 54 L. Ed. 2d 464 (1977). As stated by the court:

> "(1) * * * * the subject matter 'must be so distinctively related to some science, profession, business, or occupation *as to be beyond the ken of the average layman* [emphasis added]'; (2) 'the witness must have sufficient skill, knowledge, or experience in that field or calling as to make it appear that his opinion or inference *will*
>
> *probably aid the trier in his search for truth* [emphasis added]'; (3) expert testimony is inadmissible if 'the state of the pertinent art or scientific knowledge does not permit a reasonable opinion to be asserted even by an expert.'" McCormick on Evidence, § 13, pp. 29-31 (2d Ed. 1972)

In this case the trial judge used the criteria in *Dyas v. United States,* supra, in making his ruling. [**5] His reasons for rejecting the testimony of the expert witness, Dr. Lenore E. Walker, were set out in detail.

Dr. Walker possesses impressive academic and professional credentials and she is the pioneer in the field of the so-called "battered woman syndrome." n1 By her own characterization she is the foremost authority on that phenomenon and also describes herself as a feminist psychologist.

- - - - - - - - - - - - - - - - - -Footnotes- - - - - - - - - - - - - - - - - -

n1 Robert Menninger, M.D., The Menninger Foundation, Topeka, Kansas, during a speech at Wyoming's First State Conference, *Family Violence: A Cycle of Abuse,* defined battering as follows: "To beat with successive blows; to beat repeatedly and with violence, so as to bruise, shatter, or demolish." (Laramie, August 1978).

- - - - - - - - - - - - - - - - -End Footnotes- - - - - - - - - - - - - - - - -

During extensive voir dire by the State, it was shown that in the introduction of her book, *The Battered Woman*

(1979), Dr. Walker stated at pp. xv-xvi:

> "I think this research has raised more questions for me than it has answered. As a trained researcher, I felt uneasy about stating some of [**6] my conclusions in this book. They seemed too tentative to write down in the positive manner which I have used. Yet they are confirmed repeatedly by all the available data so far. * * * *"

In answer to a follow-up question by defense counsel, Dr. Walker explained the statement from her book as follows:

> "That's why I received the research grant, to study the matter in a much more scientific way. * * * *" [*1377]

It was further revealed on voir dire that her research was ongoing and that a deadline for completion was yet in the future. Voir dire was followed by an offer of proof by defense counsel.

Appellant's offer of proof indicated that Dr. Walker would testify that:

> 1) Mrs. Buhrle was a battered woman and a battered woman's behavior differs from that of other women.
>
> 2) Mrs. Buhrle was in a state of learned helplessness resulting in loss of free will.
>
> 3) Because of learned helplessness, Mrs. Buhrle's ability to walk away from a situation or escape was impaired.
>
> 4) Mrs. Buhrle perceived herself to be acting in self-defense.

The trial judge ruled that Dr. Walker's testimony was not admissible. The reasons for this ruling were: [**7]

> 1) Voir dire did not adequately demonstrate that the state of the art permitted a reasonable opinion.
>
> 2) The reasons for opinions were not adequately explained, were difficult to understand; and therefore, would not aid the jury.
>
> 3) Appellant's state of mind at the time of the shooting was not adequately explained; and therefore, this testimony would not aid the jury in its determination.

The record indicates that research in the "battered woman syndrome" is in its infancy; that objectives are difficult to identify; that statistical analysis was in the preparation stage; and that acceptance or recognition of the phenomenon is largely limited to the people who are actively engaged in the research and the people making research grants.

In the case at bar the shooting occurred well after the altercation with the victim in which appellant was beaten. Seven days later Mrs. Buhrle went to the victim's motel room and after arguing with him an hour and forty-five minutes she shot him. Insofar as voir dire reveals, this is not the standard battered woman self-defense situation. In explaining her opinions, Dr. Walker did not consider these factors which are departures [**8] from the standard battered woman behavior. This is not to deny a battered woman syndrome and all its ramifications. Suffice it to say defendant failed to demonstrate to the trial court that the state of the art would permit a reasonable expert opinion, nor would the proposed opinions, considering omissions in foundation, aid the jury.

The quotation from Dr. Walker's book, *The Battered Woman,* supra, and elsewhere in her voir dire suggests that Dr. Walker may make certain conclusions and state certain theories, then engage in research to attempt to substantiate those theories and conclusions. The trial judge may have concluded that she did this with Mrs. Buhrle. Dr. Walker was vague in her explanation of Mrs. Buhrle's behavior if such behavior did not fit into the pattern of battered women. For example, her explanation of why Mrs. Buhrle took a hunting rifle to the motel and why she hid the gun and gloves after the shooting apparently did not fit into the battered woman syndrome; therefore, these acts were inadequately explained and apparently ignored by Dr. Walker in arriving at an opinion.

The trial judge expressed some difficulty in understanding Dr. Walker's explanations [**9] and after he had asked several questions of Dr. Walker, said, "But you probably answered my question satisfactorily to you, but not to me. I don't understand the answer to my question." This court experienced the same difficulty. It might reasonably be assumed, therefore, that if the trial court and the appellate court had difficulty understanding the expert's explanations, so would the jury. The "aura of special reliability and trustworthiness" surrounding scientific or expert testimony, particularly calls for trial court discretion. *United States v. Amaral,* 488 F.2d 1148, 1152 (9th Cir. 1973).

In urging the admission of Dr. Walker's testimony, defendant relies principally on *Ibn-Tamas v. United States,* 407 A.2d 626 (D.C.C.A. 1979); and *State v. Thomas,* Nos. 39698, 40028 (Ohio App., filed July 24, [*1378] 1980). n2 In both of these cases wives were charged with murder of their husbands. In both, the accused presented a theory of self-defense. Each was convicted after a jury trial; on appeal *Ibn-Tamas* was remanded and *Thomas* was reversed. In both cases the accused had sought to call expert witnesses to present testimony on the psychology of battered [**10] women, and in both cases the trial judge excluded the testimony.

-----------------Footnotes-----------------

n2 Cf., *People v. White,* 90 Ill. App. 3d 1067, 414 N.E.2d 196, 46 Ill. Dec. 474 (1980).

-----------------End Footnotes-----------------

In *Ibn-Tamas,* supra, the appellate court remanded the case for specific findings on the criteria set forth in *Dyas v. United States,* supra. In the case at bar the trial judge in fact made specific findings as to the Dyas criteria.

Ibn-Tamas v. United States, supra, can also be distinguished in the opinions that the expert proposed to give. The defense proffered expert testimony in *Ibn-Tamas,* supra, p. 631, for two purposes: "To describe the phenomenon of 'wife battering,' and to give her opinion of the extent to which appellant's personality and behavior corresponded to those of 110 battered women Dr. Walker had studied." The proposed witness in *Ibn-Tamas,* supra, was not going to express an opinion on the ultimate question whether Mrs. Ibn-Tamas actually and reasonably believed she was in danger when she shot her husband. Rather, the [**11] witness would have merely supplied background data to help the jury make that crucial determination.

In the case at bar, however, Dr. Walker proposed to express such opinion. Dr. Walker also expected to express an opinion on whether or not Mrs. Buhrle was in fear of her life at the time of the shooting and whether such fear was reasonable; and she proposed to make the decision for the jury whether Edith Buhrle was capable of retreating at the instant when the victim was shot.

Ibn-Tamas and *Thomas,* supra, can further be distinguished in that the killing occurred during or immediately after a battering incident. The shooting of Kenneth Buhrle occurred a week after an altercation.

Finally, defense counsel proposed to ask Dr. Walker if in her opinion Edith Buhrle believed that she was acting in self-defense when she shot her husband. Clearly, in the case at bar, appellant proposed to go far beyond what was proposed in *Ibn-Tamas,* supra.

In *State v. Thomas,* supra, the appeals court found that the criteria in *Dyas v. United States,* supra, had been satisfied. They went on to expressly approve the use of expert testimony to substantiate the reasonableness of a claim [**12] of self-defense by a battered woman.

In our holding here we are not saying that this type of expert testimony is not admissible; we are merely holding that the state of the art was not adequately demonstrated to the court, and because of inadequate foundation the proposed opinions would not aid the jury.

The court did not abuse its discretion in rejecting the proffered expert testimony.

Wyo. Stat. § 6-1-203

§ 6-1-203. Battered woman syndrome

(a) The "**battered woman** syndrome" is defined as a subset under the diagnosis of Post-Traumatic Stress Disorder established in the Diagnostic and Statistical Manual of Mental Disorders III -- Revised of the American Psychiatric Association.

(b) If a person is charged with a crime involving the use of force against another, and the person raises the affirmative defense of self-defense, the person may introduce expert testimony that the person suffered from the syndrome, to establish the necessary requisite belief of an imminent danger of death or great bodily harm as an element of the affirmative defense, to justify the person's use of force.

HISTORY: Laws 1993, ch. 66, § 1.

JAMES ABRAHAM **TRUJILLO,** Appellant (Defendant), v. THE **STATE** OF WYOMING, Appellee (Plaintiff).

No. 96-205

SUPREME COURT OF WYOMING

953 P.2d 1182; 1998 Wyo. LEXIS 14

February 12, 1998, Decided

OPINION: [*1184] TAYLOR, Chief Justice.

Charged with the brutal beating and forced confinement of his pregnant girlfriend, appellant was convicted of aggravated assault and battery and kidnapping. Appellant now appeals the district court's evidentiary rulings. Finding that the district court properly admitted evidence of appellant's prior misconduct and the testimony of a domestic violence expert, we affirm.

In October of 1995, Natalie Newsome (Newsome) endured the last in a series of episodes of abuse by Trujillo. Having spent an hour smoking marijuana with friends, Trujillo turned upon Newsome, accusing her of stealing his marijuana. Rebuking her denials of the theft, Trujillo threatened Newsome with torture the next day if she did not tell him where she had hidden the marijuana. Using a padlock placed on [**3] the outside of the door to contain Newsome within their shared trailer house, Trujillo ordered Newsome to spend the night on the couch.

True to his word, early the next morning, Trujillo refused to allow Newsome to use the bathroom, knocked her to the floor, whipped her across the back and legs with an extension cord, and used the heated tongs of a hammer to burn the back of Newsome's leg.

Newsome, eight months pregnant at the time, repeatedly denied taking Trujillo's marijuana, and pleaded with him to stop the abuse. Dissatisfied with her protests, he used the extension cord to choke Newsome, pulling it so tight she nearly lost consciousness. He then pulled handfuls of hair from her head, and used a garden hose attached to the kitchen sink to "hose her down." Finally, Trujillo ordered Newsome to undress, gagged her, bound her, and left the trailer, again locking it from the outside.

When Trujillo returned approximately forty-five minutes later, Newsome was able to convince Trujillo she had money at a friend's home and would give it to him to replace the marijuana. Trujillo allowed Newsome to leave the trailer, and Newsome immediately called a friend who took her to the hospital and then to a safe house. After hearing Newsome's story, the safe house employees called the police.

On November 5, 1995, Newsome voluntarily left the safe house and rejoined Trujillo. [*1185] The couple traveled to Rawlins, Wyoming, where they were married on November 7, 1995. Shortly thereafter, Newsome returned to the safe house because she was afraid Trujillo would not allow her to go to the hospital to give birth. The couple's son was born on November 16, 1995.

At trial, the State presented sixteen witnesses, including the victim. Seven of those witnesses testified regarding acts committed by Trujillo either against them or against Newsome in their presence. Eight of the witnesses were police officers, safe house workers, and other social welfare workers who testified as to the result of Trujillo's acts on Newsome. In addition, the State presented testimony of two friends with whom Trujillo had been smoking marijuana on the evening in question. Both testified he had offered them bribes to testify favorably and threatened them with violence if they did not. Rosemary Bratton, Education Coordinator for the Wyoming Coalition Against Domestic Violence and Sexual Assault, testified that based upon the Newsome testimony at trial, it was Ms. Bratton's expert opinion that Newsome's description of her relationship with Trujillo resembled behavior characterized by Hostage Syndrome and Battered Woman Syndrome.

The defense contended the charges were based on Newsome's hallucinations resulting from her psychological dysfunction. Trujillo attempted to present Newsome as being mentally unbalanced, and therefore not credible, because she had stopped taking [**7] her psycotropic medication during pregnancy. Trujillo's brother and sister-in-law both testified that Newsome was happy to be married to Trujillo. Trujillo's brother further related prior incidents of explosive behavior from Newsome directed at Trujillo.

B. ROSEMARY BRATTON'S EXPERT TESTIMONY

Trujillo asserts that the testimony of Ms. Bratton, the State's expert on domestic violence, [**11] was improperly admitted because such evidence is relevant only when the victim is a minor or has claimed self-defense. Because there was no objection at trial, we must determine whether Ms. Bratton's testimony constituted plain error. This claim [*1187] fails, as we find no violation of a clear and unequivocal rule of law.

To be admissible, expert testimony must meet the requirements of W.R.E. 702:

> If scientific, technical, or other specialized knowledge will assist the trier of fact to understand the evidence or to determine a fact in issue, a witness qualified as an expert by knowledge, skill, experience, training, or education, may testify thereto in the form of an opinion or otherwise.

We have previously permitted expert testimony to explain a victim's behavior. *See, e.g., Frenzel v. State,* 849 P.2d 741, 746 (Wyo. 1993), *cert. denied,* 139 L. Ed. 2d 303, 118 S. Ct. 388 (1997); *Griego v. State,* 761 P.2d 973, 979 (Wyo. 1988); *Scadden v. State,* 732 P.2d 1036, 1047-48 (Wyo. 1987); and *Lessard v. State,* 719 P.2d 227, 234 (Wyo. 1986). In *Sorensen,* 895 P.2d at 459, we made it clear that expert testimony to explain a victim's behavior is admissible so long as it [**12] is "based on either the expert's own experience or on a syndrome * * * which has reached a sufficient level of development to warrant its admission."

The State's evidence showed a pattern of violence and abuse by Trujillo against Newsome over a period of several years. Each time she returned to Trujillo voluntarily, going so far as to marry him after the incident at issue in this case. This behavior was the subject of Ms. Bratton's expert testimony. Ms. Bratton described the characteristics of a person suffering from both Battered Woman Syndrome and Hostage Syndrome and its symptoms. Ms. Bratton opined that Newsome's continued return to Trujillo resembled both the Battered Woman Syndrome and the Hostage Syndrome.

In this case, the jury could easily have misconstrued Newsome's continuing return to the abusive environment of Trujillo's home as an indication that no abuse had occurred, thus establishing Trujillo's defense that the incident was imagined by Newsome. Ms. Bratton's expert explanation of this behavior was helpful to the jury's understanding, and was based upon recognized syndromes.

There was no violation of a clear and unequivocal rule of law, and the admission of Ms. Bratton's testimony [**14] was not error.

V. CONCLUSION

Having decided to characterize himself as the victim of Newsome's psychotic delusions, Trujillo invited the evidence of prior bad acts which corroborated Newsome's testimony. The expert opinion was properly admitted to explain the victim's repeated reconciliations with her tormentor. It is clear that Trujillo received a fair trial on all counts. The judgment and sentence of the district court are affirmed.

E. RECOMMENDED READING

L. Walker, *The Battered Woman* (Harper & Row: 1979)

L. Walker, *Terrifying Love: Why Battered Women Kill and How Society Responds* (Harper & Row: 1989)

D. Buss, N. Malamuth, *Sex, Power, Conflict: Evolutionary Perspective* (Oxford University Press: 1996)

S. Brownmiller, *Against Our Will: Men, Women and Rape* (Simon & Schuster: 1975)

CHAPTER VI
Access to Reproductive Rights

A. THE SUPREME COURT AND ABORTION

It is in the area of access to abortion that the legal gains of the modern women's rights movement have been most seriously jeopardized.. The apex of those gains was the 1973 Supreme Court decision in *Roe v. Wade*, which invalidated Texas criminal abortion statutes as violative of fundamental constitutional rights of privacy and liberty, which the Due Process Clause of the Fourteenth Amendment guaranteed to states' citizens. Justice Blackmun's majority opinion in *Roe* recognized a legitimate but limited state interest in abortion-related health concerns, as set forth in a trimester framework:

> (a) For the stage prior to approximately the end of the first trimester, the abortion decision and its effectuation must be left to the medical judgment of the pregnant woman's attending physician.
>
> (b) For the stage subsequent to approximately the end of the first trimester, the State, in promoting its interest in the health of the mother, may, if it chooses, regulate the abortion procedure in ways that are reasonably related to maternal health.
>
> (c) For the stage subsequent to viability, the State in promoting its interest in the potentiality of human life may, if it chooses, regulate, and even proscribe, abortion except where it is necessary, in appropriate medical judgment, for the preservation of the life or health of the mother.
>
> *Roe v. Wade*, 410 U.S 113 at 164-65

In the years following *Roe*, a succession of state legislatures passed new restrictions on access to abortion, and Congress prohibited funding for abortions in several federal medical programs. The Supreme Court revisited the issue periodically in a series of decisions ruling on the constitutionality of this post-*Roe* legislation. In those decisions -- notably *Harris v. McRae* (1980), *Webster v. Reproductive Health Services* (1989), and *Planned Parenthood of Southeastern Pa. v. Casey* (1992) -- the Court took pains to assert that it was not overruling *Roe's* fundamental principles. However, a broad range of state and federal funding and personal restrictions were upheld, under the new "undue burden" test (replacing the *Roe* trimester framework) enunciated by Justices O'Connor, Kennedy, and Souter in *Casey*. Following these decisions, additional states passed legislation mandating parental and spousal consent; counseling and waiting periods; and permitting abortions only in cases of danger to the mother's health, rape or incest, and other specialized situations.

ROE v. WADE, 410 U.S. 113 (1973)

Decided January 22, 1973

MR. JUSTICE BLACKMUN delivered the opinion of the Court.

I

The Texas statutes that concern us here are Arts. 1191-1194 and 1196 of the State's Penal Code.1 These make it a crime to "procure an abortion," as therein [410 U.S. 113, 118] defined, or to attempt one, except with respect to "an abortion procured or attempted by medical advice for the purpose of saving the life of the mother." Similar statutes are in existence in a majority of the States.2 [410 U.S. 113, 119]

Texas first enacted a criminal abortion statute in 1854. Texas Laws 1854, c. 49, 1, set forth in 3 H. Gammel, Laws of Texas 1502 (1898). This was soon modified into language that has remained substantially unchanged to the present time. See Texas Penal Code of 1857, c. 7, Arts. 531-536; G. Paschal, Laws of Texas, Arts. 2192-2197 (1866); Texas Rev. Stat., c. 8, Arts. 536-541 (1879); Texas Rev. Crim. Stat., Arts. 1071-1076 (1911). The final article in each of these compilations provided the same exception, as does the present Article 1196, for an abortion by "medical advice for the purpose of saving the life of the mother."3 [410 U.S. 113, 120]

II

Jane Roe,4 a single woman who was residing in Dallas County, Texas, instituted this federal action in March 1970 against the District Attorney of the county. She sought a declaratory judgment that the Texas criminal abortion statutes were unconstitutional on their face, and an injunction restraining the defendant from enforcing the statutes.

Roe alleged that she was unmarried and pregnant; that she wished to terminate her pregnancy by an abortion "performed by a competent, licensed physician, under safe, clinical conditions"; that she was unable to get a "legal" abortion in Texas because her life did not appear to be threatened by the continuation of her pregnancy; and that she could not afford to travel to another jurisdiction in order to secure a legal abortion under safe conditions. She claimed that the Texas statutes were unconstitutionally vague and that they abridged her right of personal privacy, protected by the First, Fourth, Fifth, Ninth, and Fourteenth Amendments. By an amendment to her complaint Roe purported to sue "on behalf of herself and all other women" similarly situated.

The principal thrust of appellant's attack on the Texas statutes is that they improperly invade a right, said to be possessed by the pregnant woman, to choose to terminate her pregnancy. Appellant would discover this right in the concept of personal "liberty" embodied in the Fourteenth Amendment's Due Process Clause; or in personal, marital, familial, and sexual privacy said to be protected by the Bill of Rights or its penumbras, see Griswold v. Connecticut, 381 U.S. 479 (1965); Eisenstadt v. Baird, 405 U.S. 438 (1972); id., at 460 (WHITE, J., concurring in result); or among those rights reserved to the people by the Ninth Amendment, Griswold v. Connecticut, 381 U.S., at 486

The Constitution does not explicitly mention any right of privacy. In a line of decisions, however, going back perhaps as far as Union Pacific R. Co. v. Botsford, 141 U.S. 250, 251 (1891), the Court has recognized that a right of personal privacy, or a guarantee of certain areas or zones of privacy, does exist under the Constitution. In varying contexts, the Court or individual Justices have, indeed, found at least the roots of that right in the First Amendment, Stanley v. Georgia, 394 U.S. 557, 564 (1969); in the Fourth and Fifth Amendments, Terry v. Ohio, 392 U.S. 1, 8-9 (1968), Katz v. United States, 389 U.S. 347, 350 (1967), Boyd v. United States, 116 U.S. 616 (1886), see Olmstead v. United States, 277 U.S. 438, 478 (1928) (Brandeis, J., dissenting); in the penumbras of the Bill of Rights, Griswold v. Connecticut, 381 U.S., at 484-485; in the Ninth Amendment, id., at 486 (Goldberg, J., concurring); or in the concept of liberty guaranteed by the first section of the Fourteenth Amendment, see Meyer v. Nebraska, 262 U.S. 390, 399 (1923). These decisions make it clear that only personal rights that can be deemed "fundamental" or "implicit in the concept of ordered liberty," Palko v. Connecticut, 302 U.S. 319, 325 (1937), are included in this guarantee of personal privacy. They also make it clear that the right has some extension to activities relating to marriage, Loving v. Virginia, 388 U.S. 1, 12 (1967); procreation, Skinner v. Oklahoma, 316 U.S. 535, 541-542 (1942); contraception, Eisenstadt v. Baird, 405 U.S., at 453-454; id., at 460, 463-465 [410 U.S. 113, 153] (WHITE, J., concurring in result); family relationships, Prince v. Massachusetts, 321 U.S. 158, 166 (1944); and child rearing and education, Pierce v. Society of Sisters, 268 U.S. 510, 535 (1925), Meyer v. Nebraska, supra.

This right of privacy, whether it be founded in the Fourteenth Amendment's concept of personal liberty and restrictions upon state action, as we feel it is, or, as the District Court determined, in the Ninth Amendment's reservation of rights to the people, is broad enough to encompass a woman's decision whether or not to terminate her pregnancy. The detriment that the State would impose upon the pregnant woman by denying this choice altogether is apparent. Specific and direct harm medically diagnosable even in early pregnancy may be involved. Maternity, or additional offspring, medical standards, and prenatal life, become dominant. We agree with this approach.

Where certain "fundamental rights" are involved, the Court has held that regulation limiting these rights may be justified only by a "compelling state interest," Kramer v. Union Free School District, 395 U.S. 621, 627 (1969); Shapiro v. Thompson, 394 U.S. 618, 634 (1969), Sherbert v. Verner, 374 U.S. 398, 406 (1963), and that legislative enactments must be narrowly drawn to express only the legitimate state interests at stake. Griswold v. Connecticut, 381 U.S., at 485; Aptheker v. Secretary of State, 378 U.S. 500, 508 (1964); Cantwell v. Connecticut, 310 U.S. 296, 307-308 (1940); see [410 U.S. 113, 156] Eisenstadt v. Baird, 405 U.S., at 460, 463-464 (WHITE, J., concurring in result).

In the recent abortion cases, cited above, courts have recognized these principles. Those striking down state laws have generally scrutinized the State's interests in protecting health and potential life, and have concluded that neither interest justified broad limitations on the reasons for which a physician and his pregnant patient might decide that she should have an abortion in the early stages of pregnancy. Courts sustaining state laws have held that the State's determinations to protect health or prenatal life are dominant and constitutionally justifiable.

In view of all this, we do not agree that, by adopting one theory of life, Texas may override the rights of the pregnant woman that are at stake. We repeat, however, that the State does have an important and legitimate interest in preserving and protecting the health of the pregnant woman, whether she be a resident of the State or a nonresident who seeks medical consultation and treatment there, and that it has still another important and legitimate interest in protecting the potentiality of human life. These interests are separate and distinct. Each grows in substantiality as the woman approaches [410 U.S. 113, 163] term and, at a point during pregnancy, each becomes "compelling."

With respect to the State's important and legitimate interest in the health of the mother, the "compelling" point, in the light of present medical knowledge, is at approximately the end of the first trimester. This is so because of the now-established medical fact, referred to above at 149, that until the end of the first trimester mortality in abortion may be less than mortality in normal childbirth. It follows that, from and after this point, a State may regulate the abortion procedure to the extent that the regulation reasonably relates to the preservation and protection of maternal health. Examples of permissible state regulation in this area are requirements as to the qualifications of the person who is to perform the abortion; as to the licensure of that person; as to the facility in which the procedure is to be performed, that is, whether it must be a hospital or may be a clinic or some other place of less-than-hospital status; as to the licensing of the facility; and the like.

This means, on the other hand, that, for the period of pregnancy prior to this "compelling" point, the attending physician, in consultation with his patient, is free to determine, without regulation by the State, that, in his medical judgment, the patient's pregnancy should be terminated. If that decision is reached, the judgment may be effectuated by an abortion free of interference by the State.

With respect to the State's important and legitimate interest in potential life, the "compelling" point is at viability. This is so because the fetus then presumably has the capability of meaningful life outside the mother's womb. State regulation protective of fetal life after viability thus has both logical and biological justifications. If the State is interested in protecting fetal life after viability, it may go so far as to proscribe abortion [410 U.S. 113, 164] during that period, except when it is necessary to preserve the life or health of the mother.

Measured against these standards, Art. 1196 of the Texas Penal Code, in restricting legal abortions to those "procured or attempted by medical advice for the purpose of saving the life of the mother," sweeps too broadly. The statute makes no distinction between abortions performed early in pregnancy and those performed later, and it limits to a single reason, "saving" the mother's life, the legal justification for the procedure. The statute, therefore, cannot survive the constitutional attack made upon it here.

HARRIS v. McRAE, 448 U.S. 297 (1980)

Decided June 30, 1980.

MR. JUSTICE STEWART delivered the opinion of the Court.

This case presents statutory and constitutional questions concerning the public funding of abortions under Title XIX of the Social Security Act, commonly known as the "Medicaid" Act, and recent annual Appropriations Acts containing [448 U.S. 297, 301] the so-called "Hyde Amendment." The statutory question is whether Title XIX requires a State that participates in the Medicaid program to fund the cost of medically necessary abortions for which federal reimbursement is unavailable under the Hyde Amendment. The constitutional question, which arises only if Title XIX imposes no such requirement, is whether the Hyde Amendment, by denying public funding for certain medically necessary abortions, contravenes the liberty or equal protection guarantees of the Due Process Clause of the Fifth Amendment, or either of the Religion Clauses of the First Amendment.

In the Wade case, this Court held unconstitutional a Texas statute making it a crime to procure or attempt an abortion except on medical advice for the purpose of saving the mother's life. The constitutional underpinning of Wade was a recognition that the "liberty" protected by the Due Process Clause of the Fourteenth Amendment includes not only the freedoms explicitly mentioned in the Bill of Rights, but also a freedom of personal choice in certain matters of marriage and family life.18 This implicit constitutional liberty, the Court in Wade held, includes the freedom of a woman to decide whether to terminate a pregnancy. [448 U.S. 297, 313]

But the Court in Wade also recognized that a State has legitimate interests during a pregnancy in both ensuring the health of the mother and protecting potential human life. These state interests, which were found to be "separate and distinct" and to "gro[w] in substantiality as the woman approaches term," id., at 162-163, pose a conflict with a woman's untrammeled freedom of choice. In resolving this conflict, the Court held that before the end of the first trimester of pregnancy, neither state interest is sufficiently substantial to justify any intrusion on the woman's freedom of choice. In the second trimester, the state interest in maternal health was found to be sufficiently substantial to justify regulation reasonably related to that concern. And at viability, usually in the third trimester, the state interest in protecting the potential life of the fetus was found to justify a criminal prohibition against abortions, except where necessary for the preservation of the life or health of the mother. Thus, inasmuch as the Texas criminal statute allowed abortions only where necessary to save the life of the mother and without regard to the stage of the pregnancy, the Court held in Wade that the statute violated the Due Process Clause of the Fourteenth Amendment.

Because even the compelling interest of the State in protecting potential life after fetal viability was held to be insufficient to outweigh a woman's decision to protect her life or health, it could be argued that the freedom of a woman to decide whether to terminate her pregnancy for health reasons does in fact lie at the core of the constitutional liberty identified in Wade.

But, regardless of whether the freedom of a woman to choose to terminate her pregnancy for health reasons lies at the core or the periphery of the due process liberty recognized in Wade, it simply does not follow that a woman's freedom of choice carries with it a constitutional entitlement to the financial resources to avail herself of the full range of protected choices. The reason why was explained in Maher: although government may not place obstacles in the path of a woman's exercise of her freedom of choice, it need not remove those not of its own creation. Indigency falls in the latter category. The financial constraints that restrict an indigent woman's ability to enjoy the full range of constitutionally protected freedom of choice are the product not of governmental restrictions on access to abortions, but rather of her indigency. Although Congress has opted to subsidize [448 U.S. 297, 317] medically necessary services generally, but not certain medically necessary abortions, the fact remains that the Hyde Amendment leaves an indigent woman with at least the same range of choice in deciding whether to obtain a medically necessary abortion as she would have had if Congress had chosen to subsidize no health care costs at all. We are thus not persuaded that the Hyde Amendment impinges on the constitutionally protected freedom of choice recognized in Wade.19

The remaining question then is whether the Hyde Amendment is rationally related to a legitimate governmental objective. It is the Government's position that the Hyde Amendment bears a rational relationship to its legitimate interest in protecting the potential life of the fetus. We agree.

In Wade, the Court recognized that the State has an "important and legitimate interest in protecting the potentiality of human life." 410 U.S., at 162. That interest was found to exist throughout a pregnancy, "grow[ing] in substantiality as the woman approaches term." Id., at 162-163. See also Beal v. Doe, 432 U.S., at 445-446. Moreover, in Maher, the Court held that Connecticut's decision to fund the costs associated with childbirth but not those associated with nontherapeutic abortions was a rational means of advancing the legitimate state interest in protecting potential life by [448 U.S. 297, 325] encouraging childbirth. 432 U.S., at 478-479. See also Poelker v. Doe, 432 U.S. 519, 520-521.

It follows that the Hyde Amendment, by encouraging childbirth except in the most urgent circumstances, is rationally related to the legitimate governmental objective of protecting potential life. By subsidizing the medical expenses of indigent women who carry their pregnancies to term while not subsidizing the comparable expenses of women who undergo abortions (except those whose lives are threatened),27 Congress has established incentives that make childbirth a more attractive alternative than abortion for persons eligible for Medicaid. These incentives bear a direct relationship to the legitimate congressional interest in protecting potential life. Nor is it irrational that Congress has authorized federal reimbursement for medically necessary services generally, but not for certain medically necessary abortions.28 Abortion is inherently different from other medical procedures, because no other procedure involves the purposeful termination of a potential life.

After conducting an extensive evidentiary hearing into issues surrounding the public funding of abortions, the District Court concluded that "[t]he interests of . . . the federal government . . . in the fetus and in preserving it are not sufficient, weighed in the balance with the woman's threatened health, to justify withdrawing medical assistance unless the [448 U.S. 297, 326] woman consents . . . to carry the fetus to term." 491 F. Supp., at 737. In making an independent appraisal of the competing interests involved here, the District Court went beyond the judicial function. Such decisions are entrusted under the Constitution to Congress, not the courts. It is the role of the courts only to ensure that congressional decisions comport with the Constitution.

Where, as here, the Congress has neither invaded a substantive constitutional right or freedom, nor enacted legislation that purposefully operates to the detriment of a suspect class, the only requirement of equal protection is that congressional action be rationally related to a legitimate governmental interest. The Hyde Amendment satisfies that standard. It is not the mission of this Court or any other to decide whether the balance of competing interests reflected in the Hyde Amendment is wise social policy. If that were our mission, not every Justice who has subscribed to the judgment of the Court today could have done so. But we cannot, in the name of the Constitution, overturn duly enacted statutes simply "because they may be unwise, improvident, or out of harmony with a particular school of thought." Williamson v. Lee Optical Co., 348 U.S. 483, 488, quoted in Dandridge v. Williams, 397 U.S., at 484. Rather, "when an issue involves policy choices as sensitive as those implicated [here] . . ., the appropriate forum for their resolution in a democracy is the legislature." Maher v. Roe, supra, at 479.

For the reasons stated in this opinion, we hold that a State that participates in the Medicaid program is not obligated under Title XIX to continue to fund those medically necessary abortions for which federal reimbursement is unavailable under the Hyde Amendment. We further hold that the funding restrictions of the Hyde Amendment violate neither the Fifth Amendment nor the Establishment Clause of the First Amendment. It is also our view that the appellees [448 U.S. 297, 327] lack standing to raise a challenge to the Hyde Amendment under the Free Exercise Clause of the First Amendment. Accordingly, the judgment of the District Court is reversed, and the case is remanded to that court for further proceedings consistent with this opinion.

WEBSTER v. REPRODUCTIVE HEALTH SERVICES, 492 U.S. 490 (1989)

Decided July 3, 1989

CHIEF JUSTICE REHNQUIST announced the judgment of the Court and delivered the opinion of the Court with respect to Parts I, II-A, II-B, and II-C, and an opinion with respect [492 U.S. 490, 499] to Parts II-D and III, in which JUSTICE WHITE and JUSTICE KENNEDY join.

This appeal concerns the constitutionality of a Missouri statute regulating the performance of abortions. The United States Court of Appeals for the Eighth Circuit struck down several provisions of the statute on the ground that they violated this Court's decision in Roe v. Wade, 410 U.S. 113 (1973), and cases following it.

The Act's preamble, as noted, sets forth "findings" by the Missouri Legislature that "[t]he life of each human being begins at conception," and that "[u]nborn children have protectable interests in life, health, and well-being." Mo. Rev. Stat. 1.205.1(1), (2) (1986). The Act then mandates that state laws be interpreted to provide unborn children with "all the rights, privileges, and immunities available to other persons, citizens, and residents of this state," subject to the Constitution and this Court's precedents. 1.205.2.4 In invalidating [492 U.S. 490, 505] the preamble, the Court of Appeals relied on this Court's dictum that "'a State may not adopt one theory of when life begins to justify its regulation of abortions.'" 851 F.2d, at 1075-1076, quoting Akron v. Akron Center for Reproductive Health, Inc., 462 U.S. 416, 444 (1983), in turn citing Roe v. Wade, 410 U.S., at 159-162. It rejected Missouri's claim that the preamble was "abortion-neutral," and "merely determine[d] when life begins in a nonabortion context, a traditional state prerogative." 851 F.2d, at 1076. The court thought that "[t]he only plausible inference" from the fact that "every remaining section of the bill save one regulates the performance of abortions" was that "the state intended its abortion regulations to be understood against the backdrop of its theory of life." Ibid.5

It will be time enough for federal courts to address the meaning of the preamble should it be applied to restrict the activities of appellees in some concrete way. Until then, this [492 U.S. 490, 507] Court "is not empowered to decide . . . abstract propositions, or to declare, for the government of future cases, principles or rules of law which cannot affect the result as to the thing in issue in the case before it." Tyler v. Judges of Court of Registration, 179 U.S. 405, 409 (1900). See also Valley Forge Christian College v. Americans United for Separation of Church & State, Inc., 454 U.S. 464, 473 (1982).6 We therefore need not pass on the constitutionality of the Act's preamble.

Section 188.210 provides that "[i]t shall be unlawful for any public employee within the scope of his employment to perform or assist an abortion, not necessary to save the life of the mother," while 188.215 makes it "unlawful for any public facility to be used for the purpose of performing or assisting an abortion not necessary to save the life of the mother."7 The Court of Appeals held that these provisions contravened this Court's abortion decisions. 851 F.2d, at 1082-1083. We take the contrary view.

Maher, Poelker, and McRae all support the view that the State need not commit any resources to facilitating abortions, even if it can turn a profit by doing so. In Poelker, the suit was filed by an indigent who could not afford to pay for an abortion, but the ban on the performance of nontherapeutic abortions in city-owned hospitals applied whether or not the pregnant woman could pay. 432 U.S., at 520; id., at 524 (BRENNAN, J., dissenting).9 The Court emphasized that the mayor's decision to prohibit abortions in city hospitals was "subject to public debate and approval or disapproval at the polls," and that "the Constitution does not forbid a State or city, pursuant to democratic processes, from expressing a preference for normal childbirth as St. Louis has done." Id., at 521. Thus we uphold the Act's restrictions on the use of public employees and facilities for the performance or assistance of nontherapeutic abortions.

Section 188.029 of the Missouri Act provides:

> "Before a physician performs an abortion on a woman he has reason to believe is carrying an unborn child of twenty or more weeks gestational age, the physician shall first determine if the unborn child is viable by using and exercising that degree of care, skill, and proficiency commonly exercised by the ordinarily skillful, careful, and prudent physician engaged in similar practice under the same or similar conditions. In making this determination of viability, the physician shall perform or cause to be performed such medical examinations and tests as are necessary to make a finding of the gestational age, weight, and lung maturity of the unborn child and shall enter such findings and determination of viability in the medical record of the mother."

The viability-testing provision of the Missouri Act is concerned with promoting the State's interest in potential human life rather than in maternal health. Section 188.029 creates what is essentially a presumption of viability at 20 weeks, which the physician must rebut with tests indicating that the fetus is not viable prior to performing an abortion. It also directs the physician's determination as to viability by specifying consideration, if feasible, of gestational age, fetal weight, and lung capacity. The District Court found that "the medical evidence is uncontradicted that a 20-week fetus is not viable," and that "23 1/2 to 24 weeks gestation is the earliest point in pregnancy where a reasonable possibility of viability [492 U.S. 490, 516] exists." 662 F. Supp., at 420. But it also found that there may be a 4-week error in estimating gestational age, id., at 421, which supports testing at 20 weeks.

In Roe v. Wade, the Court recognized that the State has "important and legitimate" interests in protecting maternal health and in the potentiality of human life. 410 U.S., at 162. During the second trimester, the State "may, if it chooses, regulate the abortion procedure in ways that are reasonably related to maternal health." Id., at 164. After viability, when the State's interest in potential human life was held to become compelling, the State "may, if it chooses, regulate, and even proscribe, abortion except where it is necessary, in appropriate medical judgment, for the preservation of the life or health of the mother."

PLANNED PARENTHOOD OF SOUTHEASTERN PA. v. CASEY, 505 U.S. 833 (1992)

Decided June 29, 1992

JUSTICE O'CONNOR, JUSTICE KENNEDY, and JUSTICE SOUTER announced the judgment of the Court and delivered the opinion of the Court with respect to Parts I, II, III, V-A, [505 U.S. 833, 844] V-C, and VI, an opinion with respect to Part V-E, in which JUSTICE STEVENS joins, and an opinion with respect to Parts IV, V-B, and V-D.

I

Liberty finds no refuge in a jurisprudence of doubt. Yet, 19 years after our holding that the Constitution protects a woman's right to terminate her pregnancy in its early stages, Roe v. Wade, 410 U.S. 113 (1973), that definition of liberty is still questioned. Joining the respondents as amicus curiae, the United States, as it has done in five other cases in the last decade, again asks us to overrule Roe. See Brief for Respondents 104-117; Brief for United States as Amicus Curiae 8.

At issue in these cases are five provisions of the Pennsylvania Abortion Control Act of 1982, as amended in 1988 and 1989. 18 Pa. Cons. Stat. 3203-3220 (1990). Relevant portions of the Act are set forth in the Appendix. Infra at 60. The Act requires that a woman seeking an abortion give her informed consent prior to the abortion procedure, and specifies that she be provided with certain information at least 24 hours before the abortion is performed. 3205. For a minor to obtain an abortion, the Act requires the informed consent of one of her parents, but provides for a judicial bypass option if the minor does not wish to or cannot obtain a parent's consent. 3206. Another provision of the Act requires that, unless certain exceptions apply, a married woman seeking an abortion must sign a statement indicating that she has notified her husband of her intended abortion. 3209. The Act exempts compliance with these three requirements in the event of a "medical emergency," which is defined in 3203 of the Act. See 3203, 3205(a), 3206(a), 3209(c). In addition to the above provisions regulating the performance of abortions, the Act imposes certain reporting requirements on facilities that provide abortion services. 3207(b), 3214(a), 3214(f). [505 U.S. 833, 845]

Some guiding principles should emerge. What is at stake is the woman's right to make the ultimate decision, not a right to be insulated from all others in doing so. Regulations which do no more than create a structural mechanism by which the State, or the parent or guardian of a minor, may express profound respect for the life of the unborn are permitted, if they are not a substantial obstacle to the woman's exercise of the right to choose. See infra, at 899-900 (addressing Pennsylvania's parental consent requirement). [505 U.S. 833, 878] Unless it has that effect on her right of choice, a state measure designed to persuade her to choose childbirth over abortion will be upheld if reasonably related to that goal. Regulations designed to foster the health of a woman seeking an abortion are valid if they do not constitute an undue burden.

(a) To protect the central right recognized by Roe v. Wade while at the same time accommodating the State's profound interest in potential life, we will employ the undue burden analysis as explained in this opinion. An undue burden exists, and therefore a provision of law is invalid, if its purpose or effect is to place a substantial obstacle in the path of a woman seeking an abortion before the fetus attains viability.

(b) We reject the rigid trimester framework of Roe v. Wade. To promote the State's profound interest in potential life, throughout pregnancy, the State may take measures to ensure that the woman's choice is informed, and measures designed to advance this interest will not be invalidated as long as their purpose is to persuade the woman to choose childbirth over abortion. These measures must not be an undue burden on the right.

(c) As with any medical procedure, the State may enact regulations to further the health or safety of a woman seeking an abortion. Unnecessary health regulations that have the purpose or effect of presenting a substantial obstacle to a woman seeking an abortion impose an undue burden on the right. [505 U.S. 833, 879]

(d) Our adoption of the undue burden analysis does not disturb the central holding of Roe v. Wade, and we reaffirm that holding. Regardless of whether exceptions are made for particular circumstances, a State may not prohibit any woman from making the ultimate decision to terminate her pregnancy before viability.

(e) We also reaffirm Roe's holding that, subsequent to viability, the State, in promoting its interest in the potentiality of human life, may, if it chooses, regulate, and even proscribe, abortion except where it is necessary, in appropriate medical judgment, for the preservation of the life or health of the mother. Roe v. Wade, 410 U.S., at 164-165.

Because it is central to the operation of various other requirements, we begin with the statute's definition of medical emergency. Under the statute, a medical emergency is

[t]hat condition which, on the basis of the physician's good faith clinical judgment, so complicates the medical condition of a pregnant woman as to necessitate the immediate abortion of her pregnancy to avert her death or for which a delay will create serious risk of substantial and irreversible impairment of a major bodily function. 18 Pa.Cons.Stat. 3203 (1990). [505 U.S. 833, 880]

Petitioners argue that the definition is too narrow, contending that it forecloses the possibility of an immediate abortion despite some significant health risks. If the contention were correct, we would be required to invalidate the restrictive operation of the provision, for the essential holding of Roe forbids a State from interfering with a woman's choice to undergo an abortion procedure if continuing her pregnancy would constitute a threat to her health. 410 U.S., at 164. See also Harris v. McRae, 448 U.S., at 316.

The District Court found that there were three serious conditions which would not be covered by the statute: preeclampsia, inevitable abortion, and premature ruptured membrane. 744 F.Supp., at 1378. Yet, as the Court of Appeals observed, 947 F.2d, at 700-701, it is undisputed that, under some circumstances, each of these conditions could lead to an illness with substantial and irreversible consequences. While the definition could be interpreted in an unconstitutional manner, the Court of Appeals construed the phrase "serious risk" to include those circumstances. Id., at 701. It stated: "[W]e read the medical emergency exception as intended by the Pennsylvania legislature to assure that compliance with its abortion regulations would not in any way pose a significant threat to the life or health of a woman." Ibid. As we said in Brockett v. Spokane Arcades, Inc., 472 U.S. 491,

499-500 (1985): "Normally, . . . we defer to the construction of a state statute given it by the lower federal courts." Indeed, we have said that we will defer to lower court interpretations of state law unless they amount to "plain" error. Palmer v. Hoffman, 318 U.S. 109, 118 (1943). This "reflect[s] our belief that district courts and courts of appeals are better schooled in, and more able to interpret, the laws of their respective States." Frisby v. Schultz, 487 U.S. 474, 482 (1988) (citation omitted). We adhere to that course today, and conclude that, as construed by the Court of Appeals, the medical emergency definition imposes no undue burden on a woman's abortion right.

We next consider the informed consent requirement. 18 Pa. Cons.Stat. 3205 (1990). Except in a medical emergency, the statute requires that at least 24 hours before performing an abortion a physician inform the woman of the nature of the procedure, the health risks of the abortion and of childbirth, and the "probable gestational age of the unborn child." The physician or a qualified nonphysician must inform the woman of the availability of printed materials published by the State describing the fetus and providing information about medical assistance for childbirth, information about child support from the father, and a list of agencies which provide adoption and other services as alternatives to abortion. An abortion may not be performed unless the woman certifies in writing that she has been informed of the availability of these printed materials and has been provided them if she chooses to view them.

We also see no reason why the State may not require doctors to inform a woman seeking an abortion of the availability of materials relating to the consequences to the fetus, even when those consequences have no direct relation to her health. An example illustrates the point. We would think [505 U.S. 833, 883] it constitutional for the State to require that, in order for there to be informed consent to a kidney transplant operation, the recipient must be supplied with information about risks to the donor as well as risks to himself or herself. A requirement that the physician make available information similar to that mandated by the statute here was described in Thornburgh as an outright attempt to wedge the Commonwealth's message discouraging abortion into the privacy of the informed consent dialogue between the woman and her physician. 476 U.S., at 762. We conclude, however, that informed choice need not be defined in such narrow terms that all considerations of the effect on the fetus are made irrelevant. As we have made clear, we depart from the holdings of Akron I and Thornburgh to the extent that we permit a State to further its legitimate goal of protecting the life of the unborn by enacting legislation aimed at ensuring a decision that is mature and informed, even when, in so doing, the State expresses a preference for childbirth over abortion. In short, requiring that the woman be informed of the availability of information relating to fetal development and the assistance available should she decide to carry the pregnancy to full term is a reasonable measure to ensure an informed choice, one which might cause the woman to choose childbirth over abortion. This requirement cannot be considered a substantial obstacle to obtaining an abortion, and, it follows, there is no undue burden.

Our analysis of Pennsylvania's 24-hour waiting period between the provision of the information deemed necessary to informed consent and the performance of an abortion under the undue burden standard requires us to reconsider the premise behind the decision in Akron I invalidating a parallel requirement. In Akron I we said: Nor are we convinced that the State's legitimate concern that the woman's decision be informed is reasonably served by requiring a 24-hour delay as a matter of course. 462 U.S., at 450. We consider that conclusion to be wrong. The idea that important decisions will be more informed and deliberate if they follow some period of reflection does not strike us as unreasonable, particularly where the statute directs that important information become part of the background of the decision. The statute, as construed by the Court of Appeals, permits avoidance of the waiting period in the event of a medical emergency, and the record evidence shows that, in the vast majority of cases, a 24-hour delay does not create any appreciable health risk. In theory, at least, the waiting period is a reasonable measure to implement the State's interest in protecting the life of the unborn, a measure that does not amount to an undue burden.

Subsection (12) of the reporting provision requires the reporting of, among other things, a married woman's "reason for failure to provide notice" to her husband. 3214(a)(12). This provision in effect requires women, as a condition of obtaining an abortion, to provide the Commonwealth with the precise information we have already recognized that many women have pressing reasons not to reveal. Like the spousal notice requirement itself, this provision places an undue burden on a woman's choice, and must be invalidated for that reason.

VI

Our Constitution is a covenant running from the first generation of Americans to us, and then to future generations. It is a coherent succession. Each generation must learn anew that the Constitution's written terms embody ideas and aspirations that must survive more ages than one. We accept our responsibility not to retreat from interpreting the full meaning of the covenant in light of all of our precedents. We invoke it once again to define the freedom guaranteed by the Constitution's own promise, the promise of liberty.

* * * *

JUSTICE BLACKMUN, CONCURRING IN PART AND DISSENTING IN PART IN *Casey*, 505 U.S. 833, 943:

Even if it is somehow "irrational" for a State to require a woman to risk her life for her child, what protection is offered for women who become pregnant through rape or incest? Is there anything arbitrary or capricious about a [505 U.S. 833, 943] State's prohibiting the sins of the father from being visited upon his offspring?12

But, we are reassured, there is always the protection of the democratic process. While there is much to be praised about our democracy, our country, since its founding, has recognized that there are certain fundamental liberties that are not to be left to the whims of an election. A woman's right to reproductive choice is one of those fundamental liberties. Accordingly, that liberty need not seek refuge at the ballot box.

IV

In one sense, the Court's approach is worlds apart from that of THE CHIEF JUSTICE and JUSTICE SCALIA. And yet, in another sense, the distance between the two approaches is short - the distance is but a single vote.

I am 83 years old. I cannot remain on this Court forever, and when I do step down, the confirmation process for my successor well may focus on the issue before us today. That, I regret, may be exactly where the choice between the two worlds will be made.

* * * * *

[NOTE: On June 8, 1999, the House of Representatives passed an appropriations bill amendment prohibiting the Food and Drug Administration from approving drugs that terminate pregnancy. The measure was aimed at F.D.A. approval, expected later in 1999, of the drug mifepristone (RU-486), widely used by European women.

B. VIOLENCE AGAINST ABORTION PROVIDERS

During the 1990's provision of reproductive services came under increased attack from organizations opposed to abortion rights. This opposition sometimes took the form of interference with the operation of medical clinics, as well as threats and physical -- sometimes fatal -- attacks on physicians and others. The Supreme Court, in *National Organization for Women v. Scheidler* (1994) held that those conspiring to use threats or force to stop the provision of legal abortion services could be liable under the federal Racketeer Influenced and Corrupt Practices statute. In 1999, a federal jury in Oregon granted $107 million in damages to doctors who were targeted in an internet site as "baby butchers." Practical issues including the internet's international scope and relatively easy access, as well as First Amendment considerations, make it likely that this battle will continue.

NATIONAL ORGANIZATION FOR WOMEN v. SCHEIDLER
510 U.S. 249 (1994)
Decided January 24, 1994

Chief Justice Rehnquist delivered the opinion of the Court.

We are required once again to interpret the provisions of the Racketeer Influenced and Corrupt Organizations (RICO) chapter of the Organized Crime Control Act of 1970 (OCCA), Pub. L. 91-452, Title IX, 84 Stat. 941, as amended, 18 U.S.C. §§ 1961-1968 (1988 ed. and Supp. IV). Section 1962(c) prohibits any person associated with an enterprise from conducting its affairs through a pattern of racketeering activity. We granted certiorari to determine whether RICO requires proof that either the racketeering enterprise or the predicate acts of racketeering were motivated by an economic purpose. We hold that RICO requires no such economic motive.

Petitioner National Organization For Women, Inc. (NOW) is a national nonprofit organization that supports the legal availability of abortion; petitioners Delaware Women's Health Organization, Inc. (DWHO) and Summit Women's Health Organization, Inc. (SWHO) are health care centers that perform abortions and other medical procedures. Respondents are a coalition of antiabortion groups called the Pro Life Action Network (PLAN), Joseph Scheidler and other individuals and organizations that oppose legal abortion, and a medical laboratory that formerly provided services to the two petitioner health care centers. [n.1]

Petitioners sued respondents in the United States District Court for the Northern District of Illinois, alleging violations of the Sherman Act, 26 Stat. 209, as amended, 15 U.S.C. § 1 *et seq.*, and RICO's §§ 1962(a), (c), and (d), as well as several pendent state law claims stemming from the activities of antiabortion protesters at the clinics. According to respondent Scheidler's congressional testimony, these protesters aim to shut down the clinics and persuade women not to have abortions. See, *e. g.*, Abortion Clinic Violence, Oversight Hearings before the Subcommittee on Civil and Constitutional Rights of the House Committee on the Judiciary, 99th Cong., 1st and 2d Sess., 55 (1987) (statement of Joseph M. Scheidler, Executive Director, Pro Life Action League). Petitioners sought injunctive relief, along with treble damages, costs, and attorneys' fees. They later amended their complaint, and pursuant to local rules, filed a "RICO Case Statement" that further detailed the enterprise, the pattern of racketeering, the victims of the racketeering activity, and the participants involved.

The amended complaint alleged that respondents were members of a nationwide conspiracy to shut down abortion clinics through a pattern of racketeering activity including extortion in violation of the Hobbs Act, 18 U.S.C. § 1951. [n.2] Section 1951(b)(2) defines extortion as-the obtaining of property from another, with his consent, induced by wrongful use of actual or threatened force, violence, or fear, or under color of official right." Petitioners alleged that respondents conspired to use threatened or actual force, violence or fear to induce clinic employees, doctors, and patients to give up their jobs, give up their economic right to practice medicine, and give up their right to obtain medical services at the clinics. App. 66, Second Amended complaint ¶97. Petitioners claimed that this conspiracy "has injured the business and/or property interests of the [petitioners]." *Id.*, at 72, ¶104. According to the amended complaint, PLAN constitutes the alleged racketeering "enterprise" for purposes of § 1962(c).

The phrase "any enterprise engaged in, or the activities of which affect, interstate or foreign commerce" comes the closest of any language in subsection (c) to suggesting a need for an economic motive. Arguably an enterprise engaged in interstate or foreign commerce would have a profit seeking motive, but the language in § 1962(c) does not stop there; it includes enterprises whose activities "affect" interstate or foreign commerce. Webster's Third New International Dictionary 35 (1969) defines "affect" as "to have a detrimental influence on--used especially in the phrase *affecting commerce*." An enterprise surely can have a detrimental influence oninterstate or foreign commerce without having its own profit seeking motives.

We therefore hold that petitioners may maintain this action if respondents conducted the enterprise through a pattern of racketeering activity.

Jury Finds 'Hit List,' Awards $107 Million

By Rene Sanchez
Washington Post Staff Writer

LOS ANGELES, Feb. 2—A federal jury in Portland, Ore., awarded $107 million in damages today to a group of doctors who sued antiabortion activists over an Internet site calling doctors who perform abortions "baby butchers" and listing their names, photos, addresses and license plate numbers.

The civil suit, seeking $200 million and demanding the site be closed, was viewed as an important test in defining when free speech veers into threats or incitement to violence. It came in an atmosphere of rising concern across the nation generated by recent attacks on abortion clinics and doctors who perform abortions, including the slaying of Barnett Slepian in upstate New York Oct. 23 by a sniper who is still at large.

The Web site, called the Nuremberg Files, does not explicitly threaten violence against abortion doctors. But the eight-member Portland jury agreed with the suing doctors that listing their names in a format resembling a "wanted" poster—along with crossing off names of slain doctors such as Slepian—amounted to a "hit list" that threatens violence and thus should not be protected by the First Amendment.

The jury, which did not have the prerogative to shut down the site, decided only on the damages. Attorneys for the plaintiffs immediately asked U.S. District Judge Robert E. Jones, who presided over the trial, to order the closure. The attorneys sought a temporary injunction against the site while Jones studies whether it should be shut down, or its contents changed, permanently.

Attorneys for the 14 defendants, meanwhile, vowed to appeal the decision; they were expected to argue as well that the site should remain open with its current message pending the outcome.

One of the defendants in the case is Michael Bray, a minister in Bowie, Md., who has been convicted of setting fire to abortion clinics. In an telephone interview, Bray denounced the decision and said it could set a dangerous precedent for similar First Amendment cases.

"It ought to be appealed not for my sake but for the sake of truth and free speech," he said. "These posters are nothing but a dramatic way of saying abortion is murder."

Groups that support a woman's right to abortion swiftly praised the decision, saying it will give doctors across the country a powerful new protection against threats.

"The jury confirmed what we have been saying throughout this case: These anti-choice terrorists have abused this country's precious First Amendment rights," said Lois Backus, the head of the Portland chapter of Planned Parenthood, which was one of the plaintiffs in the case.

Some free-speech activists said the jury's verdict could be vulnerable to an appeal because the judge allowed jurors to use a lesser standard to assess the case. He told jurors that they did not have to determine whether the evidence showed that contributors to the Web site actually intended to threaten doctors, just whether a "reasonable person" could consider the harsh words and graphics to be threats.

"The standard in this case will apply in many future cases and must be carefully drawn," said David Fidanque, the executive director of the American Civil Liberties Union in Oregon, "both to safeguard against any chilling effect on free speech and to prevent the First Amendment from being used as a shield by those who want to make [a] true threat of violence."

The trial, which lasted three weeks amid heavy security, marked one of the few times that a 1994 federal law created to protect abortion providers was invoked even without evidence of direct threats. In a measure of the tension it provoked, Jones ordered that jurors' names remain secret to protect them.

A computer consultant in Georgia, Neal Horsley, created the Nuremberg Files two years ago. Its name is a reference to the city in Germany where Nazi leaders were tried after World War II. Horsley and others who gather information on doctors for the Web site insist that they are doing so only in the hope that it will help them get the doctors prosecuted if abortion—legal since 1973—is again outlawed.

During the trial, several doctors testified that their lives have become nightmares of fear ever since their names appeared on the Web site. Some told jurors they wear bulletproof vests in public. Others said they resort to wearing wigs to disguise themselves and keep changing their routes to work.

One of the defendants in the case, Andrew Burnett, the publisher of Life Advocate magazine, conceded under cross-examination that the doctors may have reason to fear the Web site because of the increasing threats and incidents of violence at abortion clinics across the country.

Still, many First Amendment specialists had been suggesting that the doctors had a difficult case to prove because one standard the Supreme Court has set for limiting free speech for fear of inciting violence—a threat of "imminent lawless action"—is a high bar to clear. Court cases involving textual material have rarely reached that threshold.

Washington Post,
Feb. 2, 1999, p. A-1

C. VITAL STATISTICS

- **Almost one third of clinics (27.6%) reported one or more severe types of violence, including death threats, stalking, bomb threats, bombings, blockades, chemical attacks, invasions, arson, and arson threats, during the first seven months of 1996.** When gunfire, home picketing, and vandalism are combined with the other violence variables, the number of clinics and offices experiencing some form of violence, harassment or intimidation rises to 44.9%.

- **One in ten clinics (10.9%) during the first seven months of 1996 turned to the courts for relief from clinic violence.** Of these 34 clinics, 13 sought restraining orders, 3 temporary injunctions, and 5 permanent injunctions. In 1995, 15.2% of clinics had sought legal remedies. Less than half (41.2%) of the clinics which sought legal remedies actually won protections.

-Feminist Majority Foundation, 1997

ESTIMATED ANNUAL U.S. ABORTIONS

Year	AGI	CDC
1970	NA	193,491
1971	NA	485,816
1972	NA	586,760
1973	744,600	615,831
1974	898,600	763,476
1975	1,034,200	854,853
1976	1,179,300	988,267
1977	1,316,700	1,079,430
1978	1,409,600	1,157,776
1979	1,497,700	1,251,921
1980	1,553,900	1,297,606
1981	1,577,300	1,300,760
1982	1,573,900	1,303,980
1983	1,575,000	1,268,987
1984	1,577,200	1,333,521
1985	1,588,600	1,328,570
1986	1,574,000	1,328,112
1987	1,559,100	1,353,671
1988	1,590,800	1,371,285
1989	1,566,900	1,388,937
1990	1,608,600	1,429,577
1991	1,556,500	1,288,937
1992	1,528,900	1,359,145
1993	1,500,000	1,330,414
1994	1,435,000	1,267,415
1995	1,400,000	1,210,883
1996	1,400,000	
1997	1,300,000	

Alan Guttmacher Institute (AGI) and the Centers for Disease Control and Prevention (CDC).

SELECTED ABORTION STATUTES AND REGULATIONS

Abortion Bans (Pre-Roe)

Fifteen states and the District of Columbia have not repealed their unconstitutional and unenforceable pre-*Roe* abortion bans (AL, AZ, AR, CA, CO, DE, DC, MA, MI, MS, NM, OK, TX, VT, WV, WI).

Comprehensive Bans (Post-Roe)

Following the U.S. Supreme Court's 1989 decision in *Webster v. Reproductive Health Services*, Louisiana, Utah, and the territory of Guam enacted unenforceable laws prohibiting most abortions. The Louisiana law prohibits abortion except in cases of life endangerment, rape, or incest. The Utah law prohibits abortion before 20 weeks except in cases of life endangerment, grave damage to the woman's medical health, reported rape or incest, or grave fetal anomalies. After 20 weeks, abortions are banned except in cases of life endangerment, grave damage to the woman's medical health, or grave fetal anomalies. The Guam law prohibits an abortion unless two physicians determine that the woman's life is endangered or an abortion is necessary to prevent grave impairment to a woman's health. Courts have ruled that each of these laws is unconstitutional.

Bans on Abortion Procedures

Twenty-eight states have enacted legislation banning so-called "partial-birth" abortion or other abortion procedures (AL, AK, AZ, AR, FL, GA, ID, IL, IN, IA, KS,[1] KY, LA, MI, MS, MT, NE, NJ, OH,[2] OK, RI, SC, SD, TN, UT,[3] VA, WV, WI).

Court challenges regarding these laws have been initiated in 20 states (AL, AK, AZ, AR, FL, GA, ID, IL, IA, KY, LA, MI, MT, NE, NJ, OH, RI, VA, WV, WI).

- In 18 states, courts have partially or fully enjoined the laws (AK, AZ, AR, FL, GA,[4] ID, IL, IA, KY, LA, MI, MT, NE,[5] NJ, OH, RI, WV, WI). In 12 of these 18 states, courts have permanently enjoined the laws (AK, AZ, AR, FL, GA, IL, KY, MI, MT, NE, NJ, OH).
- In Alabama, the court has not ruled on the merits, but the Alabama Attorney General has directed the state's district attorneys to enforce the statute only after viability.
- In Virginia, the U.S. Court of Appeals for the Fourth Circuit interpreted this law to apply only to intact dilation and extraction abortion procedures and denied a motion to vacate the stay of a preliminary injunction issued by the district court. As a result, the law is in effect.
- Three U.S. Circuit Courts of Appeal have ruled on the issue. The U.S. Court of Appeals for the Sixth Circuit held Ohio's ban on dilation and extraction unconstitutional and the U.S. Supreme Court denied *certiorari* in 1998. The U.S. Court of Appeals for the Seventh Circuit reversed a denial of a preliminary injunction of Wisconsin's law in November 1998. The U.S. Court of Appeals for the Fourth Circuit

denied a motion to vacate the stay of a preliminary injunction issued by a district court in Virginia.

In eight states, the laws have not been challenged and are in effect (IN, KS, MS, OK, SC, SD, TN, UT).

Notes:

1. The Kansas statute prohibits "partial-birth" abortion after viability except when necessary to preserve a woman's life or if the pregnancy will result in "substantial and irreversible impairment of a major physical or mental function of the woman."

2. The Ohio statute prohibits dilation and extraction abortion unless the defendant proves that all other available abortion procedures pose a greater risk to the woman's health.

3. The Utah statute prohibits "partial-birth" abortion, dilation and extraction abortion, and saline abortion after viability unless all other available abortion procedures would pose a risk to the woman's life or health.

4. In Georgia, the district court approved the parties' consent order which limits enforcement of the law to post-viability intact dilation and extraction abortion procedures except when necessary to preserve the woman's life or health.

5. In Nebraska, a court has issued a permanent injunction prohibiting enforcement of the law as applied to the plaintiff, his patients, and others similarly situated.

Clinic Violence and Harassment
Twelve states and the District of Columbia have laws to protect medical personnel and women seeking health care against blockades and violence (CA, CO, DC, KS, ME, MD, MA, MN, NV, NC, OR, WA, WI). Four states have adopted resolutions condemning clinic violence (CA, MI, NM, PA).

Conscience-Based Exemptions
Forty-six states permit certain medical personnel, health facilities, or both, to refuse to participate in abortion on the basis of conscience (AK, AZ, AR, CA, CO, CT, DE, FL, GA, HI, ID, IL, IN, IA, KS, KY, LA, ME, MD, MA, MI, MN, MO, MT, NE, NV, NJ, NM, NY, NC, ND, OH, OK, OR, PA, RI, SC, SD, TN, TX, UT, VA, WA, WV, WI, WY). In three of these states, the laws have been found unconstitutional as applied to public, "quasi-public," non-sectarian, or non-profit facilities (AK, MN, NJ).

South Dakota enacted a law in 1998 that permits pharmacists to refuse to dispense medication if there is reason to believe that the medication would be used to cause an abortion.

Counseling Bans
"Gag rules" in eight states prevent health care providers employed by the

state or entities receiving state funds from counseling and/or referring women for abortion services under certain circumstances (LA, MI, MO, NE, ND, OH, PA, WI). The North Dakota law, which prohibits any organization that refers for abortion from receiving state funds for family planning, has been held unconstitutional.

Husband Consent and Notice
Nine states have unenforceable laws mandating husband consent or notice before a married woman may obtain an abortion (CO, IL, KY, LA, ND, PA, RI, SC, UT). The U.S. Supreme Court has ruled in two separate cases that a mandatory husband notice or consent provision is unconstitutional.

"Informed" Consent/Waiting Periods
Nineteen states have mandatory waiting periods that prohibit a woman from obtaining an abortion until a specified period of time after receiving a state-mandated lecture or materials (DE, ID, IN, KS, KY, LA, MA, MI, MS, MT, NE, ND, OH, PA, SC, SD, TN, UT, WI). In five states, the mandatory waiting period is not enforced (DE, MA, MI, MT, TN).

In addition, 30 states have abortion-specific "informed" consent laws, many of which require that women receive state-mandated lectures and state-prepared materials on fetal development, services available to help the woman if she continues the pregnancy, and adoption (AL, AK, CA, CT, DE, FL, ID, IN, KS, KY, LA, ME, MA, MI, MN, MS, MO, MT, NE, NV, ND, OH, PA, RI, SC, SD, TN, UT, VA, WI). In Florida, a court has issued a temporary injunction prohibiting enforcement of the law and in Missouri, a court has ruled this law is unconstitutional.

Insurance
Five states prohibit private insurance coverage for abortion unless the woman pays an extra premium (ID, KY, MO, ND, RI). The Rhode Island law has been ruled unconstitutional. One additional state, Pennsylvania, requires insurers to provide a policy alternative excluding abortion.

Eleven states prohibit insurance coverage for abortion in some circumstances in which public funds are used or public employees are insured (AR, CO, IL, KS, MA, MI, NE, OH, PA, RI, VA). The Rhode Island law has been ruled unconstitutional as applied to municipal employees.

Legislative Declarations (Anti-Choice)
Ten states have laws declaring the intent of the legislature to protect the life of the "unborn" (AR, IL, KY, LA, MO, MT, NE, ND, PA, UT).

Legislative Declarations (Pro-Choice) Five states have legislative declarations affirmatively supporting the right of a woman to choose abortion (CT, ME, MD, NV, WA). The Nevada law, which protects a woman's right to choose during the first 24 weeks of pregnancy, cannot be changed without a referendum vote.

Minors' Access

Thirty-nine states have laws that require a minor to obtain the consent of or to notify an adult, typically a parent, prior to an abortion (AL, AK, AZ, AR, CA, CO, DE, GA, ID, IL, IN, IA, KS, KY, LA, ME, MD, MA, MI, MN, MS, MO, MT, NE, NV, NM, NC, ND, OH, PA, RI, SC, SD, TN, UT, VA, WV, WI, WY).

Thirty of these laws are currently enforced (AL, AR, DE, GA, ID, IN, IA, KS, KY, LA, ME, MD, MA, MI, MN, MS, MO, NE, NC, ND, OH, PA, RI, SC, SD, UT, VA, WV, WI, WY). The Colorado law was approved by a ballot initiative in 1998 and is scheduled to become effective in January 1999. A lawsuit is expected to be filed requesting a court order enjoining enforcement of this law.

Of the 30 states that currently enforce notice or consent laws, only Idaho and Utah do not have a judicial or other bypass provision allowing a minor to secure a court order in lieu of notifying her parents.

Delaware, Maryland, and West Virginia permit a minor to obtain an abortion without parental consent or notice in certain circumstances if a physician or health professional waives the requirement. In Maine, a minor may obtain an abortion without parental consent if a physician has secured the informed written consent of the minor and the minor is mentally and physically competent to give consent. In addition, at least ten states allow a minor to obtain an abortion without parental consent or notice if she declares she is a victim of abuse, neglect, rape, or incest (AR, CO, IL, IA, KS, MN, NE, SC, VA, WI).

Eight states permit a minor to notify specified adults, other than her parents, under certain circumstances (DE, IL, IA, ME, NC, OH, SC, WI).

Connecticut does not mandate parental consent or notice, but requires that before obtaining an abortion a minor must receive counseling that must include discussion of the possibility of consulting her parents.

Physician-Only Requirements

Forty-four states provide that only a physician may perform an abortion (AL, AK, AR, CA, CO, CT, DE, FL, GA, HI, ID, IL, IN, IA, KY, LA, ME, MD, MA, MI, MN, MS, MO, MT, NE, NV, NJ, NM, NY, NC, ND, OH, OK, PA, RI, SC, SD, TN, TX, UT, VA, WA, WI, WY). The Montana law is preliminarily enjoined to the extent that it prohibits the performance of an abortion by a specified certified physician's assistant supervised by a physician.

The Kentucky law requires that first trimester abortions be performed only by a physician or by the woman herself upon the advice of a physician, and that abortion after the first trimester be performed only by a physician. The New York law requires abortions to be performed only by a physician or by a woman herself acting upon a physician's advice that such act is necessary to preserve her life or within 24 weeks from the commencement of her pregnancy. Oklahoma law provides that no woman may induce an abortion upon herself except under the supervision of a licensed physician.

The Minnesota law provides that only a physician or a supervised physician-in-training may perform an abortion.

In addition, a law in the District of Columbia provides that no abortion may be performed except under the direction of a licensed practitioner of medicine.

Post-Viability Bans
Forty-one states, including the District of Columbia, have laws that address abortion after viability (AL, AZ, AR, CA, CT, DE, DC, FL, GA, ID, IL, IN, IA, KS, KY, LA, ME, MD, MA, MI, MN, MO, MT, NE, NV, NY, NC, ND, OH, OK, PA, RI, SC, SD, TN, TX, UT, VA, WA, WI, WY).

Public Employees
Missouri is the only state that prohibits a public employee, within the scope of his or her employment, from participating in the provision of abortion services.

Public Facilities
Eight states prohibit the use of specified public facilities for the provision of abortion services in certain circumstances (AZ, IA, KS, KY, LA, MO, ND, PA).

Public Funding
Fourteen states fund abortion for women in their state medical assistance programs in all or most circumstances (CA, CT, HI, MD, MA, MN, MT, NJ, NM, NY, OR, VT, WA, WV). Five states fund abortion in cases of life endangerment, rape, incest, and under some health circumstances (ID, IL, IA, VA, WI).

Thirty states, including the District of Columbia, exclude abortion from their state medical assistance programs except in cases of life endangerment, rape, or incest (AL, AK, AZ, AR, CO, DE, DC, FL, GA, IN, KS, KY, LA, ME, MI, MO, NE, NV, NH, NC, ND, OH, OK, PA, RI, SC, TN, TX, UT, WY). Seven of these states require that the rape or incest be reported to a law enforcement or social service agency in at least some circumstances in order for the woman to receive public funds for an abortion (DE, LA, OH, OK, PA, SC, WY). Two of these make no exception for a woman judged by her physician to be too incapacitated to comply with the reporting requirement (DE, WY).

Two states exclude abortion from their state medical assistance programs except when the woman's life is endangered (MS, SD). These state policies violate federal law prohibiting participating states from excluding abortion from the Medicaid program in cases of rape or incest as well as life endangerment. 144 Cong. Rec. H11044, H11182, FY 1999 Omnibus Appropriations Act, Pub. L. No. 105-277, Tit. V, §§ 509, 510.

-National Abortion and Reproductive Rights Action League Foundation

D. RECOMMENDED READING

M. Graber, *Rethinking Abortion: Equal Choice, The Constitution, and Reproductive Politics* (Princeton University Press: 1996)

L. Gomez, *Misconceiving Mothers: Legislators, Prosecutors and the Politics of Prenatal Drug Exposure* (Temple University Press: 1998)

L. Lader, *RU-486: The Pill That Could End the Abortion Wars and Why American Women Don't Have It* (Addison-Wesley: 1991)

www.naral.org

www.choice.org

CHAPTER VII

New Directions in Family Law

A. DIVORCE, CUSTODY & SUPPORT: REASSESSMENT

The past thirty years have brought sweeping legal and societal changes to the institution of the American family. Many were the result of state legislative and litigation efforts spearheaded by the women's rights movement, but they did not always turn out as anticipated. Divorce laws underwent a massive overhaul from adversary, fault-oriented proceedings to the "no-fault" concept, which promised to make property division more equitable, banish traditional sex-role bias, and offer an easier way out of abusive marriages. While these goals were partially realized, the period also resulted in an unprecedented rise in the divorce rate and a substantial increase in the number of single-parent and other "non-traditional" families. In addition, the "no-fault" movement found many women exchanging paternalistic security for impoverishment, as many states abolished or severely limited alimony. The traditional preference for the mother in contested custody disputes was generally replaced with a facially neutral "best interests of the child" test, which, as in the Florida case of *Young v. Hector*, sometimes penalized women who entered the labor market during this period. Many states favored joint custody, which depended upon cooperation and flexibility between ex-spouses.

A re-examination of this reform era has begun, but because of the patchwork fifty-state family law system and the lack of legal or social consensus, the course of the next period in family law is not at all clear. Several commentators and a few states, such as Wisconsin, have emphasized crediting spouses monetarily for "human capital" contributed to a marriage, such as home-based support for a spouse's career, as well as child care. A growing number of states have followed the lead of the California Supreme Court in *Marvin v. Marvin* in ordering maintenance following the ending of a long-term non-marital relationship. (The Supreme Court of Canada, in M. v. H., recently interpreted its Charter of Rights and Freedoms to require that Ontario's Family Law Act, which had granted support to separating unmarried couples, be extended to lesbian and gay relationships as well.)

One legislative attempt to counteract the divorce explosion is Louisiana's 1997 Covenant Marriage statute, which gives couples the option of entering into a marriage contract which can only be broken by traditional, cruelty-based behavior by one party, or a two-year separation; both marriage and any requested divorce would be preceded by mandatory counseling. This avenue, supported by an unusual coalition of conservative Christians and female legislators and legal scholars, has yet to be followed by other states (similar legislation failed in Indiana and California).

So Who Gets the Kids?

By Susan Douglas

Ms. JUNE/JULY 1999

It's 3:47 A.M. Hour of the wolf. That deep pocket in the night when anxieties and self-doubts gnaw at already ragged psyches. I get up and go to my daughter's room. I got home from work too late the night before to put her to bed. I brush the hair off her face and kiss her warm, sweet-smelling forehead. And I wonder if Robert Young is doing the same, only with a much more desperate sense of urgency and impending loss. And is his ex-wife, Alice Hector, also up in the night, staring into her daughters' empty rooms, her stomach in a knot?

I am up because I hate this story. It's too upsetting. But that pales beside Young's and Hector's battle: for both of them, their daily relationship to their daughters, ages 10 and 13, is on the line. In a highly publicized case, Alice Hector, once a partner in a prominent Miami law firm and now head of her own, lost custody of her two daughters in June of 1998 because an all-male three-judge panel ruled that her work schedule was too demanding for her to remain their primary caretaker. They overturned a trial judge's decision to keep the girls with their mother, and awarded custody to Robert Young, the girls' father, who until two years ago was a stay-at-home dad, and who now has a job with flexible work hours. Hector appealed the ruling in December and, as of this writing, awaits a decision. Her ex-husband, by all accounts a deeply involved and devoted father, insists that their daughters get a much higher quality of love and attention with him than they would at Hector's home, because she must relegate much of their care to a housekeeper.

Young had done things like start a Brownie troop for their younger daughter when none existed, organize a soccer team for the elder daughter when that didn't exist either, and then coach the team, as well. He also volunteered at school. Hector couldn't do these kinds of things. But she did get up at the crack of dawn so she'd have time with the girls in the morning, she devoted her weekends to them, and she claimed in court that in the middle of the night, when either one of them was sick, they came to her. Young and his attorneys have been very careful not to label Hector a bad mother; on the contrary, they have praised her efforts to juggle her work as a litigator with the demands of motherhood. Young's point is simple: we're both devoted parents, we both love our kids, but I'm home much more than she is and have much more time to take care of the kids, so they should live with me.

Florida does not favor joint custody, as many other states do. Florida law assumes that moving back and forth between parents' homes is bad for kids. Instead, the law promotes "shared parental responsibility," meaning that both parents are supposed to remain active in the children's lives, but the kids maintain a primary residence with only one of the parents. This is, in part, where the battle started. Both sides say they agreed to share the house while they worked out the divorce settlement—an arrangement that kept the parents in daily touch with the kids but may have exacerbated their intense competition over who deserves custody.

Deep resentments and intransigent stereotypes snarl through the case. Hector and Young got married in New Mexico in 1982, when she was a public-interest lawyer making a moderate salary and he was a successful architectural designer and home builder. His business collapsed in the aftermath of the 1987 stock market crash, and Hector and the couple's two daughters moved to Florida in 1989 after she got a better-paying job at a major law firm. Young followed six months later, but couldn't find work in a new location where he had few professional contacts. Hector claims she never wanted Young to be a stay-at-home dad, but instead encouraged him to try to find work. She increasingly resented having the burden of supporting the family entirely on her shoulders, and clearly felt it was unfair for her to have to put in 60-hour weeks while her husband did no work outside the home.

It is very difficult for most women, however liberated, to overcome our culture's easy equation of bringing home the bacon and true manhood. Difficult for the courts, too: during the initial hearing, when Hector won custody, the judge said to Young, "Maybe I'm missing something. Why don't you get a job?" Young found himself dismissed elsewhere, as well, for staying home with the kids. He recalled a partner in his wife's law firm greeting him with "It's nice to meet you, Mr. Alice." In a comment feminists should find poignant, he told a reporter, "I was only perceived as Alice's husband." Hector, of course, has been stereotyped, too, as a selfish, uncaring mother who brought legal briefs with her to a child's recital. "There is this idea that I wanted this life and this was the life I chose," Hector said in an interview. "The opposite is true. I'm not saying I don't enjoy my work—I do—but it is not my first choice."

Which one of them should I be rooting for? Why is this a contest, a war? Does being a feminist mean that I automatically root for her, no matter what? If my husband and I ever found ourselves in divorce court, would I, too, face losing custody of my daughter because there have been nights, like last night, when I wasn't home for dinner and didn't tuck her in? Or could he be suddenly ripped out of the daily routine of her life—even though he takes her back and forth to school almost every day, helps her with her homework, and wouldn't be able to stand not seeing her for days on end—simply because I'm the mother? According to David Chambers, a professor of law at the University of Michigan, in most custody cases the courts prefer to place a child with the parent who is the primary caretaker, and in the overwhelming majority of cases, this is the mother. The primary caretaker presumption was designed, in part, to thwart the potential threat by fathers to sue for custody so their ex-wives would give in on other aspects of a divorce settlement, like money. But what if you're both the primary caretakers?

It's easy, as a feminist, to have a knee-jerk reaction to the Hector-Young case: how dare three men take away a woman's daughters just because she works? But I guess that one of the reasons I hate this story is that this case, more than many other custody battles that have received media attention, does, in fact, require us to confront our contradictory stances about what we want and expect from fathers now that we're 30 years into the women's movement. Three decades ago, we argued that our treatment before the law should be gender-blind because when it wasn't, we lost. We've also been insisting, with some limited success, that fathers become more involved in child rearing. Those of us who work outside the home are tired of the utter unfairness of the second shift, when both parents come home from work, but Dad gets to read the paper while Mom makes dinner, helps with geometry homework, fends off telemarketers, and does ten loads of laundry.

And many of our husbands have responded.

So if some men have become equal, or even more than equal, partners in child rearing, as we'd hoped, then shouldn't those men have the same rights that women would in court? I do know men who are, indeed, more conscientious and better parents than their wives and would very much merit primary custody if their marriages were to end. But if we grant this, are we opening the floodgates to thousands of frivolous and even unjust custody challenges by fathers who work but won't face the same prejudices in court about their commitment to their children as a working mother automatically does? In a custody battle, if Dad knows the name of the kids' dentist and went to one PTA meeting, he's the Albert Schweitzer of parenting; if Mom gets up at 5:00 A.M. to do the laundry and read files from work so she can have more time with her kids, she's still suspect if she isn't standing in the doorway at 3:30 P.M. in a cookie-dough-smeared apron offering baked goods to her kids as they come home from school. A 1989 report commissioned by Michigan's Supreme Court found that stereotypes bias judges against working mothers: they granted custody to fathers showing the most minimal interest in parenting, and they viewed mothers who placed emphasis on their careers to be less fit as parents than fathers who did exactly the same thing.

Many feminists, women lawyers, and women's organizations have expressed outrage over the ruling against Hector. After all, this case has not occurred in a vacuum: it comes on the heels of quite a few well-publicized and outrageous cases in which mothers lost custody of their children simply because they work outside the home, or work "too many hours." Some studies claim that when custody disputes end up in court, fathers win more than 60 percent of the time, and women lose custody for behavior that is utterly acceptable for men, such as having ambitious career goals. The list is long and infuriating. In 1994, Sharon Prost, deputy chief counsel of the Senate Judiciary Committee, lost custody of her two sons because a female judge determined that she devoted too much time to her job. It didn't matter that Prost got up at 5:30 A.M. to fix breakfast and drive her older son to school or that she brought her younger son with her to the Senate day care center every day, usually had lunch with him, and often left for home before 6:00 P.M. It didn't matter that a court-appointed psychologist affirmed that Prost's children were attached primarily to their mother. Nor did it matter that her ex-husband, Kenneth Greene, insisted that the couple retain an au pair, even when he was unemployed and at home for over a year, or that when he was employed, he put in extremely long workdays himself. After the new arrangement, according to *Time* magazine's Margaret Carlson, Greene reportedly sent along the kids' dirty laundry when he dropped them off with Prost. Recently the couple agreed to share joint custody. It came about only after Prost began to put in fewer hours at work, while her ex-husband continued to work full time.

Also in 1994, Jennifer Ireland, who had a child when she was 16 and subsequently won several scholarships to attend the University of Michigan, lost custody of her daughter because she placed the child in day care for 35 hours a week while she was in school. The child's father wasn't asserting that he would be the primary caregiver, but rather that his mother would. Judge Raymond Cashen found this arrangement superior because, as he put it, day care meant that the child would be "supervised by strangers." This case, too, ultimately ended in a joint custody solution after Cashen's ruling was successfully appealed in the spring of 199[illegible].

Meanwhile, shortly after Hector lost custody of her daughters, *Sports Illustrated* reported that Pamela McGee, who plays for the WNBA's Los Angeles Sparks, lost custody of her four-year-old daughter while the court investigated whether McGee's work prevented her from being a good mother. In his motion for temporary sole custody, McGee's ex-husband, the Rev. Kevin E. Stafford, asserted that a career and motherhood are mutually exclusive: McGee's "level of achievement," he argued, "impairs her ability to parent her daughter." At issue, according to *Sports Illustrated,* was whether McGee's travel schedule—she's on the road about four weeks a year—took her away from her daughter too much. The court was not investigating whether Stafford's travel schedule—he's on the road seven to eight weeks a year—made him an unfit father.

Many male judges are so prejudiced against working mothers and day care that they will award custody to the father and his new wife if she stays at home, insisting that a stepmom is superior to a working mother. In 1982, a father who had refused to acknowledge paternity, wouldn't pay child support, and didn't visit his son until he was 15 months old sued for custody after the mother tried to get child support. He won, because the mother had worked two jobs to support her son, while his new wife didn't have a job and could be home with the child. This mother has had to watch her child be raised by another woman. When sexist judges with outdated and inaccurate biases against day care apply the "best interests of the child" standard, working mothers can easily lose. And child care providers, whether housekeepers, baby-sitters, or day care centers, are routinely dismissed as inferior, second-rate caretakers.

So it's no surprise that we feminists have our hackles up. We see a vengeful backlash against mothers who work outside the home in which we detect a barely disguised glee in meting out the most painful punishment there can be: separating us from our children. There seems to be a real blood lust—not just in the courts, but in much of the culture—to take working women down a peg, especially if they are more successful than their ex-husbands. At its core, this trend of taking children away from their working mothers is about punishing women for having what is perceived to be too much power. This has occurred within the broader backlash against feminism that continues unabated, where we see an assault on women's reproductive rights, punitive policies toward poor mothers, ridicule of women's studies programs, trivialization of date rape, and calls by a bevy of antifeminist women for us to get back into the kitchen.

Because so much of what we fought for in the 1970s was either undermined or never realized, the prerogatives of motherhood have seemed, until recently, one of our last few privileged outposts. Of course we're going to protect our rights and interests here: we feel under siege in so many areas, and now they want to take our kids away, too? And one thing that court documents can never establish is the endless mental work of mothering: anticipating the children's immediate and long-term needs, and tending to them in advance. The kids' needs are most often in a mother's head, integrated in her psychic "to do" list, because that's what's expected of mothers, and that's what they're supposed to do.

Yet too many feminists, in our understandable outrage over this punitive trend, have been dismissive of Young. He has had to pay for every sexist judge's decision, every mother wronged in court. His feminist attorney, Barbara Green, who saw this as a case about gender equality, has been stung by reactions from other women attorneys who now treat her like a traitor. We should admit to the other truth that we also know: many fathers are deeply connected to their children and then, after a divorce, are relegated to every-other-weekend cameo appearances. I think we've let this case be too easy for us, and we've used Hector and Young as caricatures onto whom we can project a host of fears, rages, and anxieties about work and the family.

But I also wonder how many of us really want fathers to be absolutely equal partners in parenting. As gender roles shift and blur, isn't it our dirty little secret that we want to preside over at least a few of the old preserves, that we need to be seen as the better parents, that we bitch about how much more we have to do than fathers but also cherish our essentialist claims to superiority? Motherhood in America is an ongoing contest, a competition, but mostly between ourselves and celebrity moms, or our friends, or the bad mothers in the media that women are urged to feel superior to, like Susan Smith or welfare mothers. Against some of these women we lose, and against others we win. But to lose to a man?

There are other cases—L.A. Sparks player Pamela McGee's, for example—that feminists should see as emblematic of men trying to demonize working mothers. But I don't see the Hector-Young case as the exemplar of the attack on working mothers, because he truly has been a pretty unusual father. The number of stay-at-home fathers in the U.S. appears to be very small. And not many mothers make over $300,000 a year, as Hector did, or put in her hours, although increasing numbers of mothers—and fathers, for that matter—are facing expanding work schedules and speed-ups. Rather, this case embodies another crucial feminist lesson: negotiation is always preferable to battle.

As Ellen Lyons, the feminist attorney who handled Young's successful appeal, put it, "I always tell my clients to settle." The emotional costs of going through a trial and an appeal are enormous, she emphasizes, and can produce intense pain. "People should think twice before going to battle," she warns, "because the scars are so deep, so bloody." This couple should have settled, but the legal system in which divorcing parents find themselves should make it harder, not easier, to end up in court. Florida's paternalistic attitudes toward joint custody, however well intentioned, and its insistence on someone being the victor—the parent with whom the children make their primary residence—make contests over custody even more heavily charged than they already are.

The case also dramatizes how very far we still have to go as a culture to devise family-friendly work environments. For most professional people, being overworked means you're important and productive. It also means you have less time for your family. While women rightly want the same opportunities as men, feminists once had a dream that we could humanize the workplace; many of us didn't want to have to become just like workaholic, absentee men. Cases like Hector-Young allow us to focus on particular individuals—the classic way the news media covers major trends—instead of on the deep systemic problems of overwork as laid out by Juliet B. Schor in *The Overworked American.* I'm betting that despite feminists' strong reactions to this case, most of us see ourselves in neither Young nor Hector, but in the imagined parent between the two of them.

It is impossible for me not to feel torn by this case. If one is committed to gender equity, and to granting custody to the primary caretaker, Robert Young should retain custody. In my head, I am with him. But in my heart, I am with Hector. Because I know that if I ever found myself in a courtroom, it wouldn't matter that I know the names of all my daughter's dolls, or that I lie in bed with her at night to talk about friendship, or decimals, or god, or that I know which kind of socks she loves and which ones she absolutely refuses to wear. It would only matter that I work longer hours than my husband, and so, as a working mother, I am a bad mother. Until the courts banish this stereotype, it is going to be impossible for many feminists, however deeply committed they are to gender equity, to support the sort of role reversals we once celebrated in our dreams. Ms.

Model Joint Custody Statute (ABA 1989)

15 Fam. L. Rep. 1494, 1494-1495 (1989)

(2) Definitions

(a) For the purposes of this section, "joint custody" means joint legal custody, joint physical custody, or both joint legal custody and joint physical custody. In making an order for joint custody, the court may order joint legal custody without ordering joint physical custody. . . .

(3) Orders of Joint Custody; Factors Considered

(a) The court, upon the request of either or both parents, may award joint custody if joint custody is determined to be in the best interest of the child.

(b) If the court orders joint custody over the objection of a parent, the court shall make specific written findings of why joint custody is in the best interest of the child.

(c) In determining whether joint custody is in the best interest of the child, the court shall consider the factors enumerated in section ______ [reference would be made to the section, if any, in the state's statute used in determining the best interest of a child in a custody dispute] and the following factors:

(1) the agreement or lack of agreement of the parents on joint custody;

(2) the past and present abilities of the parents to cooperate and to make decisions jointly;

(3) the ability of the parents to encourage the sharing of love, affection, and contact between the child and the other parent;

(4) any history of or potential for child abuse, spouse abuse, or parental kidnapping;

(5) the geographic proximity of the parents to each other as this relates to the practical considerations of joint physical custody; and

(6) the recommendation of the representative of the child, if the child has a representative.

(4) Joint Custody Plans

In order to implement joint custody, the court shall require the parents to submit a plan on issues on which the parents are able to reach agreement, unless both parents agree to waive submission of a plan and the court approves the waiver. In the event the parents are not able to reach agreement on elements of a plan, the court shall set the plan.

134 Cal. Rptr. 815
557 P.2d 106
18 Cal.3d 660

Michelle MARVIN, Plaintiff and Appellant,

v.

Lee MARVIN, Defendant and Respondent.

L.A. 30502.

Supreme Court of California,
In Bank.

Dec. 27, 1976.

TOBRINER, Justice.

During the past 15 years, there has been a substantial increase in the number of couples living together without marriage.[1] Such nonmarital relationships lead to legal controversy when one partner dies or the couple separates. Courts of Appeal, faced with the task of determining property rights in such cases, have arrived at conflicting positions: two cases (*In re Marriage of Cary* (1973) 34 Cal.App.3d 345, 109 Cal. Rptr. 862; *Estate of Atherley* (1975) 44 Cal.App.3d 758, 119 Cal.Rptr. 41) have held that the Family Law Act (Civ.Code, § 4000 et seq.) requires division of the property according to community property principles, and one decision (*Beckman v. Mayhew* (1975) 49 Cal.App.3d 529, 122 Cal.Rptr. 604) has rejected that holding. We take this opportunity to resolve that controversy and to declare the principles which should govern distribution of property acquired in a nonmarital relationship.

We conclude: (1) The provisions of the Family Law Act do not govern the distribution of property acquired during a nonmarital relationship; such a relationship remains subject solely to judicial decision. (2) The courts should enforce express contracts between nonmarital partners except to the extent that the contract is explicitly founded on the consideration of meretricious sexual services. (3) In the absence of an express contract, the courts should inquire into the conduct of the parties to determine whether that conduct demonstrates an implied contract, agreement of partnership or joint venture, or some other tacit understanding between the parties. The courts may also employ the doctrine of quantum meruit, or equitable remedies such as constructive or resulting trusts, when warranted by the facts of the case.

In the instant case plaintiff and defendant lived together for seven years without marrying; all property acquired during this period was taken in defendant's name. When plaintiff sued to enforce a contract under which she was entitled to half the property and to support payments, the trial court granted judgment on the pleadings for defendant, thus leaving him with all property accumulated by the couple during their relationship. Since the trial court denied plaintiff a trial on the merits of her claim, its decision conflicts with the principles stated above, and must be reversed.

Plaintiff avers that in October of 1964 she and defendant "entered into an oral agreement" that while "the parties lived together they would combine their efforts and earnings and would share equally any and all property accumulated as a result of their efforts whether individual or combined." Furthermore, they agreed to "hold themselves out to the general public as husband and wife" and that "plaintiff would further render her services as a companion, homemaker, housekeeper and cook to . . . defendant."

Shortly thereafter plaintiff agreed to "give up her lucrative career as an entertainer [and] singer" in order to "devote her full time to defendant . . . as a companion, homemaker, housekeeper and cook"; in return defendant agreed to "provide for all of plaintiff's financial support and needs for the rest of her life."

Plaintiff alleges that she lived with defendant from October of 1964 through May of 1970 and fulfilled her obligations under the agreement. During this period the parties as a result of their efforts and earnings acquired in defendant's name substantial real and personal property, including motion picture rights worth over $1 million. In May of 1970, however, defendant compelled plaintiff to leave his household. He continued to support plaintiff until November of 1971, but thereafter refused to provide further support.

On the basis of these allegations plaintiff asserts two causes of action. The first, for declaratory relief, asks the court to determine her contract and property rights; the second seeks to impose a constructive trust upon one half of the property acquired during the course of the relationship.

The fact that a man and woman live together without marriage, and engage in a sexual relationship, does not in itself invalidate agreements between them relating to their earnings, property, or expenses. Neither is such an agreement invalid merely because the parties may have contemplated the creation or continuation of a nonmarital relationship when they entered into it. Agreements between nonmarital partners fail only to the extent that they rest upon a consideration of meretricious sexual services. Thus the rule asserted by defendant, that a contract fails if it is "involved in" or made "in contemplation" of a nonmarital relationship, cannot be reconciled with the decisions.

We add that in the absence of an express agreement, the courts may look to a variety of other remedies in order to protect the parties' lawful expectations.[24]

The courts may inquire into the conduct of the parties to determine whether that conduct demonstrates an implied contract or implied agreement of partnership or joint venture (see *Estate of Thornton* (1972) 81 Wash.2d 72, 499 P.2d 864), or some other tacit understanding between the parties. The courts may, when appropriate, employ principles of constructive trust (see *Omer v. Omer* (1974) 11 Wash.App. 386, 523 P.2d 957) or resulting trust (see *Hyman v. Hyman* (Tex.Civ.App.1954) 275 S.W.2d 149). Finally, a nonmarital partner may recover in quantum meruit for the reasonable value of household services rendered less the reasonable value of support received if he can show that he rendered services with the expectation of monetary reward.

[9, 10] In the present case Betty Marvin, the aggrieved spouse, had the opportunity to assert her community property rights in the divorce action. (See *Babbitt v. Babbitt* (1955) 44 Cal.2d 289, 293, 282 P.2d 1.) The interlocutory and final decrees in that action fix and limit her interest. Enforcement of the contract between plaintiff and defendant against property awarded to defendant by the divorce decree will not impair any right of Betty's, and thus is not on that account violative of public policy.[8]

[11] Defendant's third contention is noteworthy for the lack of authority advanced in its support. He contends that enforcement of the oral agreement between plaintiff and himself is barred by Civil Code section 5134, which provides that "All contracts for marriage settlements must be in writing. . . ." A marriage settlement, however, is an agreement in contemplation of marriage in which each party agrees to release or modify the property rights which would otherwise arise from the marriage. (See *Corker v. Corker* (1891) 87 Cal. 643, 648, 25 P. 922.) The contract at issue here does not conceivably fall within that definition, and thus is beyond the compass of section 5134.[9]

[12] Defendant finally argues that enforcement of the contract is barred by Civil Code section 43.5, subdivision (d), which provides that "No cause of action arises for . . . [b]reach of a promise of marriage." This rather strained contention proceeds from the premise that a promise of marriage impliedly includes a promise to support and to pool property acquired after marriage (see *Boyd v. Boyd* (1964) 228 Cal.App.2d 374, 39 Cal.Rptr. 400) to the conclusion that pooling and support agreements not part of or accompanied by promise of marriage are barred by the section. We conclude that section 43.5 is not reasonably susceptible to the interpretation advanced by defendant, a conclusion demonstrated by the fact that since section 43.5 was enacted in 1939, numerous cases have enforced pooling agreements between nonmarital partners, and in none did court or counsel refer to section 43.5.

[13, 14] In summary, we base our opinion on the principle that adults who voluntarily live together and engage in sexual relations are nonetheless as competent as any other persons to contract respecting their earnings and property rights. Of course, they cannot lawfully contract to pay for the performance of sexual services, for such a contract is, in essence, an agreement for prostitution and unlawful for that reason. But they may agree to pool their earnings and to hold all property acquired during the relationship in accord with the law governing community property; conversely they may agree that each partner's earnings and the property acquired from those earnings remains the separate property of the earning partner.[10] So long as the agreement does not rest upon illicit meretricious consideration, the parties may order their economic affairs as they choose, and no policy precludes the courts from enforcing such agreements.

[15] In the present instance, plaintiff alleges that the parties agreed to pool their earnings, and they contracted to share equally in all property acquired, and that defendant agreed to support plaintiff. The terms of the contract as alleged do not rest upon any un-

lawful consideration. We therefore conclude that the complaint furnishes a suitable basis upon which the trial court can render declaratory relief. although parties to a nonmarital relationship obviously cannot have based any expectations upon the belief that they were married, other expectations and equitable considerations remain. The parties may well expect that property will be divided in accord with the parties' own tacit understanding and that in the absence of such understanding the courts will fairly apportion property accumulated through mutual effort. We need not treat nonmarital partners as putatively married persons in order to apply principles of implied contract, or extend equitable remedies; we need to treat them only as we do any other unmarried persons.[22]

[22] The remaining arguments advanced from time to time to deny remedies to the nonmarital partners are of less moment. There is no more reason to presume that services are contributed as a gift than to presume that funds are contributed as a gift; in any event the better approach is to presume, as Justice Peters suggested, "that the parties intend to deal fairly with each other." (*Keene v. Keene, supra,* 57 Cal.2d 657, 674, 21 Cal.Rptr. 593, 603, 371 P.2d 329, 339 (dissenting opn.); see *Bruch,* op. cit., *supra,* 10 Family L.Q. 101, 113.)

[23] The argument that granting remedies to the nonmarital partners would discourage marriage must fail; as *Cary* pointed out, "with equal or greater force the point might be made that the pre-1970 rule was calculated to cause the income producing partner to avoid marriage and thus retain the benefit of all of his or her accumulated earnings." (34 Cal.App.3d at p. 353, 109 Cal.Rptr. at p. 866.) Although we recognize the well-established public policy to foster and promote the institution of marriage (see *Deyoe v. Superior Court* (1903) 140 Cal. 476, 482, 74 P. 28), perpetuation of judicial rules which result in an inequitable distribution of property accumulated during a nonmarital relationship is neither a just nor an effective way of carrying out that policy.

In summary, we believe that the prevalence of nonmarital relationships in modern society and the social acceptance of them, marks this as a time when our courts should by no means apply the doctrine of the unlawfulness of the so-called meretricious relationship to the instant case. As we have explained, the nonenforceability of agreements expressly providing for meretricious conduct rested upon the fact that such conduct, as the word suggests, pertained to and encompassed prostitution. To equate the nonmarital relationship of today to such a subject matter is to do violence to an accepted and wholly different practice.

We are aware that many young couples live together without the solemnization of marriage, in order to make sure that they can successfully later undertake marriage. This trial period,[23] preliminary to marriage, serves as some assurance that the marriage will not subsequently end in dissolution to the harm of both parties. We are aware, as we have stated, of the pervasiveness of nonmarital relationships in other situations.

The mores of the society have indeed changed so radically in regard to cohabitation that we cannot impose a standard based on alleged moral considerations that have apparently been so widely abandoned by so many. Lest we be misunderstood, however, we take this occasion to point out that the structure of society itself largely depends upon the institution of marriage, and nothing we have said in this opinion should be taken to derogate from that institution. The joining of the man and woman in marriage is at once the most socially productive and individually fulfilling relationship that one can enjoy in the course of a lifetime.

[24–26] We conclude that the judicial barriers that may stand in the way of a policy based upon the fulfillment of the reasonable expectations of the parties to a nonmarital relationship should be removed.

LOUISIANA 1997 REGULAR SESSION

ACT 1380

HOUSE BILL NO. 756

1997 La. ALS 1380; 1997 La. ACT 1380; 1997 La. HB 756

SYNOPSIS: AN ACT To amend and reenact Civil Code Articles 102 and 103 and R.S. 9:234 and 245(A)(1) and to enact R.S. 9:224(C) and 225(A)(3), Part VII of Chapter 1 of Code Title IV of Code Book I of Title 9 of the Louisiana Revised Statutes of 1950, comprised of R.S. 9:272 through 275, and R.S. 9:307, 308, and 309, all relative to covenant marriages; to provide for a declaration on the application for a marriage license; to provide prerequisites to entering into a covenant marriage, including counseling; to authorize the entering into a covenant marriage by couples already married; to provide for indication thereof on the marriage certificate; to provide the exclusive means to terminate a covenant marriage; to provide with respect to jurisdiction, venue, and incidental relief; and to provide for related matters.

Be it enacted by the Legislature of Louisiana:

[*1] Section 1. Civil Code Articles 102 and 103 are hereby amended and reenacted to read as follows:

Art. 102. Judgment of divorce; living apart one hundred eighty days prior to rule

Except in the case of a **covenant marriage,** a divorce shall be granted upon motion of a spouse when either spouse has filed a petition for divorce and upon proof that one hundred eighty days have elapsed from the service of the petition, or from the execution of written waiver of the service, and that the spouses have lived separate and apart continuously for at least one hundred eighty days prior to the filing of the rule to show cause.

The motion shall be a rule to show cause filed after all such delays have elapsed.

Art. 103. Judgment of divorce; other grounds

Except in the case of a **covenant marriage,** a divorce shall be granted on the petition of a spouse upon proof that:

(1) The spouses have been living separate and apart continuously for a period of six months or more on the date the petition is filed; or

(2) The other spouse has committed adultery; or

(3) The other spouse has committed a felony and has been sentenced to death or imprisonment at hard labor.

[*2] Section 2. R.S. 9:234 and 245(A)(1) are hereby amended and reenacted and R.S. 9:224(C) and 225(A)(3) are hereby enacted to read as follows:

Section 224. Same; information required

C. In cases wherein the parties intend to contract a **covenant marriage,** the application for a marriage license must also include the following:

"We, [D> name of intended husband <D] and [D> name of intended wife <D] , do hereby declare our intent to contract a **Covenant Marriage** and, accordingly, have executed a declaration of intent attached hereto."

Section 225. Same; attachments

A. An application for a marriage license shall be accompanied by:

(3) If applicable, the declaration of intent for a **covenant marriage,** as provided in Part VII of this Chapter.

Section 234. Time and date; indication of **covenant marriage**

The official who issues the marriage license shall show on the face of it the exact time and date of issuance.

The official shall also indicate on the marriage license whether the parties intend to enter into a **covenant marriage.**

Section 245. Marriage certificate

A.(1) The marriage certificate is the record prepared for every marriage on a form approved by the state registrar of vital records. It shall contain the information prescribed. On the face of the certificate shall appear the certification to the fact of marriage including, if applicable, a designation that the parties entered into a **covenant marriage,** signed by the parties to the marriage and by the witnesses, and the signature and title of the officiant.

[*3] Section 3. Part VII of Chapter 1 of Code Title IV of Code Book I of Title 9 of the Louisiana Revised Statutes of 1950, to be comprised of R.S. 9:272 through 275, is hereby enacted to read as follows:

PART VII. **COVENANT MARRIAGE**

Section 272. **Covenant marriage;** intent; conditions to create

A. A **covenant marriage** is a marriage entered into by one male and one female who understand and agree that the marriage between them is a lifelong relationship. Parties to a **covenant marriage** have received counseling emphasizing the nature and purposes of marriage and the responsibilities thereto. Only when there has been a complete and total breach of the marital covenant commitment may the non-breaching party seek a declaration that the marriage is no longer legally recognized.

B. A man and woman may contract a **covenant marriage** by declaring their intent to do so on their application for a marriage license, as provided in R.S. 9:224(C), and executing a declaration of intent to contract a **covenant marriage,** as provided in R.S. 9:273. The application for a marriage license and the declaration of intent shall be filed with the official who issues the marriage license.

Section 273. **Covenant marriage;** contents of declaration of intent

A. A declaration of intent to contract a **covenant marriage** shall contain all of the following:

(1) A recitation by the parties to the following effect:

"A **COVENANT MARRIAGE**

We do solemnly declare that marriage is a covenant between a man and a woman who agree to live together as husband and wife for so long as they both may live. We have chosen each other carefully and disclosed to one another everything which could adversely affect the decision to enter into this marriage. We have received premarital counseling on the nature, purposes, and responsibilities of marriage. We have read the **Covenant Marriage** Act, and we understand that a **Covenant Marriage** is for life. If we experience martial difficulties, we commit ourselves to take all reasonable efforts to preserve our marriage, including marital counseling.

With full knowledge of what this commitment means, we do hereby declare that our marriage will be bound by Louisiana law on **Covenant Marriages** and we promise to love, honor, and care for one another as husband and wife for the rest of our lives."

(2)(a) An affidavit by the parties that they have received premarital counseling from a priest, minister, rabbi, clerk of the Religious Society of Friends, any clergyman of any religious sect, or a marriage counselor, which counseling shall include a discussion of the seriousness of **covenant marriage,** communication of the fact that a **covenant marriage** is a commitment for life, a discussion of the obligation to seek marital counseling in times of marital difficulties, and a discussion of the exclusive grounds for legally terminating a **covenant marriage** by divorce or by divorce after a judgment of separation from bed and board.

(b) A notarized attestation, signed by the counselor and attached to or included in the parties' affidavit, confirming that the parties were counseled as to the nature and purpose of the marriage and the grounds for termination thereof and an acknowledging that the counselor provided to the parties the informational pamphlet developed and promulgated by the office of the attorney general, which pamphlet entitled the **Covenant Marriage** Act provides a full explanation of the terms and conditions of a **covenant marriage.**

(3)(a) The signature of both parties witnessed by a notary.

(b) If one or both of the parties are minors, the written consent or authorization of those persons required under the Children's Code to consent to or authorize the marriage of minors.

B. The declaration shall contain two separate documents, the recitation and the affidavit, the latter of which shall include the attestation either included therein or attached thereto. The recitation shall be prepared in duplicate originals, one of which shall be retained by the parties and the other, together with the affidavit and attestation, shall be filed as provided in R.S. 9:272(B).

Section 274. **Covenant marriage;** other applicable rules

A **covenant marriage** shall be governed by all of the provisions of Chapters 1 through 4 of Title IV of Book I of the Louisiana Civil Code and the provisions of Code Title IV of Code Book I of Title 9 of the Louisiana Revised Statutes of 1950.

Section 275. **Covenant marriage;** applicability to already married couples

A. On or after August 15, 1997, married couples may execute a declaration of intent to designate their marriage as a **covenant marriage** to be governed by the laws relative thereto.

B.(1) This declaration of intent in the form and containing the contents required by Subsection C of this Section must be presented to the officer who issued the couple's marriage license and with whom the couple's marriage certificate is filed. If the couple was married outside of this state, a copy of the foreign marriage certificate, with the declaration of intent attached thereto, shall be filed with the officer who issues marriage licenses in the parish in which the couple is domiciled. The officer shall make a notation on the marriage certificate of the declaration of intent of a **covenant marriage** and attach a copy of the declaration to the certificate.

(2) On or before the fifteenth day of each calendar month, the officer shall forward to the state registrar of vital records each declaration of intent of a **covenant marriage** filed with him during the preceding calendar month pursuant to this Section.

C.(1) A declaration of intent to designate a marriage as a **covenant marriage** shall contain all of the following:

(a) A recitation by the parties to the following effect:

"A **COVENANT MARRIAGE**

We do solemnly declare that marriage is a covenant between a man and a woman who agree to live together as husband and wife for so long as they both may live. We understand the nature, purpose, and responsibilities of marriage. We have read the **Covenant Marriage** Act, and we understand that a **Covenant Marriage** is for life. If we experience marital difficulties, we commit ourselves to take all reasonable efforts to preserve our marriage, including marital counseling.

With full knowledge of what this commitment means, we do hereby declare that our marriage will be bound by Louisiana law on **Covenant Marriage,** and we renew our promise to love, honor, and care for one another as husband and wife for the rest of our lives."

(b)(i) An affidavit by the parties that they have discussed their intent to designate their marriage as a **covenant marriage** with a priest, minister, rabbi, clerk of the Religious Society of Friends, any clergyman of any religious sect, or a marriage counselor, which included a discussion of the obligation to seek marital counseling in times of marital difficulties and the exclusive grounds for legally terminating a **covenant marriage** by divorce or by divorce after a judgment of separation from bed and board.

(ii) A notarized attestation, signed by the counselor and attached to the parties' affidavit, acknowledging that the counselor provided to the parties the information pamphlet developed and promulgated by the office of the attorney general, which pamphlet entitled the **Covenant Marriage** Act provides a full explanation of the terms and conditions of a **covenant marriage.**

(iii) The signature of both parties witnessed by a notary.

(2) The declaration shall contain two separate documents, the recitation and the affidavit, the latter of which shall include the attestation either included therein or attached thereto. The recitation shall be prepared in duplicate originals, one of which shall be retained by the parties and the other, together with the affidavit and attestation, shall be filed as provided in Subsection B of this Section.

[*4] Section 4. R.S. 9:307, 308, and 309 are hereby enacted to read as follows:

Section 307. Divorce or separation from bed and board in a **covenant marriage;** exclusive grounds

A. Notwithstanding any other law to the contrary and subsequent to the parties obtaining counseling, a spouse to a **covenant marriage** may obtain a judgment of divorce only upon proof of any of the following:

(1) The other spouse has committed adultery.

(2) The other spouse has committed a felony and has been sentenced to death or imprisonment at hard labor.

(3) The other spouse has abandoned the matrimonial domicile for a period of one year and constantly refuses to return.

(4) The other spouse has physically or sexually abused the spouse seeking the divorce or a child of one of the spouses.

(5) The spouses have been living separate and apart continuously without reconciliation for a period of two years.

(6)(a) The spouses have been living separate and apart continuously without reconciliation for a period of one year from the date the judgment of separation from bed and board was signed.

(b) If there is a minor child or children of the marriage, the spouses have been living separate and apart continuously without reconciliation for a period of one year and six months from the date the judgment of separation from bed and board was signed; however, if abuse of a child of the marriage or a child of one of the spouses is the basis for which the judgment of separation from bed and board was obtained, then a judgment of divorce may be obtained if the spouses have been living separate and apart continuously without reconciliation for a period of one year from the date the judgment of separation from bed and board was signed.

B. Notwithstanding any other law to the contrary and subsequent to the parties obtaining counseling, a spouse to a **covenant marriage** may obtain a judgment of separation from bed and board only upon proof of any of the following:

(1) The other spouse has committed adultery.

(2) The other spouse has committed a felony and has been sentenced to death or imprisonment at hard labor.

(3) The other spouse has abandoned the matrimonial domicile for a period of one year and constantly refuses to return.

(4) The other spouse has physically or sexually abused the spouse seeking the divorce or a child of one of the spouses.

(5) The spouses have been living separate and apart continuously without reconciliation for a period of two years.

(6) On account of habitual intemperance of the other spouse, or excesses, cruel treatment, or outrages of the other spouse, if such habitual intemperance, or such ill-treatment is of such a nature as to render their living together insupportable.

Section 308. Separation from bed and board in **covenant marriage;** suit against spouse; jurisdiction, procedure, and incidental relief

A. Unless judicially separated, spouses in a **covenant marriage** may not sue each other except for causes of action pertaining to contracts or arising out of the provisions of Book III, Title VI of the Civil Code; for restitution of separate property; for separation from bed and board in **covenant marriages,** for divorce, or for declaration of nullity of the marriage; and for causes of action pertaining to spousal support or the support or custody of a child while the spouses are living separate and apart, although not judicially separated.

B.(1) Any court which is competent to preside over divorce proceedings, including the family court for the parish of East Baton Rouge, has jurisdiction of an action for separation from bed and board in a **covenant marriage,** if:

(a) One or both of the spouses are domiciled in this state and the ground therefor was committed or occurred in this state or while the matrimonial domicile was in this state.

(b) The ground therefor occurred elsewhere while either or both of the spouses were domiciled elsewhere, provided the person obtaining the separation from bed and board was domiciled in this state prior to the time the cause of action accrued and is domiciled in this state at the time the action is filed.

(2) An action for a separation from bed and board in a **covenant marriage** shall be brought in a parish where either party is domiciled, or in the parish of the last matrimonial domicile.

(3) The venue provided herein may not be waived, and a judgment of separation rendered by a court of improper venue is an absolute nullity.

C. Judgments on the pleadings and summary judgments shall not be granted in any action for separation from bed and board in a **covenant marriage.**

D. In a proceeding for a separation from bed and board in a **covenant marriage** or thereafter, a court may award a spouse all incidental relief afforded in a proceeding for divorce, including but not limited to spousal support, claims for contributions to education, child custody, visitation rights, child support, injunctive relief and possession and use of a family residence or community movables or immovables.

Section 309. Separation from bed and board in a **covenant marriage;** effects

A.(1) Separation from bed and board in a **covenant marriage** does not dissolve the bond of matrimony, since the separated husband and wife are not at liberty to marry again; but it puts an end to their conjugal cohabitation, and to the common concerns, which existed between them.

(2) Spouses who are judicially separated from bed and board in a **covenant marriage** shall retain that status until either reconciliation or divorce.

B.(1) The judgment of separation from bed and board carries with it the separation of goods and effects and is retroactive to the date on which the original petition was filed in the action in which the judgment is rendered, but such retroactive effect shall be without prejudice (a) to the liability of the community for the attorney fees and costs incurred by the spouses in the action in which the judgment is rendered, or (b) to rights validly acquired in the interim between commencement of the action and recordation of the judgment.

(2) Upon reconciliation of the spouses, the community shall be reestablished between the spouses, as of the date of filing of the original petition in the action in which the judgment was rendered, unless the spouses execute prior to the reconciliation a

matrimonial agreement that the community shall not be reestablished upon reconciliation. This matrimonial agreement shall not require court approval.

(3) Reestablishment of the community under the provisions of this Section shall be effective toward third persons only upon filing notice of the reestablishment for registry in accordance with the provisions of Civil Code Article 2332. The reestablishment of the community shall not prejudice the rights of third persons validly acquired prior to filing notice of the reestablishment nor shall it affect a prior community property partition between the spouses.

[*5] Section 5. The office of attorney general, Department of Justice shall, prior to August 15, 1997, promulgate an informational pamphlet, entitled "**Covenant Marriage** Act", which shall outline in sufficient detail the consequences of entering into a **covenant marriage.** The informational pamphlet shall be made available to any counselor who provides marriage counseling as provided for by this Act.

[*6] Section 6. The provisions of Section 5 of this Act shall become effective upon signature by the governor or, if not signed by the governor, upon expiration of the time for bills to become law without signature by the governor, as provided in Article III, Section 18 of the Constitution of Louisiana. If vetoed by the governor and subsequently approved by the legislature, this Act shall become effective on the day following such approval.

HISTORY:
Approved by the governor: July 15, 1997

* * * *

SUPREME COURT OF CANADA

Indexed as: M. *v.* H.

File No.: 25838.

1999: May 20.

ON APPEAL FROM THE COURT OF APPEAL FOR ONTARIO

Constitutional law -- Charter of Rights -- Equality rights -- Definition of "spouse" -- Family Law Act extending right to seek support to members of unmarried opposite-sex couples -- Whether failure to provide same rights to members of same-sex couples infringes right to equality -- If so, whether infringement justified -- Canadian Charter of Rights and Freedoms, ss. 1, 15(1) -- Family Law Act, R.S.O. 1990, c. F.3, s. 29.

Family law -- Spousal support -- Definition of "spouse" -- Family Law Act extending right to seek support to members of unmarried opposite-sex couples -- Whether failure to provide same rights to members of same-sex couples infringes right to equality guaranteed by Canadian Charter of Rights and Freedoms -- Family Law Act, R.S.O. 1990, c. F.3, s. 29.

M. and H. are women who lived together in a same-sex relationship beginning in 1982. During that time they occupied a home which H. had owned since 1974. In 1982, M. and H. started their own advertising business. The business enjoyed immediate success and was the main source of income for the couple during the relationship. H.'s contribution to this company was greater than that of M. In 1983, M. and H. purchased a business property together. In 1986, they purchased as joint tenants a vacation property in the country. They later sold the business property and used the proceeds to finance the construction of a home on the country property. As a result of a dramatic downturn in the advertising business in the late 1980s, the parties' debt increased significantly. H. took a job outside the firm and placed a mortgage on her home to pay for her expenses and those of M. By the fall of 1992, M. and H.'s relationship had deteriorated. M. left the common home and sought an order for partition and sale of the house and other relief. M. later amended her application to include a claim for support pursuant to the provisions of the *Family Law Act* ("*FLA*"), and served notice of a constitutional question challenging the validity of the definition of "spouse" in s. 29, which includes a person who is actually married and also "either of a man and woman who are not married to each other and have cohabited . . . continuously for a period of not less than three years". Section 1(1) defines "cohabit" as "to live together in a conjugal relationship, whether within or outside marriage". The motions judge held that s. 29 of the *FLA* offends s. 15(1) of the *Canadian Charter of Rights and Freedoms*, and that it is not saved by s. 1. She declared that the words "a man and woman" were to be read out of the definition of "spouse" in s. 29 and replaced with the words "two persons". H. appealed the decision and was joined in the appeal by the Attorney General for Ontario. The Court of Appeal upheld the decision

Held (Gonthier J. dissenting on the appeal): The appeal and the cross-appeal should be dismissed but the remedy should be modified. Section 29 of the *FLA* is declared of no force or effect.

This denial of a benefit violates the purpose of s. 15(1). One factor which may demonstrate that legislation that treats the claimant differently has the effect of demeaning the claimant's dignity is the existence of pre-existing disadvantage, stereotyping, prejudice, or vulnerability experienced by the individual or group at issue. In this case, there is significant pre-existing disadvantage and vulnerability and these circumstances are exacerbated by the impugned legislation. The legislative provision in question draws a distinction that prevents persons in a same-sex relationship from gaining access to the court-enforced and -protected support system. The denial of that potential benefit, which may impose a financial burden on persons in the position of the claimant, contributes to the general vulnerability experienced by individuals in same-sex relationships. A second relevant factor is that the legislation at issue fails to take into account the claimant's actual situation. Being in a same-sex relationship does not mean that it is an impermanent or a non-conjugal relationship. Third, while the existence of an ameliorative purpose or effect may help to establish that human dignity is not violated where the person or group that is excluded is more advantaged with respect to the circumstances addressed by the legislation, the allegedly ameliorative purpose of this legislation does not do anything to lessen the charge of discrimination in this case. Fourth, the nature of the interest protected by s. 29 of the *FLA* is fundamental. The exclusion of same-sex partners from the benefits of s. 29 promotes the view that M., and individuals in same-sex relationships generally, are less worthy of recognition and protection. It implies that they are judged to be incapable of forming intimate relationships of economic interdependence as compared to opposite-sex couples, without regard to their actual circumstances. Such exclusion perpetuates the disadvantages suffered by individuals in same-sex relationships and contributes to the erasure of their existence.

B. VITAL STATISTICS

Marriages and Divorces in the U.S., 1920–96

Year	Marriages ('000s)	Rate per 1,000 of population	Divorces ('000s)	Rate per 1,000 of population
1920	1,274	12.0	171	1.6
1925	1,188	10.3	175	1.5
1930	1,127	9.2	19.6	1.6
1935	1,327	10.4	218	1.7
1940	1,596	12.1	264	2.0
1945	1,613	12.2	485	3.5
1950	1,667	11.1	385	2.6
1955	1,531	9.3	377	2.3
1960	1,523	8.5	393	2.2
1965	1,800	9.3	479	2.5
1970	2,163	10.6	708	3.5
1975	2,153	10.0	1,036	4.8
1980	2,390	10.0	1,036	4.8
1985	2,413	10.1	1,190	5.0
1990	2,448	9.8	1,175	4.7
1991	2,371	9.4	1,187	4.7
1992	2,362	9.3	1,215	4.8
1993	2,334	9.0	1,187	4.6
1994	2,362	9.1	1,191	4.6
1995	2,336	8.9	1,169	4.4
1996	2,344	8.8	1,150	4.3

Source: U.S. National Center for Health Statistics, *Vital Statistics of the United States* (annual) and *Monthly Vital Statistics Report*, July 17,1997.

Births and Deaths in the U.S., 1910–96

Year	Live births (000s)	Birth rate[1]	Deaths[2] (000s)	Death rate[1]
1910	2,777	30.1	N.A.	14.7
1920	2,950	27.7	N.A.	13.0
1930	2,618	21.3	N.A.	11.3
1935	2,377	18.7	1,393	10.9
1940	2,559	19.4	1,417	10.8
1945	2,858	20.4	1,402	10.6
1950	3,632	24.1	1,452	9.6
1955	4,097	25.0	1,529	9.3
1960	4,258	23.7	1,712	9.5
1965	3,760	19.5	1,828	9.4
1970	3,731	18.4	1,921	9.5
1975	3,144	14.6	1,893	8.8
1980	3,612	15.9	1,990	8.8
1985	3,761	15.8	2,086	8.8
1990	4,158	16.7	2,148	8.6
1991	4,111	16.3	2,170	8.6
1992	4,084	16.0	2,177	8.5
1993	4,039	15.7	2,268	8.8
1994	3,979	15.3	2,286	8.8
1995	3,892	14.8	2,309	8.8
1996	3,899	14.7	2,311	8.7

1. Per 1,000 total population. 2. Excludes fetal deaths. **Source:** U.S. National Center for Health Statistics, *Vital Statistics of the United States*, (annual) and *Monthly Vital Statistics Report*, July 17, 1997.

Divorced Persons per 1,000 Married Persons by Sex and Race 1960–95

Sex/race	All races	White	Black	Hispanic[1]
Both sexes:				
1960	35	33	62	N.A.
1970	47	44	83	61
1980	100	92	203	98
1990	142	133	282	129
1993	154	144	296	136
1994	163	151	310	145
1995	161	152	303	152
Male:				
1960	28	27	45	N.A.
1970	35	32	62	40
1980	79	74	149	64
1990	118	112	208	103
1993	125	119	216	114
1994	137	129	221	125
1995	134	130	212	130
Female:				
1960	42	38	78	N.A.
1970	60	56	104	81
1980	120	110	258	132
1990	166	153	358	155
1993	182	170	378	157
1994	187	173	403	165
1995	187	173	397	174

Note: Persons 18 years and over. Per 1,000 married persons with spouse present. 1. Persons of Hispanic origin may be of any race. **Source:** U.S. Bureau of the Census, *Marital Status and Living Arrangements: March 1995* (1997).

Unmarried Couple Households, 1960-95 (thousands)

Year	Total	Without children under 15	With children under 15
1960	439	242	197
1970	523	327	196
1980	1,589	1,159	431
1985	1,983	1,380	603
1990	2,856	1,966	891
1991	3,039	2,077	962
1992	3,308	2,187	1,121
1993	3,510	2,274	1,236
1994	3,661	2,391	1,270
1995	3,668	2,349	1,319

Note: Figures may not add to total due to rounding. **Source:** *Marital Status and Living Arrangements: March 1995* (1997).

Living Arrangements of Children Under 18, 1970–95 (thousands)

Arrangement	1970 Number	1970 Percent	1980 Number	1980 Percent	1990 Number	1990 Percent	1995 Number	1995 Percent
All children								
Children under 18	69,162	100.0%	63,427	100.0%	64,137	100.0%	70,254	100.0%
Living with:								
Two parents	58,939	85.2	48,624	76.7	46,503	72.5	48,276	68.7
One Parent	8,199	11.9	12,466	19.7	15,867	24.7	18,938	27.0
Mother only	7,452	10.8	11,406	18.0	13,874	21.6	16,477	23.4
Father only	748	1.1	1,060	1.7	1,993	3.1	2,461	3.5
Other relatives	1,547	2.2	1,949	3.1	1,421	2.2	2,352	3.3
Nonrelatives only	477	0.7	388	0.6	346	0.5	688	1.0

30.2 million households in 1998 about 30 percent of the nation's total were maintained by women with no husband present. In 1970, there were 13.4 million such households, comprising about 20 percent of all households.

- There were 9.8 million single mothers in 1998, no change from the number in the previous three years, but up by 6.4 million since 1970. The total includes those who maintain their own household (7.7 million in 1998), as well as those living in the homes of relatives or others. Mothers still account for most of the nation's 11.9 million single parents.

- In 1998, 58 percent of women 18 years old and over were married, 21 percent had never married and 11 percent each were widowed and divorced.

- The estimated median age at first marriage was 25.0 years for women in 1998 tying the 20th century-high reached the previous year and up almost a full five years since the early 1960s.

- The number of women living alone doubled between 1970 and 1998, from 7.3 million to 15.3 million, or 14 percent of all women 15 years old and over. Half of the women living alone were elderly; put another way, 41 percent of all elderly women lived by themselves.

- More women nowadays are either postponing or not ever having kids. Twenty-seven percent of women 30 to 34 in 1995 had never given birth; in 1976, the corresponding proportion was 16 percent. The same trend also holds for women in their late 30s (20 percent were childless in 1995, 11 percent were in 1976) and early 40s (18 percent and 10 percent, respectively).

- In 1995, 58 percent of 15- to 44-year-old women had had children: 18 percent had given birth to one child, 23 percent to two, 11 percent to three and 6 percent to four or more. For those at the end of their childbearing years (ages 40 to 44), more than 8 in 10 had had children, giving birth to an average of two each.

- Over half (55 percent) of the 3.7 million women with a newborn were in the labor force in 1995, up from 31 percent in 1976. In 1995, women with newborns were especially likely to be in the labor force (68 percent) if they had at least a bachelor's degree.

U.S. CENSUS BUREAU, 1999

Who Receives Child Support?

Not only do women have better chances of being awarded child support . . .
In spring 1992, about one-half (6.2 million) of the 11.5 million custodial parents were awarded child support; award rates were higher for mothers than for fathers (56% compared with 41%).

. . . they are more likely to actually receive payments.
Fewer than half of the custodial parents (5.3 million, or 46%) were supposed to receive child support payments in 1991. Of the 4.9 million women due payments, 76% received at least a portion of the amount they were owed. The corresponding rate for the 400,000 men owed money was 63%.

More than 5 million custodial parents were without awards of financial support from their child(ren)'s other parent. About one-third of those without awards had chosen not to pursue them. Two other common reasons they did not have awards were that they did not want an award and that the noncustodial parent was unable to pay.

Much of the child support due goes unpaid.
A total of $11.9 billion was paid in child support in 1991, $5.8 billion less than the amount due. Nearly all of the money paid ($11.2 billion) went to women.

Although women receive more child support than men . . .
Women who received child support in 1991 were paid an average of $3,011 that year, about one-third more than their male counterparts ($2,292). On average, these support payments constituted 17% of 1991 money income for the women, but only 7% for the men.

. . . they still have lower incomes.
The mothers who received child support had lower average 1991 money income than the fathers who received it ($18,144 compared with $33,579). Income was lower for custodial parents who did not receive payments.

Visitation and joint custody help.
About 6.9 million of the 11.5 million parents who did not live with their children (noncustodial parents) had joint custody and/or visitation privileges to contact their children. It was more likely for the 5.3 million noncustodial parents who owed child support in 1991 to have made payments if they had one or both of these contact privileges than if they had neither (79% compared with 56%).

Fewer than half of awards include health care benefits.
About four in ten parents with child support awards as of 1992 had health-insurance benefits included in their award. However, about one-third (31%) of the noncustodial parents who were required to provide these benefits in 1991 as part of the award failed to do so. On the other hand, some noncustodial parents (18%) not required to provide these benefits as part of the award did so anyway.

Custodial fathers and mothers differ demographically.
Race and Hispanic origin: Custodial fathers were more likely than custodial mothers to be white (85% versus 70%) and less apt to be black (12% compared with 27%). They were about as likely to be Hispanic (approximately 10% each).

Marital Status: Custodial fathers were less likely than custodial mothers to have never been married (8% versus 26%), more apt to be currently married (46% compared with 27%), and just as likely to be divorced or separated (about 47% each). Custodial fathers were as likely to be currently married as they were to be divorced or separated. Also, custodial mothers were as likely to be currently married as they were to be never married.

Age: Custodial fathers were generally older than custodial mothers. About half (46%) of custodial fathers were at least 40 years old, while only 11% were under age 30. The corresponding percentages for custodial mothers were 24% and 31%, respectively. One percent each of custodial fathers and mothers were under age 18.

Education: Custodial fathers were better educated than custodial mothers. They were twice as likely to have at least a bachelor's degree (19% compared with 10%) and less apt to have only attained a high school diploma or less (56% versus 64%).

NOTE: Data applies to the U.S. *Source:* Economics and Statistics Administration, U.S. Department of Commerce.

- About 28 percent (20 million) of all children under 18 years of age in the United States lived with just one parent.

- The majority of children who lived with just one parent in 1998 lived with their mother (84 percent).

- No other adults were present in the household for 56 percent of children living with single parents.

- About 4 million children, nearly 6 percent of all children under 18, lived in the household of their grandparents.

U.S. CENSUS BUREAU, 1999

Growth in Single Fathers Outpaces Growth in Single Mothers, Census Bureau Reports

While the number of single mothers (9.8 million) has remained constant over the past three years, the number of single fathers has grown 25 percent, from 1.7 million in 1995 to 2.1 million in 1998, according to tabulations released today by the Commerce Department's Census Bureau. Men now comprise one-sixth of the nation's 11.9 million single parents.

Other highlights for 1998 include:

- Of the 102.5 million households in the United States, 69 percent are family households. The share of family households fell 10 percentage points between 1970 and 1990 (from 81 percent to 71 percent) but has dropped only 2 percentage points since.
- About half (49 percent) of family households contain children under 18, down from 56 percent in 1970.
- The growth of one-parent families is slowing. They comprise 27 percent of family households with children, up from 24 percent in 1990 and 11 percent in 1970.
- Nearly 22 million adult (ages 18 or older) sons and daughters live in a home maintained by one or both parents, up from 15 million in 1970.
- The average U.S. family household consists of 3.18 people, down from 3.58 in 1970, but unchanged from 1990. Hispanic families are larger, with an average of 3.92 members, than either African American or non-Hispanic White families, which average 3.42 and 3.02 members, respectively.

U.S. CENSUS BUREAU, 1998

C. LEGAL STATUS OF SAME-SEX COUPLES

The Canadian Supreme Court's decision in *M. v. H.* is not, technically, legal precedent for American courts. Its message, however, has resounded legally and politically the United States, and comes just three years after the United States Supreme Court, in *Romer v. Evans*, declared unconstitutional a Colorado statewide voter referendum denying anti-discrimination protection to homosexuals. The rights of gay and lesbian citizens to marriage, adoption, spousal and child support, and employment and insurance benefits continue to be debated by legislatures, courts, and the electorate, and will likely soon be revisited by the Supreme Court. Because same-sex cases often hinge on sex -- instead of or in addition to sexual orientation -- as a legal classification, it is quite possible that key constitutional and other legal rulings with major implications for women will ensue.

This issue has been particularly compelling in Hawaii, where that state's supreme court, in *Baehr v. Lewin* (1993), ruled that denial of marriage licenses to same-sex couples violated the state constitution. The court relied heavily on *Loving v. Virginia* (1967), in which the U.S. Supreme Court held that Virginia's prohibition of interracial marriage violated the Fourteenth Amendment's Equal Protection Clause (Judge Heen, dissenting in *Baehr*, stated that no fundamental right was being denied, because marriage itself is defined as the legal union of a man and a woman). Subsequent to *Baehr*, Hawaii's constitution was amended to limit marriage to different-sex couples, and the matter is again before the Hawaii Supreme Court. *Baehr* also prompted the 1996 congressional passage of the Defense of Marriage Act, Public Law 104-199, which declared that the Constitution's Full Faith and Credit Clause, Article IV, Section 1, did not require states to recognize same-sex marriages performed outside their borders.

BAEHR v. LEWIN
SUPREME COURT OF HAWAII, 1993
852 P.2d 44 (Haw. 1993)

JUDGE LEVINSON for the Court: Lewin [Director, Hawaii Dept. of Health] contends that the fact that homosexual partners cannot form a state-licensed marriage is not the product of impermissible discrimination implicating equal protection considerations, but rather a function of their biologic inability as a couple to satisfy the definition of the status to which they aspire. We believe Lewin's argument to be circular and unpersuasive.

In a landmark decision, *Loving v. Virginia* (1967), the United States Supreme Court, through Chief Justice Warren, struck down the Virginia miscegenation laws on both equal protection and due process grounds. . . The facts in *Loving* and the respective reasoning of the Virginia courts, on the one hand, and the United States Supreme Court, on the other . . . unmask the tautological and circular nature of Lewin's argument that . . .the same-sex marriage prohibition does not violate the equality provision of the Hawaii Constitution because same-sex marriage is an innate impossibility. The Virginia courts declared that interracial marriage simply could not exist because the Deity had deemed such a union intrinsically unnatural, and in effect, because it had heretofore never been the "custom" of the state to recognize mixed marriages, marriage "always" having been construed to presuppose a different configuration. With all due respect to the Virginia courts of a bygone era, we do not believe that trial judges are the ultimate authorities on the subject of Divine Will, and, as *Loving* amply demonstrates, constitutional law may mandate, like it or not, that customs change with an evolving social order.

We hold that sex is a "suspect category" for purposes of equal protection analysis under article I, section 5 of the Hawaii Constitution and that Hawaii Revised Statutes, sec. 572-1 is subject to the "strict scrutiny" test.

JUDGE HEEN, dissenting: *Loving* is simply not authority for the plurality's proposition that the civil right to marriage must be accorded to same sex couples.

Although appellants suggest an analogy between the racial classification involved in *Loving* . . . and the alleged sexual classification involved in the case at bar, we do not find such an analogy. The operative distinction lies in the relationship which is described by the term "marriage" itself, and that relationship is the legal union of one man and one woman.

ROMER v. EVANS

517 U.S. 620 (1996)

Decided May 20, 1996

JUSTICE KENNEDY delivered the opinion of the Court.

One century ago, the first Justice Harlan admonished this Court that the Constitution "neither knows nor tolerates classes among citizens." Plessy v. Ferguson, 163 U.S. 537, 559 (1896) (dissenting opinion). Unheeded then, those words now are understood to state a commitment to the law's neutrality where the rights of persons are at stake. The Equal Protection Clause enforces this principle and today requires us to hold invalid a provision of Colorado's Constitution.

I

The enactment challenged in this case is an amendment to the Constitution of the State of Colorado, adopted in a 1992 statewide referendum. The parties and the state courts refer to it as "Amendment 2," its designation when submitted to the voters. The impetus for the amendment and the contentious campaign that preceded its adoption came in large part from ordinances that had been passed in various Colorado municipalities. For example, the cities of Aspen and Boulder and the City and County of Denver each had enacted ordinances which banned discrimination in many transactions and activities, including housing, employment, education, public accommodations, and health and welfare services. Denver Rev. Municipal Code, Art. IV 28-91 to 28-116 (1991); Aspen Municipal Code 13-98 (1977); Boulder Rev. Code 12-1-1 [ROMER v. EVANS, ___ U.S. ___ (1996) , 2] to 12-1-11 (1987). What gave rise to the statewide controversy was the protection the ordinances afforded to persons discriminated against by reason of their sexual orientation. See Boulder Rev. Code 12-1-1 (defining "sexual orientation" as "the choice of sexual partners, i.e., bisexual, homosexual or heterosexual"); Denver Rev. Municipal Code, Art. IV 28-92 (defining "sexual orientation" as "[t]he status of an individual as to his or her heterosexuality, homosexuality or bisexuality"). Amendment 2 repeals these ordinances to the extent they prohibit discrimination on the basis of "homosexual, lesbian or bisexual orientation, conduct, practices or relationships." Colo. Const., Art. II, 30b.

Yet Amendment 2, in explicit terms, does more than repeal or rescind these provisions. It prohibits all legislative, executive or judicial action at any level of state or local government designed to protect the named class, a class we shall refer to as homosexual persons or gays and lesbians. The amendment reads:

"No Protected Status Based on Homosexual, Lesbian, or Bisexual Orientation. Neither the State of Colorado, through any of its branches or departments, nor any of its agencies, political subdivisions, municipalities or school districts, shall enact, adopt or enforce any statute, regulation, ordinance or policy whereby homosexual, lesbian or bisexual orientation, conduct, practices or relationships shall constitute or otherwise be the basis of or entitle any person or class of persons to have or claim any minority status, quota preferences, protected status or claim of discrimination. This Section of the Constitution shall be in all respects self-executing." Ibid.

It is not within our constitutional tradition to enact laws of this sort. Central both to the idea of the rule of law and to our own Constitution's guarantee of equal protection is the principle that government and each of its parts remain open on impartial terms to all who seek its assistance. "`Equal protection of the laws is not achieved through indiscriminate imposition of inequalities.'" Sweatt v. Painter, 339 U.S. 629, 635 (1950) (quoting Shelley v. Kraemer, 334 U.S. 1, 22 (1948)). Respect for this principle explains why laws singling out a certain class of citizens for disfavored legal status or general hardships are rare. A law declaring that in general it shall be more difficult for one group of citizens than for all others to seek aid from the government is itself a denial of equal protection of the laws in the most literal sense. "The guaranty of `equal protection of the laws is a pledge of the protection of equal laws.'" Skinner v. Oklahoma ex rel. Williamson, 316 U.S. 535, 541 (1942) (quoting Yick Wo v. Hopkins, 118 U.S. 356, 369 (1886)).

A second and related point is that laws of the kind now before us raise the inevitable inference that the disadvantage imposed is born of animosity toward the class of persons affected. "[I]f the constitutional conception of `equal protection of the laws' means anything, it must at the very least mean that a bare . . . desire to harm a politically unpopular group cannot constitute a legitimate governmental interest." Department of Agriculture v. Moreno, 413 U.S. 528, 534 (1973). Even laws enacted for broad and ambitious purposes often can be explained by reference to legitimate public policies which justify the incidental disadvantages they impose on certain persons. Amendment 2, however, in making a general announcement that gays and lesbians shall not have any particular protections from the law, inflicts on them immediate, continuing, and real injuries that outrun and belie any legitimate justifications that may be claimed for it. We conclude that, in addition to the far-reaching deficiencies of Amendment 2 that we have noted, the principles it offends, in another sense, are conventional and venerable; a law must bear a rational relationship to a legitimate governmental purpose, Kadrmas v. Dickinson Public Schools, 487 U.S. 450, 462 (1988), and Amendment 2 does not.

The primary rationale the State offers for Amendment 2 is respect for other citizens' freedom of association, and in [ROMER v. EVANS, ___ U.S. ___ (1996) , 13] particular the liberties of landlords or employers who have personal or religious objections to homosexuality. Colorado also cites its interest in conserving resources to fight discrimination against other groups. The breadth of the Amendment is so far removed from these particular justifications that we find it impossible to credit them. We cannot say that Amendment 2 is directed to any identifiable legitimate purpose or discrete objective. It is a status-based enactment divorced from any factual context from which we could discern a relationship to legitimate state interests; it is a classification of persons undertaken for its own sake, something the Equal Protection Clause does not permit. "[C]lass legislation . . . [is] obnoxious to the prohibitions of the Fourteenth Amendment . . . ." Civil Rights Cases, 109 U.S., at 24.

We must conclude that Amendment 2 classifies homosexuals not to further a proper legislative end but to make them unequal to everyone else. This Colorado cannot do. A State cannot so deem a class of persons a stranger to its laws. Amendment 2 violates the Equal Protection Clause, and the judgment of the Supreme Court of Colorado is affirmed.

D. RECOMMENDED READING

A. Parkman, *No-Fault Divorce: What Went Wrong?* (Westview Press: 1992)

W. Eskridge, *The Case For Same-Sex Marriage, From Sexual Liberty to Civilized Commitment* (Free Press: 1996)

L. Weitzman, "The Economics of Divorce: Social and Economic Consequences of Property, Alimony, and Child Support," 28 *U.C.L.A. Law Review* 1181 (1991)

C. Starnes, "Divorce and the Displaced Homemaker: A Discourse on Playing with Dolls," 67 *U. Chicago Law Review 60* (1987)

CHAPTER VIII
The Intersection of Sex, Race and Culture

A. MULTICULTURAL CONSIDERATIONS

The individuals and organizations involved in gender- related issues have, of course, come from a variety of ethnic backgrounds. Issues of race and ethnicity continue to inform key legal developments surrounding gender equality. Issues of race can be critical to case dispositions, but results vary greatly. In *Rogers v. American Airlines* (1981) and similar cases, courts have not been sympathetic to female employee seeking the right to particular clothing or grooming styles as a reflection of cultural identity. As a matter of law, courts have generally held that plaintiffs alleging discrimination on the basis of the *combination* of race and sex have no special legal protection under Title VII of the 1964 Civil Rights Act or other statutes. As a matter of social and political thought, commentators disagree regarding the relative status of, and interaction between, race and sex

In a pair of highly-publicized 1999 custody decisions, two state courts came to different conclusions. The Maryland Court of Appeals [In Re: Adoption No. 12612, February 17, 1999] awarded adoptive custody of a black child to a white caretaker, when the black natural mother had killed the child's sibling. In Illinois, a state juvenile court judge [In the Matter of Baby T., Cook County Juvenile Court, March 8, 1999] ordered a black child returned to his African-American mother, following temporary placement with a politically-powerful white family due to the mother's drug addiction.

Women's rights issues have played a prominent role in recent years in the areas of immigration and human rights. Women seeking political asylum in lieu of expected genital mutilation, physical and sexual abuse, and similar treatment in their countries of origin often find that their predicaments do not necessarily find a sympathetic ear in the U.S. Immigration and Naturalization Service. This area may well be a fertile one for future legal reform.

ROGERS v. AMERICAN AIRLINES

U.S. District Court, Southern District of New York (1981)

Plaintiff is a black woman who seeks $10,000 damages, injunctive, and declaratory relief against enforcement of a grooming policy of the defendant American Airlines that prohibits employees in certain employment categories from wearing an all-braided hairstyle. Plaintiff has been an American Airlines employee for approximately eleven years, and has been an airport operations agent for over one year. Her duties involve extensive passenger contact, including greeting passengers, issuing boarding passes, and checking luggage. She alleges that the policy . . . discriminates against her as a woman, and more specifically as a black woman . . .

Defendant's motion to dismiss is meritorious with respect to the statutory claims insofar as they challenge the policy on its face. The statutory bases alleged, Title VII and section 1981, are indistinguishable in the circumstances of this case, and will be considered together. The policy is addressed to both men and women, black and white. Plaintiff's assertion that the policy has practical effect only with respect to women is not supported by any factual allegations. Many men have hair longer than many women. Some men have hair long enough to wear in braids if they choose to do so. Even if the grooming policy imposed different standards for men and women, however, it would not violate Title VII. It follows, therefore, that an evenhanded policy that prohibits to both sexes a style more often adopted by members of one sex does not constitute prohibited sex discrimination. This is because this type of regulation has at most a negligible effect on employment opportunity. It does not regulate on the basis of any immutable characteristic of the employees involve. It concerns a matter of relatively low importance in terms of the constitutional interests protected by the Fourteenth Amendment and Title VII, rather than involving fundamental rights such as the right to have children or to marry. The complaint does not state a claim for discrimination.

The considerations with respect to plaintiff's race discrimination claim would clearly be the same, except for plaintiff's assertion that the "corn row" style has a special significance for black women. She contends that it:

"has been, historically, a fashion and style adopted by black American women, reflective of the cultural, historical essence of the black woman in American society. The style was 'popularized' so to speak within the larger society, when Cicely Tyson adopted the same for an appearance on a nationally-viewed Academy Awards presentation several years ago . . . It was and is analogous to the public statement by the late Malcolm X regarding the Afro hair style . . . At the bottom line, the completely braided hair style, sometimes referred to as corn rows, has been and continues to be part of the cultural and historical essence of black American women.

There can be little doubt that, if America adopted a policy which foreclose black women/all women from wearing hair styled as an 'Afro/bush', that policy would have very pointedly racial dynamics and consequences reflecting a vestige of slavery unwilling to die (that is, a master mandate that one wear hair divorced from one's historical and cultural perspective and otherwise consistent with the 'white master'-dominated society and preference thereof)."

Plaintiff is entitled to a presumption that her arguments, largely repeated in her affidavit, are true. But the grooming policy applies equally to members of all races, and plaintiff does not allege that an all-braided hair style is worn exclusively or even predominantly by black people. Moreover, it is proper to note that defendants have alleged without contravention that plaintiff first appeared at work in the all-braided hairstyle on or about September 25, 1980, soon after the style had been popularized by a white actress in the film "10." Plaintiff may be correct that an employer's policy prohibiting the "Afro/bush" style might offend Title VII and section 1981. But if so, this chiefly would be because banning a natural hairstyle would implicate the policies underlying the prohibition of discrimination on the basis of immutable characteristics. In any event, an all-braided hairstyle is a different matter. It is not the product of natural hair growth but of artifice. An all-braided hairstyle is an "easily changeable characteristic," and, even if socio-culturally associated with a particular race or nationality, is not an impermissible basis for distinctions in the application of employment practices by an employer . . .

Moreover, the airline did not require plaintiff to re-style her hair. It is suggested that she could wear her hair as she liked while off duty, and permitted her to pull her hair into a bun and wrap a hairpiece around the bun during working hours . . . Plaintiff has done this, but alleges that the hairpiece has caused her severe headaches. A larger hairpiece would seem in order. But even if any hairpiece would cause such discomfort, the policy does not offend a substantial interest.

Plaintiff has failed to allege sufficient facts to require defendants to demonstrate that the policy has a bona fide business purpose. In this regard, however, plaintiff does not dispute defendant's assertion that the policy was adopted in order to help American project a conservative and business-like image, a consideration recognized as a bona fide business purpose. Rather she objects to its impact with respect to the "corn row" style, an impact not protected against by Title VII or section 1981.

Nigerian Fights Deportation, Fearing Mistreatment by Tribe

By SYLVIA MORENO
Washington Post Staff Writer

They parted that morning with a hug and tiny whispered words of encouragement from daughter to mother.

"Bye, Mommy," said Chenidu Anikwata, a lanky, bespectacled fifth-grader. "Good luck."

For three weeks, Chenidu's mother, Virginia, has been in a detention center on Maryland's Eastern Shore, fighting deportation to Nigeria.

Virginia Anikwata contends that if she is forced to return to Nigeria after 12 years in the United States, her daughter, a U.S. citizen, would be doomed to female circumcision. She says that under Ibo tribal custom, she and her daughter also would be considered property of her late husband's family and both would be forced into polygamous marriages against their wills.

"My fear is if I go back, I will be mistreated, that they might even kill me . . . and that my husband's family would take my child away from me," Anikwata, 36, said in a recent interview.

The alternative, she said, is to leave the 10-year-old girl behind in a country where she has no relatives. And that is something she cannot do.

"It's outrageous . . . to put a parent in that position: dump the kid or take the child back to female genital mutilation or early marriage," said Lois Whitman, director of the children's rights division of Human Rights Watch in New York.

But U.S. immigration officials, who have been trying to deport Anikwata as an illegal alien since 1991, have said that her persecution claims are "speculative and fantastic" and that, in any case, the child's fate is not their immediate concern.

While the issue is fought out in court, Chenidu is winding down her sixth year at Garrett Park Elementary School, where she is classified as a gifted and talented student. This month, she won an academic excellence award given to select African American students.

She recently reenacted a pioneer trek with her class during a field trip, and she played a spider in the drama club play, "James and the Giant Peach." Her fifth-grade graduation is coming up, as is the class trip to Williamsburg—events that Virginia Anikwata, who worked as a licensed practical nurse until this month, had neatly penciled in on the kitchen calendar.

"My mother has been so much a part of my life," Chenidu said as she stood in a bedroom decorated with pictures she drew of herself and of her and her mother ("We'll Be a Family Forever," reads the caption). "And they have to take custody of her at such an important time in my life."

Chenidu, who is known at school by her middle name—Sharon—was born in Washington in July 1987, a year after her parents legally entered the United States on her father's student visa. Godfrey Anikwata was an aspiring urban planner enrolled in graduate studies at Morgan State University in Baltimore.

But in spring 1987, he was diagnosed with lung cancer, and eight weeks after Chenidu's birth, he died at the age of 28. It was at that moment that Virginia Anikwata's status in the United States, which hinged on her husband's visa, went from legal to illegal.

Anikwata's initial attempt to legalize her status after her husband's death was denied by the U.S. Immigration and Naturalization Service, which issued a letter advising her to leave the country. She then started to explore other avenues to remain here legally.

In 1989, a Silver Spring family for whom she worked as a nanny agreed to sponsor her for her green card. But a brush with the INS in mid-1991, when immigration agents came to her apartment looking for another Nigerian suspected of marriage fraud, forced her into deportation proceedings because Anikwata was technically still here illegally.

Since then, Anikwata has been fighting her deportation in the hopes that, at some point, her request for a visa to stay in the United States legally would be granted, said her attorney, Martha Saenz.

But changes in federal immigration law significantly reduced the number of visas available for unskilled workers, and other revisions in the law eventually worked against

Anikwata, Saenz said.

In 1994, Anikwata filed an affidavit with the U.S. Board of Immigration Appeals that said her daughter "will face a hardship due to the laws and customs of my tribe" if she were deported.

"My husband's family will take her away from me and that has been my main concern," Anikwata wrote.

Then in January—after exhausting appeals for a suspension of deportation—Anikwata filed a petition for political asylum on the grounds that she had been persecuted in Nigeria by being forced to undergo circumcision. The procedure includes cutting and removing parts of the female genitalia, usually done without anesthesia and under unsanitary conditions. The operation has been condemned by human rights organizations worldwide and is outlawed in the United States.

However, Anikwata's asylum claim can be considered only with the permission of the Baltimore INS district office or the Board of Immigration Appeals. The district office rejected her request, and last Wednesday the appeals board rejected her request to delay her deportation further and indicated it was not likely to consider her asylum petition.

A spokesman for the Baltimore district office said Anikwata has already had her fair hearing before various immigration officials.

"All the information has been heard by an immigration judge and the Board of Immigration Appeals, and they have found her claims have no merit," John Shallman said.

In addition, a key INS official filed a motion with the Board of Immigration Appeals opposing the reopening of Anikwata's case.

"Her characterization of what would happen to her if she returned to Nigeria is entirely speculative," wrote Lawrence O. Burman, the former assistant district counsel in the Baltimore INS office.

"Claims that her U.S. citizen daughter would be circumcised and enslaved if taken to Nigeria are even more speculative and fantastic," said Burman, who is now an immigration judge in Los Angeles. "Of course, her daughter will not go to Nigeria unless (Anikwata) takes her."

Human rights officials have written on Anikwata's behalf to INS Commissioner Doris M. Meissner, Baltimore INS District Director Benedict J. Ferro and to the Board of Immigration Appeals in an attempt to get the merits of the asylum case reviewed.

"Getting sent out of the country without ever having had an opportunity to have a claim like this be heard is a fundamental denial of due process," said Jessica Neuwirth, president of Equality Now, a New York-based organization that works to protect the human rights of women.

"This circumstance that she's raising about her daughter is new, but it's extremely valid and it should not be dismissed," said Morton Sklar, head of the World Organization Against Torture in Washington. "And when you're talking about an American citizen, that makes it even more compelling."

Just being a U.S. citizen could make Chenidu a target for "greater persecution" in Nigeria, Anikwata said in her application for political asylum.

What she says she is sure about, however, is that she would not be able to protect her daughter from being circumcised or sold into marriage.

"She would be subjected to female genital mutilation. I went through it when I was a young child," she said, as she cried in the visitor's booth at the detention center. "That would hurt me so bad. She is the only thing I have. She is my only hope."

Washington Post, May 28, 1998 p. A-1

Immigration Ruling Reflects Split Over Gender Persecution

By Fredric N. Tulsky
Special to The Washington Post

A foreign woman fleeing a violently abusive spouse cannot gain asylum in the United States even if she faces a direct and serious threat of harm in her home country, a federal immigration panel has ruled in a case that is drawing protests from asylum advocates and women's groups.

The decision this month by a sharply divided Board of Immigration Appeals, the Justice Department panel that sets and interprets U.S. immigration policy, reflects a growing philosophical tension within the immigration system over how to treat women's claims of gender persecution.

Since issuing guidelines intended to recognize gender-based persecution under U.S. asylum laws, the federal government has sent mixed signals about whether women fleeing persecution from their husbands—as opposed to persecution by a government—should be allowed to seek refuge here.

The subject in the case, Rodi Alvarado Peña, now 33, was abused for years by her husband in Guatemala in ways that U.S. officials agree were horrific. Her husband, a former soldier, beat her unconscious, raped her and kicked her so badly she hemorrhaged, she has told authorities. He broke windows and mirrors with her head, pistol-whipped her and threatened her with a machete.

Alvarado attempted suicide and vainly sought protection from Guatemalan police and courts, who told her it was a private matter. Finally, Alvarado said, in desperation she fled Guatemala and sought protection in the United States. An immigration judge granted her asylum claim in September 1996.

But in its 10 to 5 decision, the Board of Immigration Appeals ruled that Alvarado does not qualify for asylum under U.S. immigration policy. The board found she had not proven that she suffered persecution under any of the five categories enumerated under international and U.S. law: race, religion, nationality, political opinion or membership in a social group.

The majority's opinion reflects the caution that many immigration judges and U.S. officials feel about allowing new categories of eligible asylum seekers that would open the floodgates to large numbers of new claims by people seeking residence in the United States.

Already, U.S. immigration courts wrestle routinely with the difficulties of evaluating evidence of government persecution claims presented by asylum seekers whose experiences and travels pose huge challenges of documentation and corroboration. A new category of claims involving domestic violence would impose further burdens on the immigration courts.

With persecution based on gender status [illegible]ng as a relatively new area of asylum [illegible]e board's majority said that it would [illegible]to Congress to step in and provide [illegible] detailed guidance about how new [illegible]ards should be applied.

[illegible] the five dissenting appeals board [illegible]bers contended that the board's deci[illegible]ot to recognize domestic abuse victims [illegible]atemala as a social group "cannot be [illegible]led either with the reality of the [illegible]dent's situation in Guatemala, or with [illegible]." They said the United States has an [illegible]ion to protect those who fear harm [illegible]e of "some fundamental aspect of [illegible]dentity."

[illegible] asylum policies offer protection for [illegible]ees who demonstrate a "credible fear" [illegible]secution if they are sent home. But [illegible]must show that their persecutor is [illegible]the government itself or someone the [illegible]ment is unable or unwilling to con[illegible]e persecution must be on account of [illegible]the five enumerated grounds.

In Alvarado's case, the board majority said in the June 11 decision that resolution of her spousal abuse claim "does not lie in our asylum laws as they are currently formulated."

The case illustrates the latest zigzag in U.S. immigration policies toward women. In 1995, the Immigration and Naturalization Service first issued guidelines intended to recognize gender-based persecution under the asylum laws. But asylum advocates contend that the guidelines have been erratically applied and interpreted.

The guidelines are not binding on the immigration judges, who work for a sister agency within the Justice Department. The board majority concluded at any rate that the guidelines do not resolve whether domestic violence victims are a protected social group.

The board factions split over whether the majority was departing from the reasoning that it used in overturning an immigration judge and granting asylum in 1997 to Fauziya Kasinga, who said she faced female genital mutilation if returned to Togo. The board ruled then that women who opposed the practice were singled out for persecution because of their opposition. In contrast, the majority said in Alvarado's case, Guatemalan women were not singled out because they opposed domestic violence.

"The record in this case reflects that the views of society and of many governmental institutions in Guatemala can result in the tolerance of spousal abuse at levels we find appalling," states the majority opinion, written by board member Lauri S. Filppu. "The record also shows that abusive marriages are not viewed as desirable, that spousal abuse is recognized as a problem, and that some measures have been pursued in an attempt to respond to this acknowledged problem."

The INS does not tally asylum claims by sex, but says that 20,459 people applied between last October and May, and 8,028 were granted protection during that period.

Women's rights advocates condemned the Alvarado decision. San Francisco attorney Jane Kroesche, who represents Alvarado, on Thursday said she plans to appeal to federal court. While the Board of Immigration Appeals is the highest administrative authority for asylum cases in the federal system, its decisions can be appealed directly to the U.S. Appeals Court.

"She suffered prolonged torture, and did everything in her country she could to help herself," Kroesche said. "At great sacrifice, she left behind her country, her family and her children, knowing she might not see them again. If she is not protected, what kind of woman would be?"

Karen Musalo, resident scholar at the University of California at Hastings, who was Kasinga's attorney and who advised Kroesche, called the similarities in the cases "striking."

"What is so distressing is that the board seems either to have not understood its decision in Kasinga, or is refusing to apply its own principles," she said.

Maria T. Cardona, INS spokeswoman, said Friday, "The INS is absolutely committed to gender protection where the claims can be supported by law." But Cardona added that defining a "social group is complicated, and is a difficult legal standard."

U.S. officials do not dispute Alvarado's account of brutal treatment by her husband. "We struggle to describe how deplorable we find the husband's conduct to have been," the board majority wrote.

In an interview conducted through a translator, Alvarado, now a maid in San Francisco, recounted in Spanish how the abuse began when she was a 16-year-old newlywed and continued throughout 11 years of marriage. The couple has a 12-year-old daughter and 6-year-old son, now living with relatives in Guatemala.

"Some nights I don't sleep at all," she said. "I think of all that has happened. I'm very sure if I were not here, I would be dead."

Usually her husband put the children in the yard while he abused her, she said. But once, when she tried to take the children and flee to a new house, she said, he tracked them down and beat her unconscious in front of them.

On occasion, she called the police and even filed a formal complaint. But she said she was told that "he was my husband. They couldn't insert themselves in the matter of a couple." The courts told her the same thing.

She said she tried to take an overdose of pills. When she was revived, she said, her husband told her that she was not going to die or leave him. "You're going to stay here, even without any feet or any arms," she quotes him as telling her. Finally, she waited until her children were away in May 1995, got on a bus and left for good. She ended up in San Francisco with no money or knowledge of the United States, she said.

Just days after Alvarado's arrival in the United States, INS issued its gender guidelines. The guidelines warned that female refugees might fear authority figures during questioning and that sexually abused women "may appear numb ... or show emotional passivity."

Alvarado's asylum claim was granted by Immigration Judge Mimi S. Yam of San Francisco in 1996, but the INS promptly appealed. It said she did not fall under one of the five protected categories under the law.

Deborah Anker, head of Harvard University's immigration and refugee clinic, said Thursday that the appeals board decision was contrary to a growing body of international authority.

"Gender is an immutable characteristic, and persecution on account of gender violates the most fundamental rights that the Refugee Convention was clearly intended to address," she said, referring to the 1951 international agreement on which U.S. asylum law is based.

Even as they issued the decision, the board majority acknowledged the possible danger facing Alvarado if she returned home.

"The respondent in this case has been terribly abused and has a genuine and reasonable fear of returning to Guatemala," the opinion says.

Nevertheless, the majority concluded that "the solution to the respondent's plight" does not exist in U.S. asylum laws "as they are currently formulated."

The dissent, written by board member John Guendelsberger, contends that the majority opinion is contrary to U.S. law, prior board decisions and federal court decisions.

"The respondent has a fundamental right to protection from abuse based on gender," the dissenting opinion states.

Washington Post, June 20, 1999 - p. A-1

Racism, Civil Rights, and Feminism

Kathleen Neal Cleaver

The roots of the extraordinary protest movement culminating with the passage of the 1964 Civil Rights Act and the 1965 Voting Rights Act reach deep into the century-long struggle blacks waged to end slavery and secure full citizenship.[1] Feminists have drawn inspiration and legal ammunition[2] from those passionate struggles during both the nineteenth and twentieth centuries. Yet despite appropriating legal gains paid for in blood during the civil rights era, and benefiting in great numbers from legislation banning employment discrimination, white women who represent the dominant voice of American feminists seem nearly inaudible in their opposition to racism. The perceptions that motivated the radical feminists, Third World feminists, and progressive women devoted to ending racial oppression have become peripheral among leading feminist authors.

This silence, which seems especially paradoxical to me in light of the crucial role women played in the modern civil rights movement, demonstrates how profound efforts at collective transformation can remain trapped within deeply entrenched boundaries. For in many ways, the Southern-based struggle to end segregation during the 1950s and 1960s, which can be seen as a human rights movement, a struggle for community empowerment, or a collective effort to expand democracy, was a women's movement. If it were not for black women, there would have been no Montgomery Bus Boycott, few voting rights campaigns, far less marvelous educational impact—in short, the civil rights movement as we know it could not have occurred.

Black women supported the churches that sustained the movement; raised money for the National Association for the Advancement of Colored People (NAACP), the Southern Christian Leadership Conference (SCLC), and other groups; encouraged their children to become plaintiffs in desegregation suits, and fed and sheltered the young student activists who took the challenge against white supremacy to the countryside. Women sat in at lunch counters, boarded the buses that became Freedom Rides, walked in the boycott lines, marched in demonstrations, went to jail, and became civil rights leaders in their communities. The visual record always documents the presence of women, but in the printed texts of academic accounts women's participation tends to fade. Yet it was the women in the movement who insisted on the more radical approaches, showed the most determination, and kept the fires for radical change lit. And it was black women in the movement whose example transformed white women's understanding of what women could do.[3]

Ella Baker, whose lifelong civil rights career spanned the NAACP, the Urban League, the SCLC, and the Student Nonviolent Coordinating Committee, has stated that "the number of women who carried the movement is much larger than the number of men."[4] Baker, raised in North Carolina by grandparents who had been enslaved, continued that spirited resistance that animated the struggle against slavery in her lifework. And it was that concrete, real-time devotion to the destruction of oppression, which I think characterized the socialization of daughters in many Southern black families, that accounted for their deep attraction to the civil rights struggle. For the movement of that era was about *Freedom*—praying, singing, marching, planning, reaching, and organizing for freedom. And in Southern black communities it was patently obvious that freedom was not withheld simply because of gender, but denied to every man, woman, and child who was black.

What the women who financed, mobilized, and joined civil rights campaigns knew, what those whose community work empowered the charismatic leaders who rose to represent the civil rights cause knew was that the price of black women's freedom was freedom for the entire community. Historical accounts concentrate largely on national leadership figures, but most of the mass protests and insurgencies that exploded during the 1950s and 1960s were grassroots movements that emerged with little direction from national organizations or leaders.[5] And where there were grassroots, there were women, as Kay Mills wrote in her biography of Fannie Lou Hamer.[6] The intertwining of the concerns of women and the struggle to end black oppression have a long history. As far back as 1892, the African American feminist, scholar, and human rights activist Anna Julia Cooper wrote that "only the *Black Woman* can say 'when and where I enter, in the quiet, undisputed dignity of my womanhood, without violence and without suing or special patronage, then and there the whole Negro race enters with me.' "[7]

I was in high school when I first saw defiant young women engaged in civil rights protest. Those students who went to jail in Albany, Georgia, during the early voter registration campaigns impressed me immensely. The courage it took for them to challenge white racist laws and their determination not to let jail or mob violence turn them away were awe-inspiring. I learned what heroism and leadership meant from Diane Nash, who led student demonstrations in Nashville, Tennessee, and later organized Freedom Rides, from Gloria Richardson, who mobilized the black community to fight segregation in Cambridge, Maryland, and from Ruby Doris Robinson, who helped coordinate the 1964 Mississippi Summer Project. It never once entered my head that women could not be civil rights leaders or organizers.

Like hundreds of women of my generation, I was thrilled to get a chance to join the movement. Shortly after the Meredith March, which galvanized national attention on the cry of "Black Power" in the summer of 1966, I began working at the Student Nonviolent Coordinating Committee's office in New York. I moved on to the national office in Atlanta, where I helped organize a black student conference held at Fisk University. Eldridge Cleaver was invited to speak at the conference. We fell in love and were married at the end of 1967. I became the communications secretary of the Black Panther Party and devoted most of my effort to our campaign to prevent Huey Newton, the defense minister of the Black Panther Party, from going to the gas chamber on charges of murdering an Oakland policeman.

My involvement with the Black Panther Party began during a turbulent era marked by frequent urban rebellions, profound dissent over the Vietnam War, and extremist political violence. Leaders with progressive views—from the Democratic president Kennedy to the NAACP leader Medgar Evers to Malcolm X to Black Panther Fred Hampton—were all assassinated because their eloquent pleas for change inspired a generation. The Black Panthers were being subjected to constant police surveillance, harassment, and terrorism. By that I mean people were followed, our telephones were tapped, our mail was opened, our homes were raided, our offices were shot up, and our organization was infiltrated. Members were frequently arrested and jailed, our leaders were framed, and our organization was sabotaged by a secret counterintelligence program spearheaded by the director of the FBI.[8] The news media were enlisted to portray Black Panthers as dangerous criminals instead of young people engaged in a struggle for self-determination. We sought power for the people, and in return the power of the state came crashing down on our heads.

Such conditions made it obvious to women within the Black Panther Party that liberation was not something we could obtain separately, nor would consciousness-raising groups serve as an appropriate channel for our rage. Of course, as in the larger community, conflicts occurred between men and women, and sexism was an issue that Panthers struggled to confront. Yet we could see how these conflicts arising from sexism within our community were subordinate to the overwhelming violence of the domination imposed on our community by the armed representatives of the state.

The women's liberation movement was coalescing around this same time, but women in the Black Panther Party did not believe that the discussions white women were launching would derive solutions to the difficulties we faced. While white women were addressing the specific form of oppression they experienced within the dominant culture, we came to fight side by side with men for black liberation. In fact, the way we engaged the culture in our struggle against racism deeply encouraged white women to strike out against sexism.

As revolutionaries, we rejected the conventional definition of our economic, political, and social relationship to the dominant society as "second-class citizenship." That citizenship extended after the Civil War continued the subjugation historically enforced during slavery, and we analyzed the regime of segregation as a variant of colonialism. Instead of being separated by land, as was Angola from Portugal, for example, black colonies were dispersed throughout the American "mother country" in separate communities that police controlled like occupying armies. Under international human rights law, we saw blacks as colonial subjects just as entitled to fight for human rights and self-determination as Africans, Asians, and Latin Americans who were waging revolutionary wars against imperialist domination.

The first point in the Black Panther Party Ten Point Program stated, "We want power to determine the destiny of our own black community." Our colonized status was the basis on which we organized for liberation; therefore all members of the Black Panther Party were drawn from the colonized community. We worked with other peoples and groups on the principle of coalition, not combination within the same organization. We formed coalitions with the electoral Peace and Freedom Party, which was predominantly white, with the Chicano Brown Berets, with the Puerto Rican Young Lords, and with the Asian Red Guards. We challenged racism with solidarity, and violence with self-defense.

While the ultimate domination that we all struggled to destroy during that era may have been the same, that did not mean its distinct historical and social articulations were interchangeable. The ancient dynamic that elevated white men over white women was not rooted in the same historical economic processes that allowed them to extract forced labor from African slaves and their descendants in North America. Although both unequal power relationships were embedded within hierarchical structures of authority, the barbarism involved in constructing New World slave societies transcended the bounds of patriarchy and laid the foundation for imperialist domination of the world.[9] Nothing has so profoundly chiseled the contours of our national heritage as those formative centuries of American slavery. The central paradox of American history is that the rise of liberty and equality was accompanied by the rise of slavery.[10] And the stigma of that social death inherent in the slave condition has imprinted itself on the entire cultural fabric.[11]

When Supreme Court justice Roger Taney, a former slaveowner, refuted Dred Scott's claim to freedom in the middle of the nineteenth century, he wrote that blacks were "beings of an inferior order . . . altogether unfit to associate with the white race in either social or political relations."[12] Their social position was so degraded, Taney wrote, "that they had no rights which the white man was bound to respect."[13] He did not support his assertion with legal citations, but instead pointed to the fact that "the negro [was] justly and lawfully . . . reduced to slavery for his benefit. He was bought and sold and treated as an ordinary article of merchandise . . . whenever a profit could be made by it."[14]

In a society defined by its creation of a class of human property, gender has maintained the demarcation that race historically imposed between those who owned that property and those who became property. The alleged benefits of the cult of femininity did not accrue to the black woman, who was neither protected within the white patriarchal structure nor excluded from the market.[15] When the slave woman's children, her labor, and her person legally became a commodity, white women were both protected and subordinated by the authority, autonomy, and property of their fathers or husbands. An irony of the system that extracted the greatest labor benefits conceivable from its workers was that it released enslaved women from the conventions evoked by gender among the dominant group. But, as Angela Davis has cautioned, the onerous nature of this brutal equality with black men should never be overlooked.[16]

Eliminating gender discrimination in itself does not remove the contortion blighting the lives of women whose color, race, national origin, or economic marginalization causes them such pain. As a rule, the subtleties of entrenched racism are no better understood by whites, women or men, than sexual harassment is by men, whether they are black or white, rich or poor. Until white feminists discover how to see the insidious way that racism constricts the lives of millions of women, they cannot oppose it. Worse, they may blindly fail to perceive how their ancestry positions them to benefit passively from racism's perpetuation, and remain oblivious to the racialized nature of gender.[17] Cultural, political, and economic institutions that mask deeply entrenched patterns of thought and action sustain white superiority almost automatically, as they have sustained male power. This enables racism to function with very little conscious individual attention.

Educated, well-meaning whites will insist, "I am not a racist," which is quite true if one accepts their fragmentary definition of "racist."[18] But what is the source of those slights, remarks, insults, or overt behavior that blacks interacting with them interpret as revealing a belief in black inferiority? What explains the gross media stereotypes that pervert the image of blacks? Why are blacks singled out for suspicious or fearful treatment because of their appearance, even in the hallowed halls of the Ivy League? How did it happen that over 80 percent of white Americans live where they have no black neighbors?

Just like sexism, racist behaviors flourish unless conscious, systematic, organized opposition to their manifestation, including but not limited to administrative and legal regulation, is in place. Thirty years of civil rights law have not eliminated those social conditions molded by three centuries of black subjugation. Feminism does not inoculate women against racism, because gender for black women has represented a category differentiated from white women,[19] whose race reserved them a place within the dominant society from which black women were barred.[20] Not only did gender limit the earning power of black women pushed to the lowest rungs of the economic ladder, but it left them outside the realm of glorified white womanhood. Patriarchal norms, economic exploitation, and racial denigration give a polydimensional character to the sexism that oppresses black women, which one-dimensional feminism cannot combat. Instead, the feminism appropriate to African Americans requires a complex recognition of the gendered dimension of racial subjugation.

The social isolation, economic deprivation, and blatant terrorism meted out to blacks make it difficult for many to appreciate the subtler subordination and intimidation that women within the dominant community endure. Lacking an appreciation of these women's realities, many black people fail to recognize that women whom they perceive as privileged may in fact feel weak, and therefore they discredit the validity of the feminist movement. Further, the sexist attitudes that belittle and exclude women's contributions from major black institutions, including churches, colleges, and reform organizations, is rarely given the public acknowledgment and condemnation it deserves. The presence of a significant underclass, masses of solid working people, and an affluent middle class among blacks shows that we are neither liberated nor integrated, but have become a fragmented population, scattered through all levels of society from the Pentagon to the prison yard. To elevate awareness of feminist concerns within black communities requires facing hostile opposition and uncomprehending denial. Yet this work may become a new focus for black women's activism. Concern for gender equity knows no color line, and women of every community desperately need more respect.

Unless we intend to remain locked up in self-righteous boxes, it is time to replace cross-racial silence and hostility on gender with communication. But no one can speak truth to power until they find out what is true. The weaknesses, aspirations, and histories that divide as well as unite us need to be examined, understood, and demythologized. That may get us to the starting gate to look for the solution that seems to elude us. Those progressive organizations that advocate on behalf of black concerns must adopt stronger antisexist positions if they intend to mobilize their constituencies and retain their relevance. More attention must be devoted to problems facing black women, particularly those juggling poverty and motherhood, fending off domestic violence and community crime waves.

These changes may take place before mainstream feminists become motivated to develop antiracist positions, because whites have a stake in failing to examine the interplay of racism with their cultural identity. During the heyday of European imperialism, when race became elevated to the primary indicator of cultural achievement, the hierarchical theory of race placed whites at the pinnacle of historical development.[21] Masterfully fabricated justifications in science, religion, industry, politics, and art that entitled whites to live on the labor and property of the inferior colored peoples of the world distinguished the nineteenth century.[22] Everything great, everything fine, everything really successful in human culture was seen as white.[23] As that legacy has yet to be repudiated entirely, it abets American feminist scholarship in which race remains peculiarly invisible.

The analytical task is to include gender and race within the same critique instead of polarizing them. If these constructs are extracted separately from the cultural matrix that defines them both, each category loses layers of its coherence. As we look back on the twentieth century, we see that W. E. B. Du Bois was prophetic when he wrote in 1903 that the problem of the twentieth century was the problem of the color line.[24] Race, particularly in the United States, has come to serve as a "metalanguage" for the construction of social relations.[25] Not only is race manipulated to subsume gender and class, but it blurs, disguises, and suppresses their interplay, precluding unity within gender and permitting cross-class solidarity.[26] Without an understanding of the complex encoding that our mutual and interdependent identities acquire within racism's language, those women who seek to engage America in social reconstruction will be left whistling in the dark.

CATHARINE A. MacKINNON, FROM PRACTICE TO THEORY, OR WHAT IS A WHITE WOMAN ANYWAY?

4 Yale J.L. & Feminism 13, 18, 20–22 (1991).

In recent critiques of feminist work for failing to take account of race or class,[14] it is worth noting that the fact that there is such a thing as race and class is assumed, although race and class are generally treated as abstractions to attack gender rather than as concrete realities, if indeed they are treated at all. * * * [R]ace and class are regarded as unproblematically real and not in need of justification or theoretical construction. Only gender is not real and needs to be justified. Although many women have demanded that discussions of race or class take gender into account, typically these demands do not take the form that, outside explicit recognition of gender, race or class do not exist. That there is a diversity to the experience of men and women of color, and of working class women and men regardless of race, is not said to mean that race or class are not meaningful concepts. I have heard no one say that there can be no meaningful discussion of "people of color" without gender specificity. * * *

Beneath the trivialization of the white woman's subordination implicit in the dismissive sneer "straight white economically-privileged women" (a phrase which has become one word, the accuracy of some of its terms being rarely documented even in law journals) lies the notion that there is no such thing as the oppression of women as such. If white women's oppression is an illusion of privilege and a rip-off and reduction of the civil rights movement, we are being told that there is no such thing as discrimination on the basis of sex. What I am saying is, to argue that oppression "as a woman" negates rather than encompasses recognition of the oppression of women on other bases, is to say that there is no such thing as the practice of sex inequality.

Let's take this the other way around. As I mentioned, both Mechelle Vinson * and Lillian Garland ** are African-American women. Wasn't Mechelle Vinson sexually harassed as a woman? Wasn't Lillian Garland pregnant as a woman? They thought so. The whole point of their cases was to get their injuries understood as "based on sex," that is, because they are women. The perpetrators, and the policies under which they were disadvantaged, saw them as women. What is being a woman if it does not include being oppressed as one? When the Reconstruction Amendments "gave Blacks the vote," and Black women still could not vote, weren't they kept from voting "as women"? When African-American women are raped two times as often as white women, aren't they raped as women? That does not mean their race is irrelevant and it does not mean that their injuries can be understood outside a racial context. Rather, it means that "sex" is made up of the reality of the experiences of all women, including theirs. It is a composite unit rather than a divided unitary whole, such that each woman, in her way, is all women. So, when white women are sexually harassed or lose their jobs because they are pregnant, aren't they women too?

In my view, the subtext to the critique of oppression "as a woman," the critique that holds that there is no such thing, is dis-identification with women. One of its consequences is the destruction of the basis for a jurisprudence of sex equality.

SCLC Split With Women's Group

By Caryle Murphy
Washington Post Staff Writer

The Southern Christian Leadership Conference, which recently named Martin Luther King III its fourth president, has stunned many of its followers by deciding to sever ties to one of its most active components, the women's division.

The move, taken during a board meeting in Atlanta in April but not made widely known, has created tensions within the SCLC just before its annual convention in Washington. The convention is to kick off July 25 with King's formal installation at Jericho City of Praise in Landover, a huge congregation with many female members, whose pastor is the Rev. Betty P. Peebles.

The SCLC board's 10 to 9 vote does not mean the women's division, which is incorporated as a separate entity under Georgia law, will disappear. But the board's move to end the SCLC's relationship with it has shocked and puzzled many longtime SCLC supporters.

"I'm gravely concerned and would like answers," said Melanie Hill, a longtime member and resident of Prince George's County who is executive director of a District-based nonprofit group. "I was upset. I'm just concerned that what happens with women [is] we get marginalized."

"I've had women all over the country call to say they are concerned and can't understand it," said Evelyn G. Lowery, of Atlanta, founder and head of the women's group. "It was hurtful to us."

Former D.C. Council member Wilhelmina Rolark, who serves on the SCLC board, declined to discuss the board's decision and referred questions to King. So did the Rev. Walter E. Fauntroy of Northeast Washington's New Bethel Baptist Church, another board member, who said he did not attend the April board meeting.

SCLC spokesman David Stokes in Atlanta said on three occasions that he would pass along a reporter's request to speak with King about the board's action, but the SCLC president did not return any of the calls.

Peebles, one of the area's most prominent female members of the clergy, declined to comment. "Not having been aware of [the decision] and since I don't know all the ramifications of it, I don't have a comment on it," Peebles said. "I don't know what the reasons were" for it.

The SCLC was founded in 1957 by a group of ministers including Martin Luther King Jr., who made the organization into a major force in the civil rights movement of the 1960s. But in recent years, the SCLC has had trouble defining its mission and raising money. King's son, who is 40, was named president last November.

SCLC/W.O.M.E.N., which stands for Women's Organizational Movement for Equality Now Inc., was founded in 1979 by Lowery, a veteran of the civil rights struggle and wife of Joseph E. Lowery, who stepped down as SCLC president last fall.

After the board's vote in April, Evelyn Lowery urged her division's members not to complain publicly. But contacted last week by The Post, Lowery said the move came without warning or prior discussion with King. "The reason given was that we were competing with them . . . for money, I guess," Lowery said.

According to a June 9 letter sent by Lowery and others to supporters of the women's division, "the new president felt that the women's group was 'competitive' and that he had difficulty raising funds because of the women. Mind you, the new president had ignored our written requests to meet with him so he could understand our work."

The letter goes on to say: "Never did we dream that we would be targets of abusive and oppressive assaults from some members of the board of SCLC and the president. . . . To add insult to injury . . . we have not been invited to engage in any discussions about the 1998 convention. We have been totally ignored."

The letter also says that on June 5, King informed the women's group's administrative assistant, LaSean Lane, that her salary would no longer be paid by the SCLC's national office. "This was the only link SCLC financially had with SCLC/W.O.M.E.N.," Lowery's letter states.

She said the women's organization runs programs in about eight cities but works mainly in Atlanta, where it has a mentoring program for low-income women and has given out $300,000 in scholarships in recent years. The group also raised money to buy a building it uses for its programs but has deeded to the SCLC.

"We didn't want to be a cookie-eating, tea-sipping group," Lowery said. "We wanted to be involved helping the least of these, and that's what we've been doing."

"SCLC/W.O.M.E.N, thank God, is incorporated, so male men cannot just come together and decide to eliminate a women's entity," said Felicia Davis-Gilmore, a Miami consultant and former Howard University student who is another longtime SCLC activist. "I find [the SCLC action] personally offensive," Davis-Gilmore added. "We've all struggled too hard to let it be done the way it was."

<u>Washington Post</u>, July 14, 1998 - P. A-5

B. VITAL STATISTICS

Numbers are in thousands, except averages and medians

Characteristics	All families	Married couple families: All races	White	Black	Hispan
All families	70,880	54,317	48,066	3,921	4,8
Size of family /2					
2 people	30,282	22,042	20,228	1,196	9
3 people	16,231	11,639	10,190	869	1,0
4 people	14,633	12,402	10,715	1,030	1,3
5 people	6,555	5,633	4,829	535	8
6 people	2,047	1,746	1,440	186	3
7 or more people	1,130	855	663	105	2
Average size	3.18	3.24	3.18	3.58	4.
Own children under 18					
Without own children under 18	36,120	29,048	26,156	1,865	1,6
With own children under 18	34,760	25,269	21,910	2,055	3,1
One own child under 18	14,363	9,507	8,231	723	1,0
Two own children under 18	13,122	10,241	8,913	830	1,1
Three or more own children under 18	7,275	5,521	4,766	502	9
Total own children under 18	64,323	47,931	41,265	3,996	6,8
Average per family with own children under 18	1.85	1.90	1.88	1.94	2.
Age of own children /3					
Of any age	44,979	31,288	27,057	2,586	3,6
Under 25 years	40,006	28,871	25,057	2,323	3,4
Under 18 years	34,760	25,269	21,910	2,055	3,1
Under 12 years	26,030	19,279	16,739	1,549	2,6
Under 6 years	15,532	11,773	10,278	880	1,7
Under 3 years	8,927	7,053	6,205	507	1,0
Under 1 year	3,160	2,527	2,240	163	3
Six to 17 years	26,298	18,927	16,360	1,609	2,3
Members 65 and older					
Without members 65 and older	57,338	43,542	38,316	3,275	4,2
With members 65 and older	13,542	10,775	9,750	646	5
Family without own children under 18	12,873	10,252	9,371	598	5
Family with own children under 18	669	524	379	47	
Householder's age					
Under 25 years	3,019	1,373	1,221	111	3
25 to 34 years	13,639	9,886	8,557	858	1,3
35 to 44 years	18,872	14,180	12,382	1,066	1,4
45 to 54 years	14,694	11,734	10,324	884	8
55 to 64 years	9,387	7,936	7,125	485	5
65 to 74 years	6,989	5,841	5,338	369	2
75 years and over	4,282	3,368	3,118	149	1
Median age	45.0	46.4	46.7	44.3	40

Householder's marital status					
Married, spouse present	54,317	54,317	48,066	3,921	4,8
Married, spouse absent	2,506	(X)	(X)	(X)	(
Separated	1,905	(X)	(X)	(X)	(
Other	601	(X)	(X)	(X)	(
Widowed	2,698	(X)	(X)	(X)	(
Divorced	5,910	(X)	(X)	(X)	(
Never married	5,449	(X)	(X)	(X)	(

1 People of Hispanic origin may be of any race.

2 Note that "size of family" and "size of household" are different. Household household, whereas family members include only the householder and his/her re

3 Age categories are not mutually exclusive.

(X) Not Applicable

Source: U.S. Bureau of the Census, Current Population Survey (CPS)

Numbers are in thousands, except averages and percentages.

		Family households		
				Other
Characteristics	All households	Total	Married couple	Female householder
All households	102,528	70,880	54,317	12,652
Race and Hispanic origin				
White	86,106	59,511	48,066	8,308
White not Hispanic	77,936	52,871	43,423	6,826
Black	12,474	8,408	3,921	3,926
Hispanic /1	8,590	6,961	4,804	1,612
Size of household				
1 person	26,327	(X)	(X)	(X)
2 people	32,965	28,722	21,833	5,290
3 people	17,331	16,640	11,595	3,858
4 people	15,358	15,090	12,427	2,008
5 people	7,048	6,972	5,743	924
6 people	2,232	2,195	1,807	293
7 or more people	1,267	1,260	911	278
Average size	2.62	3.24	3.26	3.18
Percent with own children under 18	33.9	49.0	46.5	60.6
Age of householder				
Under 25	5,435	3,019	1,373	1,095
25 to 34	19,033	13,639	9,886	2,887
35 to 44	23,943	18,872	14,180	3,637
45 to 54	19,547	14,694	11,734	2,260
55 to 64	13,072	9,387	7,936	1,099
65 to 74	11,272	6,989	5,841	938
75 and over	10,225	4,282	3,368	738
Median age	46.3	45.0	46.4	41.4

1 People of Hispanic origin may be of any race.
(X) Not applicable.

U.S. CENSUS BUREAU.
1998

Source: U.S. Bureau of the Census, Current Population Survey (CPS).

FGM IN AFRICA: STATISTICS.

There are no definite studies that have been conducted on the prevalence of FGM in Africa and the Middle East. Therefore, it is important to keep in mind that these are only estimates. They are based on Fran Hosken's estimates and date from 1992. In 1982, Ms. Hosken conducted a study that was published in "The Hosken's Report". She estimated that there are more than 79.97 (about 80 million) mutilated females in the world. Today there are more than 114 million women who have undergone some form of FGM in the world. That's almost double of what the 1982 estimates show.

COUNTRY	PREVALENCE	ACTUAL NUMBER
Benin*	50%	1,200,00
Burkina Faso*	70%	3,290,000
Cameroon*	--	--
Central African Republic*	50%	750,000
Chad	60%	1,530,000
Cote d'Ivoire*	60%	3,750,000
Djibouti	98%	196,000
Egypt	50%	13,625,000
Ethopia and Eritrea	90%	23,940,000
Gambia*	60%	270,000
Ghana	30%	2,325,000
Guinea*	50%	1,875,000
Guinea Bissau*	50%	250,000
Kenya	50%	6,300,000
Liberia*	60%	810,000
Mali*	75%	3,112,500
Mauritania*	25%	262,500
Niger*	20%	800,000
Nigeria	50%	30,625,000
Senegal	20%	750,000
Sierra Leone	90%	1,935,000
Somalia	98%	3,773,000
Sudan (North)	89%	9,220,400
Tanzania	10%	1,345,000
Togo*	50%	950,000
Uganda*	5%	467,500
Zaire*	5%	945,000
Total		114,296,900

Country	% of girls operated on	female life expectancy against male male = 100	maternal mortality rate (per 100,000 births)	under one year mortality (per 1,000 live births)	under five mortality (per 1,000 live births)	female literacy rate %
Somalia	100%	109.1	1,100	127	215	6.0%
Djibouti	NA	NA	NA	NA	NA	NA
Ethiopia/ Eritrea	90%	106.8	NA	130	259	46.7%
Mali	90%	109.3	2,000	164	292	11.0%
Sudan (north)	90%	104.0	660	104	181	15.0%
Sierra Leone	90%	110.0	450	149	266	21.0%
Burkina Faso	70%	106.4	810	133	233	6.1%
Gambia	60%	NA	NA	NA	NA	15.1%
Ivory Coast	60%	105.8	NA	92	NA	NA
Kenya	60%	106.9	170	68	113	49.0%
Senegal	50%	104.3	600	84	136	19.0%
Egypt	80%	105.1	320	61	125	30.0%
Guinea	50%	102.3	800	140	NA	NA
Guinea Bissau	50%	107.3	700	146	NA	17.3%
Nigeria	50%	106.0	800	101	174	31.0%
Maurtinia	25%	108.9	NA	122	220	NA
Central African Republic	20%	110.6	600	100	223	29.0%
Niger	20%	106.8	700	130	228	9.0%
Chad	20%	106.7	960	127	223	11.0%
Benin	20%	108.9	160	88	185	15.7%
Togo	20%	107.7	920	90	153	28.0%
Ghana	20%	107.5	1,000	86	146	43.0%
Tanzania	10%	107.7	340	102	176	31.4%
Uganda	Under 5%	106.0	300	99	169	45.0%
Zaire	Under 5%	107.8	800	79	138	45.0%
Sub-Saharan Africa	NA	106.9	540	108	179	25.2%
Industrial Countries	NA	110.1	24	NA	NA	NA

C. RECOMMENDED READING

E. Higginbotham, "African-American Women's History and the Metalanguage of Race," *SIGNS: Journal of Women in Culture and Society*, Winter 1992

b. hooks, *Talking Back* (South End Press: 1989)

M. Hodes, *Sex, Love, Race: Crossing Boundaries in North American History* New York University Press: 1999)

N. Toubia, *Female Genital Mutilation: A Call for Global Action* (Rainbow: 1990)

CHAPTER IX
The Future of Women's Rights

All of the issues examined in this book remain in play. All will be pursued legally into the 21st Century, but on different paths. Gender disparities at the upper reaches of industry and education may narrow to some extent as pools of upwardly-mobile candidates increase, but history has shown that equity does not necessarily follow, and new litigation, under Titles VII and IX as well as constitutional theories, will likely become more innovative. More effective investigation and prosecution of violence against women and the "second wave" of family law reform will continue to be pressed in state legislatures, where, as with Congress, increased female membership will surely be a major political priority. Efforts for better access to reproductive and other medical procedures may well focus on two areas: (a) increased participation in the federal regulatory process for testing and approval of contraceptive and other drugs, and (b) presidential campaigning, with an eye toward Supreme Court nominations. The issue of equal access to medical procedures appears increasingly amenable to constitutional litigation, as Justice Blackmun pondered in his opinion, concurring in part and dissenting in part, in *Planned Parenthood of Southeastern Pa. v. Casey:*

> A state's restrictions on a woman's right to terminate her pregnancy also implicate constitutional guarantees of gender equality. State restrictions on abortion compel women to continue pregnancies they otherwise might terminate. By restricting the right to terminate pregnancies, the State conscripts women's bodies into its service, forcing women to continue their pregnancies, suffer the pains of childbirth, and in most instances, provide years of maternal care. The state does not compensate women for their services; instead, it assumes that they owe this duty as a matter of course. This assumption – that women can simply be forced to accept the "natural" status and incidents of motherhood – appears to rest upon a conception of women's role that has triggered the protection of the Equal Protection Clause.
> *Planned Parenthood of Southeastern Pa. v. Casey,* 505 U.S. 833, 929 (1992).

Similarly, concurring in the Supreme Court's invalidation of the gender-discriminatory military benefits laws in *Frontiero v. Richardson,* Justice Powell noted an even more compelling, potential constitutional basis for broad-based gender equality:

> I agree that the challenged statutes constitute an unconstitutional discrimination against servicewomen . . .but I cannot join the opinion of MR. JUSTICE BRENNAN, which would hold that all classifications based upon sex, "like classifications based upon race, alienage, and national origin" are "inherently suspect and must therefore be subjected to close judicial scrutiny."

> . . .There is another, and I find compelling, reason for deferring a general categorizing of sex classifications as invoking the strictest test of judicial scrutiny. The Equal Rights Amendment, which if adopted will resolve the substance of this precise question, has been approved by the Congress and submitted for ratification by the States. If this Amendment is adopted, it will represent the will of the people accomplished in the manner prescribed by the Constitution.
>
> *Frontiero v. Richardson*, 411 U.S. 677, 692 (1973)

The Equal Rights Amendment, however, fell three states short of ratification. While it would not be a complete panacea for the women's rights movement, it remains its most potentially powerful, if temporarily dormant, legal instrument. A glimpse of the E.R.A.'s legal potential can be had by revisiting the *Vorchheimer* case from Chapter III, in which the Third Circuit Court of Appeals rejected an Equal Protection challenge to Philadelphia's sex-segregated, competitive academic high schools. A subsequent group of female students filed suit in Pennsylvania state court, seeking admission to the same male-only high school which had, among other facilities, superior mathematics and science curricula. This time, the result was different.

In *Newburg v. Board of Education,* No. 5822 (Common Pleas Court of Philadelphia County, August 30, 1983), Judge Marutani held that the Pennsylvania State Equal Rights Amendment, whose language was substantially identical to the unratified federal E.R.A., required that all gender classifications be viewed with strict scrutiny. Accordingly, the system of sex-segregated high schools was ordered dismantled.

> The thrust of the [Pennsylvania] Equal Rights Amendment is to insure equality of rights under the law and to eliminate sex as a basis for distinction. The sex of citizens of this Commonwealth is no longer a permissible factor in the determination of their legal rights and legal responsibilities. The law will not impose different benefits or different burdens upon the members of society based on the fact that they may be man or woman.
>
> Pennsylvania's ERA and the . . . federal ERA are essentially mirror copies . . . Thus, with ERA placed on the scale, at least a majority of the justices of the Supreme Court would categorize classifications based upon sex as being "inherently suspect" and therefore subject to strict judicial scrutiny.
>
> *Newburg v. Board of Education*, pp. 23, 25 (1983).

Because the Equal Rights Amendment was not ratified within the Congressionally-mandated time period, it has been generally assumed that the process would have to begin anew in Congress. An alternate theory, noting that the Twenty-seventh Amendment was passed by Congress in 1789 but was not ratified until 1992, holds that Congress could re-extend the E.R.A. deadline (one extension was previously granted), and declare the amendment ratified when three additional state legislatures vote for ratification. The requisite resolutions have been introduced in both Congress and the remaining state legislatures, where they await the new Century.

The Future Is Ours to Lose

Without historical awareness, women could still believe that their fate rests in their cleavage and in their stars.

By Naomi Wolf

THE NEW YORK TIMES MAGAZINE / MAY 16, 1999

Standing at the turn of the millennium, how odd it seems that women, the majority of the human species, have not, over the course of so many centuries, intervened successfully once and for all on their own behalf. That is, until you consider that women have been trained to see themselves as having no relationship to history, and no claim upon it. Feminism can be defined as women's ability to think about their subjugated role in history, and then to do something about it. The 21st century will see the End of Inequality — but only if women absorb the habit of historical self-awareness, becoming a mass of people who, rather than do it all, decide at last to change it all. The future is ours to lose.

Since there has always been some scattered awareness that women's low status was unfair, you could say that there has always been a women's movement. And just as you could say that there has always been a women's movement, you could also say that there has always been a backlash. It is truly striking how often Western humanity has taken the leap forward into more egalitarian, rational and democratic models of society and government, and made the decision — for a decision it had to be — to leave women out. At every turn, with a heroic effort of the will to ignore the obvious path of justice, men were granted, and granted themselves, more and more equality, and women of all races were left in history's tidewater.

Once again, we are at a turning point. This decade has seen one new landmark after another: the Family and Medical Leave Act; a feminist sitting on the Supreme Court; a woman in charge of American foreign policies that now include opposition to clitoridectomy. Indeed, feminism has become mainstream: Betty Friedan has met Betsy Ross; Barbie's ads now read "Dream With Your Eyes Wide Open" and "Be Your Own Hero." Oprah is talking about how to walk out of an abusive marriage, and Tori Amos and Fran Drescher speak out in the celebrity press about sexual assault. This flood tide could either crest further to change the landscape forever, or it could recede once again. This is what historians call an "open moment," and women have blown such moments in the past. What determines the outcome is the level of historical awareness we reach before the tide inevitably turns.

There are four ways that our culture militates against historical consciousness in women. One is the steady omission of women from history's first draft, the news. Women, Men and Media, a national watchdog project, reports that women are featured in only 15 percent of the front-page news — and then usually as victims or perpetrators of crime or misconduct. It is not because no one is interested in what women are doing that this ceiling of visibility is kept so low; nor is it a conscious conspiracy. But if tomorrow the editors in chief and publishers of national news media were to see front sections dominated by 53 percent female newsmakers, they would not shout, Stop the presses! Too many women! Rather, there would be the impression that somehow these publications had, by featuring newsmakers who are part of a majority, marginalized themselves. So women's advances take place with little day-by-day, let alone month-by-month, popular analysis.

The second pressure, which complements the omission of women from historical culture, is the omission of history from women's culture. One example: under its previous editor, Ruth Whitney, Glamour magazine ran a political column. Bonnie Fuller, a new editor fresh from Cosmopolitan, has deleted this monthly column and added a horoscope. It's a shift from real-time — historical-political time — back into that dependent, dreamy, timeless state of Women's Time. In Women's Time, your fate is not in your own hands as an agent of historical change. Rather — Hey, are you a Pisces? Why bother running down your Manolo Blahniks to do something as *mousy* as voting? Your fate is in your cleavage, and in the stars.

Emerging naturally from this is the third pressure: the recurrent ideological theme that if women take themselves seriously they will lose femininity and, therefore, social status. If what they do, think, worry about and long for doesn't matter, surely it's not important that history pays them attention.

The fourth pressure is forgetfulness. Young women I have met on real college campuses think sex discrimination is a thing of the past. Or that the struggle for the vote lasted maybe 10 years, not more than 70. Or that women got the vote when African-Americans did. Or that it has always been legal to get an abortion in America. They are stunned to discover that in their mothers' lifetimes women could not get credit on their own. They are amazed to learn that it was African-American middle-class women's clubs that led the movement against lynching. They didn't know that women chained themselves to the gates of Congress, or went on hunger strikes and were force-fed — so that young women far into the future could take their rights for granted. These young women are shocked, in other words, to find that they have a history.

As a result, women remain dependent on other

models of "revolution" for their own. They must catch the taste and techniques of activism like a hit song of the month wafting through the air. So one sees women slumbering and then "waking up" every 30 years or so; periods of feminism always follow periods of agitation by women on behalf of other, more respectable causes.

This past century shows how fragile conscious feminism has been. The 1910's, with their wave of populist reform, saw the crescendo of women's push for the vote. But the year before it was granted, in 1919, the term "post-feminist" had already expediently been coined. By the 20's, pop culture was once again ridiculing the suffragists' generations as being man-hating old battle-axes, irrelevant and out of touch with "today's women."

A long sleep followed, with fitful waking. After Betty Friedan's 1963 book helped middle-class white women identify the causes of their deeper malaise, the magical 15 years, from 1965 to 1980, began, representing a high point of historical self-awareness for Western women. Again, other movements had to set the stage: the anti-war movement, the free-speech movement and the hippie movement all contributed to the idea that it was all right to break free of social roles. The civil rights movement trained a generation of African-American activists. The 70's were astonishing: the statutes against sex discrimination labeled Title VII and Title IX; Shirley Chisholm's 1972 race for the Democratic Presidential nomination. That era, personified by Steinem and Jong, NOW and the National Women's Political Caucus, showed what could happen for women when, as an energized mass in a democracy, they wanted change badly enough to make noise about it.

The predictable backlash came, as it always does; the evil 80's were a time of shoulder pads, silicone and retrenchment. Again — so quickly, so thoroughly — women "forgot." A Time/CNN poll found that only 33 percent of women called themselves feminists — and only 16 percent of college-age women. "Guilt" and "the Mommy Track" were the catchwords of the day. Once again, feminists were represented as hairy-legged man-hating shrews.

The heartbreak of those times was in seeing newly clueless young women come of age. Once, when I visited Yale as a speaker, a brilliant young Asian-American student joined her male debating society peers in loudly ridiculing feminism. Later, when we were alone for a moment, she confided that she didn't really believe what she said — but the guys were in charge of the club and she just wanted to get along with them. "Besides," she had said, as if parroting some women's magazine, "women my age just have to accept that we can't have it all." It was as if all those words — flextime, family leave, egalitarian marriage — had vanished, taking with them the ways in which that young woman could have reconsidered her life.

Enter the explosive 90's. Women are now the most important voting mass in America. "Women's Issues" dominate the agenda. The word "feminism" is as taboo as ever, but does it matter if you call yourself a feminist if you are living feminism? And American women are doing that, considering the number of their new businesses, and their new judgeships, new elected officials and new spending power. Feminism today is not a label; it's a way of life.

But here's the catch: if we remain indifferent to history, we risk losing it all. The bad old days are always ready to knock at your door, sisters: while you're packing your briefcase or getting into your truck, feeling confident, having thrown out the mailing from that advocacy group, you could just find that you can't get a legal abortion anymore; or that your boss knows that those sexual harassment statutes can be managed with a wink and a nod.

Women who are ignorant of their own history forget the main lessons, like: Here's how you mobilize; being nice is never as good as getting leverage; the nature-nurture debate has been going on forever, and neither side is going to win; your representatives pay attention when you use your money, your voice and your will. And voting millions can provide the will.

Maybe we will learn at last. Maybe we will create institutions that are willing to share influence with younger women coming up, rather than hoarding power for one generation. Maybe we will learn to honor our heroines and role models while they are still alive: maybe Gloria Steinem and Shirley Chisholm will get their commemorative stamps and parades in their own lifetimes, so our daughters will grow up with some one to turn to more powerful in their imaginations than Kate Moss and Calista Flockhart. Maybe we will learn at last that dissent and disagreement among women across the political spectrum is a sign of our diversity and strength. Maybe we will turn from the horoscope page to the Congressional Quarterly, and understand at last that our salvation lies not in our stars, but in ourselves. ■

* * * * * * * *

BEYOND GENDER

BY BETTY FRIEDAN

Sexual Politics Can Advance the Women's Movement for Equality Only So Far

In the summer of 1994, I had lunch with a friend near her office in New York City. She happens to be the top woman there and she gets lonesome at lunchtime. The guys at her level all go out together and never have lunch with the women anymore. Is this some new kind of sex discrimination? "Oh no," she says, "It's just that there's so much talk about sexual harassment suits these days. No one knows what it is or isn't, so they figure 'Why risk it?' "

But my friend wasn't looking for feminist advice. Her husband, who was "downsized" at one of our biggest corporations three years earlier, hadn't been able to find a job and had almost stopped looking. "I'm carrying it all," she said. "It's OK, we'll make it. But it's not good at home, the way he feels now. It's as if he's given up. I could get a divorce, I suppose. But he is the father of my children, and I still love him. So that's not an option. But, ambitious as I am, I never figured it would end up like this."

That same week, I saw an item in *The New York Times* which reported that in the previous five years there had been a nearly 20 percent drop in income among college-educated white American men. Not minority, high school educated, or blue-collar men, but white management men in their 40s and early 50s, the masters of the universe. And while women on the whole still do not earn as much money as men, the *Times* noted that college-educated women in the same age group had seen their incomes rise slightly over the same period. Meanwhile, new national studies were indicating that women were now carrying half of the income burden in half of all U.S. families.

Downsizing had not yet hit the headlines in 1994; the "angry white male" had not yet surfaced in that year's election campaign. But my inner Geiger counter had begun to click, the way it does when something foreign to definition, expectation, and accepted truth happens. I trust that click; it set me on the search that led to the concept of "the feminine mystique," which led to the women's movement for equality. And now, though my and many other women's lives in the 30 years since had been conducted within that liberating frame of reference, I feel again that urgent change is required. My inner Geiger counter does not lie. I sense something that cannot be evaded or handled in the usual feminist terms.

I sense the need for a paradigm shift beyond feminism, beyond sexual politics, beyond identity politics altogether—a new paradigm for women and men. Since then, the more I've thought about this and begun to try to make it happen, the more I realize that many other people from very different political persuasions than mine are moving in the same direction. There's a mounting sense that the crises we are now facing, or denying, cannot be solved in the same terms that we used to conduct our personal, political, business, or family lives. They can no longer be seen in terms of gender. The old paradigm still shaping our thinking may keep us from seeing these problems for what they are, much less solving them.

Competing Paradigms

Before the modern women's movement, every map in every field of endeavor defined women in relation to men. It was a paradigm shift when we began to challenge the rubrics that had been developed only from male experience. This shift opened up every field, as women began to move in great numbers from the 1960s onward into law, medicine, science, business, art, politics, and the humanities. It opened life in complex new directions.

But today I look back and admit anomalies that kept me trying to stretch the box of feminism long before this crisis. For me, the unwritten, inviolable law against which all thinking about women must be tested is life itself. Does it open or close real life as women live it? Does it permit more choice, autonomy, freedom, and control? Does it empower or restrict?

For those of us who started the modern women's movement, the new paradigm was simply the ethos of American democracy—equality of opportunity, our own voice in the decisions of our destiny, but applied to women in concrete terms as the theory and practice of democracy had never been applied to us before. But for the younger women who came from the 1960s student movement and who had not yet experienced the life that most women led, the paradigm was sexual politics: women as a whole rising up against men as a whole, the oppressed against the oppressors. While seeing women in these terms did open women's lives to new growth and development, I had trouble with this paradigm from the beginning. It didn't fit *life*—life as I and other women had known it, even scientific knowledge about life.

When I left the presidency of the National Organization for Women in 1970, sexual politics was already dividing our strength. I began putting my energy into teaching, lecturing, and writing again—all of it geared to what I saw as the need for feminist thought to evolve. In my 1981 book *The Second Stage,* I proposed going beyond the impossible dilemmas of the sexual politics paradigm and coming to new terms with family, motherhood, men, and careers. My views were bitterly attacked by the "politically correct" voices of feminism, as if I was betraying the women's movement. Though deeply hurt, I had no desire to mount a divisive counter-feminist movement. I bowed out of feminist organizational politics altogether, except when asked for help.

Women as a "Special Interest"

In the 1980s, when feminist consciousness was supposedly at its apex, women of childbearing years were dividing into two antagonistic camps. They were being forced to make no-win choices that pit motherhood against career. The women's movement for equality was spreading throughout society; women in great numbers were graduating from law, medical, and business schools as well as community colleges and moving into jobs and professions. Yet polls began to show that younger women were reluctant to identify themselves as feminists, though they identified with every item of the women's agenda of equality.

A backlash was growing. Women, blacks, Latinos, gays, the handicapped—all were being labeled "special interests," with a moral claim on society no greater than that of the oil industry or the lumber barons. Women, who constitute 52 percent of the American people, never should have let ourselves be defined this way. Had we weakened ourselves by increasingly organizing over separate, single issues? Did we cloud the vision of the common good by defining our cause in terms of women versus men?

The energy of the leading feminist organizations had been focused on abortion or on sexual politics—rape, date rape, pornography. I have no doubt that the far right has deliberately focused on abortion as symbol and substance of a woman's independence, autonomy, control over her own body, and destiny. But did we somehow let those who opposed our rights, our very personhood as women, box us in and define the terms of our unfinished battle too narrowly?

Year after year we spend all our organizational energy and funds fighting for the right to an abortion, a battle we have already won in Congress and in the courts of law and public opinion. Shouldn't we put at least as much energy into breaking down the remaining barriers to women's advancing to equality with men in our economy? The key to achieving that goal is changing the structures that make it difficult for American women to combine childbearing with advancement in business and the professions.

An Impossible Paradox

In the early 1990s, the Center for Policy Alternatives and the Ms. Foundation conducted a poll to discover the true concerns of women. To the amazement of the politically correct, it revealed that none of the sexual issues ranked among the main problems of women young or old, black or white.. For the great majority of the women polled, the main problem was jobs—how to get them, keep them, and get ahead in them; and how to meet the responsibilities of family life while living the equality we'd fought for.

My sense of crisis came in the summer of 1994 as I prepared to come to Washington as a guest scholar at the Woodrow Wilson International Center for Scholars. While packing up my papers, I stumbled across the *Times* article on income losses among middle-aged white male professionals and gains among similarly aged and educated women. Citing the same trend, another article published in *The Economist* posed this question: Have women driven men from the workplace?

At once, I saw the impossible paradox for women: *We are achieving what begins to look like equality because the men are doing worse.* Is their loss really our gain?

Women today enjoy more control over their lives than their mothers ever dreamed of. The great majority have jobs that may not be the greatest, but which give them a life in their 40s and 50s after their kids are off (though the juggling of children and job in their 30s is tough). Many women are doing as well as or better than those downsized men.

Studying the pattern in the news clippings, I sensed a truly serious backlash ahead. I had noticed the court rulings in which divorced women lost custody of a child because they had a demanding job or were pursuing a degree and placed their child in day care for part of the day. The fathers won custody because their new wives or mothers would stay home all day with the child. I also noticed how the religious right marched under the banner of "family values" even as its zealots continued to bomb abortion clinics. Feminist groups have mobilized to defend those clinics. But who is mobilizing to confront the economic inequality and dislocation that threatens the survival and stability of families far more than abortion or pornography?

There has to be a paradigm shift in our thinking about women, not just from sexual politics but from the whole focus of our status vis-a-vis men. If women are winning while men are losing, since most women continue to live with men in families, how long can women really win? If jobs, work, and family are the issues that concern women most now, we have to mobilize to protect our children, our families, and ourselves in a new coalition with men.

Toward a New Vision

Our economy is in need of basic restructuring—one which counters income inequality, confronts the needs of family that can't be ignored in a workplace where women now equal or outnumber men, and insists that more and more men share in the responsibilities of parenting. This restructuring can't be accomplished in terms of women versus men, blacks versus whites, old versus young, conservative versus liberal.

We need a new political movement in America that puts the lives and interests of people first. It can't be done by separate, single-issue movements now, and it has to be political, to protect and translate our new empowerment with a new vision of community, with new structures that open the doors again to real equality of opportunity for the diverse interests of all our children—a new evolution of democracy as we approach the new millennium.

The New Democrat, July/August 1997

Appendix A:
Women in Government: A Turn-of-the-Century Snapshot

- Among citizens, women were significantly more likely than men to have voted in the 1996 presidential election (60 percent versus 57 percent). In 1984, women's voting rates in presidential elections surpassed those of men for the first time since the Census Bureau began collecting voting data in 1964

Women's voting rates have been higher than men's ever since.

U.S. CENSUS BUREAU, 1999

Year	National Convention Delegates (% Women) Dem.	Rep.
1968	13	17
1972	40	30
1976	34	31
1980	50	36
1984	50	44
1988	49	37
1992	50	42

Women Barely a Quarter of Top Hill Staffers

Despite the women's movement, the percentage of women in the top jobs in the Senate and House is still only 27 percent, according to a new survey out today in the National Journal of nearly 300 top committee and leadership aides—some of the least-known but most powerful people in town.

Women hold about one-third of the Senate's top committee and leadership aide jobs, but barely over 20 percent of those on the House side—and there's no difference between Republicans and Democrats.

"The typical staffer is a 40-something male who's more likely to be from the Northeast than the West," the Journal said.

WOMEN IN U.S. STATE LEGISLATURES

Year	Number	Pct.
1969	301	4
1975	604	6
1981	908	12
1987	1170	16
1993	1516	20
1999	**1652**	**25**

Other Female Government Officials, 1999

U.S. Cabinet Level Positions:	7*
State Governors:	3
State Lt. Governors:	19
Statewide Executive-Level:	89**

*Highest number ever

**All five statewide elected officials in Arizona are female.

Number of Women in Congress, by Year

Election	Congress	President	President's Party	Number of Women in Congress	Percentage
1922	68	Warren G. Harding	R	1	0.2
1924	69	Calvin Coolidge	R	2	0.5
1926	70	Calvin Coolidge	R	5	0.9
1928	71	Herbert C. Hoover	R	9	1.6
1930	72	Herbert C. Hoover	R	8	1.5
1932	73	Franklin D. Roosevelt	D	8	1.5
1934	74	Franklin D. Roosevelt	D	8	1.5
1936	75	Franklin D. Roosevelt	D	9	1.6
1938	76	Franklin D. Roosevelt	D	9	1.6
1940	77	Franklin D. Roosevelt	D	10	1.8
1942	78	Franklin D. Roosevelt	D	9	1.6
1944	79	Franklin D. Roosevelt	D	11	1.9
1946	80	Franklin D. Roosevelt	D	8	1.4
1948	81	Harry S. Truman	D	9	1.6
1950	82	Harry S. Truman	D	9	1.6
1952	83	Dwight D. Eisenhower	R	13	2.3
1954	84	Dwight D. Eisenhower	R	16	3.0
1956	85	Dwight D. Eisenhower	R	15	2.8
1958	86	Dwight D. Eisenhower	R	19	3.4
1960	87	John F. Kennedy	D	20	3.6
1962	88	John F. Kennedy	D	14	2.5
1964	89	Lyndon B. Johnson	D	13	2.4
1966	90	Lyndon B. Johnson	D	12	2.2
1968	91	Richard M. Nixon	R	11	2.0
1970	92	Richard M. Nixon	R	15	2.7
1972	93	Richard M. Nixon	R	16	2.9
1974	94	Gerald R. Ford	R	19	3.5
1976	95	Jimmy Carter	D	19	3.5
1978	96	Jimmy Carter	D	17	3.1
1980	97	Ronald Reagan	R	24	4.4
1982	98	Ronald Reagan	R	25	4.4
1984	99	Ronald Reagan	R	25	4.6
1986	100	Ronald Reagan	R	26	4.8
1988	101	George Bush	R	28	5.2
1990	102	George Bush	R	32	6.0
1992	103	Bill Clinton	D	54	10.0
1994	104	Bill Clinton	D	55	10.4
1996	105	Bill Clinton	D	59	11.0
1998	106	Bill Clinton	D	65	13.0

Gender Gap in 1996 on Voting, Partisanship, and Selected Issues

	Men (%)	Women (%)	Gender Gap (%)
Voting			
Clinton for President	47	60	13
Democrat for House	44	52	8
Partisanship			
Democrat*	46*	58*	12
Republican*	46	33	−13
Liberal	21	30	9
Conservative	52	37	−15
Economic Issues			
Government should do more	44	63	19
Spend more on child care	46	56	10
Spend more on homeless	50	64	14
Spend more on social security	39	54	15
Culture Wars Issues			
Pro-choice	39	44	5
Like Women's Movement	59	71	12
Like gays & lesbians	17	29	12
Support gun laws	34	57	23
Like fundamentalists	41	45	4
Alienation from Government			
Trust fed govt most of time	29	29	0
Fed govt run for big interests	73	72	−1

Source: Computed from data from the 1996 National Election Study of the Survey Research Center, distributed by the International Consortium for Political and Social Research.

INTERNATIONAL LEGISLATIVE REPRESENTATION

SOURCES: European Union, International Foundation for Election Systems

Percentage of Female Judges, Percentage of Women Receiving Law Degrees, and Percentage of Female Lawyers

Women	1980	1987	1993	1997
Federal Judges	5.4%	7.0%	11.1%	17.4%
State Supreme	3.6	6.5	11.2	20.0
State Trial	2.4	7.3	8.5	9.0*
Lawyers	8.0	13.0	19.0	25.0*
Law Degrees	30.0	40.0	45.0	47.0*

*Estimates

Table 6–7 Women on the Federal Judiciary, 1976–1996

Year	1976	1981	1989	1992	1996
Seats	534	686	754	837	837
Women	6 (1.1%)	45 (6.6%)	64 (8.5%)	90 (10.8%)	140 (16.7%)

Source: Alliance for Justice

Table 6–6 Gender Appointments to the Federal Bench by Administration, 1969–1996

	Women
Clinton (202)	63
1992–1996	(31.2%)
Bush (194)	36
1989–1992	(18.5%)
Reagan (378)	31
1981–1988	(8.2%)
Carter (258)	40
1977–1980	(15.5%)
Ford (65)	1
1974–1976	(1.5%)
Nixon (227)	1
1969–1974	(.4%)

Source: Alliance for Justice

RECOMMENDED READING

L. Whitaker, ed., *Women in Politics: Outsiders or Insiders?* (Prentice Hall: 1999)

B. Burrell, *A Woman's Place Is in the House* (University of Michigan Press: 1994)

N. McGlen, K. O'Connor, *Women, Politics, and American Society* (Prentice Hall: 1998)

M. Conway, D. Ahern, G. Steuernagel, *Women & Public Policy: A Revolution in Progress* (C.Q. Press: 1999)